Sociology 2C06

MW01515585

TABLE OF CONTENTS
& ACKNOWLEDGEMENTS

PAGE

Gomme - The Shadow Line

CHAPTER 1

Determining Deviance

Learning Objectives

After reading this chapter, you should be able to:

- Describe the objective/subjective dichotomy.
- Describe four definitions of deviance traditionally associated with the objective side of the objective/subjective dichotomy, and explain their limitations.
- Describe the definitions of deviance traditionally associated with the subjective side of the objective/subjective dichotomy, and summarize the concept of social construction.
- Explain how the study of deviance is influenced by how the researcher defines it. Depict the role of change, negotiation, opposition, and diversity in the "deviance dance" in Canadian society.
- Outline the three components of the social typing process through which someone is defined as "deviant." Explain the role of power, and identify who holds this power in Canadian society.

"Conformity makes everything easier, if you can still breathe." (Mason Cooley)[1]

"You have to be deviant if you're going to do anything new." (David Lee)[2]

The two above quotations both make some very pointed claims about the nature of **deviance** and **conformity**. The first quotation makes the claim that our lives will run more smoothly if we conform; however, it also makes the claim that conformity will constrict and limit us. The second quotation makes a related claim, that acting or thinking in a novel way is necessarily deviant; although "thinking outside the box" is a popular corporate phrase, the source of this quotation suggests that only "deviants" will actually do so.

Taken together, the claims made in these quotations raise questions about deviance and conformity. Who are the conformists in our society and in our world? Is life easier for them? Who are the deviants? Are they really the innovators of our world, or do they represent some sort of problem that we need to control? How can we distinguish between a "deviant" and a "conformist"? These are the kinds of questions that will guide us through this textbook.

Who Is Deviant?

Who is deviant? One way to try to answer this question is by looking at the topics covered in deviance textbooks. Historically, certain themes have prevailed—what have been referred to as "nuts, sluts, [and] preverts [sic]" (Liazos, 1972, p. 103). Criminality has also dominated the topics covered in some deviance textbooks. However, a growing number of recent books have moved away from these tendencies, and toward broader notions of deviance—welfare recipients (Doherty, 2000), smokers (Tuggle & Holmes, 1997), overweight people (Degher & Hughes, 2003), and motherhood (Wachholz, 2000) have all been analyzed in the context of deviance. A second way to try to answer the question of who is deviant is to ask people. Just as many other deviance professors have done (e.g. Goode, 1997), over several years of teaching I have conducted polls of students in my classes. Certain responses have predominated, and may bear a striking resemblance to the list you created in the *Ask Yourself* exercise. People who commit crimes, especially violent crimes, are thought of as deviant by large numbers of students.

There is also considerable consensus that those who glaringly perpetuate injustice, such as racists, are deviant as well. However, once going

Ask Yourself

Before going on, take out your notebook and make a list of types of people whom you consider to be deviant. Remember, no one will see your list, so just write down whatever comes into your mind. We will come back to your list in a little while.

Ask Yourself

• • • • • • • • • • • • • • • • • • •

Look back at your personal list of "deviant" people. Which people on your list are there primarily because you personally do not approve of them or are annoyed by them? Are there people on your list who you think may have characteristics which go beyond the level of your personal dislike and instead point to processes occurring at the societal level?

Ask Yourself

• •

Go back to the list you made of people whom you consider to be deviant. Take a look at the list. What do all of the people on your list have in common? That is, is there a characteristic that all of them share, which might point to how deviance can be defined or how we can recognize a deviant when we see one? This issue will be addressed in the next section of the chapter.

beyond the top three or four types of people listed, perceptions of deviance become as diverse as the students making those lists. Anyone the student dislikes or is annoyed by is added to the list—classmates who twirl their hair, people who will not hold the door open for you when you are carrying a heavy bag, country singers, and professors who wear too much beige are just some of the hundreds of unique responses students have given. However, although using the term "deviance" in reference to our own individual pet peeves may be common practice, the concept of deviance transcends the individual level and instead exists at the societal level. That is, deviance is not about people of whom I personally disapprove, but rather is about characteristics of the broader society and sociocultural processes. In other words, just because I personally might not like country singers does not mean that country singers are deviant in Canadian society. Although each of us (along with our individual opinions) is an important participant in the social processes that occur in Canadian society, social processes constitute more than the sum of their parts, and more than the sum of each of our personal points of view. Thus, studying deviance requires moving beyond individual belief, and instead analyzing the broader social processes that occur in the society you live in, regardless of whether those processes correspond to your individual beliefs or challenge them.

In addition to focusing analytical attention on social processes rather than on personal points of view, understanding deviance also requires an exploration of its absence. What is the absence of deviance? The quotation by Mason Cooley that opened this chapter utilizes the term "conformity," which is commonly used to refer to the absence of deviance; in fact, some courses in deviance are titled "Deviance and Conformity." However, the term **"normal"** can also be used, referring to a behaviour or person that conforms (Merriam-Webster, 2002). What is considered deviant exists only in conjunction with what is seen as normal or conforming. But how is it that some people come to be seen as deviant while others are perceived as normal?

How Can We Recognize Deviance When We See It?

Asking the question of how we are able to determine who is deviant and who is normal brings us to the issue of definitions. The dictionary tells us the following:

Deviant: "deviating [straying] from an accepted norm." Synonyms: "abnormal, atypical, aberrant, unrepresentative." Contrasted words: "normal, natural." (Merriam-Webster, 2002)

At first glance, the dictionary seems to make the concept of deviance quite clear. Deviance involves violating norms that have been accepted in society, and apparently this is quite serious, because doing so makes one abnormal and unnatural. Clearly, breaking the rules has significant consequences. Perhaps Mason Cooley, quoted at the beginning of this chapter, was correct in saying that conformity makes one's life easier.

We could stop with the dictionary definition of deviance and let that serve as the foundation for our exploration through the remainder of this book. However, the ways that the word "deviance" is used in academic research and in common usage often differ from the dictionary definition—defining deviance is not as straightforward as the dictionary implies. In the academic realm, deviance is studied by **deviance specialists** who analyze criminal and/or non-criminal forms of deviance; those who focus exclusively on criminal forms of deviance are more specifically known as **criminologists**. Among deviance specialists (including criminologists), the study of deviance has historically been characterized by considerable disagreement over the concept of deviance, and this "problem of definition" (Ben-Yehuda, 1990, p. 4) continues to the present day. That is, even deviance specialists cannot entirely agree on what deviance is. Although contradictory definitions of deviance have co-existed for many decades, some researchers suggest that a broader shift in definitions has become evident over time (Hathaway & Atkinson, 2001). Older definitions, which suggested there is an *objective* way of determining what is deviant, have shifted to more recent definitions that have essentially deconstructed the notion of objectivity, and instead point out that deviance is necessarily *subjective*. **Objective** views of deviance claim that the presence of certain characteristics defines deviance; that is, behaviours or people with those characteristics are deviant, and those lacking such characteristics are normal. By looking for these characteristics, we can all identify deviance. In contrast, **subjective** views of deviance claim that there is no shared, observable characteristic that can clearly tell us who or what is deviant, and who or what is normal—instead, someone must tell us who is deviant in Canadian society. Both the objective and subjective ways of defining deviance will be outlined and explored in more detail as the chapter progresses.

Proposing that there has been a shift from objective to subjective ways of defining deviance implies certain underlying assumptions. The core underlying assumption is that there is an unmistakable distinction between objective and subjective definitions of deviance, so that an objective definition can be clearly differentiated from a subjective definition. The distinction between objective and subjective is typically described as a dualism, or dichotomy, wherein objective and subjective represent two oppositional and mutually exclusive categories (e.g. Ben-Yehuda, 1990; Adler & Adler, 2003). These categories are analagous to the two sides of coin which, when tossed, will show *either* heads or tails, but not both. However, the recent shifts in definitions of deviance often go beyond this notion of objective and subjective as mutually exclusive categories, and instead combine aspects of both. And if it is possible to combine objective and subjective notions of deviance, this raises the question of whether the objective/subjective dichotomy that has been so frequently referred to is even a useful one to talk about in contemporary deviance research. In the following sections, the traditional objective/subjective distinction will be explored. We will look at the different objective definitions of deviance that have been utilized in the academic arena as well as in common usage. Subjective definitions of deviance will also be reviewed. Finally, we will look at how these two different types of definitions may not be so different after all, and how many contemporary ways of looking at deviance are blends of both objective and subjective approaches. Although this section of the chapter began with what looked like a very clear dictionary definition of deviance, when you finish reading the chapter you will see that the subject of this book—deviance—is a far more complex and multifaceted phenomenon than what the dictionary definition suggests.

The Objective/Subjective Dichotomy

Objectivism: Deviance as an Act

The objective side of the dichotomy, as it has typically been depicted, emphasizes the assumption that there is something inherent in a person, behaviour, or characteristic that is necessarily deviant. All "deviants" have something in common that enables us to recognize them when we see them. However, the precise nature of that shared trait is a matter of debate. The traits that have been most frequently postulated include statistical rarity, harm, a negative societal reaction, and normative violation (e.g. Deutschmann, 2002; Sacco, 1992). Each of these traits is emphasized by different deviance specialists, as well as by various laypersons. Each of these traits, when used as a defining characteristic of deviance, has also been subject to criticism by other deviance specialists, particularly those working from a subjective approach.

Statistical Rarity. One of the definitions of deviance that has been associated with the objective side of the objective/subjective dualism is based on **statistical rarity**. Although this is a definition that is not commonly utilized in academic research, it is a definition that is "often heard in everyday conversation" (Clinard & Meier, 2001, p. 7); as a result of its popular usage, it is an important conception of deviance to analyze (Becker, 1963; Ward, Carter, & Perrin, 1994). According to this definition, if a behaviour or characteristic is not typical, it is deviant. Thus, smokers may be thought of as deviant in contemporary Canada, because only 19% of adult Canadians smoke daily (Shields, 2005a). Ex-cons may be thought of as deviant because most people have not been in prison. People with spiked green hair may be thought of as deviant because most people do not have spiked green hair. Because most people are heterosexual (Bagley & Tremblay, 1998), homosexuals may be thought of as deviant.

While this definition of deviance has popular credibility, and although there are particular instances where statistical rarity can be observed, postulating statistical rarity as the defining characteristic of deviance has its limitations. First of all, how we define "rare" presents a problem. Is a behaviour rare if its prevalence is less than 50%? Or does it have to be less than 30%? Tjepkema (2004) has found that 38% of 18- and 19-year-olds are current users of marijuana, as are almost 29% of 15- to 17-year-olds. A significant proportion of Canadian university undergraduates have engaged in binge drinking in the previous month, ranging from 34% in Quebec to 49% in the Atlantic provinces (Adlaf, Demers, & Gliksman, 2005). Are these behaviours rare? The difficulty in determining the criterion for rarity illustrates one of the limitations of this definition of deviance.

A second limitation is that some behaviours are *not* statistically rare, but are still perceived as being unacceptable in the larger society, and are subjected to control efforts. For example, 66% of Canadian youth ages 12 to 15 have consumed alcohol (Hotton & Haans, 2004). Thus, alcohol consumption among young teenagers is statistically *common* rather than rare, and yet most of us would say that it is not acceptable for 12-year-olds to drink. Furthermore, extensive efforts to prevent this behaviour are found in the school curriculum, community programs, and families. A similar illustration of this limitation comes from the study of adolescent sexuality. It might surprise you that as many as 57% of students in Grade 9 and 74% of those in Grade 11 have participated in "heavy petting" (i.e. manual genital stimulation of a partner) (Alberta Medical Association, 1991). Even though this behaviour is not statistically rare, as a society we still initiate efforts to control and reduce it through sex education programs in schools, religious teachings, and socialization in the families.

Third, we must also consider that there are many rare behaviours or characteristics that are not considered deviant in Canadian society. Left-handed people are statistically rare, but they are not treated as deviant, although they were seen that way historically (Barsley, 1967). Sports prodigies (like Wayne Gretzky) are statistically rare, but are respected and envied. Only 26% of Canadians over the age of 12 are physically active (Statistics Canada, 2004a), but few of us would say that people who are physically active are considered deviant in our society.

The proportion of people who are physically active (26%) is actually lower than the proportion of adults ages 20–34 who smoke at least occasionally (30%) (Statistics Canada, 2004b). And yet being physically active is not considered deviant, while smoking is, and has also been subjected to significant levels of social control. This apparent contradiction, as well as the limitations mentioned above, suggests that it is *more than* the statistical number of people who engage in a specific behaviour that determines what is considered deviant in our society. Some deviance specialists propose that the important factor is actually harmfulness.

Harm. The second definition of deviance associated with the objective side of the objective/subjective dichotomy is based on the concept of **harm** (Deutschmann, 2002; Sacco, 1992). That is, if an action causes harm, then it is deviant. The most obvious type of harm is *physical harm.* Thus, if someone harms someone else—for example, through assault, drunk driving, or exposing others to secondhand smoke—then the perpetrator of that harm is deviant. Physical harm can also be done to oneself; for example, smoking may be considered deviant because of the harm caused to the smoker by increased risks of heart disease and various types of cancer. *Emotional harm* can be done to others (e.g. emotional abuse) and to oneself (e.g. repeatedly dating partners with addictions), as well.

Harm may also be directed not at a human being but at society itself; that is, certain behaviours or people may constitute *social harm*, because they interfere with the smooth running of society as a whole. In this context, criminals can be considered deviant because they threaten the safety of the population at large and the social order as a whole. If everyone committed crimes, then anarchy would rule. In fact, implicit in criminal law is the assumption that certain acts must be prohibited because of their harmfulness. In Canada, *all* crimes are considered to harm society itself; the court case is between the Crown (i.e. the state) and the defendant, not the victim and the defendant.

Finally, harm may be directed at something far more abstract and ethereal than a person or society; harm may occur in the form of a *threat to the way we understand the world and our place in it.* Historically, religious belief systems have frequently provided us with this means of abstract understanding on a large scale. Even in contemporary societies, religious belief systems provide many people with a fundamental way of understanding existence. With the example of religion, we can see many instances of this more abstract notion of harm. For example, Joan of Arc was seen as deviant (Brower, 1999), in part because she claimed that she did not need the fathers of the church as a pipeline of communication to God. This violated the dominant religious-based belief system of the time, which claimed only the fathers of the church were able to communicate with God (Read, Armstrong, Pettigrew, & Johansson, 1994). In contemporary society, Muslim women who do not cover their heads may be seen by some other Muslims, who hold a particular interpretation of their religious doctrine, as threatening the fundamental assumptions upon which the religious belief system is based (Fernea, 1998; Todd, 2001).

At first glance, notions of physical or emotional harm to someone, harm to the social order, and harm to abstract world views appear to be useful in

Exercise Your Mind

Since Al-Qaeda orchestrated the attacks on the World Trade Center and the Pentagon in 2001, "terrorism" has become a word we hear daily in the media. Within the context of "harm," terrorism can be perceived as causing all three types of harm, and in multiple ways. Identify the ways that terrorism causes (a) physical harm to others and/or to oneself, (b) emotional harm to others and/or to oneself, (c) harm to the social order and the smooth running of society, and (d) harm to the way people understand the world and their place in it.

recognizing and defining deviance. Many different forms of deviance, from murder and smoking to the behaviour of persecuted historical figures such as Joan of Arc, can be seen as causing harm to someone or something. And perceptions of harm frequently do galvanize social action, such as the creation of non-smoking bylaws. However, a more critical look at the idea of harm is useful.

The very idea of physical harm is not as clear as it might initially appear, and has sometimes changed. Claims of physical harm can be, and have been, disputed. For many years, the tobacco industry claimed that smoking did not cause the harm that anti-smoking activists suggested it did. In the past, some claims of physical harm were greatly exaggerated. A century ago, doctors argued that masturbation caused hairy palms, acne, and outright insanity. For example, look at the following excerpt from a lecture by 19th-century health reformer Sylvester Graham: "'This general mental decay. . .continues with the continued abuses [of masturbation], till the wretched transgressor sinks into a miserable fatuity, and finally becomes a confirmed and degraded idiot, whose deeply sunken and vacant glassy eye, and livid, shriveled countenance, and ulcerous, toothless gums, and fetid breath, and feeble broken voice, and emaciated and dwarfish and crooked body, and almost hairless head—covered, perhaps, with suppurating blisters and running sores—denote a premature old age—a blighted body—and a mined soul'" (cited in Whorton, 2001, p. 3).

Elaborate measures were taken to curb children's masturbation in orphanages, hospitals, boarding schools, and middle-class homes. This included behavioural controls, such as cold baths, intense exercise, sleeping on hard beds, and moderate eating (Hunt, 1998). It also included a wide range of anti-masturbation devices (e.g. see photograph on p. 9). Bondage would prevent children from touching themselves at night. The Stephenson Spermatic Truss prevented erections from occurring. The Bowen Device would pull on the wearer's pubic hair if an erection occurred. Steel armour was padlocked shut at night, and a key was required to allow trips to the bathroom. Penis-cooling devices splashed cold water on the genitals if an erection occurred (Hunt, 1998).

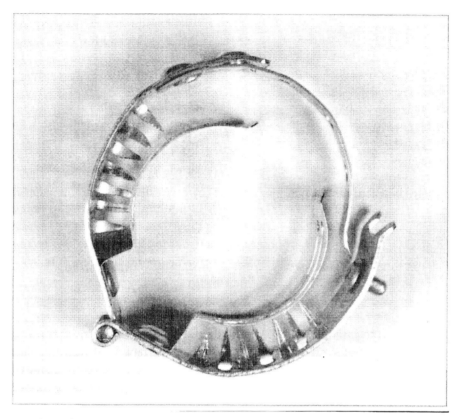

A variety of anti-masturbation devices were used on children during the Victorian era and the early 20th century, because of the harm that the behaviour was thought to cause.

Exaggerated claims about the dangers of marijuana use were also common in the past. In the years leading up to the criminalization of marijuana in 1923, social activists, community leaders, and law enforcement officials spoke out about the physical harm it caused. As can be seen in Box 1.1, marijuana use was alleged to cause horrific violent crimes, murder, idiocy, and ultimately complete insanity and even death. Today, such claims are perceived as greatly exaggerated; however, debates over the physical harm caused by marijuana use continue, as do debates over the physical *benefits* for medical purposes, both of which are fundamental to discussions of the issues of decriminalization and legalization.

When it comes to the idea of interfering with the current social order, or threatening a belief system or world view, the limitations of defining deviance by virtue of harm become more evident. First, whether or not society or a belief system is being *harmed* can be subjective. Are Muslim women who do not cover their heads actually a threat to the belief system contained in Islam? While some people would say so, these women themselves often say there is nothing in the belief system itself that requires it. During the 20th century, there were several

---

Box 1.1 Emily Murphy's Marijuana Campaign

Emily Murphy, the first female judge in the British Empire and a leading Canadian suffragist in the early 20th century, was dismayed at what she saw as the horrors of Canada's drug trade. After interviewing both drug users and law enforcement officials from across North America, in 1922 she wrote the book *The Black Candle* about drug use. One chapter focuses specifically on the harms caused by marijuana use, quoting police officials: "[Marijuana] has the effect of driving the [user] completely insane. The addict loses all sense of moral responsibility. Addicts to this drug, while under its influence, are immune to pain. . . . While in this condition they become raving maniacs and are liable to kill or indulge in any form of violence to other persons, using the most savage methods of cruelty. . . . They are dispossessed of their natural and normal will power, and their mentality is that of idiots. If this drug is indulged in to any great extent, it ends in the untimely death of its addict" (Murphy, 1973 [1922], pp. 332–333). These types of claims are somewhat humorous to today's reader, but had a significant influence on changing drug laws at the time.

---

times when women in North America were accused of harming the social order or abstract belief systems or both. Early feminists who fought for the right of women to vote faced such accusations, as did later groups of women in the 1960s and 1970s when they questioned the "natural" role of women as homemakers and moved outside the home into paid employment. Were these women causing harm to society or to beliefs? Because the word *harm* implies a negative impact, many would say that these women were not *harming* society; they were simply *changing* society. Others would say that by changing society, they were having a negative impact on the social order of the time, and thus were technically causing harm, but that it was a social order that needed to be changed.

All of the above limitations of defining deviance on the basis of harm illustrate the necessity of going beyond the idea of harm in seeking the defining characteristic of deviance. The nature of these limitations is such that this definition of deviance is rarely used in academic literature, although it does enjoy popular usage among laypersons, politicians, and social activists.

Despite the fact that academic literature rarely suggests that harm is *the* defining characteristic of deviance, some literature does acknowledge that harm, or a characteristic similar to harm (i.e. threat or dangerousness), is *one of* the characteristics of deviance. For example, Lianos (with Douglas, 2000) proposes that what is most significant to the study of deviance is not whether someone actually causes harm or is actually dangerous, but rather whether someone *seems* dangerous. Deviance specialists from the subjective side of the objective/subjective dualism suggest we look at the social processes that result in someone being seen as potentially dangerous, and not consider whether that person actually is dangerous. The next *Ask Yourself* exercise has you further explore the concept of harm within the context of contemporary social debates.

Ask Yourself

• •

What are some of the controversial or hotly debated issues that are occurring in your community or in the larger society at the present time? Are you aware of any current debates over whether certain forms of behaviour or certain groups of people should be subjected to measures of control? Are claims of "harm" being made in any of these debates? In those instances, is harm (a) *actually* present, (b) a perception on the part of some groups of people but not others, and/or (c) merely being used as a justification for implementing particular actions?

Societal Reaction. Another one of the definitions of deviance that has been associated with the objective side of the objective/subjective dichotomy is based on the nature of **societal reaction**. People may respond to others in a number of different ways. If the responses of society's "masses" are primarily negative (such as dislike, anger, hatred, stigmatization, and teasing) rather than positive (such as like, admiration, envy, or tolerance), then the person or act being responded to is deviant. Seeing this negative societal evaluation enables us to determine who or what is deviant.

However, focusing on a negative societal reaction as the defining characteristic of deviance raises many questions. Why does society react negatively to some actions, characteristics, or people, and not others? Whose reaction counts? Does my reaction, as a college professor and social scientist, count more than your reaction as a student? Does the Prime Minister's reaction count more than mine? How many individual negative reactions must exist before we can say that "society" is reacting negatively?

The gaps that emerge when defining deviance on the basis of societal reaction are revealed by numerous examples. For instance, Canadian surveys consistently find that "a strong majority. . . favour[s] a limited fine as the maximum penalty for cannabis possession" (i.e. decriminalization), and survey questions about full legalization reveal "an almost even split" (Fischer, Ala-Leppilampi, Single, & Robins, 2003, p. 277). However, despite this data on societal reaction, the current federal government explicitly states that it will "prevent the decriminalization of marijuana" (Conservative Party of Canada, 2006, p. 25). In contrast, the government's position on same-sex marriage is that it will "hold a truly free vote on the definition of marriage, [and]. . . if the resolution is passed, the government will introduce legislation to restore the traditional definition of marriage" (Conservative Party of Canada, 2006, p. 33). Elected officials in Parliament presumably consider a free vote representative of Canadian public opinion—that is, a proxy for societal reaction. The comparison of these two issues shows that the legislative action regarding one issue (i.e. same-sex marriage) is to be based on a representation of societal reaction, while the legislative action on another issue (i.e. the decriminalization of marijuana) is to be independent of societal reaction, and in fact may directly oppose public opinion. These inconsistencies reveal that the law and, more broadly, determinations of who/what is deviant in Canadian society are based upon processes that go beyond societal reaction.

Surveys of public opinion reveal diverse points of view. That is, not everyone shares the same opinion. More than half of Canadians (54%) are in favour of marriage rights for same-sex couples (Matthews, 2005), but that means 46% are not in favour or have no opinion about those rights. A large majority of Canadians (85 to 90%) support the full legalization of medicinal marijuana (Stein, cited in Fischer, Ala-Leppilampi, Single, & Robins, 2003), but that means 10 to 15% do not support it or are indifferent. These types of diverse survey results reveal that societal reactions are not uniform, and different groups of people react in various ways to the same behaviour or issue. Given the plurality of points of view on many issues, it appears that societal reaction alone does not determine how a particular behaviour is treated in Canadian society.

Normative Violation. The dictionary (as cited on p. 4), as well as many deviance specialists, suggests that recognizing deviance is quite straightforward—a behaviour or characteristic is deviant if it violates norms. The "general statement that deviance is focused around the violation of norms" (Ben-Yehuda, 1990, p. 4) is shared extensively among deviance specialists from both the objective and subjective sides of the objective/subjective dichotomy, as well as those who transcend this traditional dualism. However, the manner in which **normative violation** is integrated into a definition of deviance varies among deviance specialists working in the various approaches.

Among deviance specialists working in the objective side of the dichotomy, the violation of norms has been proposed to be *the* defining characteristic of deviance. Indeed, the dictionary definition of deviance makes this point quite clearly as well. Yet even among those recognized as objectivists, the nature of the normative violation seen as constituting deviance has changed. Early objectivists utilized what may be considered an "absolutist" (Adler & Adler, 2003, p. 2) or a value-based (Clinard & Meier, 2001) conception of normative violation, wherein a particular behaviour or characteristic was perceived as being inherently and universally deviant (Ward, Carter, & Perrin, 1994; Adler & Adler, 2003; Clinard & Meier, 2001). According to this view, there are certain immutable norms and values that should be held in all cultures and at all times—norms and values that emerge from an "absolute moral order" (Adler & Adler, 2003, p. 3) based upon the word of God, the laws of nature, or some other immutable source. Because of that absolute moral order, what is considered wrong in one place should be considered wrong everywhere; cross-cultural and trans-historical norms prohibiting incest, murder, and lying are perceived as evidence of this absolute moral order.

The simplistic view of norms in the absolutist view led many objectivists to abandon the absolutist view. However, still working in the objective side of the objective/subjective dualism, another view of normative violation has developed. Among these more modern objectivists, norms are perceived as being culturally specific rather than universal—based on a given society's moral code rather than on any type of absolute moral order (Ward, Carter, & Perrin, 1994). This perspective is still identified as objective, in that someone who violates the norms of the society they live in is seen as deviant. From birth, we are socialized into the norms that govern our society; we learn the standards or the expectations of the society we live in. In Canadian society, as we grow up we are taught to share with others, to be polite, to work hard, to listen to our teachers—in essence, most of us are taught by our parents, teachers, community leaders, and religious leaders to follow the rules. We learn what behaviours will be rewarded (like arriving at work on time) and what behaviours will be punished (like breaking the law). Knowing these expectations, if we then go on to violate the norms, we are "deviant." The *Ask Yourself* exercise requires you to take a closer look at some of the norms in Canadian society.

Ask Yourself

· · · · · · · · · · · · · · · · · · ·

List the norms that are being violated by each of the following people: an obese person; a student that plagiarizes by downloading a term paper from the internet; someone on social assistance; a drug addict or alcoholic; a thief. Remember, norms refer to standards or expectations of behaviour, so ask yourself what expectations each of these people are not living up to—what "rules" of society are they breaking?

Looking at the examples in the *Ask Yourself* exercise, one can see that not all norms are the same. While violating some norms may result in prison (as for the thief), violating other norms has different (and some might say less severe) consequences. The obese person, alcoholic, social assistance recipient, or plagiarizing student will not be entered into the criminal justice system for their normative violations. These differential outcomes of normative violation emerge from the existence of various types of norms, ranging from *folkways* to *morés* to *laws* (Kendall, Murray, & Linden, 2000; Stebbins, 1996). Norms, as standards or expectations of behaviour, can refer to informal, everyday behaviours, such as rules of etiquette, choice of clothing, and behaviour in the college classroom. These kinds of informal norms are called **folkways**, and if you violate these norms, you might be thought of as odd (Adler & Adler, 2003), rude, or a troublemaker. Other norms are taken more seriously. **Morés** are those standards that are often seen as the foundation of morality in a culture, such as prohibitions of incest or homosexuality. If you violate these norms, you may be thought of as immoral (Adler & Adler, 2003) or even evil. Finally, some norms are considered to be so central to the smooth running of society that they are enshrined within the legal system; for example, in Canada's Criminal Code. If you violate the Criminal Code, you will be thought of as a criminal. At times, the legal system integrates morés (e.g. incest is included in the Criminal Code of Canada, and homosexual activities remain criminal offences in several American states); however, other acts that are not perceived as the foundation for morality in our culture (e.g. marijuana possession) are also integrated into the legal system.

AN INTERNET MOMENT

You can find a copy of the Criminal Code of Canada at http://laws.justice.gc.ca/en/C-46/. Look at the Table of Contents to see the kinds of normative violations that have been enshrined within Canada's legal system. You might find it particularly interesting to look at the behaviours that are prohibited in the section on Offences against the Person (which include assault, hate crimes, and bigamy) and the section on Sexual Offences, Public Morals, and Disorderly Conduct. What, if anything, do all of the norms that are being supported in this document have in common, such that they are considered important enough to enshrine within our criminal justice system?

The way that norms are integrated into objectivist definitions of deviance presumes a certain level of consensus (McCaghy, Çapron, & Jamieson, 2003; Miller, Wright, & Dannels, 2001; Ward, Carter, & Perrin, 1994). Although cross-cultural variations in norms are acknowledged, it is assumed that, in a given society, the majority of citizens agree upon the norms. However, deviance specialists working in the subjective side of the objective/subjective dualism find this view of social norms problematic. Some have reservations about the presumption of normative consensus, and question the extent to which a given expectation must be shared in order to be considered a "norm" and then used as an objective standard against which deviance is judged (Ward, Carter, & Perrin, 1994). Some even question whether it is possible to determine the level of consensus that does or does not exist for a given expectation. They point out that there are countless numbers of groups in society having innumerable different sets of rules; even a single individual belongs to multiple groups having varying sets of expectations. Given the multiplicity of individuals, groups, and sets of expectations that coexist in a society, normative consensus is difficult to determine (Adler & Adler, 2003; Becker, 1963). In fact, given all of these different sets of expectations that exist in society simultaneously, which expectations are the ones that constitute society's "norms" and are then used to judge deviance and normality?

In response to these critiques, some deviance specialists have elected to focus on those norms that they suggest are characterized by some consensus, "assuming that the agreed-upon norms of a society can be found in its criminal law" (McCaghy, Capron, & Jamieson, 2003, p. 8). Following this chain of logic, deviance becomes equated with criminality, and the forms of deviance studied include prostitution, drug use, white-collar crime, gang behaviour, and other forms of law-violating behaviour. The practice of equating deviance with criminality has resulted in an academic debate over the differences between the fields of criminology and the sociology of deviance, and whether the sociology of deviance has been subsumed under the umbrella of criminology (Miller, Wright, & Dannels, 2001). Whether focusing on criminal law violations is more illustrative of criminology or the sociology of deviance, the claim that agreed-upon norms can be found in a society's criminal law has itself been questioned.

Some criminologists and other deviance specialists working in the subjective side of the objective/subjective dichotomy draw our attention to the fact that law creation is a political activity, wherein those norms that are embodied in law do not necessarily reflect the opinion of the majority of citizens (Ward, Carter, & Perrin, 1994). Indeed, the creation of a new law in Canada does not require the support of a majority, nor are the opinions of all Canadians sought prior to its creation. Marijuana possession remains illegal, even though since the late 1990s, the courts, the Senate Special Committee on Illegal Drugs, the Canadian Centre on Substance Abuse, the Centre for Addictions and Mental Health, the Canadian Association of Police Chiefs, and public opinion have all recommended its decriminalization (Fischer, Ala-Leppilampi, Single, & Robins, 2003). In this case, "consensus" seems to contradict the law rather than support it. The **consensual view of law**, wherein the law is perceived as arising out of social consensus and is then equally applied to all, is only one of the possible views of crime and law (Siegel & McCormick, 2003).

Critiques of the consensual view of law point to conflict and interactionist views. Criminologists who utilize the **conflict view** perceive the law as a tool used by the ruling class to serve its own interests, and believe that the law is more likely to be applied to members of the powerless classes in society. For example, some research suggests that young offenders who belong to the lower classes are more likely to be drawn into the justice system than are youth of the middle and upper classes. In Canada, self-report surveys of youth crime show us that middle- and upper-class youth are underrepresented in official crime statistics; they are, in fact, committing more crimes than official statistics indicate (Bell, 2002). Why might this be the case? Howard Becker (1963), one of the first deviance specialists to critique objectivist views and propose a subjectivist view of deviance, suggested that even given similar behaviours by lower-class and middle-class youth, police are more likely to enter the former into the justice system, while letting middle-class youth go with a warning or into their parents' custody. Another view of crime, the **interactionist view**, also presents a non-consensual view of criminal law. In this view, it is suggested that society's powerful define the law at the behest of interest groups, who appeal to those with power in order to rectify a perceived social ill. Again, the criminal law is not seen as emerging out of consensus, but rather out of the interests of certain groups in society. Finally, some criminologists portray a more complex view of criminal law, pointing out that the nation's law must attempt to strike some sort of a balance between the interests of the powerful, the opinion of the majority, and the views of special interest groups (Linden, 2000). Looking at these different views, we can see that criminal law is based on more than a simple consensus over what society's norms are.

The normative objectivity of the law has also been critiqued on the question of the situational applicability of broad social norms. For example, in a rather objective fashion we might say that legal prohibitions against murder reflect normative clarity in society—we know that murder is wrong. However, some deviance specialists point out the many situational characteristics that can modify this abstract norm. Depending upon the laws of a particular country, self-defence, capital punishment, military action in wartime, and euthanasia are all circumstances in which taking a human life may be considered acceptable. So, is taking another human life deviant? Looking at the above, we see that the answer to that question is that taking another human life is deviant at some times but not at others. In fact, in situations where taking another human life is considered acceptable, the behaviour is not called "murder"; for example, during wartime, the death of innocent civilians is not "murder," but "collateral damage." Consequently, given the situational variations in which even the most basic norms do or do not apply, some deviance specialists have come to ask whether norms, as reflected in criminal law, are even useful in trying to define deviance (Ward, Carter, & Perrin, 1994).

Some deviance specialists step into this debate over the degree of consensus involved in social norms by proposing that there are some norms that do have higher levels of consensus. For example, despite the situational variations in prohibitions against taking another human life, it is likely that most (if not all) Canadians support the inclusion of homicide in the Criminal Code; the same can also likely be said for auto theft, sexual assault, and break-and-enter. Thio (1983) utilizes the concepts of **high-consensus deviance** and **low-consensus deviance** to distinguish between forms of deviance that have differential levels of support in the broader society. The norms reflected in criminal law are characterized by relatively more consensus than are society's non-legislative norms (such as norms governing physical appearance). And within the law, certain laws are characterized by relatively more consensus than are others.

Although the dictionary defines deviance on the basis of normative violation, the limitations of that definition make this definition problematic. In fact, limitations are associated with each of the objectivist definitions of deviance—not only normative violation, but also statistical rarity, harm, and a negative societal reaction. Some deviance specialists suggest that these limitations have caused a large-scale shift to the subjective side of the objective/subjective dichotomy (Hathaway & Atkinson, 2001).

TIME TO REVIEW

- What does the "problem of definition" refer to, and how is it related to the objective/subjective dichotomy?
- What is the core assumption underlying the objective side of the objective/subjective dichotomy?
- What are the four different objective definitions of deviance? Provide examples of each.
- What are the limitations of each of the objective definitions of deviance? Provide examples of each.

- What are the different types of harm that can occur, according to those who define deviance on the basis of harm?
- How has the objectivist notion of normative violation changed over time?
- What are the different views of the role of consensus in the development of criminal law?

Subjectivism: Deviance as a Label

Having looked at the objective side of the traditional objective/subjective dichotomy, we now turn our attention to the subjective side. From this point of view, there is a very different answer to the question "How can we recognize deviance when we see it?" While objectivists suggest that deviance can be recognized by the presence of a particular characteristic, subjectivists say that we cannot recognize deviance when we see it; someone has to tell us that a person, behaviour, or characteristic is deviant. There is no singular trait or characteristic that is shared by all deviant people throughout history and across cultures, other than the fact that people with some influence on society have said they are deviant (Becker, 1963).

Just as objective conceptions of deviance have changed over time, so have subjective conceptions of deviance. Early subjectivism focused primarily on the process of labelling—deviance is anything that is labelled as such. This form of subjectivism has a negative reaction as its foundation, with Becker (1963) saying that if there is no negative reaction, there is no deviance; in other words, deviance lies in the reaction rather than in the act. The distinction between the ways the concept of "negative reaction" is used by these early subjectivists and the way it is used by objectivists (as discussed earlier in the chapter) is somewhat hazy. The objective use of negative reaction focuses on a *societal* reaction—particular behaviours or characteristics *are* deviant in our society, and we can see that they are deviant by the negative societal reaction that occurs. In contrast, the early subjective use of negative reaction is more abstract, pointing to the reaction as being almost arbitrary—any behaviour may be reacted to negatively, such that we can never know how a particular act will be responded to. The abstract way that early subjectivists used the concept of negative reaction has been subject to criticism, particularly for ignoring the act that stimulated a negative reaction in the first place (Ward, Carter, & Perrin, 1994). The reaction itself does not create the initial act that people are reacting to; in other words, people are reacting to a specific act for a reason—their reactions do not arise out of a purely arbitrary process. It is the processes that contribute to that reaction, and the nature of the reaction itself, that must be analyzed.

Consequently, the **dominant moral codes** (Goode, 1997, p. 29) of a society serve as the foundation for determining who or what is deviant. These are the "lists" of right/wrong, appropriate/inappropriate, moral/immoral that predominate in a particular society at a given time in history and are enforced in multiple ways (e.g. by the criminal justice system, media, and education system). A society's dominant moral codes are shaped by the interests and the actions of groups that hold some level of power.

Contemporary subjective deviance specialists point to the complex nature of power relations. Social processes involve far more than simply the control and oppression of the powerless by the powerful. The use and legitimization of power interacts with negotiations about moral boundaries—negotiations that the less powerful groups in society are also able to participate in. Consequently, "this process does mean that the powerless can resist deviantization" (Ben-Yehuda,

1990, p. 7), rather than simply being at the mercy of the interests of the powerful. Continual negotiations are occurring, such that the social construction of deviance and normality/conformity is in a constant state of flux (Ben-Yehuda, 1990).

Subjectivity and the "Social Construction" of Deviance

Referring to the subjective nature of deviance means focusing on deviance as a *social construction*. In other words, there is nothing inherent in a behaviour or characteristic that makes it deviant; a particular behaviour or characteristic is deviant only if the dominant moral codes of a specific society at a certain time in history say that behaviour is deviant. The subjective view also recognizes that a society's dominant moral codes are influenced by powerful groups. Similarly, what is considered to be normal is also socially constructed, given that notions of deviance and normality exist only in relation to each other (Freud, 1999). **Social constructionism** refers to the perspective proposing that social characteristics (e.g. "thin," "delinquent") are creations or artifacts of a particular society at a specific time in history, just as objects (e.g. houses, cars) are artifacts of that society; consequently, a person, behaviour, or characteristic that is considered "deviant" in one society may be considered "normal" in another society or at another time in history.

Social constructionism has become a dominant force in the study of deviance today. In fact, Goode (1997) suggests that "Most deviance specialists [today] are *constructionists*" (p. 35). However, there are different levels or different types of constructionism. One type of constructionism is labelled **radical** (Goode, 1997) or **strict** (Best, cited in Rubington & Weinberg, 2002); the other type is labelled **soft** or **contextual** (Best, cited in Rubington & Weinberg, 2002). Radical constructionists postulate a distinct theoretical perspective claiming that the world is characterized by endless relativism, that "there is no essential reality to the social world at all, that if everything and anything is simply looked at in a certain way, that is the way it is" (Goode, 1997, p. 35). However, "most [contemporary deviance specialists] are not *radical* constructionists. What I mean by this is that most do *not* believe that *everything* is a matter of definition, that there is *no* essential reality to the social world at all. . . . Rather, most sociologists of deviance believe that there are limits to social constructionism" (Goode, 1997, p. 35). Consequently, sociologists who are soft or contextual constructionists emphasize the processes by which certain social phenomena come to be perceived and reacted to in particular ways in a given society at a specific time in history. In such cases, social construction is addressed in terms of a process rather than a theory, and therefore can be combined with a number of different theoretical approaches, approaches that will be addressed in Chapter 3.

Viewing social constructionism as a process implies that what is of sociological significance is not the individual behaviour or characteristic itself, but rather: (a) its place in the social order; (b) the roles assigned to people who exhibit that behaviour or characteristic; and (c) the meanings attached to that behaviour or characteristic. For example, homosexuality is "universal" in the sense that it has existed across the world and throughout history. What varies is the way that homosexuality is perceived and reacted to in particular societies; thus, while homosexuality is a part of nature, and therefore "biological," it is also "socially constructed." The way deviance is socially constructed emerges from several ongoing multilevel processes (see Figure 1.1) (Nelson & Robinson, 2002). The first process to consider is the *sociocultural* level: beliefs, ideologies, values, and systems of meaning have an influence on the path of social construction. The second is the *institutional* level: the structures of our society, such as government, the education system, and religion that affect social construction. Third is the *interactional* level: our interactions with other people influence the way we think and feel about others, thereby determining the role that each of us plays in social construction. Fourth is the *individual* level: at this level our own identities, concepts of self, and ways of understanding our own existence in the world affect the path of social construction.

Transcending the Objective/Subjective Dichotomy

The objective and subjective sides of the objective/subjective dichotomy, as it has been traditionally expressed, appear to be considerably distinct. On the objective side of the dualism, deviance specialists claim that there is a shared trait that all deviants have in common, a trait that enables us to recognize

Figure 1.1   LEVELS OF SOCIAL CONSTRUCTION

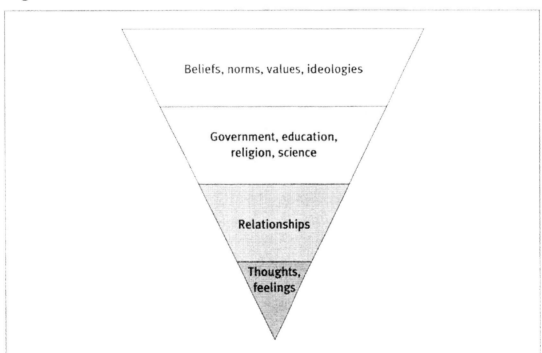

TIME TO REVIEW

- What is the core assumption of definitions of deviance on the subjective side of the objective/subjective dichotomy?
- What are the roles of *power* and *dominant moral codes* according to subjective definitions of deviance?
- What does it mean when we say that deviance and normality are socially constructed?

- What are the two types of social constructionism, and how do they differ?
- What are the four levels at which the social construction of deviance and normality occurs?

deviance when we see it. Although statistical rarity, harm, and a negative societal reaction have each been identified as that shared trait (whether by academics, laypersons, or social activists), the defining characteristic of deviance that is most often identified is that of normative violation. On the subjective side of the dualism, deviance specialists claim that there is no shared trait among deviants; instead, a person, behaviour, or characteristic is deviant if enough important people say so. Through the processes of social construction, which are influenced by power, a dominant moral order emerges that then serves as the standard against which deviance and normality are judged.

The conception of the objective/subjective dichotomy serves as the foundation for the claim that a shift in definitions of deviance has recently occurred, from objective to subjective (e.g. Hathaway & Atkinson, 2001; Goode, 1997). In fact, some deviance specialists suggest that using the subjective, constructionist view in exploring both legal and illegal norm-violating behaviour defines the sociology of deviance as a discipline. However, recent shifts in the study of deviance may, in fact, transcend the objective/subjective dualism, with elements of objectivism and subjectivism being integrated to varying degrees.

We have already seen some evidence of this in the previous discussions of dualism. For example, we have seen that, over time, objective deviance specialists have changed their conceptions of norms from that of an absolute moral order to that of a culturally specific moral order. Similarly, over time, subjective deviance specialists have acknowledged the role of norms in defining deviance, but in terms of norms that may be socially constructed and determined by processes of power. For example, Evans (2001) suggests that small group–specific normative systems *can* be identified. Evans delineates the set of norms that governs behaviour in Married Life chat rooms, which then serves as the standard against which certain types of chat room behaviour are judged deviant and made subject to a negative reaction by other group members. Tittle and Paternoster (2000) also propose that group-specific normative systems can be identified, and on a different level, they identify the normative system of middle-class America. Their discussion of norms goes a step further by suggesting that, although this is only one of countless numbers of normative systems in society, it is the one that has come to dominate American society as a whole, through the power that the middle class holds in processes of social construction: ". . . [T]he middle class dominates U.S. society, both by imposing its standards through the schools, the mass media, and the law and by enjoying a degree of natural hegemony in behavior styles and thinking that flows from the admiration and emulation of those with higher status" (p. 29).

Many contemporary definitions of deviance combine normative violation, negative reaction, harm, power, and/or social construction (Hathaway & Atkinson, 2001; Ward, Carter, & Perrin, 1994; McCaghy, Capron, & Jamieson, 2003). For example, Stebbins (1996) defines deviance as normative violation, but goes on to say that the nature of society's response to that violation depends upon the level of perceived threat the normative violation entails, and that the structures and processes of power relations in society influence this entire process. In fact, a retrospective look at work by earlier deviance specialists reveals that the distinction between objective and subjective has always been somewhat blurred. Even Howard Becker (1963), one of the leading proponents of the subjective view of deviance, integrated the notion of harm into his definition of deviance. He stated that deviance is that which is so labelled, but that this process of labelling depends on who has committed the act and who feels harmed by it.

The boundaries of objective and subjective become further blurred when looking at the extent to which the objective traits that have been discussed are present within processes of social construction. For instance, interest groups that are opposed to same-sex rights sometimes argue that homosexuality is statistically rare, a violation of the laws of nature or the word of God, or a threat to "the family" and to any children being raised by gay or lesbian parents. People who work toward toughening young offender legislation bring arguments of harm into their work. Those trying to decriminalize marijuana possession often refer to changing public attitudes that reflect a positive societal reaction to the issue of marijuana use. All of these groups are involved in the process of social construction in that they are attempting to influence the meanings attached to a particular behaviour, its place in the larger social order, and the roles assigned to individuals who engage in that behaviour. Yet they also draw upon objectivist concepts as a foundation for their arguments, so that objectivist traits are embedded within the subjectivist process of social construction.

Examining the complexities of the work of both past and present deviance specialists indicates that perhaps the traditional objective/subjective dualism that has served as the foundation for discussing definitions of deviance in the field has always been an oversimplification. The actual nature of the work done by sociologists of deviance frequently transcends the dichotomy, blending aspects of both objective and subjective. Rather than being embedded in a dichotomy, definitions of deviance and research on deviance may actually fall along more of a continuum, with more objective assumptions lying at one end of the continuum and more subjective assumptions lying at the other (see Figure 1.2).

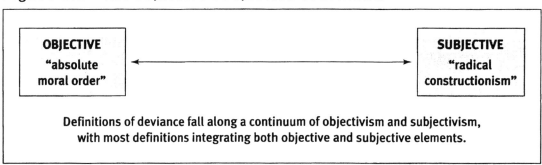

Figure 1.2   THE OBJECTIVE-SUBJECTIVE CONTINUUM

| OBJECTIVE "absolute moral order" | ⟷ | SUBJECTIVE "radical constructionism" |

Definitions of deviance fall along a continuum of objectivism and subjectivism, with most definitions integrating both objective and subjective elements.

At the extreme objective end of the continuum are those deviance specialists who have proposed an absolute moral order as the standard for determining deviance; at the extreme subjective end are the most radical constructionists, who suggest that there is no reality outside of perception. The definitions and analyses of each deviance specialist fall somewhere along this continuum, with some being more objective in nature and some being more subjective in nature. Those researchers who lean toward objectivism may be more likely to study those forms of deviance that Thio (1983) referred to as high-consensus forms of deviance, such as homicide, gang membership, white-collar crime, police corruption, and prostitution. Those researchers who lean toward subjectivism may be more likely to study those forms of deviance that Thio referred to as low-consensus forms of deviance, such as marijuana use, pornography, swinging, gambling, and aspects of physical appearance (e.g. tattoos, body piercing, punk rockers, goths, and being overweight).

Studying Deviance

The way that deviance is defined along the objective-subjective continuum has implications for the way deviance is studied. That is, deviance specialists who lean more toward objectivism will study deviance in ways that those who lean more toward subjectivism will not (and vice versa).

Studying the Act: Why People Behave the Way They Do

Those who perceive more objectivity in deviance shine their analytical spotlight on a particular act or characteristic in question. The deviant nature of these behaviours/characteristics is, to some extent, taken for granted (because, after all, they *are* violating norms, or *are* causing harm, etc.), and then the details of the deviance are studied—who the people are, how they became deviant, what their lives are like (Richardson, Best, & Bromley, 1991; Rubington & Weinberg, 2002). In essence, the interest lies in explaining the person, behaviour, or characteristic in question.

Studying Social Processes: The "Deviance Dance"

Deviance specialists who focus more on the subjective aspects of deviance are less interested in shining their analytical spotlight on the "deviant," and more interested in shining it on society and social processes—the perceptions of and reactions to the act, as well as the role of power in those perceptions and reactions. The focus becomes the "**deviance dance**"—the interactions, negotiations, and debates among groups with different perceptions of whether a behaviour or characteristic is deviant and needs to be socially controlled and, if so, how. The participants in this "dance" each take certain "steps" in order to move the dance in the direction they desire, whether that direction is the creation of a new law, the legalization of a behaviour that was previously illegal, achieving public recognition of a new social problem or one previously ignored, or changing public perceptions that will reduce the prejudices faced by certain groups. In some cases, this "dance" may be characterized by considerable cooperation among the participants in achieving a consensual goal—analogous to a country line dance in which everyone does precisely the same steps. In other cases, it is characterized by participants taking opposing steps, but still moving together in their negotiation over the outcome—analogous to a waltz, where one partner moves backward and the other forward as they set their joint course across the dance floor. And in some cases the "dance" may look more like a mosh pit at a heavy metal or punk rock concert—with each participant moving independently of the others and in varying and often opposing directions, intentionally pushing, shoving, and ramming into other participants in order to move in his or her own individually desired direction.

Exercise Your Mind

List some current examples of each of these types of "dances": (a) groups who agree that a particular behaviour is deviant and work together in trying to control that behaviour (i.e. a "country line dance"); (b) groups whose perceptions are somewhat different (e.g. they may agree that a behaviour is deviant, but disagree as to how to best control it) but who still cooperate in some way (i.e. a "waltz"); and (c) groups who have completely different perceptions (e.g. they disagree as to whether a behaviour is deviant at all) and try to impose those perceptions on others (i.e. a "mosh pit").

Studying struggles and debates over deviance requires going beyond the problem of "radical phenomenalism" (Ben-Yehuda, 1990, p. 5) that some researchers see as plaguing the sociology of deviance, wherein countless numbers of specific phenomena (e.g. call girls, drug users, swingers) have been studied in tremendous detail but without paying attention to larger social structures. Ben-Yehuda (1990) suggests that the "study of deviance should be reframed. . .

within general societal processes [of change and stability], in a dynamic historical and political perspective" (p. 5). In this vein, understanding an act of deviance requires understanding its larger context in a society's value systems, and understanding the configuration of power relationships that influence the negotiation of moral boundaries among different groups of people.

Studying Acts and Social Processes

Both the more objective and the more subjective approaches lend to our understanding of deviance. The most comprehensive knowledge emerges from combining an analysis of the social processes involved in the "deviance dance" and an explication of the act or characteristic in question. For example, information about why people become overweight can be combined with knowledge of the processes by which certain people come to be perceived as "too fat" and are then made subject to various measures of social control. Similarly, an understanding of why people engage in certain sexual behaviours can be combined with knowledge of the processes by which certain sexual behaviours are typed as deviant and made subject to measures of social control, while other sexual behaviours are labelled as conforming and thereby become the standard against which other behaviours are judged. Each of these levels of understanding paints an important part of the picture of deviance that will be integrated into this textbook—that is, at various points we will analyze acts/characteristics, perceptions of and reactions to those acts, and the role played by power in these perceptions and reactions.

The Role of Powerful People

Who are the "important" people that are able to influence the dominant moral codes of society, from which emerge standards of deviance and normality? In Canadian society, some of the most powerful groups involved in this process are politicians/government, scientists, religious institutions, media, and commercial enterprise. Each of these groups of people may act as or have a relationship with **moral entrepreneurs**. Becker (1963) coined this term to describe those individuals and groups who take action to try and influence or change the development and enforcement of society's moral codes. For example, participants in the temperance movement, the abolitionist movement, and the "child-savers" movement all acted as moral entrepreneurs during the Victorian era.

In the temperance movement, members of church-based groups (frequently women's groups) throughout North America and Great Britain declared the "demon liquor" a social evil, and sought to reduce alcohol consumption; that is "temperance." In Canada and the United States, groups of people acting as moral entrepreneurs sought abolition (the eradication of slavery under the law) and demanded voting rights for women (see the photograph on p. 26). And throughout North America and Western Europe, the "child-savers" influenced child labour laws, sought the criminalization of child abuse and neglect, and encouraged compulsory education for children. During the 1950s and 1960s, North America's

Ask Yourself

. . . .

Make a list of groups of people that you are aware of who try to influence society's dominant moral codes by seeking to influence our notions of right/wrong, bad/good, deviant/normal, acceptable/unacceptable. At its simplest level, these are groups that you feel are trying to change people's perceptions of a particular behaviour or group of people.

civil rights activists acted as moral entrepreneurs in their efforts to end segregation and gain rights for African-Canadians and African-Americans. All of these groups had an influence on society's dominant moral codes, and thereby on perceptions of what was considered deviant and normal. In contemporary society, we continue to see groups of moral entrepreneurs, as illustrated in the *Ask Yourself* exercise.

Perhaps the most central group in society that acts as or has a relationship with moral entrepreneurs is composed of *politicians*. Politicians are the people in whom ultimate power has been vested in modern state systems: they have powers to invoke, revoke, and determine the enforcement of legislation and social policy. Interest groups, acting as moral entrepreneurs who have identified a social ill that they think must be solved in some way, often lobby the government to initiate change.

A second group, comprised of *scientists*, is able to effectively make claims that influence society's moral codes. The claims made by scientists are backed by the domain that is granted perhaps the highest level of credibility in our society—that of science. As we will see in the chapter on science and deviance later in the textbook, when scientists proclaim truths, many of us will believe those claims simply because scientists say so. When scientists tell us that smoking is harmful, or that having sex too frequently indicates an addiction, or that hearing voices indicates mental illness, they have a persuasive impact on what we see as being "normal." When making such claims, scientists themselves may be acting as moral entrepreneurs; in addition, the claims made by scientists may be used as convincing support for the efforts of other moral entrepreneurs, such as anti-smoking activists.

Religious institutions have also played a central role in the creation of the dominant moral codes that determine deviance and normality. For example, during the Middle Ages and into the early Renaissance, the Christian church was the instigator of witch persecutions and the Spanish Inquisition, both of which resulted in countless numbers of people being tortured and killed for their deviance. In the present day, the power of religious institutions can be seen in the many nations in which religious-based governments are the source of social order. For instance, the displaced Taliban government imposed a particular and extreme interpretation of Islamic beliefs on the people of Afghanistan. Contemporary Canadian society is characterized by a separation of church and state; however, the influence of religion on perceptions of deviance and normality maintains its presence in many ways. Canadian society itself is built upon a Judeo-Christian foundation. For example, two of our national statutory holidays,

In the early 20th century, groups of women in the United States and Canada acted as "moral entrepreneurs," and demanded the right to vote.

those days when most businesses are closed, are Christian holidays—Christmas Day and Easter Sunday. Our criminal law is based on the Judeo-Christian ethic of free will—we are responsible for our own actions, and redemption can occur through punishment (Linden, 2000). At a more individual level, many Canadians adhere to various religious belief systems. Their belief systems provide them with moral codes that subsequently affect the role individuals play in larger social processes. For instance, the Victorian prohibitionists, abolitionists, and child-savers described earlier were typically members of various Christian church-based groups. A later chapter in this book looks more closely at the relationship between religious institutions and the "deviance dance."

In our 21st-century world, the *media* serves as the central battleground in the struggles over moral codes. The media is a powerful tool used by a wide range of moral entrepreneurs. When politicians, medical doctors, or interest groups endeavour to raise awareness of an issue or sway public opinion, they turn to the media. Public service announcements, press conferences, and issue-driven advertisements all appear in the media. The media is not just a tool used by moral entrepreneurs, however; it also acts as a moral entrepreneur itself in terms of the choices made about what will and will not be included on a particular program or in a particular commercial segment. For example, when the television news program *Dateline* features child molesters being captured through sting operations, it contributes to the construction of pedophilia as a deviant (and criminal) activity.

Finally, in a modern capitalist economy, *commercial enterprise* has a significant level of power as well, frequently in conjunction with the use of the media; in fact, most components of the media itself are commercial enterprises driven by a profit motive. Ads, commercials, magazines, television programs, and movies tell us how we are and are not supposed to look: punk rock characters in a movie are the butt of the movie's jokes; magazine articles tell us we will be happier if we can just lose those 10 pounds by Labour Day; Seth and Marissa on the television program *The O.C.* show us the right clothes to wear. They tell us how we are supposed to act: beer commercials show us that drinking is the best way to have fun with friends; a fictional television show tells us that "potheads" are losers; and a nighttime news program tells us that joining a cult is problematic.

Commercial enterprise has power outside of the media as well. For example, Giesbrecht (2000) discusses the power of the alcohol industry over the content and form of alcohol policies created by government. The manner in which alcohol production, marketing, and consumption is controlled in both Canada and the United States is determined, in part, by the influence of the alcohol industry itself. A similar example can be seen in the historical development of the institution of law in modern state systems. It is the law that delineates those actions considered to require the greatest level of control by society; historically, English law developed on the basis of merchant and commercial interests. With the end of feudalism, kings had much to gain from the wealth of merchants involved in international trade. Feudal lords no longer had the means to finance the nation's warfare and colonial expansion, but merchants did. It was in the best financial interests of the king, as he oversaw the development and growth of a centralized state, to form it in accordance with commercial interests. These origins serve as the foundation for modern Canadian law, wherein most legal infractions by those involved in commercial enterprise are dealt with under the more lenient civil law rather than the more punitive criminal law (Linden, 2000).

This brief discussion of politicians, scientists, religion, media, and commercial enterprise demonstrates the complexity of the notion of power. People are powerful for many different reasons, and their power operates in diverse ways. The moral entrepreneurship of one group of powerful people may contradict or even oppose the moral entrepreneurship of another group of powerful people; for instance, the efforts of commercial enterprise might oppose the efforts of members of a religious-based group. But regardless of whether one group's involvement in social construction contradicts or, conversely, coincides with another group's involvement in social construction, the process through which they operate is the same—that of social typing.

The Social Typing Process

As moral entrepreneurs influence the content and enforcement of society's dominant moral codes, the foundation is laid for the standards that subsequently determine deviance and normality. A closer look at the process by which some people come to be seen as deviant and others come to be seen as normal reveals what Rubington and Weinberg (2002) label **social typing**. This three-component process has the end result of changing the way society treats people who are typed or categorized as deviant.

The first component of the social typing process is **description**, wherein a label is placed on an individual because of an observed or presumed behaviour or characteristic. The exact nature of the label that is applied is dependent on the culture in question (Rubington & Weinberg, 2002). For example, in contemporary Canada we are more likely to label someone a "terrorist" than a "heretic"; in contrast, in Europe during the 16th century, people were more likely to be labelled "heretics" than "terrorists." Terrorism is a social phenomenon that has become an integral part of our world view in the 21st century, while the concept of heresy reflected the religious foundations of the European world view in the 16th century.

The second component of the social typing process is **evaluation**. This occurs when a judgment is attached to the individual by virtue of the label that was previously attached or the category that individual was placed in under the description component. If someone is socially typed as deviant, this judgment is characteristically negative in nature.

The third component of the social typing process is **prescription**. This is where the processes of social control or regulation emerge. Because of the label that has been given and the resulting judgment that occurs, the individual is treated in a particular way—a way she or he would not be treated if the initial label had not been applied. In other words, individuals are made subject to a range of social treatments designed to regulate or control their deviance. Just as the larger culture determines the initial label that is used, it also shapes the nature of the prescription that is utilized (Rubington & Weinberg, 2002). For example, a Canadian woman who violates standards of female dress is likely to be teased or stared at rather than made subject to stoning, as women in Taliban-controlled Afghanistan were.

Exercise Your Mind

Go through the three components of the social typing process, using the example of someone who is obese. What description or label is given to this person? What judgments or evaluations are attached to this person because of the label you have just given him or her? Finally, how is this person treated or socially controlled?

Forms of Social Control

The regulation or social control of a person who has been subjected to the social typing process can occur at multiple levels. It may be *formal* or *informal* in nature (Rubington & Weinberg, 2002; Edwards, 1988; Becker, 1963). The informal aspect of the prescription component emerges at the level of patterns of informal social interaction—patterns of interaction with diverse people—such as family members, friends, acquaintances, colleagues, or strangers. As you go about your day seeing many different people, you react to them and interact with them in various ways. You may smile at, frown at, stare at, tease, laugh at, agree with, disagree with, talk to, avoid, ignore, criticize, applaud them, and more. These are all means by which **informal regulation or social control** can occur. You can see one example if you think back to your adolescent years. Perhaps as you were leaving the house, your parents saw what you were wearing and clearly disapproved. They may have asked, "What do you think you're wearing?" They may have said, "In those baggy pants you look like a bum!" Or they may have even sent you back to your room to change. That is informal regulation. Alternatively, you may have noticed people staring at you and laughing when you walked down the street. Informal social controls can include staring, laughing, frowning, avoiding, shaming, and more (Goode, 1997; Edwards, 1988; Braithwaite, 2000). Informal regulation comprises much of our daily lives today, and prior to industrialization it served as the dominant way that deviance was controlled (Spector, 1981). Take a moment to look at the *Ask Yourself* exercise, and consider how informal social control affects your life.

Ask Yourself

• • • • • • • • • • • • • • • • • • •

As a student at the college or university you attend, how is your behaviour or appearance informally controlled? In other words, how is your behaviour or appearance controlled at the level of everyday social interaction?

In answering the *Ask Yourself* question, you may have referred to peer pressure; that is, the desire to fit in with your classmates might have an effect on the clothes you wear to class, the way you style your hair, or whether you go to the library versus the bar after class. Maybe you recall a time when you were whispering to a friend during class and two of your classmates gave you a dirty look or even asked you to keep it down. When you first became a post-secondary student, perhaps an older sibling gave you advice on what it would be like and how you should act. These are all examples of informal control.

Formal social controls involve processing at some type of an organizational or institutional level. Prior to industrialization in the Western world, church prohibitions served as the central means of formal social control. With industrialization and the creation of a centralized government, there was a dramatic increase in organizations and agencies involved in regulation and social control (Spector, 1981). A wide range of types of formal regulation can serve as controls for deviant behaviour—a nation's laws (such as Canada's Criminal Code); a school or work dress code; regulations governing driver's licences or hunting permits; a teacher punishing a student for misbehaviour; or the psychiatrists' handbook that lists the symptoms of various forms of mental illness.

Look at the next *Ask Yourself* question regarding formal social controls in your life. In answering it, you could have referred to registration requirements—you are permitted to take Class B only if you have already passed Class A. You could have referred to the regulations governing student conduct at your college or university. What behaviours are considered unacceptable and what are the consequences for those behaviours? Perhaps you referred to a course syllabus, which tells you what exams and assignments you must complete in order to pass a particular course. Maybe you attend a college that has a student dress code. After an outburst in class, possibly the chair of the department gave you a written reprimand or made you see a student counsellor. These are all examples of **formal regulation**.

Ask Yourself

• • • • • • • • • • • • • • • • • •

As a college or university student, how is your behaviour or appearance formally regulated? How is it controlled at an organizational or institutional level?

Social control may be *intentional* at times, such as through the creation of rules that must be followed by a child, student, employee, or citizen of the state. At other times regulation might be the result of a more *general influence*; for instance, professionals such as doctors and lawyers have a general influence on their clients' lives (Edwards, 1988). Social control may be either **retroactive** (treating a known deviant in a certain way) or **preventative** (trying to prevent deviance in the first place—through socialization, for example) (Edwards, 1988). Social control may be directed at an individual by someone else (e.g. a doctor, a parent, or a judge), or may occur at the level of **self-regulation** or self-control, where people regulate their own behaviours (such as by dieting to try and conform to an idealized body image, by joining a self-help group to end an addiction, or by avoiding behaviours that they know will be stigmatized) (Foucault, 1995; Gottfredson & Hirschi, 1990).

Of course, because the social construction of deviance and normality are embedded within a bigger "dance," it means that a particular behaviour, characteristic, or person is not subjected to only one social typing process at any given moment. Multiple social typing processes may be going on simultaneously, processes that may even contradict each other. One segment of society may socially type someone as "deviant," while another segment of society may claim that same person is "normal." In some arenas of society, for example, someone who is perceived as overweight is labelled "too fat," has negative judgments attached to them, and is then treated in particular ways as a result; however, in other arenas of society that person may be seen as "normal" or "healthy."

Even if there is some agreement that a person, behaviour, or characteristic is deviant, there may be differing views on what the appropriate forms of social control are. For example, while some people suggest that addiction is a disease and should be medically regulated, other people disagree and argue that another form of social control, such as punishment, should be instituted. Thus, within these multiple social typing processes, the claims made by one group often must compete with the claims made by another; claimsmakers compete with other claimsmakers "in a [deviance] marketplace" (Richardson, Best, & Bromley, 1991, p. 5). But the principal role of power in this process ultimately means that some people's claims count more than other people's, and that some people's claims have a greater bearing on the society at large—its norms, its structure, its institutions, and its people.

The consequences of the social typing process, whereby a person, behaviour, or characteristic becomes typed as deviant or, in other words, **deviantized**, are far-reaching. Through this process ". . . description becomes prescription, which is then transformed into a desirable standard of normal behaviour to be upheld and maintained by the educational system, the religious system, the legal system, and of course the psychotherapeutic system, and to which every section of the population has to measure up or be found deficient" (Freud, 1999, p. 2).

TIME TO REVIEW

■ Why is the notion of an objective-subjective *continuum* more accurate than that of a *dichotomy*?

■ In what way do researchers' locations on the objective-subjective continuum influence their study of deviance?

■ What is the "deviance dance," and why is it relevant to the study of deviance?

■ What are moral entrepreneurs? Provide examples.

■ What role do politicians, scientists, religion, media, and commercial enterprise play in the development of society's dominant moral codes?

■ What are the three components of the social typing process, and why do multiple social typing processes coexist?

■ What are the different types of social control or regulation? Provide examples of each.

Our Journey through this Book

In the process of transcending the objective/subjective dualism and of integrating analyses of acts, perceptions/reactions, and power relations, many questions will serve as a guide in the remaining chapters of this book:

■ Where does a particular act or characteristic come from?

■ What is the nature of the social typing process? What are the descriptions, evaluations, and prescriptions that are being applied to this person, behaviour, or characteristic?

■ Who has done the social typing?

■ What is the foundation for their arguments?

■ Who benefits from the deviantizing of this behaviour, characteristic, or person?

- What larger social conditions support the social typing process?
- How is the "deviance dance" evident?

These kinds of questions will guide us in our understanding of deviance in relation to sexuality, youth, physical appearance, mental disorder, religion, and science. The choice of these topics is intended to provide you with critical insight into some of the core processes, as well as the people, that make up the foundation of our society. Such critical insight will be based on both specific structures and processes of deviance as described in the particular topics above, as well as at a level of theoretical understanding and explanations of deviance more generally. By the end of this book, you will see that you are not an outsider looking in at deviance in society, but instead will see that deviance is a part of *your* life every day.

CHAPTER SUMMARY

- We all can make a list of people we find annoying. However, the concept of deviance exists at the level of social processes, not personal opinion.

- The study of deviance is characterized by disagreement about how deviance should be defined. Some deviance specialists suggest that there has been a general shift from *objective* to *subjective* definitions, drawing upon the notion of an objective/subjective dualism or dichotomy.

- The *objective* side of the dualism suggests that there is a single characteristic that distinguishes "deviant" people from "normal" people. The four different defining traits that laypersons, social activists, politicians, or academics have mentioned are *normative violation, statistical rarity, societal reaction*, and *harm*.

- According to the subjective side of the dichotomy, the only characteristic all deviant people have in common is that *enough important people have called them deviant*. In other words, deviance is a *social construction*.

- Looking at deviance from a social constructionist point of view, what is of interest are a particular behaviour's place in the social order, the roles assigned to people who exhibit that behaviour, and the societal meanings attached to it.

- Recent work in the study of deviance integrates both objective and subjective components. Thus, objectivism and subjectivism may be thought of as existing along a continuum, rather than as a dichotomy.

- The way that deviance is defined has implications for the way it is studied. Some researchers focus their analyses on the deviant act without further contextualizing it, assuming that the act can be classified as a form of deviance, while others focus their analyses on the processes involved in the perception of and reaction to the act.

- The perceptions of *powerful groups* play the central role in the creation of the *dominant moral codes* that underlie the construction of deviance. In our society, powerful groups include politicians, religious institutions, scientists, media, and commercial enterprise.

- Central to issues of deviance are the processes of *social typing*, wherein someone is labelled in a particular way, judged on the basis of that label, and subjected to measures of social control. Such treatment can occur through various levels of regulation or social control—formal, informal, preventative, retroactive, and via the self.

RECOMMENDED READINGS

Becker, H. (1963). *Outsiders: Studies in the Sociology of Deviance*. London: Free Press of Glencoe.

Edwards, A. R. (1988). *Regulation and Repression: The Study of Social Control*. Sydney, Australia: Allen & Unwin.

RECOMMENDED VIEWING

Read, D. (Director), Armstrong, M., Pettigrew, M., & Johansson, S. (Producers). (1990). *The Burning Times*. Available from the National Film Board of Canada. (56 minutes).

This documentary explores the European witch persecutions. It serves as an excellent opportunity to apply the core concepts introduced in this chapter. Viewers can look for the objective characteristics of deviance (i.e. rarity, harm, normative violation, and negative societal reaction), the three components of the social typing process, and the role of powerful groups.

Apatow, J. (Writer/Director), & Carell, S. (Writer). (2005). *The 40-Year-Old Virgin*. United States: Universal Pictures. (116 minutes).

In this comedy, a man who is a virgin at the age of 40 is socially typed as deviant by his co-workers and made subject to various measures of social control as they attempt to "cure" him of this problem.

ENDNOTES

1 Mason Cooley [b.1927]. Columbia World of Quotations. City aphorisms, fourteenth selection. New York. Retrieved August 23, 2006, from **www.bartleby.com**

2 David Lee (producer of Frasier). Rand Lindsly's quotations from The Quotations Page. Retrieved August 23, 2006, from **www.quotationspage.com**

KEY TERMS

deviance,   **p. 2**

conformity,   **p. 2**

normal,   **p. 3**

deviance specialists,   **p. 4**

criminologists,   **p. 4**

objective,   **p. 4**

subjective,   **p. 4**

statistical rarity,   **p. 5**

harm,   **p. 7**

societal reaction,   **p. 11**

normative violation,   **p. 12**

folkways,   **p. 13**

morés,   **p. 13**

consensual view of law,   **p. 15**

conflict view of law,   **p. 15**

interactionist view of law,   **p. 15**

high-consensus deviance,   **p. 16**

low-consensus deviance,   **p. 16**

dominant moral codes,   **p. 17**

social constructionism,   **p. 18**

radical/strict constructionism,   **p. 18**

soft/contextual constructionism,   **p. 18**

deviance dance,   **p. 23**

moral entrepreneurs,   **p. 24**

social typing,   **p. 28**

description,   **p. 28**

evaluation,   **p. 28**

prescription,   **p. 28**

informal social control/regulation,   **p. 29**

formal social control/regulation,   **p. 29**

retroactive social control,   **p. 30**

preventative social control,   **p. 30**

self-regulation,   **p. 30**

deviantized,   **p. 31**

CHAPTER 3

The Chicago School

Excerpts from: Part Two - Theories of Deviance and Crime

The aims of this chapter are to familiarize the reader with:

- the ways in which the early work of Guerry and Quetelet influenced the later work of Shaw and McKay and Cohen and Felson
- the adaptation of ideas from plant and animal ecology in the explanation of deviant and criminal behaviour in urban settings
- the substance of the ecological and routine activities approaches
- connections between Sutherland's differential association and the ecological perspectives of the Chicago school
- the nine propositions of differential association
- the ways in which Glaser's differential identification and Burgess and Akers's differential reinforcement complement differential association
- the policy implications of human ecology, routine activities, and differential association
- deficiencies in the human ecology, routine activities, and differential association perspectives
- the contributions of the human ecology, routine activities, and differential association approaches to the understanding of deviance and crime

INTRODUCTION

A deeply rooted interest in the urban environment was perhaps the central concern of the sociological tradition that originated at the University of Chicago in 1892. Chicago's population grew at an impressive pace from 1850 to 1900, and the social fabric of this dynamic and changing city formed the basis of much of the school's empirical research. On the basis of their observations of city life and the process of **urbanization,** Chicago sociologists developed explanations for a variety of social phenomena, including deviance and crime (Park, 1952). Their approach resembles that of Guerry and Quetelet of the early ecological school, except that the Chicago ecologists used their empirical observations to develop explanations of deviance.

This chapter examines the **Chicago school's** contributions to the understanding of deviance and crime. Contained within the Chicago tradition are macro-level theories (human ecology and routine activities) and a micro-level theory (differential association). The discussion begins with ecological theory in its general form and focuses on how ecological theories account for deviant and criminal behaviour. The chapter then outlines the routine activities perspective as a contemporary extension of ecological ideas. The micro approach — differential association — is then examined to show how it is rooted in the theory of human ecology. The chapter continues with a discussion of the policy strategies inherent in each of the Chicago school approaches and concludes with an assessment of their deficiencies and contributions.

HUMAN ECOLOGY

One of the most noticeable patterns observed by social scientists at the University of Chicago was that city areas inhabited predominantly by the poor, by recent immigrants, and by ethnic minorities displayed high rates of nonconformity. Their task became to explain this relationship by modifying and applying ecological theory, a schematic framework borrowed from the biological sciences (Hawley, 1986).

The ecological approach to understanding the organization of living matter in natural environments focuses on the relationships of plants and animals both to each other and to their physical surroundings. This interaction strongly affects the activity and survival of all organisms. Human ecology likens human communities to plant and animal communities and, in the process, makes two simple observations: racial, class, and other groups affect one another's daily lives; and these groups are also affected by a variety of conditions in the urban environment, including land use, property values, the location of industry, and natural boundaries such as rivers, highways, and railroad lines.

Chicago sociologists argued that all these intricate relationships form a social system, or "web of life." They believed that the "normal" conditions of this complex system are equilibrium and order. They envisaged change as an evolutionary process involving the gradual adaptation of people and groups to alterations in the characteristics either of one another or of their physical surroundings (Faris, 1967).

In particular, two central and interrelated concepts from the science of plant ecology were adapted and applied to the sociological analysis of city life. The first was the notion of symbiosis, and the second was the idea of invasion, dominance, and succession (Vold and Bernard, 1986). *Symbiosis* refers to a condition of mutual interdependence among organisms in an environment that is necessary for their survival. Forms of life compatible with each other and with the environment survive. When species become incompatible with one another or when the nature of the environment changes, some forms of life inevitably suffer or perish. In the world of nature, plants produce oxygen that is vital to the survival of animals. Animals produce carbon dioxide that is equally essential to the survival of plants. This mutually dependent relationship among plants and animals exemplifies symbiosis. The slow destruction of large masses of plant life through industrial expansion and pollution, however, undermines this equilibrium. The ultimate loss of food and shelter caused by acid rain, for example, is dramatically changing the nature of animal and bird life in affected areas. The demolition of urban slums represents an analogous change in the physical surroundings of city dwellers. The elimination of housing affordable to disadvantaged class and ethnic

groups requires both their adaptation and relocation. An important point emphasized in the ecological approach is that change in one part of the system invariably affects other system components.

The sequential process of invasion, dominance, and succession in biology involves species competing with each other for scarce resources, thus changing the balance of relationships in any given geographical area. The balance of nature changes as new species drive out competitors, come to dominate the environment, and eventually form stable interdependencies themselves. After a forest fire, for example, weeds and grasses move in, followed by scrub brush, which eventually gives way first to coniferous and later to deciduous trees. These changes in plant life affect the distribution of animals, which depend on various plants for survival. In a similar process, industrial and commercial establishments reclaim slum areas. New and modern banks, business establishments, and government offices replace dilapidated housing. In the process, people living in these run-down areas are displaced to other locations.

An examination of Chicago's growth patterns suggested an evolutionary process whereby urban expansion occurs radially from the city core outward in a series of concentric bands, each of which is continually expanding (Burgess, 1925) (see Figure 3.1). The Chicago school maintained that this series of concentric zones emerges from the ecological process of competition; in this instance, for valuable land. The Chicago ecologists noted that each concentric zone reflects a different land value, land use, residence pattern, and cultural character. They did not, however, believe that all cities necessarily perfectly exemplified the concentric zonal pattern. Rather, they employed this image as an ideal type against which to assess actual urban patterns.

According to Chicago ecologists, land is most expensive in the core of the city. Only commerce, industry, and government can afford the high prices there. They dominate the core by erecting banks, stores, theatres, hotels, public transportation centres, and government offices. The band immediately adjacent to the central business district is the transitional zone. Located next to the ever-expanding industrial core, the transitional zone's property values are sharply eroded. Since property owners believe that buildings in this sector will eventually be torn down to make room for industrial and commercial expansion, they do not maintain the buildings. Residential

FIGURE 3.1

CHICAGO'S CONCENTRIC ZONES

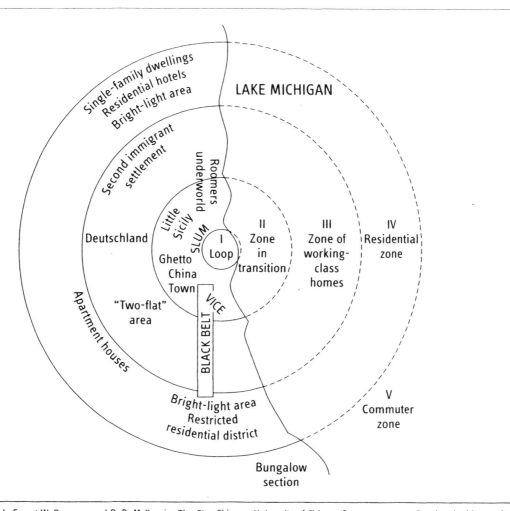

Source: Robert E. Park, Ernest W. Burgess, and R. D. McKenzie, *The City*. Chicago: University of Chicago Press, 1925. p. 55. Reprinted with permission of University of Chicago Press.

areas in this zone deteriorate as higher-status residents flee to the suburbs. Their low rents make these dilapidated and run-down dwellings attractive to impoverished ethnic and immigrant populations.

The third zone contains relatively inexpensive two- and three-family dwellings inhabited by members of the working class, who had previously migrated outward from the transitional zone. In the fourth zone are the more expensive apartments and single-family dwellings occupied by the middle class. Small business and professional offices are also present in this ring. In the outermost sector are the residences of the more affluent commuter population. This outlying suburban area has more recently become the contemporary satellite city.

Each of the five zones contains "natural areas." In the transitional band, these natural areas are ghettos. In the third and fourth zones, the natural areas are communities united by ethnic or religious ties. Often physical boundaries such as railway tracks, rivers, or roads separate these areas from other parts of the city.

CLIFFORD SHAW AND HENRY McKAY AND SOCIAL DISORGANIZATION

While examining the geographical distributions of deviant and criminal activity in Chicago, Clifford Shaw and Henry McKay (1969 [1942]) noted that

FIGURE 3.2

SOCIAL DISORGANIZATION THEORY

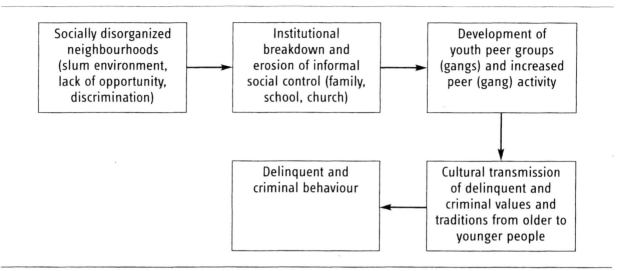

rates of nonconformity and illegal conduct are highest in the **transitional zone.** They contend that industrial growth and urban expansion erode the traditional social controls inherent in the family, the church, and the community, and they argue that this erosion is particularly severe in the transitional zone. Areas where social controls are weakened or severed are "disorganized" and consequently susceptible to increased levels of deviance.

Shaw and McKay explain the social disorganization in these neighbourhoods by referring to the combined impacts of industrialization and urbanization. Industrial expansion requires labour power, and when workers arrive to meet the employment needs of industry, population size and density increase. Groups of people with vastly different social backgrounds and cultural traditions are brought together. Given the diversity of ethnic origin, language, religion, and occupation, conflicts over differing values, norms, beliefs, and behaviours are inevitable. Moreover, high rates of geographical and social mobility also converge to weaken the ties binding people in a community to one another. Primary social relationships are particularly difficult to sustain in the transitional zone because this band is under constant pressure from the ever-expanding commercial centre.

As the spectre of invasion by industry and commerce becomes a reality, land values in adjacent areas plummet and the population flees for more desirable locations farther from the city core. Consequently,

living conditions in the transitional area deteriorate, and the area fills with a heterogeneous mix of marginally employed or unemployed lower-class immigrant groups. The deleterious effects of diversity, geographical mobility, and conflict are compounded in the transitional zone by poverty, substandard housing, and inadequate social services, education, and recreation. Shaw and McKay argue that these conditions continue to erode traditional social controls and encourage unconventional activity and illegal conduct (see Figure 3.2).

LAWRENCE COHEN AND MARCUS FELSON AND ROUTINE ACTIVITIES THEORY

The routine activities approach developed by Lawrence Cohen and Marcus Felson (1979) and the **lifestyle–exposure perspective** advanced by Hindelang et al. (1978) explain crime by charting the way in which everyday living creates a structure of opportunity that brings people into direct contact with predatory criminals. In this fashion, **routine activities theory** provides a detailed explanation of a particular type of victimization, one in which a predator definitely and intentionally takes or damages the person or property of another. The intellectual foundations of the lifestyle–exposure approach rest in the pioneering work of the ecological sociologists of the Chicago school.

FIGURE 3.3

ROUTINE ACTIVITIES ANALYSIS

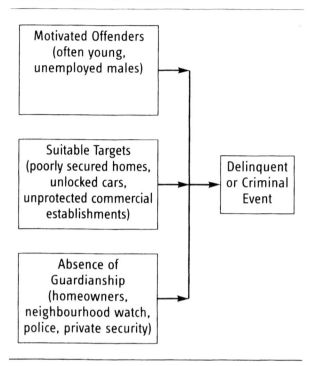

Cohen and Felson (1979) link fluctuations in crime rates to changes in people's routine activities that create the convergence in space and time of three elements: a **motivated offender,** a suitable target, and the absence of guardianship against predation (see Figure 3.3). The convergence or separation in time and space of these three factors, Cohen and Felson maintain, explains increases and decreases in crime rates in the absence of alterations in society's economic and social structure. Structural conditions such as economic recession, racial heterogeneity, rising unemployment, and heightening rates of family dissolution are less relevant as direct explanations of intentional predatory crime than are alterations in space and time of patterns of behaviour that bring together offenders and targets in the absence of guardianship. Indeed, Cohen and Felson maintain that a target without protection is the key element that produces victimization.

Before examining the central propositions of the theory itself, three important facets of the time dimension should be considered. The first, *periodicity,* refers to regular cycles of behaviour such as going to work from Monday to Friday, visiting the bars on Friday and Saturday nights, and walking the dog after

dinner. The second element, *tempo,* concerns the number of events in a particular period. The number of visits to bars on Friday night, the number of times church is attended on Sunday mornings, and the number of vacations taken away from home during the winter school break are examples. The final consideration is *timing,* the coordination among different but interdependent activities that comprise the rhythm of life for potential offenders and prospective victims. The meeting in time of victim and offender may well leave the victim feeling that he or she was in the wrong place at the wrong time. The successful offender would respond more positively.

With respect to motivation, routine activities analysis does not try to explain why certain individuals or groups are criminally inclined. The theory treats the motivation of offenders largely as a given. It is the "spatio-temporal" organization of social activities that translates criminal proclivity into action.

Target suitability varies on a number of important dimensions. First, some targets are more valuable than others, either monetarily or symbolically. To a car thief, a Corvette may be worth more than a Toyota Tercel. Second, some targets are more visible and accessible than others. A case of beer on the passenger seat of an unattended vehicle is more vulnerable than a case hidden in the trunk. Finally, targets vary in terms of their "inertia." By target inertia, Cohen and Felson refer to such considerations as the size and weight of the object to be stolen and the strength and combat skill of the person to be accosted. In the former case, the large and the heavy are usually less vulnerable than the small and the light. In the latter case, young males may be less at risk than elderly females.

Guardianship refers to the degree to which targets are protected. In routine-activities terms, vulnerability is a function of social organization and technology. The organization of groups and the technology available affect not only access to targets and the ways and means of attack, but also resistance to assailment. In general terms, women's participation in the labour force is a broad change in social organization that has varied over time and across regions. In places and times where most women work at home providing care to young children, burglary rates might be lower than they would be in places and times where most women work outside the home and where children are nonexistent, in day care, or fully grown. Larger numbers of people at home for extended periods of time each day dampens the enthusiasm of all but the most intrepid or stupidest of burglars. Furthermore, the impacts upon target accessibility and target guardianship have changed dramatically over the past fifty years as a result of new technologies. Armoured trucks, automatic weaponry, telephones, closed-circuit televisions, credit cards, time-locked safes, automated teller machines, and exploding dye bombs have had a considerable impact on both the execution and control of robbery.

Routine activities analysis relates deviant and illegal conduct to other legitimate social behaviours in which people normally engage. Patterns of everyday legitimate activities determine the location, type, and frequency of illegality in a given community or society. Some locations and types of behaviour entail greater risks of victimization than do others (Messner and Blau, 1987). Work and leisure are two spheres of activity that figure prominently in the production of intentional crime because they largely determine the amount of time that people spend in their dwellings. In considering the risk of victimization in relation to recreation, for example, one's lifestyle governs where one is during the day and in the evening, whether one is in the company of friends or strangers, whether or not those in one's immediate environment are the same or different in terms of demographic characteristics, and whether the locations of activity are characterized by the presence or the absence of criminogenic conditions such as alcohol consumption, the availability of weapons, architectural blind spots, and poor lighting.

Routine activities theory posits that social structural variables affect criminal opportunity, which in turn affects the rates of certain types of crime. Structural variables worthy of consideration vis-à-vis their impact on lifestyle include a community's ratio of males to females, its age distribution, its family organization, its affluence, and the nature of its marketplace. Cohen and Felson note that changes in these variables have altered lifestyles from what they were before the Second World War. Canadian society in the 1970s, for example, was younger and more affluent than it was in 1935. Changes in the economy and in the labour force reduced the number of women spending their days toiling within the home. Compared with the situation in 1935, the market during the 1970s involved a vastly larger number of valuable, small, and light goods. This trend continues,

and Cohen and Felson suggest that increases in rates of theft, shoplifting, burglary, and robbery should not be surprising.

EDWIN SUTHERLAND AND DIFFERENTIAL ASSOCIATION

The theory of **differential association** is one of the most influential and popular explanatory frameworks in the sociology of deviance. It was outlined by Edwin Sutherland of the University of Chicago in his 1934 criminology text, was first set out in proposition form in 1939, and was refined to its present structure in the 1947 edition of the textbook (Sutherland, 1947). The theory of differential association has remained largely unchanged since that time (see Figure 3.4).

Sutherland's perspective was influenced by the ecological approach. Shaw and McKay had provided an explanation of why crime rates varied across certain social groups. They had observed from official crime data that urban dwellers, nonwhites, members of the lower classes, and males were consistently more involved in crime than were rural residents, whites, the affluent, and females. In developing their explanation, Shaw and McKay (1931) observed that various geographical areas have different levels of social disorganization, which undermine traditional forces of social control and are the root cause of high rates of deviance. Once established in a particular area, the high rates of deviance and crime are transmitted from one generation of inhabitants to the next.

Sutherland, building on these ideas, suggests that some social groups possess pro-criminal traditions and that others have anti-criminal traditions. Both types of tradition, he maintains, are passed down through generations in a process of socialization. Groups with cultural traditions encouraging deviance (e.g., urbanites, blacks, the poor) have higher crime rates than groups with cultural traditions promoting conformity (e.g., rural inhabitants, whites, the rich). This part of Sutherland's thinking is a "cultural transmission" explanation of deviance and crime. According to cultural transmission theory, two primary factors affect deviant behaviour. The first is the degree to which cultural traditions stimulating nonconformity characterize the group. The second is the extent to which these traditions are passed on from generation to generation.

FIGURE 3.4

DIFFERENTIAL ASSOCIATION THEORY

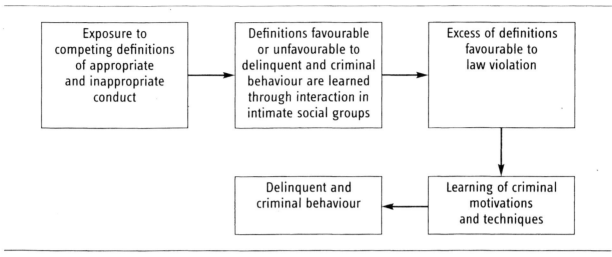

Sutherland's major concern, however, is to explain why participation in deviant and criminal activity varies from one individual to the next. Why are some people more criminal than others? To answer this question, Sutherland modifies ideas from the ecological and cultural transmission traditions and constructs his theory of differential association. He outlines his theory in nine propositions (Sutherland and Cressey, 1970):

1. *Criminal behaviour is learned.* People learn to act criminally in the same way that they learn other behaviours. The propensity for deviance is neither inherited nor the result of a personality defect. Stealing a car, using a computer to embezzle funds from a bank, driving a truck, and removing a brain tumour are all learned behaviours.
2. *Criminal behaviour is learned in interaction with other persons in a process of communication.* Through words and gestures exchanged with others, people learn how to perform criminal acts just as they learn conventional behaviours.
3. *The principal part of learning criminal behaviour occurs in intimate personal groups.* The greater the intimacy among group members, the more effective is the communication of the message. Sources of information can vary from the personal (e.g., family and friends) to the impersonal (e.g., television and newspapers). Personal sources of information, particularly families, are

more powerful because of their higher degrees of intimacy.

4. *When criminal behaviour is learned, the learning includes (a) the techniques of committing the crime, which sometimes are very complicated and sometimes very simple, and (b) the specific direction of motives, drives,* **rationalizations,** *and attitudes.* Corporate price fixing, drug smuggling, burglary, and prostitution require skills varying tremendously in complexity and sophistication. In addition, each of these crimes requires the perpetrator to justify the illegal act as an acceptable way to acquire money. For example, embezzlement by computer requires computer programming and accounting skills. Transgressors might rationalize the act by arguing that the victimized organization "owes" the embezzler the money or that the embezzled funds are merely being "borrowed."
5. *The specific directions of motives and drives are learned from definitions of legal codes as favourable or unfavourable.* Their **reference group**'s view of the law affects people's commitment to criminal or conforming behaviour. There is an increased probability that individuals will develop an aversion to criminal behaviour if their reference group respects the law. However, if the reference group has contempt for the law, the individual is more likely to engage in crime. Where members of the reference group have mixed feelings about legal codes, a person is more likely to be ambivalent about crime.

6. *A person becomes criminal because of an excess of definitions favourable to violation of the law over definitions unfavourable to violation of the law.* This proposition is the core of differential association theory. It states that if people associate more with patterns of ideas encouraging participation in deviance and crime, they are more likely to violate the rules. Two important points related to this proposition must be emphasized.

First, the notion of criminal patterns refers to ideas, not persons. Strictly speaking, proposition 6 does not state that if a person associates with criminals, he or she, on that basis alone, is more likely to become criminal. Rather, it refers to connections with *definitions of the situation* or with ideas that support the commission of crime. Thus, law-abiding persons may transmit definitions conducive to law violation. For example, law-abiding parents who complain about the unfairness of income tax may provide their children with a rationalization for cheating on their tax returns later in life.

Second, differential association comprises more than one type of association. The key word in proposition 6 is *excess*. People are exposed differentially to two types of definitions, criminal and law-abiding. While everyone is influenced to some degree by both types of definition, one type probably has greater primacy than the other. What is important is the ratio of pro-deviance definitions to pro-conformity definitions. Association with more criminal ideas than conventional ideas is the root source of nonconforming and illegal conduct (Thio, 1988).

7. *Differential association varies in terms of frequency, duration, priority, and intensity.* When individuals are frequently confronted with messages promoting deviance and infrequently confronted with messages encouraging conformity, they are more likely to deviate from the straight and narrow. The longer the time during which deviant ideas are conveyed, the greater the probability that the person will engage in nonconforming activity. Priority refers to the time of life at which a person is presented with ideas favouring deviance or conformity; the younger the person, the more influential the ideas are likely to be. Finally, the level of affectivity or emotional commitment between an individual and those persons providing the deviant and conforming definitions sways the person's behaviour. Intense bonds to deviant associates, combined with weak ties to conventional comrades, increases the likelihood that the person will choose a deviant path.

These four aspects of differential association are not entirely independent. Their effects may be cumulative. Where definitions favourable to violation of the law are relatively frequent, take place over a long period of time, are experienced early in life, and emanate from people held in high regard, the probability of nonconformity and illegal conduct increases significantly.

8. *The process of learning criminal behaviour by association with criminal and anti-criminal patterns involves all the mechanisms involved with any other type of learning.* Criminal and law-abiding patterns differ in terms of content but not in terms of the process through which knowledge is acquired. Learning how to research and write an essay, how to invest money wisely, how to cheat on exams, and how to rob banks all require the same learning process.

9. *Although criminal behaviour is an expression of general needs and values, it cannot be explained by them, because noncriminal behaviour is an expression of the same needs and values.* Most people value material acquisitions in general and money in particular. These motivations do not explain why some people commit burglary, robbery, or fraud since many other people choose legitimate ways to attain these same goals. Rather than break the law to get what they want, they work overtime or take on a second job.

The ecological theory of Shaw and McKay and Sutherland's differential association approach are mutually complementary. Differential social organization across different social groups results in their embodying, to varying degrees, criminal or conventional traditions. Exposure by birth or by migration to these differing group traditions causes individuals to differentially associate with mainly criminal or mainly law-abiding definitions. This differential association with patterns of ideas in turn results in criminal or conforming behaviour, depending on the degree to which the balance of these associations is tipped one way or the other. Where the associations are mostly favourable to law violation, people will break the law. Where the associations are mostly

FIGURE 3.5

DIFFERENTIAL IDENTIFICATION THEORY

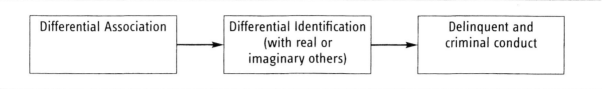

unfavourable to law violation, people will obey the law. Individuals are more likely to engage in crime if they are members of groups with criminal traditions. Conversely, they are more likely to avoid participation in illegal action if they are members of groups with law-abiding traditions.

Differential association theory has spawned a good deal of research and much critical debate. Part of this debate concerns the generality of the theory. Some critics argue that the mechanisms through which differential association produces crime need to be specified in more detail. Consequently, refinements of the theory have been offered by Daniel Glaser in the form of differential identification and by Robert Burgess and Ronald Akers in the form of differential reinforcement.

DANIEL GLASER AND DIFFERENTIAL IDENTIFICATION

Daniel Glaser (1956) criticizes Sutherland on two counts. He argues that differential association theory presents an overly mechanistic image of criminality, in which the individual is mechanically propelled into involvement with crime as a result of excessive association with criminal traditions. According to Glaser, Sutherland does not sufficiently emphasize individual role taking and choice making. He also points out that Sutherland's theory was developed when mass media were less influential than they now are. As a result, Sutherland does not take sufficient account of the potential impacts of indirect interactions.

To remedy these deficiencies, Glaser constructs a theory based on differential association but with an additional component that he terms "identification." Glaser maintains that, to be influenced by criminal traditions, the individual must identify with definitions of deviance conveyed by real or

imaginary others who deem nonconforming behaviour acceptable (see Figure 3.5). Importantly, while **differential identification** operates in the context of both deviant and conforming groups, it does not necessarily involve groups of which the individual is actually a member. Criminal traditions need not be transmitted to the individual by persons in close proximity. Attachment may occur between an individual and either a real or a fictional character if that character is attractive and admirable. The notion of identification is useful in explaining media contributions to deviance and crime. Differential identification also provides an account of how a nonconformist might be part of a conforming group and how a conformist might belong to a nonconforming group.

ROBERT BURGESS AND RONALD AKERS AND DIFFERENTIAL REINFORCEMENT

Robert Burgess and Ronald Akers's dissatisfaction with Sutherland's differential association theory stems from their feeling that it is not sufficiently specific about the nature of the learning process. They maintain that Sutherland fails to clearly demarcate the mechanisms alluded to in proposition 8, which refers to the way in which learning occurs. To correct this deficiency, they identify differential reinforcement as the necessary but missing link between the initial cause, excessive association with traditions encouraging deviance, and the effect — deviant behaviour (Burgess and Akers, 1966). Drawing on behavioural psychology, they introduce the concept of **operant conditioning** as an intermediary stage in the process, as shown in Figure 3.6.

FIGURE 3.6

DIFFERENTIAL REINFORCEMENT THEORY

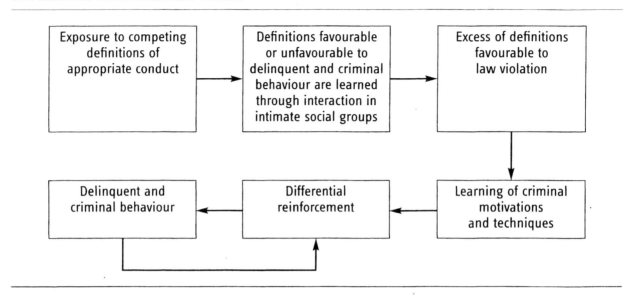

Burgess and Akers claim that people engage in deviant conduct if and only if its social or material rewards outweigh those attached to conformity. In short, one continues activities that are rewarded and desists from activities that are punished. For example, through interactions with friends, teenagers learn the skills and rationalizations necessary for becoming "high" on drugs. To the extent that the sensations are pleasurable and rewarding, drug use is likely to continue. Conversely, feeling guilty or having a "bad trip" will likely reduce subsequent use.

THE CHICAGO SCHOOL AND SOCIAL POLICY

Human Ecology

Shaw and McKay cite as a key cause of deviance and crime the social disorganization that results from rapid industrialization and urbanization. Since it is impossible to halt industrial growth and urban expansion, human-ecology policy initiatives focus on countering the social disorganization that frequently accompanies this growth. Policymakers have attempted to provide communities in transitional areas with the means to encourage social organization. Community-building initiatives such as improving schools, building recreational facilities, and providing

on-the-street social services are attempts to strengthen traditional social controls and improve the quality of neighbourhood life (Liska, 1987).

Routine Activities

Cohen and Felson argue that motivated offenders in contact with suitable targets without adequate guardianship affect the likelihood of illegal conduct in more than an additive fashion; the effects are multiplicative. Therefore, their convergence results in sharp increases in crime that are relatively immune to control through doctrines and policy initiatives aimed at deterrence. Rather than try to increase the effectiveness of police and court crime-control tactics, routine activities and lifestyle–exposure theorists reason that modest alterations in lifestyle are likely to meet with greater success. Since high material standards of living create opportunities for crime, policy directives based on routine activities analysis stress the importance of controlling victimization through increased guardianship or "target hardening" — steps must be taken to make targets either less suitable or less accessible.

Differential Association

Differential association states that nonconformity and crime are consequences of the excessive transmission, through group members, of an excess of deviant over

TABLE 3.1

THE CHICAGO SCHOOL

Theory	Theorist(s)	Central Premise	Key Concepts	Principal Contributions
Human ecology: Social disorganization	Clifford Shaw and Henry McKay	Institutional breakdown and a lack of social control give rise to values and norms conducive to illegal conduct; older youth socialize their younger counterparts to law violation in stable slum environments	Web of life; symbiosis; invasion, dominance, and succession; social disorganization, mobility, heterogeneity, and poverty; concentric zones (zone of transition); differential social organization	Explains enduring patterns of illegal behaviour in impoverished inner-city areas over time
Routine activities	Lawrence Cohen and Marcus Felson	People's everyday behaviours are linked to a structure of opportunity that renders them vulnerable to intentional property and personal crime. Crime occurs where three essential ingredients – motivated offenders, suitable targets, and the absence of guardianship – converge in space and time. The suitability of target varies in terms of value, accessibility, and inertia. Guardianship also varies on the bases of social organization and technology. The theory considers three dimensions of space and time: periodicity, tempo, and frequency.	Offender; target; guardianship; value; accessibility; inertia; periodicity; tempo; frequency	Highly relevant to the practice of crime prevention in modern society; policy based on the theory is relatively inexpensive, politically palatable, and effective
Differential association	Edwin Sutherland	Individuals learn to commit crime from exposure to an excess of pro-deviant definitions	Differential association; learning; frequency, duration, priority, and necessity	Explains crime across the social structure
Differential identification	Daniel Glaser	Individuals learn to commit crime through a process of identification with definitions of deviance conveyed by real or imagined others who favour rule violation	Differential identification	Explains potential for media contribution to deviant and criminal activity
Differential reinforcement	Ronald Akers and Robert Burgess	Individuals' learning to commit crime is enhanced by having criminality more often rewarded than punished	Differential reinforcement; operant conditioning	Augments differential association with principles of learning theory (operant conditioning); incorporates psychological principles

conforming definitions. The policy implications are clear: to reduce deviance, the ratio of nondeviant to deviant associations must be increased. Since the theory identifies socialization in reference-group contexts as the principal conduit through which individuals internalize illegal traditions, much of the policy stemming from differential association theory aims at reducing contacts between individuals and criminal groups and increasing contact between individuals and law-abiding groups. Typical strategies include diverting individuals from the correctional system altogether or placing them in secure settings that limit their contact with hardened criminals. These initiatives stem from the widely held view that correctional institutions are training centres in which inmates refine their skills and motivations on the road to career criminality (West, 1984).

Other initiatives grounded in differential association theory include the use of helping professionals and the establishment of self-help groups. In the first instance, psychiatrists, social workers, and correctional personnel may serve as sources of conventional definitions. These professionals meet with clients regularly to provide advice, support, and treatment to assist rehabilitation and reintegration into conventional society. Self-help groups like Alcoholics Anonymous and Synanon, consisting of reformed alcoholics and former drug addicts, promote the development of nondeviant definitions through resocialization. Group members who have themselves experienced alcohol and drug addiction seek to help others break the habit and return to more productive lives.

The frequency, **duration,** and **intensity** of contacts between deviants and their pro-conformist referents affect the success of these efforts. These factors are likely to be less influential for the clientele of the helping professions than for the voluntary members of self-help organizations (Liska, 1987).

Table 3.1 summarizes the development of the Chicago school's ideas.

EVALUATION OF THE CHICAGO SCHOOL
Human Ecology

Human ecology has been criticized for overemphasizing social disorganization. Critics argue that the terms "organizational diversity" or "differential social organization" better capture the reality of the situa-

tion. The essence of the critics' claim is that the transitional zone merely has different forms of social organization, which appear disorganized only from a staunchly middle-class point of view (Matza, 1966).

In addition to confusing differential social organization with disorganization, human ecologists display another middle-class bias. Shaw and McKay assume that middle-class areas of cities are more homogeneous and more cohesively organized (and hence less deviant) than inner-city neighbourhoods (Mills, 1943). However, these presumed high levels of social integration and cohesion do not always exist in affluent neighbourhoods. Moreover, while the official data used by Shaw and McKay reveal a strong concentration of deviance and crime in transitional zones, other sources such as crime surveys suggest that residents of middle-class neighbourhoods also perform large numbers of nonconforming and illegal acts (Jensen and Rojek, 1980). Furthermore, since police patrols tend to be more concentrated in impoverished slum neighbourhoods than in affluent middle-class districts, and since the types of crime committed by the lower classes are of the more visible street variety, the profile of criminal activity is distorted. The essence of these criticisms is that crime is simply more easily detected in lower-class ghettos than in higher-class neighbourhoods.

Measurement problems have made the determination of cause and effect particularly problematic in earlier human ecology research. The theory holds that social disorganization results in higher rates of deviance. All too often, however, disorganization itself is measured by the existence of a high rate of rule violation. It is hardly surprising that social disorganization (measured by high rates of deviance) is highly predictive of deviance (measured by high rates of deviance). Since the measurements of cause and effect are virtually identical, the exercise represents a rather circular analysis (Kornhauser, 1978).

Recent assessments of the ecological approach have employed indicators other than rates of deviance as measures of social disorganization (Chilton, 1964). These improved measures include degrees of ethnic differentiation, ratios of owners to renters, and ratios of singles to families. High degrees of ethnic difference, more renters than owners, and more singles than families are taken to indicate less social cohesion and community attachment. Conversely, ethnic homogeneity, home ownership, and resident families indicate greater cohesion.

The prediction is that less neighbourhood integration will result in more nonconformity. Research based on the ecological model has consistently supported this hypothesis. Deviance and crime, at least as it is measured in official data, are consistently concentrated in city areas characterized by poverty, transience, urban decline, and ethnic diversity (Brantingham and Brantingham, 1981).

The success of programs for improving the quality of life and reducing crime in disadvantaged urban areas is uncertain. Although many of these programs have operated for a long time, their impacts on crime reduction have not been subjected to methodologically rigorous research (Miller, 1962). While improved services and facilities may have many positive consequences, their direct relationship to the control of deviant and criminal activity is difficult to assess.

Critics have attacked the policy of the ecological approach by charging that it advocates treating symptoms rather than alleviating causes. They maintain that the problems in disadvantaged areas are consequences of an economy that advantages some groups at the expense of others. The ecological perspective advocates providing slum residents with sufficient resources to increase their educational and occupational opportunities and to otherwise adjust to the problems they face. Many sociologists argue that these efforts do not seriously address issues of inequality. Providing genuine solutions to the problem of urban decay, they maintain, requires more radical social and economic change (Vold and Bernard, 1986).

When it was introduced in the early part of this century, the ecological approach did much to counter the dominant biological and psychological theories of deviance and crime. Residents of disadvantaged urban neighbourhoods were widely considered deviant as a result of racially inherited biological and psychological deficiencies. What Shaw and McKay and others demonstrated was that various class and ethnic groups were deviant only while residing in slum areas. Once they abandoned the transitional zone for the more affluent outlying sectors, they joined the ranks of the law-abiding (Faris, 1967). This finding was powerful evidence that social and economic conditions associated with certain urban areas were more responsible for increased rates of drug addiction, alcoholism, mental illness, suicide, and crime than were the individual traits of residents.

Routine Activities

Routine activities theory has received a good deal of support empirically. It has, however, been criticized on several grounds. First, its treatment of offender motivation as both given and constant offers little insight into what propels some but not others, under identical circumstances, to commit crimes. Second, the relative weights of the three central components — motivated offenders, suitable targets, and the absence of guardianship — remain unclear. Finally, routine activities theory ignores expressive crime. While it provides a good account of intentional instrumental illegal conduct, it provides little insight into crimes such as murder and assault, in which passion frequently plays a role (Meithe, Stafford, and Long, 1987).

Differential Association

Both differential identification and differential reinforcement are supported by empirical testing. Differential identification, however, is unclear about whether identification consistently occurs before or after the deviant activity it is supposed to explain. If identification with a criminal figure, real or imaginary, occurs after the deviant or criminal act, it cannot be considered to have contributed to that act (Thio, 1988).

Burgess and Akers emphasize the positive experience of reward that results in deviant acts being repeated time and again. However, critics point out that the theory does not explain why someone would commit a deviant act in the first place (Thio, 1988).

Differential association emphasizes the learning of skills and motives in group contexts. Some sociologists have pointed out that much of deviance and crime requires no special skills and that nonconformity comes naturally (Glueck, 1956). They cite violence, vandalism, and ordinary theft as examples of unsophisticated acts that often occur in the heat of passion or on impulse. Moreover, they argue that deviant acts for which there are no cultural or subcultural supports are not well accounted for by differential association. Incest and child molesting, for example, appear universally unsupported by the traditions of any group.

Developing concrete empirical measures has also been problematic for differential association theory. It is difficult to isolate and identify empirically the presence, in an individual, of too many definitions favouring either deviance or conformity. Similarly, indicators and accurate estimates of frequency, duration, priority, and intensity have proven elusive (Nettler, 1984).

The difficulty of measuring excesses of definitions has led researchers to employ a proxy indicator — group membership. Persons who are members of deviant groups are assumed to be associated with deviant traditions. This "bad companions" conceptualization of deviance causation, while departing significantly from Sutherland's initial conceptualization, has received considerable empirical support (West, 1984).

While members of deviant groups are indeed more deviant than members of conforming groups, a major debate revolves around this fact. Differential association, as presented in this revision, suggests that membership in deviant groups results in the learning of skills and motivations that encourage and result in deviant behaviour. Several critics point out that an alternative sequence is equally plausible: deviants may seek out persons with similar predispositions. The question is which comes first — membership in deviant groups or deviant behaviour (Gomme, 1985b).

SUMMARY

Human ecology approaches examine the geographical distribution of deviance and crime in urban areas. Districts plagued by social and economic deprivation also experience more deviant and criminal activity. Ecologists explain this empirical association between deprivation and deviance by arguing that traditional forms of social control in these areas have broken down and left these neighbourhoods socially disorganized. This erosion of traditional social control is seen as a result of industrial expansion and urbanization. Human ecology recommends various forms of urban renewal and community building, but their effectiveness in reducing crime awaits methodologically rigorous evaluation.

The human ecology approach has been criticized for overemphasizing "disorganization," for unequivocally asserting that crime is concentrated among the lower classes, and for imprecisely measuring central concepts. The consistency of human ecology research findings and the challenge they presented to the established accounts of deviance are the major contributions of the human ecology approach.

Routine activities analysis links people's everyday behaviours to a structure of opportunity that renders them vulnerable to intentional property and personal crime. This perspective accounts for crime on the basis of the convergence in space and time of three essential ingredients: motivated offenders, suitable targets, and the absence of guardianship. The theory treats the motivation of offenders as a given. The suitability of targets varies in terms of value, accessibility, and inertia. Guardianship also varies on the bases of social organization and technology. Finally, routine activities theory considers three dimensions of space and time. Periodicity refers to cyclical behaviours, and tempo involves the frequency of certain events in time. Timing refers to the crossover of offenders' and victims' lifestyle patterns. Although the routine activities or lifestyle–exposure perspective enjoys solid empirical support, it is criticized for sidestepping the question of motivation, for being imprecise about the relative criminogenic importance of its central elements, and for ignoring expressive crime.

Differential association builds on several of the tenets of the ecological approach, including the notion of cultural transmission, to explain how individuals are socialized to deviant behaviour by their reference groups. In nine propositions, the theory suggests that the skills and motives of deviance are learned from intimate others through various communication processes. When individuals, through social interaction, are exposed to more definitions favouring deviance than favouring conformity, rule breaking becomes likely. Two major extensions of differential association are the theories of differential identification and differential reinforcement. Differential identification explains how definitions favouring deviance develop in contexts other than face-to-face interaction. Differential reinforcement explains continuing deviant behaviour in terms of operant conditioning: the rewards and costs of most behaviours affect the extent to which they are continued. Differential reinforcement explains more specifically than does differential association the precise way in which people learn deviant and conforming behaviours. Policies grounded in differential association aim to reduce deviant associations and bolster conforming associations.

The deficiencies of differential association include its inadequate account of deviance engaged in alone or in the absence of cultural support, its imprecise measurements, and its uncertainty with respect to the sequence of cause and effect. That the theory spawned considerable research and challenged the conception of deviance as primarily a product of personality deficiencies are among its major contributions.

QUESTIONS FOR CRITICAL THINKING

1. Can you identify a neighbourhood in a town or city in which you have lived that represents a transitional zone? What characteristics does the area have that exemplifies this zone? Has the neighbourhood experienced relative constancy with respect to crime rates regardless of the time period considered and the racial, ethnic, or cultural composition of its residents?

2. The theoretical construct "differential association theory" is difficult for researchers to measure. Many studies have used peer group membership as a proxy, but this operationalization of the concept departs significantly from the theory. Develop a test of Sutherland's differential association that conforms more closely to the theoretical concept. Specifically, how would you measure an excess of definitions toward criminality as opposed to conformity?

3. Differential identification highlights the role of media such as TV and film in the production of criminal activity. What are the policy implications of differential identification theory in terms of control of sexual and violent content in the media? Do you think Canada is proceeding appropriately on this issue? Can observed relationships between exposure to media on one hand and violent behaviour on the other have an alternative explanation?

4. As a student at a postsecondary educational institution, document your routine activities over a week's time. Use insights provided by the routine activities theory to assess your risk of victimization. What alterations could you or others in your situation make to reduce the probability of becoming a victim of property or violent crime?

5. Rural communities have their fair share of crime. To what extent can social disorganization theory be used to explain crime in rural areas?

RECOMMENDED READINGS

Akers, R., and G. Jensen. (2003). *Social Learning Theory and the Explanation of Crime: A Guide for the New Century.* New Brunswick: Transaction Publishing.
> Recent collection of papers focusing on advances, or lack thereof, in applications of social learning principles to various forms of deviance in diverse settings.

Burgess, R., and R. L. Akers. (1966). "A Differential Association–Reinforcement Theory of Criminal Behaviour." *Social Problems* 14:128–47.
> Original formulation of social learning theory that has influenced contemporary thinking in the sociology and psychology of crime.

Felson, M., and L. Cohen. (1980). "Human Ecology and Crime: A Routine Activities Approach." *Human Ecology* 4:389–406.
> Presents the original articulation of the routine activities or lifestyle exposure approach to the understanding of criminal victimization and crime prevention.

Glaser, D. (1956). "Criminality Theories and Behavioral Images." *American Journal of Sociology* 61:433–44.
> Classic presentation of differential identification theory and its extension of Sutherland's ideas of differential association.

Kennedy, L. W., and D. R. Forde. (1999). *When Push Comes to Shove: A Routine Conflict Approach to Violence.* Albany: SUNY Press.
> Uses Canadian survey data to analyze various conflictual situations. Points out the importance of lifestyle, daily routine, and respondent experience with crime and conflict as important predictive variables. Also includes an analysis of the violent conduct of conflict-prone street youth.

Shaw, C., and H. D. McKay. (1969). *Juvenile Delinquency and Urban Areas.* Chicago: University of Chicago Press.
> Presents the fundamental thesis of social disorganization in Chicago that has strongly influenced contemporary analyses of crime in urban contexts.

Sutherland, E., and D. Cressey. (1978). *Criminology.* Philadelphia: Lippincott.
> Contains Sutherland's classic articulation of the highly influential theory of differential association.

Wilcox, P., K. Land, and S. Hunt. (2003). *Criminal Circumstance: A Dynamic Multicontextual Criminal Opportunity Theory.* New York: Aldine de Gruyter.
> Extends routine activities perspective by discussing opportunity (targets and guardianship) as multilevel. Incorporates economic market theory and shows how opportunity shifts across time and space.

CHAPTER 4

Functionalism

The aims of this chapter are to familiarize the reader with:

- the organic analogy, manifest and latent functions, and the idea of the social system
- the concept of anomie, developed by Durkheim to explain suicide and later modified by Merton to explain deviance and crime generally
- Merton's theory of anomie and the five adaptations to strain
- Cohen's extension of Merton's theory with his use of status frustration
- Cloward and Ohlin's extension of Merton's theory with their use of differential illegitimate opportunity
- Agnew's contemporary adaptation — general strain theory
- the four functions of deviance
- the policy implications of functional theories
- the deficiencies of the functionalist perspective
- the contributions of the functionalist perspective to an understanding of deviance and crime

INTRODUCTION

Functionalism, like the ecological branch of the Chicago school, uses a biological analogy to explain how society operates. It draws parallels between organic life and the social order. This chapter begins by outlining the general mechanics of the functionalist perspective. The two central thematic frameworks applied to the explanation of deviant and illegal conduct, both of which originate in the work of Émile Durkheim, are described. The anomie approach emphasizes the violation of social norms, while the functions-of-deviance approach seeks to explain the contributions to the social order made by nonconformity and illegality.

THE FUNCTIONALIST APPROACH

Like a living organism, society is conceived of as a series of integrated parts, each of which plays a role in ensuring the continuance of the system (Parsons, 1951). Just as the heart, lungs, stomach, and veins of an animal operate to keep it alive and well, society's parts — its social structures — function in an orderly manner to meet its goals: maintenance, solidarity, and survival. The parts of society that operate in harmony to sustain the entire system are usually called social structures and are analogous to parts of the body.

An elementary example of the functionalist perspective illustrates its central propositions. The family, the educational system, organized religion, and the economy are four parts of the social system that ensure the persistence of society and the well-being of its members. The family produces children and instils in them fundamental values, including respect for others, regard for their property, and belief in the merit of hard work. Later, the school provides the child with basic knowledge and work-related skills. Organized religion supports, in its teachings, many of the basic values learned at home and at school and provides a spiritual means of coping with life's problems. Then, properly socialized by the family, the school, and the church, the individual participates in the marketplace by working, earning, and spending. The healthier the parts of the social system, the more vital is society and the better off are its members.

Functionalism, like the organic analogy from which it derives, asserts that the ideal condition of any system is balance and stability. An important implication of equilibrium is that changes in one part of the system affect all other parts. Increased heart rates require arteries and veins to cope with a greater volume of blood. With regard to society, the same principle pertains. If families produce more children, the educational system must expand to accommodate more students, religious institutions must increase their services to youth, and the economy must incorporate an enlarged cohort of workers.

Functionalists assert that there are two types of function: manifest and latent (Merton, 1957). **Manifest functions** are those that society intends and that are often formally set out as institutional goals. For example, society seeks to punish criminals so that they and others will obey its laws. It tries to protect the public from continued criminal activity by incarcerating career criminals, and attempts to rehabilitate and reintegrate offenders by treating their psychological maladies, by instilling in them the values of diligence and honesty, and by training them for re-entry into the labour market and society at large (Griffiths and Verdun-Jones, 1989).

Latent functions differ from manifest functions in that they are unintended and almost always informal. Among the latent functions of the corrections system are the provision of an underground training school for criminals, which in turn creates an enormous number of jobs in crime control and related fields (Toch, 1977).

Functionalism assumes that society is integrated and orderly and that there is considerable consensus among its members regarding the form and nature of normative rules, values, and beliefs. Since functionalists presume that no pattern of behaviour perseveres unless it serves a function, they explain persisting social structures in terms of the functions they perform. Marriage, worship, and work are patterns of behaviour that have been around for a long time; so is crime. Functionalist analysis first identifies persistent societal patterns and then analyzes how they maintain the social system.

FUNCTIONALIST EXPLANATIONS OF DEVIANCE AND CRIME

Functionalism has two basic theories of deviance and crime, both of which originate in the writings of Émile Durkheim. The first perspective focuses on norm violations as a disruption of natural order and equilibrium. This approach includes the work of the anomie theorists Merton, Cohen, and Cloward and Ohlin. The second perspective argues that deviance is normal and functions to maintain society.

ÉMILE DURKHEIM AND ANOMIE

In explaining the incidence of one particular type of deviance — suicide — Durkheim emphasized the importance of variations in external social regulation. The relative absence of social regulation resulting in a state of normlessness is a condition Durkheim calls **anomie**. He considers it a pathological state indicating a breakdown in social order and solidarity (Durkheim, 1951).

In a healthy society where anomie does not exist, citizens know exactly what goals are appropriate for their particular social positions and precisely how they are supposed to realize those goals. Under normal conditions, social ethics and individuals' sense of what is morally proper limit their aspirations. Durkheim conceptualizes anomie as a state of confusion about the legitimacy of various social aspirations and the propriety of certain ways of pursuing those aspirations.

Using the concept of anomie, Durkheim develops his theory of suicide in the following fashion. He theorizes that a person's physical and social needs are governed differently. Nature regulates physical needs. For example, hungry people eat until they are full and then they stop; internal regulatory mechanisms automatically discourage people from eating too much. Social needs, however, are not regulated naturally. A person's desires for wealth, power, and prestige, for example, are unlimited if not checked by external and social constraints. Unregulated by external social norms, these goals escalate until they become virtually unattainable. The inability to satisfy unregulated and heightened desires for wealth, power, and prestige results in disappointment, unhappiness, and frustration. This disillusionment is accompanied by

FIGURE 4.1

DURKHEIM'S THEORY OF ANOMIE AND SUICIDE

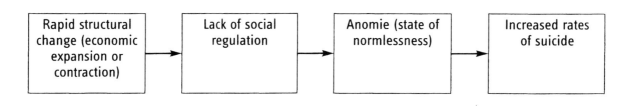

| Rapid structural change (economic expansion or contraction) | → | Lack of social regulation | → | Anomie (state of normlessness) | → | Increased rates of suicide |

stress and subsequently by an increased propensity to commit suicide, as shown in Figure 4.1.

In explaining how anomie is produced, Durkheim focuses on the relationship between suicide and sudden dislocating changes in economic conditions. Noting that suicide rates are lowest when the economy is stable, he argues that under such conditions, both culturally defined goals and the rules relating to their attainment are closely governed by strong and unequivocal social norms. Both rapid economic contraction and rapid economic expansion, however, weaken the constraining power of normative regulation and produce anomie. During severe economic depressions, for example, individuals experience declining wages and increasing unemployment. They do not, however, reduce their wants to reflect the new economic realities. As the disparity increases between high aspirations and the failing economic means of realizing such aspirations, feelings of distress intensify. The resulting strain manifests itself, according to Durkheim, in higher rates of suicide.

The alternative case, unbridled economic growth and expansion, produces equally stressful conditions. Although individuals are able to achieve their long-standing goals more readily, at least initially, they are encouraged in the long run to aspire to increasingly lofty ends. Where rising expectations outstrip the opportunities for their realization, frustration and disillusionment increase and so does the frequency of suicide.

ROBERT MERTON — SOCIAL STRUCTURE AND ANOMIE

Robert Merton revised Durkheim's original discussion of anomie and suicide into a more general theory of social deviance (Merton, 1938).

From a very early age, according to Merton, people are taught the value of being successful. In North American society in particular, success means making money and acquiring material possessions. Under ideal conditions of structural integration, the culturally defined goals of success and material acquisition align sufficiently well with the institutionalized means of attaining them (e.g., education and work) that individuals are able to legitimately achieve the rewards to which society has encouraged them to aspire. Winners are regularly rewarded in school, on the job, in sports, and in other spheres of human activity. Media depictions reinforce this view; they often feature a rags-to-riches story wherein some downtrodden soul "makes good" through intelligence and effort. Indeed, individuals frequently assess their social worth mainly in terms of their material success.

Merton argues that what is implied in North American culture is that success is available to anyone who has the necessary intelligence and drive, regardless of social characteristics such as class, ethnicity, and gender. He suggests, however, that these ideal conditions do not exist in North American society; rather, inequality produces **differential opportunity** for people of different circumstances.

According to Merton, the combined overemphasis on ends and underemphasis on means produces an imperfect state of affairs (anomie). With all their energies focused on winning (goals), the way people play the game (means) may lose much of its importance. Inattention to the rules eventually results in their becoming imprecise and less explicit. This lack of structural balance results in a condition of mal-integration or anomie that in turn produces strain, which is most acutely felt by lower-status individuals. Legitimate mechanisms of attainment, mainly educational and occupational opportunities, are more restricted for these individuals. Compared with white people from the middle and upper classes, members

FIGURE 4.2

MERTON'S THEORY OF SOCIAL STRUCTURE AND ANOMIE

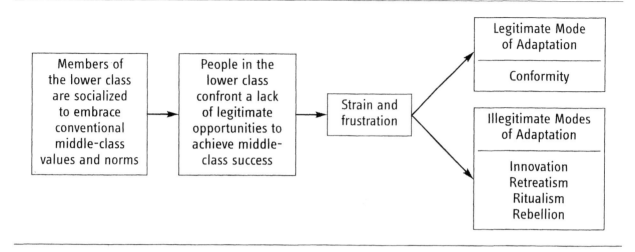

Members of the lower class are socialized to embrace conventional middle-class values and norms → People in the lower class confront a lack of legitimate opportunities to achieve middle-class success → Strain and frustration → Legitimate Mode of Adaptation / Conformity ; Illegitimate Modes of Adaptation / Innovation Retreatism Ritualism Rebellion

of certain ethnic groups and of the lower classes are significantly disadvantaged in the competition to become successful. The dilemma facing lower-status individuals is that society has encouraged them to aspire highly while denying them equal access to legitimate avenues of opportunity (education and work). As a result, the disadvantaged experience frustrations and strains that encourage them to engage in deviance as a way of adapting to the gap separating social goals and the means of attaining them.

Merton specifies five modes of personal adaptation to anomie: conformity, innovation, **retreatism, ritualism,** and rebellion (see Figure 4.2). All except conformity are deviant responses. Conformists accept the legitimacy of both social goals and the legitimate means of reaching them. They seek success through the socially acceptable avenues of educational and occupational advancement. Most middle- and lower-class people are conformists. Although members of the lower classes are less likely than members of the middle classes to attain their desired ends, most of them still obey the rules. While accepting both goals and means does not ensure that goals will be met, it does imply faith in the system. Conforming members of the lower classes who are less successful than they wish to be accept responsibility for their own poor showing and continue to strive by sticking with it and by encouraging their children to compete within the rules.

Innovation occurs when individuals experiencing strain adhere to the culturally defined goals of material success but abandon the legitimate ways of

pursuing them. Seeking material gain through illegal means, innovators typically engage in a variety of predatory offences, including theft, burglary, and robbery.

The archetype of the innovator is the gangster (Liska, 1987). Stories abound of impoverished young immigrants coming to North America in search of a better life. Excluded from legitimate avenues of success by discrimination and prejudice, many young immigrants with considerable intelligence and ambition have turned their talents to organized crime and amassed considerable fortunes. The affluence of several wealthy and influential North American families began with alcohol trading in the Prohibition era.

Retreatism is a deviant adaptation to stress that involves renouncing not only the legitimate means of attaining goals but also the very goals themselves. Merton suggests that when an individual's socialization equally emphasizes success goals and the legitimate means of their attainment, and when the individual is unable to soothe feelings of strain by depreciating goals over means (ritualism) or means over goals (innovation), the solution is likely to be withdrawal. Those who retreat neither value success nor wish to actively pursue it. Retreatists include alcoholics, drug addicts, psychological misfits, tramps, and hippies.

Ritualists reduce strain by lowering their aspirations so that their goals correspond more closely with what is attainable in light of the insufficient legitimate means available. The ritualist is usually lower-middle class; a good example is the aging junior-level bureaucrat who gradually becomes aware that he or she will not be promoted. The ritualist accepts this worrisome reality, comes to work each day, and toils relatively compulsively as an honest employee. For ritualists, means become ends in themselves. While ritualists break no formal rules they do violate informal cultural norms, since everyone is expected to strive continuously for success. Since ritualism is only a minor social problem, this adaptation has received little attention from sociologists of deviance.

In rebellion, the rebel rejects both the goals and the legitimate means of their acquisition and seeks to replace them with new ones. Into this category fall revolutionaries and terrorists who seek radical change in the social order, perhaps by replacing one form of government (tyranny) with another (democracy).

In his typology of adaptations, shown in Table 4.1, Merton presents four deviant reactions to the structural malintegration of social goals and legitimate means, the latter of which he views as differently distributed among social segments. Innovation, retreatism, ritualism, and rebellion are not meant to represent personality types. An individual might vary his or her adaptive strategy from time to time or engage in more than one adaptation concurrently. In this way, Merton is somewhat vague as to why one adaptation might be selected over another. In

TABLE 4.1

MERTON'S THEORY OF ANOMIE

Mode of Adaptation	Cultural Goal	Institutionalized Means
Conformity	+	+
Innovation	+	−
Ritualism	−	+
Retreatism	−	−
Rebellion	+	+
	−	−

Source: Robert Merton (1938). "Social Structure and Anomie." *American Sociological Review* 3(1938):676.

explaining differing propensities for innovation and ritualism, however, he does point out that differing degrees of socialization against the use of illegitimate means affect the person's choice of adaptation. Lower-class individuals more frequently innovate because they are less likely to be socialized against the use of illegitimate means in the pursuit of success. Lower-middle- and middle-class individuals, because they are more effectively socialized to conformity, are reluctant to break the law to achieve success. As a result of their presumably more adequate socialization, lower-middle- and middle-class persons are more likely to adapt to strain by simply reducing their aspirations and becoming ritualists.

ALBERT COHEN AND STATUS FRUSTRATION

In 1955, Albert Cohen modified Merton's theory of anomie to explain higher rates of delinquency among lower-class youth. Cohen developed the idea that lower-class delinquency occurs as a subcultural adaptation to problems generated by the societal predominance of middle-class culture (Cohen, 1955).

Like Merton, Cohen argues that North American society encourages all its members to aspire highly but at the same time makes it very difficult for some groups to be successful. With compulsory attendance, the school becomes a competitive arena in which youth of all classes pursue the all-important goal of elevated social status. While both lower- and middle-class youth desire high status, lower-class boys are much more likely to fail in attaining the rewards commonly accorded to achievers in the public school system. In the competition for academic and social success in school, children from middle-class backgrounds have a decided advantage over their lower-class counterparts. Middle-class parents have already socialized their offspring into the system of values and behaviours represented, promoted, and rewarded in schools. Academically, middle-class children are more highly motivated, more diligent, more articulate, and better able to defer gratification. Behaviourally, they are more likely to be obedient, polite, and respectful.

Lower-class youths, having learned different norms and values, do not readily meet the standards of attitude and performance that the education system demands of them. Unable to compete

FIGURE 4.3

STATUS FRUSTRATION THEORY

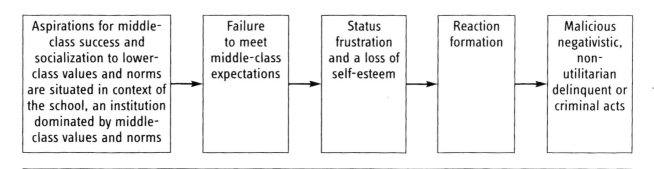

| Aspirations for middle-class success and socialization to lower-class values and norms are situated in context of the school, an institution dominated by middle-class values and norms | → | Failure to meet middle-class expectations | → | Status frustration and a loss of self-esteem | → | Reaction formation | → | Malicious negativistic, non-utilitarian delinquent or criminal acts |

effectively and faced with constant failure to achieve middle-class status, lower-class children experience considerable frustration. According to Cohen, the consequence of this **status frustration** is the formation of a subculture that incorporates a rival hierarchy of statuses through a process of reaction formation (see Figure 4.3). In this subculture, lower-class youth can compete on more equal terms for status that is meaningful in their own eyes. The criteria for status in the lower-class youth subculture are precisely the opposite of those valued in the dominant middle-class culture. Acts worthy of accolades in the lower-class subculture are, as Cohen puts it, "nonutilitarian, malicious, and negativistic." Performed not out of need but in pursuit of status, these acts symbolize the rejection of the middle-class value system. Stealing, fighting, and vandalizing property are intended to improve one's position in a delinquent subculture that itself defies conventional, law-abiding, middle-class behaviour.

For both Merton and Cohen, the decisive causal factor in the production of deviant behaviour is the disjunction between the social goals of material success and elevated status on the one hand, and the legitimate means of their attainment — occupational and educational achievement — on the other. The lower classes lack sufficient access to legitimate means and consequently engage in delinquent and criminal activity. Cohen extends the horizons of anomie theory by using it to explain nonutilitarian as opposed to utilitarian deviant acts. He also expands the explanatory framework by documenting the connection between status frustration and the formation of delinquent subcultures.

RICHARD CLOWARD AND LLOYD OHLIN AND DIFFERENTIAL ILLEGITIMATE OPPORTUNITY

Richard Cloward and Lloyd Ohlin (1960) extended Merton's theory by developing the concept of **differential illegitimate opportunity.** They agree with Merton that individuals are compelled to become deviant in circumstances where success goals are highly emphasized but where the legitimate strategies of attainment are severely restricted. Cloward and Ohlin differ from Merton in one major respect, however. They point out that while lower-class persons frequently lack access to socially acceptable ways of achieving success, many are also denied equal access to the illegitimate ways of meeting their goals. As with the legitimate avenues to success, like education and work, illegitimate routes range from the highly restricted to the wide open. Cloward and Ohlin criticize Merton's implicit assumption that, faced with the disjunction between ends and legal means, all lower-class individuals enjoy equal access to illicit techniques of goal attainment. Rather, they assert that both the extent of deviance and the form it takes are strongly influenced by the availability of unlawful options.

The degree to which opportunities exist for people to learn illicit techniques and put them to use affects participation in deviant activity. To make a living as a burglar, one must have the opportunity to learn how to execute the crime and how to sell stolen merchandise without getting caught. These endeavours are likely to be greatly facilitated by the immediate presence of criminal role models; of instructors expert in

FIGURE 4.4

DIFFERENTIAL OPPORTUNITY THEORY

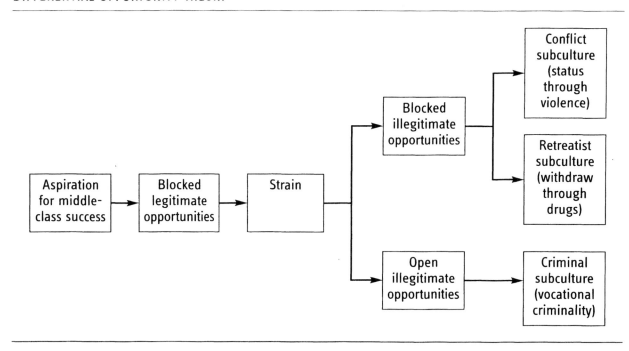

the skills required for break, enter, and theft; and of a reliable "fence." The lack of such an illegitimate opportunity structure markedly reduces the likelihood of taking up burglary as a vocation.

Cloward and Ohlin outline three types of deviant subculture that offer different access to illicit opportunities: criminal, conflict, and retreatist (see Figure 4.4). A neighbourhood characterized by an illegitimate opportunity structure has developed a criminal subculture. Individuals learn the skills required for theft, burglary, robbery, and the like from more seasoned members of the neighbourhood subculture. Fences convert stolen goods into cash. Illegal conduct of this type is less likely if, for whatever reason, integration into the **criminal subculture** is impossible. According to Cloward and Ohlin, the criminal subculture is most prevalent in established and stable slum areas of large cities, where various criminal organizations have become firmly entrenched.

Conflict subcultures characterize neighbourhoods that offer neither legitimate nor illegitimate routes to success. The only way to obtain high status in these cases is through violence. Combat skill, physical strength, and enthusiasm for risking one's safety form the bases of prestige in the violent gang. This type of subculture, Cloward and Ohlin suggest, is prevalent in the disorganized slum.

Membership in conflict subcultures has prerequisites that cannot be met by all. For those who lack the physical prowess and taste for violent action and for whom both legitimate and illegitimate opportunities are unavailable, retreat is a likely alternative. **"Double failures,"** those who are not able to take advantage of either legitimate or illegitimate opportunity structures, form retreatist subcultures in which drugs and alcohol are used frequently to escape.

Cloward and Ohlin, like Cohen before them, extend Merton's theory of anomie by further specifying the way in which the gap between aspirations and opportunities translates into deviant behaviour. Cohen specifies the intervening mechanism as status frustration, while for Cloward and Ohlin differential illegitimate opportunity is the mechanism through which the rift separating goals and means produces conduct that violates social norms.

ROBERT AGNEW AND GENERAL STRAIN THEORY

Robert Agnew has developed a contemporary version of the strain perspective that he calls **general strain theory** (Agnew, 1999; Passas and Agnew, 1997). Adopting a more micro-sociological stance, the theory continues to view delinquency and crime as products of stress but broadens the conception of strain beyond the simple ends–means gap stressed by earlier versions. General strain theory incorporates explanatory variables such as frustration and aggression from social psychology, and peer pressure and eroded societal bonds from alternative sociological perspectives such as differential association and social control. In comparison to its predecessors, Agnew's version presents strain as being generated by a broader array of stressors and as forming three distinct types — the failure to achieve positively valued goals, the removal of positive and desired stimuli, and confrontation with negative stimuli.

1. **The failure to achieve positively valued goals.** Included in this category are three subtypes of strain. The first closely resembles Merton's strain theory, arguing that strain results from a disjunction between a person's aspirations and expectations. Agnew extends this argument, incorporating not only ideal or future goals but also more immediate objectives. Furthermore, he presents failure as a product not only of blocked opportunities but also of inadequate skills and abilities. The second subtype emphasizes the separation between expectations and actual achievements. As this gap widens, people experience feelings of disappointment, resentment, and anger. The final subdimension stresses the discrepancy between what individuals see as a fair and equitable outcome and the actual outcome. In this process, the positive results for people of their investments in activities or relationships fail to match their perceptions of appropriate returns given the amount of effort expended. Strain may also ensue from perceptions of unfairness inherent in the observation that one has invested more than others in comparison and has received less in return.

2. **The removal of positive and desired stimuli.** This type of strain focuses attention on people's experiences with stressful events frequently experienced in day-to-day living. It involves losses of objects, statuses, or persons of significant value. Examples are disintegrating relationships among romantic partners, friends, or family members, or their deaths or illnesses. Also included are such alterations as moving from one place to another and being suspended from school or losing a job.

3. **Confrontation with negative stimuli.** This subtype incorporates the idea that people's life experiences frequently involve being the object of others' negative actions. Such noxious occurrences include being the victim of child abuse, neglect, bullying, and adverse school and work experiences. Such sources of strain are particularly significant for adolescents, who often cannot legally escape the confines of family and school. They have less power to control or eliminate negative stimuli in these contexts. Unable to easily avoid abusive parents, difficult teachers, and obnoxious classmates, youth experience considerable pressure to deviate.

Like Merton's version, general strain theory notes that deviance and crime represent only one set of adaptations to strain. One can, for example, simply ignore the strain-producing element, minimize it, or take responsibility for the discomfort by blaming oneself. The theory posits that deviant acts emerge as means of dealing with stress by trying to circumvent its sources or to seek retaliation or numb the effects by withdrawal into a world of alcohol or drugs. These outcomes are more likely where the individuals' responses to strain involve frustration and anger, blaming others rather than themselves. General strain theory suggests that internal and external constraints work to determine whether people under stress choose to conform or deviate. Among these conditional factors are the presence or absence of alternative goals, values, and identities; coping resources such as intelligence, self-esteem, and problem-solving skills; social support networks; non-conforming peer groups; and larger environmental factors such as education and material resources.

THE FUNCTIONS OF DEVIANCE

Academic interest in Merton's anomie theory and its variants declined significantly in the early 1960s. The publication of K. T. Erikson's *Wayward Puritans* in 1966, however, renewed interest in functionalist theories of deviance. In this work, Erikson studies deviance in a seventeenth-century Massachusetts colony. He explains incidents of heresy and witchcraft in terms of their contributions to the social cohesion and social stability of the community. In developing the notion that deviant behaviour is functional for society and social groups within it, Erikson leans heavily on ideas developed by Durkheim (1962) in his *Rules of Sociological Method*. In this book, Durkheim further explores his interests in both the creation of social solidarity and the nature of legal sanctions.

Durkheim points out that while there is tremendous variation across societies with regard to what is considered crime, no society is entirely crime-free. Given the considerable range of this variation, it cannot be said that anything intrinsically makes acts criminal. Rather, what defines an act as criminal in any society is the fact that it elicits social condemnation. An act is a crime, Durkheim maintains, "because it shocks the common conscience." Further, crime can be distinguished from minor social infractions by virtue of the fact that the social disapproval is intense. Crime and punishment, Durkheim notes, are universal and persistent features of human society. Since patterns of norm violation and their punishment are both widespread and enduring, he argues that they must perform vital functions for the social system.

Four functions are served for society by crime and by the social reactions it elicits (see Table 4.2) (Erikson, 1966). When community standards are seriously violated, the ensuing outrage and contempt felt by citizens brings them together in an expression of common indignation. Crime and the reaction it entails on the part of both citizens and the media promote the creation of social solidarity. For example, on September 11, 2001 Islamic terrorists crashed commercial airliners into the World Trade Center and the Pentagon. The attacks, the rescue efforts, the massive destruction of property, and the

loss of several thousand lives on the ground became the central focus of public and media attention for months following the incident. The horror and outrage people felt over this brutal act of aggression were widely shared and traversed international boundaries. Public emotions were communicated in such a way that common values of right and wrong and good and evil were reconfirmed. In this sense, crime functions to integrate members of a social system who unite with a common sentiment against a common enemy.

The second **function of deviance** and its condemnation is the clarification of the moral boundaries of the community. The precise borders separating the acceptable from the unacceptable are not always clear. Social reactions to behaviour that "crosses the line" clarify how far one can go in a particular direction. What constitutes an act of sexual harassment in the university? Can sexual harassment be a longing glance? Is a professor's compliment on a student's attire sexual harassment? Do requests by an instructor for a graduate-student assistant to work late, to go for a drink after work, or to share a room at a conference constitute sexual harassment? Is an overt request for sex necessary? Must a student be threatened with lower grades or the loss of a research position if sexual demands are not met? Is any sexual reference that makes a student feel uncomfortable equivalent to harassment? Cases in which complaints are formally examined and punitive actions taken do much to clarify the bounds of acceptable behaviour. In a celebrated case at the University of Toronto, for example, a tribunal held a professor responsible for harassing a female student. Wearing skin-diving equipment, he had repeatedly followed and stared at her underwater in a university swimming pool.

Functionalists consider conformity to social values and norms on the part of the majority necessary for society to operate harmoniously. Conformity, they suggest, must be rewarded; saintly behaviour must be visibly condoned. By inflicting punishment on those who violate society's rules, those who obey them can compare themselves with deviants and feel virtuous. Fining the motorist who drinks and drives or jailing the executive who cheats on an income tax return allows law-abiding drivers and businesspeople to compare themselves with their lawbreaking counterparts and to feel respectable for having remained honest and upright. These penalties accent the

TABLE 4.2

FUNCTIONS OF DEVIANCE AND REACTION TO DEVIANCE

Integrate members of the society

Clarify moral boundaries of communities

Reward and thereby motivate saintly behaviour

Provide avenue for social flexibility and change

TABLE 4.3

FUNCTIONALIST APPROACHES TO EXPLAINING DEVIANCE AND CRIME

Theory	Theorist(s)	Central Premise	Key Concepts	Principal Contributions
Anomie	Émile Durkheim	Anomie or a breakdown in social regulation increases dissatisfaction, which produces stress and leads to suicide	Social regulation; anomie	Provides a social structural explanation for behaviour (suicide) that is often taken to be highly individualistic with purely psychological causes
Anomie	Robert Merton	Disjunction between ends and means produces strain, thereby increasing the probability of deviant behaviour	Structural integration: conformity; innovation; retreatism; ritualism; rebellion	Emphasizes the role of social structural conditions, as opposed to personality, in generation of illegal conduct
Status frustration	Albert Cohen	Lower-class males' experience of failure to achieve middle-class success creates a subculture in which status attainment involves engagement in nonconforming conduct that is nonutilitarian, malicious, and negativistic	Status frustration; reaction formation	Demonstrates mechanism by which lower-class living conditions produce illegal conduct that is violent and destructive and is often seen as senseless
Differential opportunity	Richard Cloward and Lloyd Ohlin	Blocked conventional and available illegitimate opportunity pressures lower-class youth to embrace a criminal subculture; blocked conventional and illegitimate opportunity pressures lower-class youth to embrace conflict or retreatist subcultures	Differential legitimate opportunity; differential illegitimate opportunity; criminal subculture; conflict subculture; retreatist subculture	Illustrates how the presence or absence of legitimate and illegitimate opportunities structures criminal involvement; indicates why one type of subculture activity is chosen over another
General strain theory	Robert Agnew	Views delinquency and crime as products of stress but broadens the conception of strain beyond the simple ends–means gap stressed by earlier versions	Failure to achieve positively valued goals; removal of positive and desired stimuli; confrontation with negative stimuli	Extends conceptualizations of strain and incorporates variables from psychology and other criminological approaches; less tied to race and class; explains gender differences
Functions of deviance and punishment	Émile Durkheim	Some level of deviance and crime are inevitable, necessary, and functional for the operation of society	Manifest function; latent function	Demonstrates the commonly overlooked fact that deviance and crime at a certain level are not without their positive aspects; emphasizes contribution of deviant behaviour, and reaction to it, to social solidarity and community

rewards for conformity and reinforce the commitment to moral uprightness.

Finally, Durkheim argues that crime is a precondition of society's capacity for flexibility and change, and that it can sometimes promote progress:

> How many times, indeed, it is only an anticipation of future morality — a step toward what will be! According to Athenian law, Socrates was a criminal, and his condemnation was no more than just. However, his crime, namely, the independence of his thought, rendered a service not only to humanity but to his country. (Durkheim, 1962:71)

Many consider it progressive to defy certain laws if the cause is worthy. In recent years, various groups of Canadians have defied the law to promote an end to wars and nuclear-weapons testing, discrimination against disadvantaged groups, and environmental destruction.

Crime, according to Durkheim, performs four functions for society: it increases social solidarity, clarifies norms, accents the rewards of conformity, and has the potential to stimulate social progress. Deviance is a normal, necessary, inescapable characteristic of society. Even in a "perfect" group, some behaviours will be considered criminal:

> Imagine a society of saints, a perfect cloister of exemplary individuals. Crimes, properly so called, will there be unknown: but faults which appear venal to the layman will create there the same scandal that the ordinary offence does in ordinary consciousness. If then, this society has the power to judge and punish, it will define these acts as criminal and will treat them as such. (Durkheim, 1962:69)

While some level of deviance can have positive consequences for society, too much nonconformity can be pathological and encourage social breakdown. While the social and economic destruction generated by the coordinated terrorist attacks in New York and Washington on September 11, 2001 resulted in increased solidarity among Americans and Canadians alike, rampant acts of crime have the opposite effect. The killing of hundreds of men, women, and children over a protracted period of time in the Sudan does not have the same effect. Excessive deviance and crime inspires fear, fuels terror, and can seriously undermine social order. Too much crime, in short, can be dysfunctional (Liska, 1987).

Table 4.3 summarizes functionalist approaches.

FUNCTIONALISM AND SOCIAL POLICY

Durkheim identified several interrelated causes of deviance and crime: social disintegration, social deregulation, and rapid social and economic change. To reduce deviance, the integration and regulation of society must be increased and economic expansions and contractions stabilized.

The Mertonian version of anomie as a gap between cultural goals and means of achievement has led to policy initiatives aimed at either broadening access to lawful educational and occupational means or redistributing existing resources more equitably. Programs designed to provide more training and more jobs to members of socially and economically disadvantaged groups and to stimulate economic growth are offshoots of this perspective (Liska, 1987).

EVALUATION OF THE FUNCTIONALIST PERSPECTIVES

Critics have subjected both the anomie and functions-of-deviance approaches to careful scrutiny. Some argue that there is no evidence that individuals from lower-class backgrounds are more deviant than people from the middle and upper classes (Thio, 1975). In initially proposing his theory, Merton observed that official crime data demonstrate that illegal conduct is concentrated among the lower classes. However, official data on crime are obtained from police and court records. This information base produces a clear bias, because police are more likely to detect types of deviance perpetrated by members of the lower classes. Alternatively, they are much less likely to uncover and proceed against the deviant activities of the middle and especially of the upper classes. Murder, assault, and bank robbery are much more likely to be brought to police attention than are the marketing of unsafe products, the polluting of the environment, and theft by computer. Thus, critics charge that anomie theory, by dwelling on the explanation of lower-class deviance, effectively ignores the wide range of violations committed by more advantaged members of society (Taylor, Walton, and Young, 1973).

The assumption that the same aspirations are held by the lower, middle, and upper classes is questionable. Although society may encourage everyone to aspire highly, members of the lower classes may have more realistic expectations of what is achievable (Nettler, 1984; Kornhauser, 1978). Their aspirations may not be as high as those of members of the middle classes.

Sociologists have also questioned the notion of value consensus, which is central to the anomie framework. The heterogeneity and pluralism that are the hallmarks of Canadian and American postindustrial societies call into question the assertion that everyone is committed to material success. Divisions of class, ethnicity, region, age, and sex may promote competing sets of values. Thus, it is likely that various minority groups engage in different types of deviance for reasons other than frustration with their inability to reach material goals. For example, gambling, the use of prohibited drugs, and excessive alcohol consumption may be motivated not by strain but by the fact that they are a normal part of a culture (Lemert, 1967; Ribordy, 1980).

Anomie theory represents lower-class people as frustrated and miserable with their lives, but some critics suggest that this image is an exaggeration. In arguing that untenable conditions create strain that in turn forces basically good people to become deviants, anomie theory does not explain deviant and criminal activities that inject fun and excitement into otherwise routine and dull lives (Bordua, 1961).

Anomie theory fails to spell out adequately why lower-class persons choose one form of deviant adaptation over another. For example, it does not explain why, under the same conditions, one person innovates and one retreats while another rebels. While each of these three adaptations occurs as a result of restricted access to legitimate means of achieving success, innovators continue to pursue lofty ends (albeit illegally), retreatists give up the chase, and rebels seek to institute entirely new goals. The reasons for these choices are not explicitly articulated.

Anomie theory cites the gap separating ends and means as the primary source of deviant behaviour. It argues that this disjuncture is disproportionately experienced by lower-class persons. Given that the gap presumably endures over time, the prediction follows that deviant and criminal behaviour should also be continuous. However, evidence suggests that for many lower-class people who do engage in some illegal conduct, deviance is far more episodic than continuous. Why some lower-class persons never start, why some stop entirely, why some engage in deviant acts only occasionally, and why others perpetrate deviant acts systematically over long careers are questions not adequately addressed by the theory (Liska, 1987).

Violence is frequently more expressive than instrumental. Beating a child, killing a spouse, or assaulting a bar-room acquaintance are usually expressive acts of violence and, because they occur in the heat of the moment and do not involve the pursuit of material success, they are not well explained by anomie theory. Nonetheless, violence occasionally is used for material gain. Abduction, robbery, some murders (e.g., contract killing, homicide for insurance or inheritance money), and some terrorist activities are violent crimes rationally undertaken to enrich the lawbreaker.

Anomie theory also fails to take proper account of the impact upon individuals of their major reference groups (Farrell and Swigert, 1982). People compare their circumstances with the situations of those with whom they associate, who resemble them in terms of occupation and income. Thus, lower-class persons comparing themselves with others similarly circumstanced or possibly even worse off will not experience much strain.

Some commentators concede that anomie theorists are correct in assuming that the dissonance between one's goals and legitimate opportunities encourages deviance. Those who see themselves as deprived in comparison with their reference groups will experience greater strain and thus will be more likely to deviate. This mismatch of goals and opportunities, however, may not be entirely class-related. Anyone whose aspirations outstrip the legitimate means of their achievement may be prone to deviate, regardless of his or her class (Farrell and Swigert, 1982).

Cloward and Ohlin's version of anomie theory posits the existence of three subcultures that promote different forms of deviance. Researchers have attacked their presentation of three separate and distinct subcultures in light of data indicating that this threefold typology oversimplifies the varied and complex specialties of delinquent gangs and that it fails to consider shifting membership patterns across these subcultural forms (Schrag, 1962; Bernard, 1984).

Cohen's version of anomie focuses exclusively on nonutilitarian delinquency. This focus, say some critics, ignores the profit-making rationale for much delinquent behaviour (Bordua, 1961).

General strain theory holds some promise of providing an account of gender difference in deviant and criminal conduct given its suggestion that the experience of strain may differ for males and females. Proponents argue that for females stressors more likely produce depression, insecurity, anxiety, and self-blame, while for males they generate anger directed not at themselves but at others. Furthermore, there is some suggestion that the availability of coping mechanisms varies by gender, with females more than males avoiding, downplaying, or taking responsibility for their situation and also making greater use of support networks to ameliorate problems.

Empirical testing provides some support for general strain theory in that various but by no means all measures of strain predict delinquency and crime. More recent specifications and tests of the theory suggest that strain is most strongly linked to delinquency and crime where stress is high in magnitude and stress-producing conditions incorporate the element of injustice. The strength of the relationship of strain to deviance is enhanced in situations where social controls are undermined and where deviant peer groups encourage nonconformity.

General strain theory represents a revival of the strain tradition and exhibits several advantages over earlier versions of the theory. First, while it stresses the primacy of structural pressures it broadens the perspective by extending conceptualizations of strain and incorporating variables from psychology and other criminological approaches, namely differential association and social control. Second, it is less tied to class and race interpretations given the variety of potential stressors incorporated into the perspective. Third, the more recent version points the way to understanding gender group differences in propensity for deviance and crime. Finally, while not without room for improvement in design and measurement, empirical tests provide more support for general strain theory than for earlier forms.

The functions-of-deviance branch of the functionalist perspective proposes that deviance and reactions to it promote social solidarity. Critics dispute that deviance and crime always produce consensus. Although the murder of a child may unite the community in indignation, the provision of abortion services on demand may result in considerable divisiveness. The opening of the Morgentaler abortion clinics across Canada is a case in point. The heated dispute about the legitimacy of these clinics has split public opinion, with each side of the controversy impassioned in its stance. Thus, while serious crimes like murder, rape, and robbery may produce community cohesion, acts upon which there is less consensus may have the opposite effect. Where there is less agreement on the wrongfulness of certain illegal practices like drug use, prostitution, and gambling, these illegal acts and reaction to them may undermine social solidarity (Box, 1981).

Functionalists have not clearly established the point at which the incidence of deviance and crime becomes dysfunctional. At some point (unspecified by the theory), the number of crimes may become so large that people's fears of victimization erode community integration (Liska, 1987).

Criticisms of the policy implications of anomie theory focus mainly on their feasibility. Significantly reducing the gap between goals and means would necessitate a radical redistribution of wealth and property in society. Meaningful redistributions of goods and services across social strata would negatively affect middle- and particularly upper-class groups, which are already affluent, privileged, and powerful. Even relatively conservative initiatives such as expanding unemployment-insurance benefits, increasing welfare payments, and developing guaranteed-income schemes are unpopular among those whose income taxes would support them. More drastic steps, such as compelling corporations to absorb the costs of keeping their workers employed despite fluctuations in markets, are costly and unlikely to be embraced by economic elites. For these reasons, policies based upon anomie theory that are aimed at dramatically reducing the disjuncture between material goals and legitimate means are unlikely to be widely implemented. More limited initiatives advocating the modest expansion of legitimate opportunities through job training and job creation are much more likely to be undertaken. Such measures are, however, less likely to have a significant impact on the reduction first of anomie and then of crime (Maris and Rein, 1973).

For obvious reasons, the argument that deviance is functional for society has not been reflected in social policy. Crime-creation programs to ensure social solidarity and clarify social norms would be met with less than enthusiasm by most people. In any case, such efforts are clearly unnecessary; the current volume of deviance and crime appears sufficient to meet these requirements.

Although it has been heavily criticized, anomie theory has made major contributions to the explanation of deviance and crime. Before Merton proposed his theory in the 1930s, scholars and laypersons alike commonly assumed that deviant behaviour resulted from personality deficiencies and psychopathologies. That the structure of society could cause deviant and criminal behaviour was a truly innovative insight. The fact that this premise is now commonplace is testimony to the importance of the idea (Bernard, 1984).

SUMMARY

Anomie theory and the functions-of-deviance approach are the two basic themes of functionalism. Durkheim's theory of anomie asserts that deregulation in society produces conditions wherein individuals' aspirations and the means of their achievement fall out of phase with one another. The widening gap between ends and means produces strain, which in turn increases rates of suicide. Durkheim cites both rapid economic expansion and rapid economic contraction as major forces in creating the disjunction between ends and means.

While Durkheim argues that both ends and means fluctuate, Merton maintains that goals are firmly set at high levels for all social groups. He argues that the means through which these goals may be legitimately attained, however, are differentially distributed, with the poor having restricted access. As a result, deprived groups adapt in five distinct ways to anomic conditions: they conform, innovate, retreat, become ritualistic, or rebel.

Following Merton's lead, Cohen constructs a theory positing that delinquency occurs because lower-class youths lack the means to be successful in a world dominated by middle-class values. Faced with continual frustration over their failure to acquire middle-class status, they adapt by forming deviant subcultures that patently reject middle-class values and offer meaningful ways of attaining status in lower-class contexts.

Cloward and Ohlin extend Merton's anomie formulation by suggesting that illegitimate opportunity structures affect involvement in various forms of delinquency. The availability of illegal opportunities encourages people experiencing strain to become embroiled in criminal subcultures. The presence of neither legitimate nor illegitimate options increases the likelihood of involvement in violent-conflict subcultures or of entry into the retreatist world of drug use.

General strain theory represents a revival of the strain tradition. It stresses the primacy of structural pressures and broadens the perspective by extending conceptualizations of strain and incorporating variables from psychology and other criminological approaches, namely differential association and social control.

The functions-of-deviance approach maintains that some level of deviance in society is inevitable and that deviance serves several distinct functions. Central among these functions are the creation of social solidarity, the clarification of social norms, the emphasis on the rewards of conformity, and the stimulation of social change. Too much deviance and crime, however, can be dysfunctional in that they erode social cohesion.

Functional theories have been heavily criticized, partly because they have existed for a long time. Deficiencies of the anomie approach include the middle-class biases inherent in the theory, the ignoring of value pluralism in modern society, the lack of information as to why certain adaptations are chosen over others, the inability to account for episodic deviance among the lower classes, and the failure to consider deprivation as a relative concept. The functions-of-deviance point of view has been attacked for its naïve assumption that all deviance and crime produce an element of cohesion and for its failure to specify the point at which deviance becomes dysfunctional.

Anomie theory implies that social and economic resources should be redistributed more equitably to reduce the considerable gap between ends and means experienced by some groups in society. Radical change in this regard is unlikely to be accomplished because affluent and powerful groups with nothing to gain and something to lose would resist it.

The major contribution of functional theory is the idea that social structure profoundly affects the distribution of deviance and crime in society.

QUESTIONS FOR CRITICAL THINKING

1. Have you ever been in the position to observe directly the conditions associated with Merton's conceptualization of anomie? What forms, conformity or deviance, did the response to anomie take? What determined the nature of the response?

2. How might Merton's anomie theory account for the higher rates of deviance and crime among Canada's aboriginal people? Can the theory point policymakers in the right direction to develop effective solutions to this problem?

3. How could Merton's framework be used first to explain middle-class crime and second to explain corporate crime? Can the theory be used as it is? How would you modify the perspective to incorporate the idea of relative deprivation to explain the illegal conduct of professional workers on one hand and society's rich and powerful elites on the other?

4. According to Cohen, the middle-class school environment is a source of frustration for lower-class children. Based on Cohen's theory, is it justified to have segregated schools for lower-class children? Why or why not?

5. How closely tied to the ideas of Durkheim and Merton is Agnew's theory of anomie? Does it make more sense to characterize Agnew's formulation as an integrated theory drawing upon insights and variables from a variety of criminological perspectives and psychology? Are there sources of strain that Agnew has overlooked?

RECOMMENDED READINGS

Cloward, R., and L. Ohlin. (1960). *Delinquency and Opportunity.* New York: Free Press.
   Provides the seminal account of the role of illegitimate opportunity structures in understanding the formation and reinforcement of criminal, conflict, and retreatist subcultures and gangs.

Cohen, A. (1955). *Delinquent Boys: The Culture of the Gang.* New York: Free Press.
   Sets out influential ideas concerning development of delinquency among lower-class youth in middle-class-dominated schools.

Merton, R. (1968). *Social Structure and Anomie.* New York: Free Press.
   Represents an expansion and refinement of Merton's classic formulation of anomie and its relation to various forms of lower-class criminality in America.

Messner, S., and R. Rosenfeld. (2001). *Crime and the American Dream,* 3rd edition. Belmont, CA: Wadsworth.
   Presents a contemporary version of anomie or strain theory that incorporates the idea of the American Dream and its pursuit in an era of weakened societal connections that might have constrained illegality more effectively in the past.

Passas, N., and R. Agnew. (1997). *The Future of Anomie Theory.* Boston: Northeastern University Press.
   Re-examines empirical research based on anomie theory and finds support for the original formulation. The authors provide responses to criticism and attempt to extend the theory.

CHAPTER 5

Social Control Theory

The aims of this chapter are to familiarize the reader with:

- the differences between inner and outer controls
- the differences between informal and formal controls
- the major elements of Reckless's containment, Nye's family ties, and Hirschi's social bonding versions of social control theory
- the key components self-control theory as a general theory of crime
- the fundamentals of the deterrence perspective
- the similarities and differences among the versions of the theory presented by Reckless, Nye, and Hirschi
- the historical antecedents of deterrence theory
- the concepts of specific and general deterrence
- the three major elements of the deterrence perspective
- the policy implications of social control theories that stress informal and formal controls
- the deficiencies of the social control perspectives
- the contributions of the social control perspectives to the understanding of deviance and crime

INTRODUCTION

Social control theory differs fundamentally from the human ecology, differential association, and anomie theories by asking not what causes people to violate social norms but rather what causes them to conform to the rules. It accepts the Freudian notion that the natural state of humankind is base and animalistic

and that, if not inhibited or constrained by social controls, these inborn animal impulses will burst forth in free expression (Freud, 1961 [1930]). Deviant behaviour, then, requires no special motivation. Incentives to deviate need not be created by structural malintegration, and they need not be learned. Without social controls, everyone would succumb to the enjoyment, excitement, and profit that frequently accompany deviant and criminal conduct.

This chapter begins by examining the broad divisions between the two basic themes of social control theory: inner control and outer control. The remainder of the chapter discusses particular versions of the social control perspective: containment theory, the family ties approach, the social bonding perspective, self-control theory, and deterrence theory. The policy implications of **informal** and **formal control** perspectives are examined, and the strengths and shortcomings of these perspectives are assessed.

INNER AND OUTER CONTROL

Social control theory, outlined in Figure 5.1, focuses on two types of control: inner and outer. Inner social controls consist of norms internalized through the socialization process. People learn most rules of proper behaviour in the family during the formative years of childhood.

Inner Controls

Subjected to **inner controls**, people conform because doing so makes them feel good about themselves. Children first learn to be honest in order to curry

FIGURE 5.1

GENERAL MODEL OF INFORMAL SOCIAL CONTROL THEORY

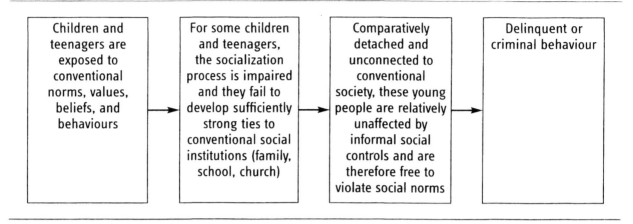

favour with their parents. Continuous socialization during childhood and adolescence gradually transforms honesty into an internal value that guides exchanges with other people. Being honest and forthright in dealings with others bolsters self-worth and creates a feeling of personal moral satisfaction. Dishonesty, alternatively, gives rise to feelings of guilt and self-deprecation. Preferring feelings of personal satisfaction to feelings of guilt, the individual conforms to a fundamental social value — honesty. In this sense, constraints internalized in the personality control the person. The process of socialization is extremely important to the development of internal social controls. Not surprisingly, control theorists frequently cite inadequate socialization as the primary reason for weak social controls and consequently for deviance.

Outer Controls

Outer controls manifest themselves in the potential loss of social or economic rewards experienced by a norm violator. They can be both informal and formal. Informal outer controls include concerns about what friends and relatives will think, about being the subject of gossip, and about being ostracized. The threat of apprehension, conviction, and "correction" with legally imposed fines and jail terms are examples of formal outer controls. Operating together, informal and formal external controls can be powerful suppressors of behaviour that violates community standards.

For example, in an effort to deal more effectively with intoxicated drivers in St. John's, Newfoundland, authorities not only subjected violators to the punish-

ments provided by the *Criminal Code* but also published the names of miscreants in the newspaper. This strategy used informal social control mechanisms to bolster the existing formal ones to more effectively deter drinking and driving. Although this practice has been discontinued, rumour has it that this column was avidly read. According to the social control perspective, when both inner and outer controls are strong, levels of deviance will be low. Alternatively, where both inner and outer controls are weak or absent, rates of deviance will be high.

Social control theory has several variations, each of which differs somewhat in the degree of emphasis it places on inner and outer informal and formal controls.

WALTER RECKLESS AND CONTAINMENT THEORY

Walter Reckless developed one of the earliest and best-known versions of the social control perspective (Reckless, 1973). In his **containment theory,** outlined in Figure 5.2, Reckless points out that many powerful societal and psychological forces propel individuals into nonconforming acts. Social forces that push and pull people toward deviant behaviour include poverty, membership in an ethnic minority, restricted access to legitimate opportunities, involvement in deviant subcultures, and exposure to media influences. Reckless calls these mechanisms *external forces* because they reside outside the individual personality. Inner psychological pressures that promote

FIGURE 5.2

RECKLESS'S CONTAINMENT THEORY

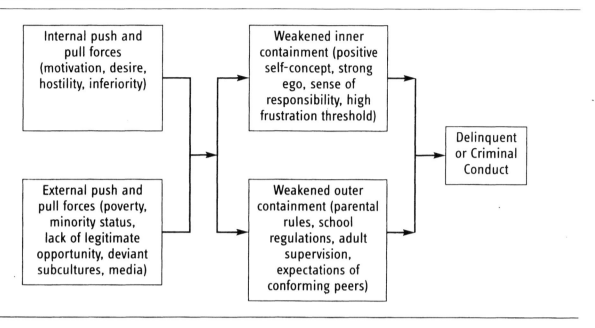

deviant activity include motives, desires, hostilities, and feelings of inferiority and inadequacy. While Reckless views these outer and inner forces as impelling people to violate rules, he notes that not everyone becomes deviant. Reckless answers the question of why some become rule breakers while others do not with the concept of containment.

While internal and external forces promote deviance, inner and outer containments insulate people from these pressures. According to Reckless, **inner containments** are qualities of personality acting as impediments to deviance. These include a positive self-concept, a strong **ego,** an intense sense of personal responsibility, and a high frustration threshold. People acquire these components of **self** largely during childhood through socialization to the "proper" social values. **Outer containments,** on the other hand, are external to the individual and take the form of parental rules, school regulations, supervision by adults, and the expectations of rule-abiding friends.

Deviant behaviour, Reckless argues, is a function of the interaction of inner and outer pro-deviance pressures on the one hand and the internal and external anti-deviance containing forces on the other. When predisposing factors are strong and containing forces are weak, deviant behaviour will result.

Conversely, where predisposing factors are weak and containing forces are strong, the outcome will be conformity. This framework predicts that moderate involvement in deviant activity might be produced by intermediary combinations such as strong external pressures but weak internal pressures, coupled with weak inner constraints but strong outer constraints.

IVAN NYE AND FAMILY TIES

Ivan Nye's version of social control theory, outlined in Figure 5.3, emphasizes the family's role as an agent of socialization (Nye, 1958). Drawing on Freudian psychology, Nye accounts for pro-deviance motivations by pointing to the baser animal instincts ingrained in the human psyche. Nye, in short, assumes that all humans are born with the same tendencies toward deviance. He explains why only a few actually violate social norms by identifying four types of social control stemming from the family environment: internal control, indirect control, direct control, and legitimate need satisfaction. Nye contends that each type mitigates the negative forces exerted by people's natural animal instincts.

Children acquire internal control through a process of socialization wherein they learn from their

FIGURE 5.3

NYE'S THEORY OF FAMILY TIES

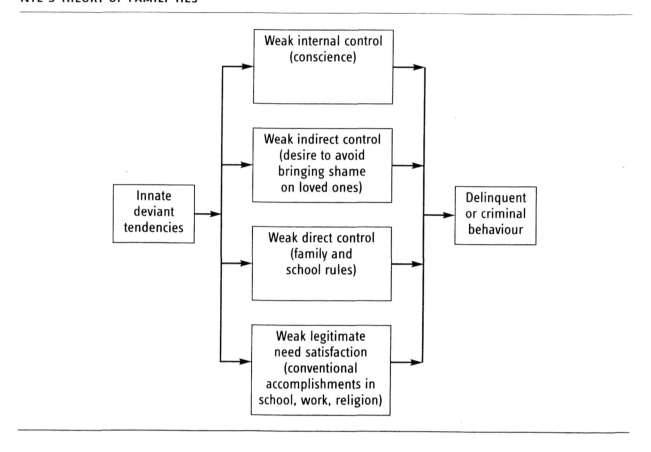

parents the values and norms governing acceptable social conduct. Conditioned through rewards and punishments, children over time internalize family and social values and in so doing develop a conscience. If families properly socialize their progeny at this stage, children's consciences will exert considerable controlling power over them as they mature. People with healthy consciences will feel good when they conform to social rules; they will feel bad when they do not.

In addition to being guided by internalized notions of right and wrong, behaviour is also governed by indirect control. Most people do not wish to shame, hurt, or heap disrespect on those for whom they care deeply. The feeling that being observed or apprehended while engaging in deviance might distress loved ones, Nye suggests, is a strong inhibitor.

Direct controls are the efforts of conventional groups like the family and the school to restrict the activities of youth. Rules concerning curfew, leisure

time use, studying, and the company one keeps are examples of direct controls. The threat and application of informal and formal sanctions can be powerful inhibitors of deviant conduct. The child who plays hooky faces not only parental disapproval but also the legalistic penalties handed down by an irate principal or a disgruntled truant officer.

Nye's final form of social control is need satisfaction. If families prepare children to become successful in school and at work and society enables individuals to find affection, security, and recognition, their legitimate needs will be satisfied. The satisfaction of these legitimate needs by family, friendship circles, the school, and organized religion knits the individual securely into the social fabric.

Variation in the strengths of these controls results in variations in conduct ranging from conformity to deviance. Strong controls overcome people's baser instincts and produce obedience to social regulations. Weak controls, alternatively, permit innate animal impulses to surface and to be more freely expressed.

TRAVIS HIRSCHI AND SOCIAL BONDING

Travis Hirschi, like Reckless and Nye before him, also takes the position that people's natural predisposition is to behave deviantly. Despite this, few conduct themselves reprehensibly. For the most part, they conform. According to Hirschi, people obey the rules because they are tied to conventional society by social bonds, which are similar to the inner and outer controls identified earlier by Reckless and Nye. Specifically, Hirschi (1969) presents four strands constituting the ties that bind: attachment, commitment, and involvement, which are analogous to outer controls; and belief, which is comparable to inner control (see Figure 5.4).

FIGURE 5.4

HIRSCHI'S SOCIAL BONDING THEORY

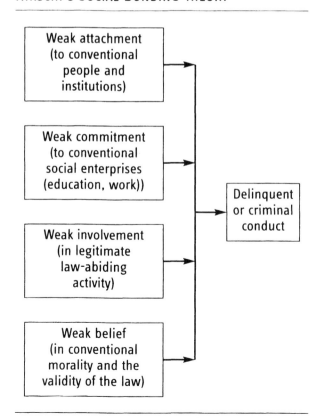

Attachment refers to the connection between individuals and other conventional people and institutions. Sensitivity to the wishes and expectations of conforming others whose opinions are valued is the main idea behind attachment. Children and adolescents who love their parents, who respect their teachers, who admire their conventional friends, and who care deeply about what these people think, are attached. Conversely, a person who does not care about the degrees of affection or respect accorded by others is detached. High degrees of detachment make rule violation possible if not likely.

Acquiring an education, securing a challenging and well-paying job, and otherwise building a good reputation in the community are conventional achievements that require considerable time and energy. Hirschi suggests that those who enjoy the rewards of these and other conformist activities are unwilling to risk their loss. Consequently, they avoid being publicly identified as deviant. Working long and hard at building a conventional way of life, enjoying present rewards, and anticipating bright prospects in the future increase one's stake in conformity. With vested social and economic interests such as these, many people have considerably more to lose by deviant action than they have to gain. Strong *commitments* to the social system reduce the probability of deviant behaviour.

The idea that idle hands are the devil's helper is the central point of Hirschi's third social bond. *Involvement* refers to the amount of time spent pursuing legitimate undertakings. Taken to its extreme, if conformist activities consume every waking minute, no time remains for hatching plots and getting into mischief. Adolescents who are heavily involved in school, extracurricular activities, and homework during the week, who work at a part-time job on Saturday, and who spend Sunday morning in church and Sunday afternoon at home, entertaining younger brothers and sisters, have little time for delinquency.

While attachment, commitment, and involvement are external to the individual, *belief* is an internal control. Intense beliefs in the rightness of conventional morality and in the legitimacy of social norms reduce the likelihood of misconduct. Hirschi's notion of belief is comparable to Nye's idea of internalized control. One is likely to be bothered by one's conscience if one were to break a rule that one believed should be obeyed. Those whose internalized beliefs support conventional social values and norms are morally constrained from committing anti-social acts. Those who do not feel these moral obligations are free to deviate as they wish.

SELF-CONTROL THEORY AS A GENERAL THEORY OF CRIME

Gottfredson and Hirschi's (1990) general theory of crime is an extension of Hirschi's social control theory. It differs from its predecessor in that it emphasizes only one type of control, self-control, while incorporating such additional components as individual choice, life course events, and psychological constructs. The self-control perspective sets out to explain all individual differences in the propensity to commit crime or to refrain from it. As a general theory, the self-control approach explains all acts of deviance and crime, at all ages, under all circumstances. In so doing, it presents individual differences in criminal propensity as inherently stable. The theory states that individuals with high levels of self-control are less likely, at all periods of life, to engage in criminal acts. Those with low levels of self-control, conversely, are highly likely to commit crimes. Since low self-control can be counteracted by a variety of circumstances, it does not always result in illegal conduct. Circumstances must be right for low self-control to result in a criminal act.

The theory, outlined in Figure 5.5, maintains that low self-control is a product of inadequate socialization, particularly in the family domain. Parents effectively socialize their children when their relationship to their offspring is one of attachment, when they provide close supervision, and when they actively punish rule breaking. Ineffective child-rearing, on the other hand, produces low self-control, which causes people to break laws in a more or less impulsive fashion. People with low self-control engage in crime because it is easy and provides immediate gratification. In contrast, legitimate work involves effort and deferred gratification, both of which require high self-control. Work is an unattractive option for those who are drawn to such easy pleasures as smoking, drinking, gambling, and sex and who are captivated by action involving stealth, danger, agility, speed, and power.

The social control theories discussed thus far concentrate largely on informal inner and outer controls. The discussion of social control theory will now focus on formal external controls.

DETERRENCE THEORY

The threat or application of punishment can deter behaviour that violates formal norms. Formal codes governing proper conduct characterize many formal organizations, including the military, industry, the professions, mental hospitals, and universities. Formal normative systems also characterize nations. The *Criminal Code* of Canada, for instance, governs the proper conduct of its citizens.

Contemporary deterrence theory, outlined in Figure 5.6, has its roots in the works of the classical theorists, principally Beccaria and Bentham. Deterrence theory views people as rational beings capable of calculating the costs and benefits of

FIGURE 5.5

A GENERAL THEORY OF CRIME

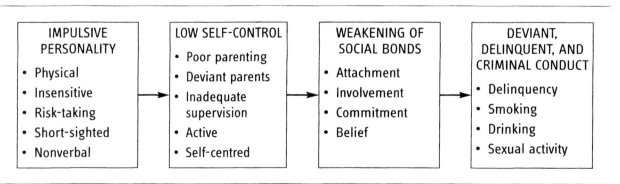

FIGURE 5.6

DETERRENCE THEORY

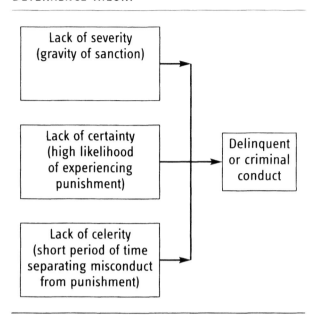

breaking the law (Cook, 1980; Gibbs, 1975; Zimring and Hawkins, 1973). If an individual believes that the benefits of committing a crime outweigh the potential liabilities of detection, apprehension, and punishment, criminal action is encouraged. Conversely, when the costs of punishment appear to outweigh the benefits of committing a crime, the probability of obeying the law increases. For example, the average "take" for a bank robbery in Canada is slightly more than $4,000 (McLean, 2000). Clearance rates for this offence are typically less than 30 percent (Brannigan, 1984). Conviction for robbery in Canada carries a maximum sentence of life imprisonment. A potential robber of a Canadian bank who is aware of these facts and who decides that the risks of the crime outweigh its benefits demonstrates the deterrent value of the criminal law pertaining to bank robbery.

There are two types of **deterrence**, specific and general. **Specific deterrence** embodies the idea that the direct experience of punishment will dissuade those convicted from repeating their crimes. The ideal for the deterrence enthusiast is that the person convicted of fraud, who must repay the amount owing to the government and who must serve a two-month jail sentence, will be reluctant to repeat this action. In **general deterrence,** the punishment of the criminal

serves a symbolic purpose. It warns members of the public about the potential costs that they might incur if they were to commit the same offence. This warning signal, transmitted through the criminal justice system, operates to deter those who might be contemplating but who have not yet committed the crime. Affluent businesspeople and influential politicians whose marriages are deteriorating may be reluctant to hire killers to dispatch their spouses, given the dismal track records of Peter Demeter, Helmuth Buxbaum, and Colin Thatcher. Those of lesser means may be even more strongly deterred by the knowledge that it is difficult for even the rich to terminate marriages in this fashion.

Three dimensions of punishment affect the efficacy of deterrence: the severity of the sanctions, the **certainty** that the sanctions will be applied, and the **celerity** or speed with which they are administered (Cook, 1980; Gibbs, 1975; Zimring and Hawkins, 1973). According to the theory, more severe punishments increase the level of deterrence. The more costly the fines and the longer the periods of incarceration, the less likely is the commission of the crime.

Certainty refers to the risk of being punished. If a potential culprit is virtually certain of receiving a fine or a jail term, his or her likelihood of committing the crime decreases commensurately. Deterrence theory also hypothesizes that the *celerity* or speed with which one is punished increases the deterrent value of a particular sanction. A short time interval between the crime and the punishment heightens the deterrent value of the sanction. The thinking underlying this proposition is that more immediate punishments are somehow more real in the minds of potential offenders.

Interest in deterrence theory and its applications declined after the Second World War as the emphasis in Canadian corrections shifted to a concern for rehabilitating and reintegrating prisoners. Rehabilitation and reintegration, however, have been very costly and, in the opinion of much of the Canadian public, have failed (Moore, 1985; Gomme, 1987). The widespread perception of rapidly increasing crime rates, despite being erroneous, has generated considerable interest in a return to punishment as the primary if not sole function of Canadian prisons. In light of these contemporary correctional trends in Canada and the United States, deterrence theory has recently undergone a rejuvenation.

SOCIAL CONTROL THEORY AND SOCIAL POLICY

Some social control theories call for the implementation of strategies designed to curb deviant behaviour by increasing the strengths of inner and outer informal controls. In this vein, various intervention techniques, including individual, group, and family counselling, have been undertaken to increase intrafamily unity and develop a stronger sense of right and wrong in youth. Social service agencies have also promoted education and work projects designed to involve youths in conventional activities, thereby fostering greater conformity in them. These initiatives enjoy a good deal of popularity because they fit nicely with commonsense notions that delinquency and crime originate in the poor upbringing of the young (Vold and Bernard, 1986). The policy implications of self-control theory suggest that official initiatives aimed at deterring crime in adulthood are misplaced and doomed to failure. Preventive policies must be implemented that take effect early in the life course and benefit families.

Policy based on deterrence theory is equally straightforward in principle. Deterrence theory predicts that increases in the severity, certainty, and celerity of punishment will reduce criminal infractions. Recommendations favouring harsher punishments enjoy considerable public support because they coincide with the public's conception of better crime control. Efforts to increase the punitiveness and efficiency of criminal justice are not merely popular, they are simpler to implement and easier to evaluate than are alterations in informal social control mechanisms. Lengthening sentences and hiring more police are much more straightforward undertakings than altering belief systems, strengthening ties to family and conventional peers, and instilling commitment to school and work (Liska, 1987).

Table 5.1 presents a summary of social control theories.

THE EVALUATION OF SOCIAL CONTROL THEORIES

Informal Social Control Theories

Critics point out that informal social control theories (such as those of Reckless, Nye, and Hirschi) contain concepts that are vague and overlap conceptually (Nettler, 1984). For example, it is difficult to separate analytically some of Hirschi's elements of the social bond. An adolescent's investment of a great deal of time in homework and study projects could indicate involvement in conventional activities, attachment to a charismatic teacher, belief in the values of knowledge and diligence, or commitment to a conventional course of action. These elements are neither theoretically nor empirically distinct.

The relative importance of the various forms of inner and outer controls remains largely undetermined (West, 1984). Does an inner control, such as a person's conscience, have a greater impact on deterring deviant behaviour than an external control, such as ostracism? Also, control theorists have paid insufficient attention to the way in which the various dimensions of informal social control interact with one another. Does a highly developed self-concept (inner containment) render the individual more or less susceptible to external controls such as parental expectations and levels of supervision?

Researchers have extensively tested containment, family ties, and social bond explanations of deviance with data gathered primarily on adolescents. These tests support the hypothesis that strong controls foster conformity and that weak or nonexistent controls unleash deviant impulses (Hagan, 1985).

Theories emphasizing informal controls have not been carefully tested with adults and the utility of the theories of informal social control in explaining adult deviance is dubious. As control theorists present it, the world of children and adolescents is comparatively simple — rules regarding right and wrong are relatively clear-cut. Parents socialize their offspring to the basic values and norms of society. The young learn to eat and dress properly, to observe the rights of others, to respect property, to be honest, and to work hard. With some variations, in the early stages of life social values are comparatively straightforward and the norms governing conduct are relatively simple. Moreover, the child is subject to socialization in only a few groups. In the earliest formative years, the family alone is responsible for inculcating a single set of norms, values, and beliefs.

As a person grows older, the surrounding world becomes increasingly complex. Right and wrong become more equivocal, and the norms governing proper conduct become more ambiguous. The combination of occupying more roles, holding memberships in a larger number of groups, and playing for

TABLE 5.1

THEORIES OF SOCIAL CONTROL

Theory	Theorist(s)	Central Premise	Key Concepts	Principal Contributions
Containment	Walter Reckless	Different levels of external and internal social and psychological pressures to deviate are neutralized by different levels of inner and outer containment; high internal and external pressures and weak inner and outer containments result in delinquent and criminal behaviour	External pressure; internal pressure; inner containment; outer containment	Emphasis on societal and psychological forces in encouraging conformity or deviance
Family ties	Ivan Nye	While everyone is innately inclined to deviate, strong connections to the family through internal, indirect, and direct control and high need satisfaction encourage conformity; weak controls facilitate deviant behaviour	Internal control; indirect control; direct control; need satisfaction	Focuses attention on the family as the primary institution of socialization to conformity or deviant behaviour
Social bonding	Travis Hirschi	Nonconformity is impeded by attachment to conventional people and institutions, commitment to conventional social enterprises, involvement in legitimate undertakings, and belief in conventional morality	Attachment; commitment; involvement; belief	Presents a popular reformulation of informal social control theory that has been widely tested and empirically supported
Self-control theory as a general theory of crime	Travis Hirschi; Michael Gottfredson	Variations in self-control produce variations in the propensity to commit crime. Low self-control is a product of inadequate socialization, primarily in the family context.	Self-control	Refined version of Hirschi's earlier formulation of social control theory. It offers a theory of crime designed to explain all forms of illegal behaviour
Deterrence theory		Severe, certain, and swift punishment deters crime; certainty of punishment is more important than its severity	Specific deterrence; general deterrence; severity; certainty; celerity	Forms the cornerstone of crime control and correctional policy in many countries, including Canada and the United States

higher stakes renders the adult world more complicated, confusing, and conflict-ridden (Thio, 1988).

The manner in which external controls like Hirschi's attachment and commitment channel the adolescent into conforming conduct has already been examined. Attachment refers to the child's love and respect for and desire to please parents, while commitment refers to the investment of the child's time and energy in conventional activities like doing well in school. Consider, however, how attachment and commitment might operate in the world of adults.

Intense affective attachments to their families often place adults in difficult moral positions. Executives who inform the media about their companies' violations of pollution regulations and who later testify in court may be worthy of our commendation for their honesty and courage. The consequences of whistle-blowing, however, might very well be the denial of promotion or the loss of a job. Attachment to family members might well preclude ensuring that one's company be forced to follow anti-pollution legislation to the letter. Being a good parent and spouse in one's own eyes and in the eyes of family members might mean keeping one's job and maintaining family security, or it might mean being honest and preserving the environment for future generations. Either choice has major ethical implications.

Presumably, a highly committed adult would be one who worked very hard and who sought to improve his or her status. For example, for the well-educated, high-performing, ambitious executive employed by General Motors, promotion requires diligence, intelligence, and following the instructions of superiors. It is not impossible that company directives might involve carrying out morally debatable actions. Suppose the executive is required to assist in the speedy marketing of an unsafe vehicle. To refuse to do so might have dire consequences for a person with an immense stake in the conventional occupational world. Life becomes complicated when consensus on what is good and what is evil declines and when commitment to conventional success necessitates participating in actions that may be harmful to others.

Being highly committed to conventional courses of social action can encourage deviant and criminal activity in another manner. Committed and successful people may climb to positions of higher status and greater power in the conventional occupational hierarchy. Many sociologists of deviance seriously question the notion that lower-class people are more frequently involved in deviant and criminal activity than are higher-status people. They maintain that what varies by status is not the frequency of wrongdoing but the type of misconduct. Put simply, people from all status groups, in more or less equal proportions, commit acts that harm others. The type of rule violation or the manner in which it is carried out, however, differs as a consequence of status in general and occupational status in particular. Assembly-line workers steal tools, salespeople abscond with merchandise and pad expense accounts, physicians overbill government health-insurance plans, and oil executives conspire and fix prices (Snider and West, 1980). Broadly construed, each of these acts is theft.

Consider another example. People near the bottom of the status hierarchy kill. The act is usually performed swiftly, in anger, at home or in a bar, and often in the presence of witnesses. However, those at the top of the status hierarchy are also responsible for the deaths of others (Hills, 1987). Industrial safety standards that are not observed (Frank, 1987; Reasons, Ross, and Paterson, 1981), potentially unsafe automobiles and pharmaceutical drugs that are marketed nonetheless (Braithwaite, 1984; Dowie, 1977), and toxic chemicals that are improperly disposed of (Tallmer, 1987) have killed, are killing, and will kill — albeit without anger — slowly and from a considerable distance. Safety standards, marketing strategies, and waste disposal practices are frequently matters of policy. They are rational, planned decisions made by "responsible" people. As a final point, of course, status is related not only to the type and means of commission of certain illegitimate acts but also to the chances of being detected, prosecuted, and convicted. All such probabilities tend to be greater for members of the lower classes.

While there are many acts of deviance and crime for which social controls may not serve as constraints for adults, there are some for which controls do curb participation. Social control theory may inform our understanding of adult involvement in such activities as shoplifting, petty theft, and certain sex offences. Fear of apprehension and the ensuing embarrassment and shame effectively deter the commission of these offences.

The social control theories elaborated by Reckless, Nye, and Hirschi have been very well received, for two reasons. First, empirical research strongly confirms them. Second, they provide logical explanations for the ways in which a large number of variables are associated with deviance and lawbreaking. School, family, peer group, community, and religion are all subsumed under the social control umbrella. Common sense has long suggested that these factors are important in accounting for delinquency.

While self-control theory is logically consistent, parsimonious, broad in scope, and enjoys some empirical support as a general theory of crime, it is new and requires more testing. Because self-control is a psychological variable, its existence and levels are very difficult to measure. A second criticism is that self-control cannot be easily separated from propensities for criminal activity and therefore the theory is tautological or circular in its reasoning. Low and high self-control are labels for differential propensity to commit crime, and measures of low self-control are not clearly separated conceptually from the tendencies to commit crime that low self-control is meant to explain (Akers, 1997).

Formal Social Control Theories

Deterrence theory applies specifically to the formalized efforts of the state to enforce the conformity of its citizens. Attempts to evaluate the impacts of criminal laws and the dimensions of deterrence (e.g., severity, certainty, and celerity) have resulted in findings that are neither entirely consistent nor easily synthesized (Liska, 1987). That all types of crime are equally affected by deterrence seems unlikely. The idea of deterrence assumes that individuals rationally calculate the costs and benefits of committing a particular illegal act. Rational calculation requires a period of thought. People commit certain crimes, some of them serious, on the spur of the moment and often under considerable emotional strain. Most assaults and murders are unpremeditated and, as such, are prime examples of acts of passion.

While there is a low probability of deterring crimes that are not carefully thought through, the same may be less true of predatory offences such as robbery, burglary, consumer fraud, and restriction of trade, all of which require planning. Planned crimes leave time for contemplation. To the extent that people perceive the costs of apprehension to outweigh the profits of crime, penalties may have some deterrent impact. Deterrence is especially the case where there is a high probability that sanctions will be administered (Avio and Clark, 1976, 1978; Tittle and Rowe, 1974).

For any punishment to accomplish the goal of general deterrence, a knowledgeable public is required. The citizenry must know about the potential liabilities of committing a particular crime in order to properly calculate its costs and benefits. Some critics of deterrence theory maintain that potential offenders do not understand the penalty structure (Liska, 1987). To be properly informed, a potential offender should be able to answer, for the jurisdiction in which the crime is to be carried out, the following questions. For the proposed crime, what is the rate of offence cleared by charge (that is, in how many instances are charges laid)? What are the minimum and maximum sentences set out in the *Criminal Code?* What is the average sentence actually meted out? To bring this point home, do you yourself know the answers to these questions for any of the following crimes: selling narcotics, impaired driving, burglary, forgery, or armed robbery?

Theories of formal social control tend to ignore the idea that the control efforts of police forces may actually cause some criminal activity (Marx, 1981). Police often assume false identities to trap criminals. They may pose as drug buyers, sellers of stolen goods, and "johns" in search of sexual services from prostitutes. In some instances, through tempting the unaware, crime-control strategies induce criminal acts where they would not otherwise have taken place. Unofficially, informal aspects of police–citizen encounters may result in lawbreaking. The demeanour with which police treat citizens may either encourage cooperation or provoke flight or retaliation, both of which are illegal.

The idea of specific deterrence implies that if someone commits a crime and is apprehended and punished, the direct experience of negative sanctions decreases the likelihood of re-offending. That incarceration reduces a person's lawbreaking, given the recidivism rates reported for Canadian correctional facilities, seems questionable. Despite punishment, many ex-inmates re-offend, are re-convicted, and return to serve time in a correctional institution (Ekstadt and Griffiths, 1988).

It has long been recognized that lengthy prison sentences may have effects opposite to those intended. There are two reasons why this may be the case. Time served in prison in the company of more experienced and more hardened criminals provides a setting in which crime-oriented skills and values can be learned (Ekstadt and Griffiths, 1988). The incarcerated find it easy to learn how to "case" a house, how to gain entry efficiently, what to steal, and how to turn a profit on the goods. In this context, incarcerated persons also develop the beliefs that they are downtrodden, that they have been unfairly treated by "the system," and that society owes them a living by whatever means.

The second reason offered for the frequent re-commission of crime by ex-inmates is that they emerge from prison with a criminal record (Ekstadt and Griffiths, 1988). The socially devalued status of ex-convicts has a number of very real implications. Ex-offenders often face rejection both by family and by former conventional associates and exclusion from the job market. Branded in this fashion, many ex-convicts renew acquaintances with lawbreaking friends and return to making a living through illegal enterprise. Socialization in the correctional institution and the social stigma after release may outweigh or totally negate the power of punishment as a specific deterrent.

Deterrence theory specifies neither the relative strengths of severity, certainty, and celerity nor the nature of interactions among these dimensions (Gibbs, 1975). On the first point, the theory offers no reasons why one of these three elements might be more powerful than the others. On the second point, explanations as to why certain combinations of elements might have different deterrent effects have not been forthcoming. Is the impact of severity reduced or eliminated for crimes for which punishment is rarely meted out (lack of certainty) or where considerable time elapses between the commission of the act and the experience of negative sanction (lack of celerity)?

While some variations exist from one research study to the next, empirical findings generally suggest that increasing the severity of punishments does not increase deterrence (Tittle, 1969). Comparing jurisdictions where the lengths of sentences differ for the same offence indicates that more severe penalties produce no greater deterrent impact. Similarly, comparisons of regions in which the penalty for murder is execution with those in which it is life imprisonment show that capital punishment does nothing to reduce the rates of homicide (Bailey, 1974; Fattah, 1972).

Although increasing severity does not appear to curb criminal activity, increasing the certainty of arrest does seem to have some deterrent effect (Avio and Clark, 1976, 1978). Jurisdictions in which arrests more frequently result in charges seem to have lower

crime rates than those in which arrests do not so often lead to the laying of charges. The effects of celerity of the negative sanction have, to date, not been seriously investigated.

Research concerning the elements of deterrence presents an interesting dilemma for policymakers. Increasing severity as a crime-control strategy is unsupported by the data but widely called for by the public. Alternatively, making punishment more certain might, according to research findings, heighten the impact of punitive sanctions. Increasing the certainty of punishment, however, would require restructuring and expanding the various agencies of the criminal justice system, including police, courts, and corrections. By comparison, lengthening sentences is much less expensive, disturbs fewer vested interests, and incurs less resistance from justice-system personnel. The coping strategies called for by political expediency do not coincide with the best advice offered by existing research.

Finally, the theory and research on social control have yet to carefully assess the relative impacts and interactions of informal and formal controls. Are informal controls more or less important than formal controls in enforcing conformity? What levels of informal control (conscience and attachment) must exist for formal controls (threat or application of punishment) to deter deviant acts?

SUMMARY

Social control theory posits that people are not propelled into deviance by external forces beyond their control. Rather, control theorists argue that everyone would be deviant if they were not constrained by inner and outer controls. The impacts of informal controls are emphasized by Reckless (containment), Nye (family ties), and Hirschi (social bonds). The general theory of crime is an extension of social control theory that emphasizes a single causal variable — self-control. Variations in self-control produce variations in the propensity to commit crime. Low self-control is a product of inadequate socialization, primarily in the family context. Deterrence theory concerns itself with formal controls and, in so doing, directs attention to the impacts of three dimensions of punishment, namely, severity, certainty, and celerity.

Criminologists criticize informal control theories on the bases of conceptual overlap, measurement deficiencies, the failure to specify the relative impacts and interactions of different types of informal control, and the dubious ability of these theories to explain adult deviance and crime. An additional criticism of self control theory is that it is tautological. Approaches stressing informal social control have two strengths: juvenile-delinquency research confirms many of their principal propositions, and these theories convincingly incorporate many variables empirically associated with delinquency.

The deterrence perspective, which examines the formal aspects of social control, has been criticized on a number of grounds. First, deterrence theory does not explain passionate or impulsive crime. Second, since many people are unfamiliar with the penalties for a variety of crimes, finer distinctions regarding the deterrent values of particular sanctions are difficult to determine. Third, the deterrence approach fails to consider that crime-control efforts can produce rather than deter crime. Incarceration provides exposure to criminal learning opportunities, and a criminal record results in the experience of stigma; both these factors may negate the deterrent value of sanctions. Finally, the relative impacts or interactions of severity, certainty, and celerity are unspecified by the theory. Research casts doubt on the overall efficacy of deterrence, particularly increases in the severity of punishment.

Social control theories prescribe the strengthening of inner and outer social ties through socialization. This objective is unlikely to be accomplished easily. Deterrence research indicates that an increased certainty of punishment may reduce crime, while increasing severity is unlikely to have this effect. Increasing the severity of punishment, although unsupported by research, is nonetheless heavily favoured by the public.

QUESTIONS FOR CRITICAL THINKING

1. What are the implications of theories emphasizing informal social controls on family issues such as dual-income families, blended families, extended families, divorce, and single parenthood? In terms of policy, how amenable to change are criminogenic conditions associated with the family?

2. Hirschi's social control theory suggests that involvement in conventional activities reduces delinquency. In Canada, however, there is much debate on whether the involvement of youth in organized hockey encourages violence. What do you think? Is it important to consider whether or not the violent conduct is confined to the ice?

3. Much research supports the claim that children who do well in school are less likely to commit criminal acts than those who are failures at school. Based on your knowledge of social control theory, what changes would you make to the Canadian public school system to reduce delinquency and crime? Can you think of other theoretically grounded arguments for the link between deviance and illegal conduct and school failure and dropout?

4. How is self-control theory a logical extension of the earlier informal social control theories not only of Hirschi but also of Reckless and Nye? Can you identify any problems created by subsuming earlier articulations of various dimensions of social control under the heading of self-control? Are there dimensions that do not fit well within the Gottfredson-Hirschi formulation? If so, consider the implications for the explanatory power of self-control theory.

5. Significant proportions of the Canadian and American public champion the efficacy of capital punishment, and many supporters cite deterrence as their primary rationale. Few accept empirical findings challenging the utility of this practice. Considering the components of deterrence, do you think that it is possible either in theory or in practice to strengthen the deterrent value of the death penalty? Should, as some Americans have suggested, executions be televised to increase general deterrence? What might the intended and unintended consequences of such a practice be?

RECOMMENDED READINGS

Gottfredson, M. R., and T. Hirschi. (1990). *A General Theory of Crime*. Stanford, CA: Stanford University Press.

Represents an extension and refinement of Hirschi's early theory of informal social control into a general theory applicable to the explanation of all forms of criminality.

Hirschi, T. (1969). *Causes of Delinquency*. Berkeley: University of California Press.

Provides the classic statement of social bonding theory. Hirschi explains the approach in detail and convincingly emphasizes its superiority to competing frameworks.

Nye, F. I. (1958). *Family Relationships and Delinquent Behaviour*. New York: John Wiley.

Nye sets out his version of informal social control in the context of family relationships and their power to constrain delinquent conduct.

Reckless, W. C. (1973). *The Crime Problem,* 3rd edition. New York: Appleton Century Crofts.

Contains the fundamentals of a version of social control theory that emphasizes the importance of inner and outer containments in the constraint of adolescent misconduct.

Varma, K. N., and A. N. Doob. (1998). "Deterring Economic Crime: The Case of Tax Evasion," *Canadian Journal of Criminology* 40:165–184.

Study of tax evasion in Canada suggesting that severity is less important in deterring crime than certainty.

CHAPTER 6

Symbolic Interactionism and the Labelling Theory of Deviance

The aims of this chapter are to familiarize the reader with:

- the bases of symbolic interactionism: verbal and nonverbal symbols and communication through interaction
- self-image, self-concept, and identity as social constructs
- Blumer's propositions on symbolic interaction: the importance of meaning, the origin of meaning, and the active creation of meaning
- definitions of self: Mead's "self as a social construct" and Cooley's "looking-glass self"
- definitions of society
- definitions of situations
- the links between the general theory of symbolic interaction and the labelling perspective on deviance and crime
- labelling approaches: Tannenbaum's dramatization of evil, Lemert's primary and secondary deviance, and Becker's deviant career
- the basic arguments of reintegrative shaming
- the policy implications of the symbolic interactionist and labelling perspectives
- the deficiencies of the symbolic interactionist and labelling frameworks
- the contributions of symbolic interactionism and labelling to the understanding of deviance and crime

INTRODUCTION

The two basic concepts providing the foundation for symbolic interactionist theory are, not surprisingly, symbols and interaction. This chapter explores the interactionist framework and its contribution to an understanding of deviance and crime. It begins with a discussion of the general principles of symbolic interactionism as developed by philosopher George Herbert Mead and sociologists Charles Horton Cooley and Herbert Blumer. It then examines the development of the labelling perspective, an orientation focusing on deviance and heavily grounded in symbolic interactionism. Subsequent sections introduce reintegrative shaming as an extension of labelling (and deterrence), and discuss the policy implications of labelling theory. The chapter concludes with an assessment of deficiencies and contributions to an understanding of deviance, crime, and social control.

THE THEORY OF SYMBOLIC INTERACTIONISM

Symbols are signs that stand for things. They can be either nonverbal or verbal. The red light in front of many old houses in the seedier districts of turn-of-the-twentieth-century Canadian cities is a good example of a nonverbal symbol; it ensured that all who passed by understood the service available from the establishment. Similarly, hoisting one's arms over one's head, shaking one's clenched fist, or holding the gaze of another are nonverbal symbols intended to communicate surrender, displeasure, or sexual interest, respectively. As verbal symbols, words provide representation for objects, emotions, and behaviours. The words gun, car, and mask are abstract signs that stand for concrete objects. Fear is a word representing a real feeling, while shoot, drive, and hide are verbal symbols representing different kinds of behaviour. Moans, screams, and whistles, although they are not words, are verbal signs nonetheless.

To the extent that people have internalized symbols and share their meanings, symbolic interactionists say that society and culture exist. From the symbolic interactionist perspective, society is a large collectivity of people held together by a common culture that itself is composed of shared symbols. That people interpret red lights, arms held above the head, and screams in approximately the same way and that they attach similar meanings to words like shoot, drive, and hide indicate that they share the same basic culture.

People use symbols to communicate, and communication requires interaction. Prominently displaying the red lantern allows the madam to communicate a marketing idea to the passerby with a sexual desire. The robber pointing a .45-calibre pistol at an unarmed man on a deserted street clearly communicates a desire for his money. In the process of interaction, people use symbols to convey meanings. Madam and robber interact with john and victim and in so doing communicate intentions through both verbal symbols ("Need a date, honey?", "Give me the money!") and nonverbal symbols (red light, gun).

The context in which interaction occurs affects the way in which people interpret symbols. A red light on a doorway on December 25, a red light on a post at an intersection, and a red light on the bow of a houseboat convey different meanings, none of which has anything to do with the sale of sexual services. As the context changes, so too does the meaning attached to the symbol.

A central focus of **symbolic interactionism** is the development of self-image, self-concept, and identity. Interactionists view a person's self-concept as the product of long-term social interaction during which an individual develops a positive or negative sense of self in response to the perceived reactions of others who surround and are important to the individual. Being able to date physically attractive persons is a symbol of worth in our society. People whose phones ring constantly and whose date books are filled are likely to interpret this enthusiasm for their company as a sign of extraordinary personal value. Alternatively, those for whom the phone never rings, for whom the answer is always no, and for whom owning a date book is entirely superfluous are equally likely to interpret this continuous indifference as unflattering. Interactionists claim that the long-term

experience of either favourable or unfavourable responses produces varying degrees of positive or negative self-image.

Philosopher George Herbert Mead is generally acknowledged as the founder of symbolic interactionism (Mead, 1943). Although Mead wrote little, many of his ideas have been widely disseminated by his students. One such student, Herbert Blumer, has written extensively on symbolic interactionism. Blumer (1969) summarizes the perspective more formally in the following manner.

First, Blumer stresses the importance of social meaning. He states that humans act toward things on the basis of the meanings that those things have for them and not simply as a consequence of something inherent in those things. Other theoretical explanations of deviance suggest that factors such as economic hardship, involvement in deviant groups, or severed social bonds produce deviance. Symbolic interactionists, alternatively, take the position that it is not the existence of these conditions per se but rather the meaning that people attach to them that is vital in explaining deviance. People interpret things differently. Some see growing up in poverty, being surrounded by a neighbourhood full of delinquents, or having a parent die an untimely death as intolerably stressful. Others view these same circumstances as great personal challenges. According to symbolic interactionists, behaviour is not simply determined in any straightforward way by conditions; rather, it is affected by the variable meanings that a condition has for a particular individual in a particular context.

Second, having asserted that meaning affects action, Blumer addresses the issue of where the meanings that people attach to things originate. He contends that the meaning of things arises out of social interaction with others. Neither the thing itself nor the person alone provides meaning. Rather, people create, modify, and transmit meaning through a process of social interaction in social and cultural contexts. The precise meanings attached to specific objects and actions in the multitude of contexts in which deviance occurs develop in this way. Observing and interpreting the verbal and nonverbal symbols manipulated by others communicates the meanings of objects (e.g., crowbars, marijuana cigarettes, pool tables, submachine guns), conditions (e.g., poverty, broken homes, unemployment), and acts (e.g., murder, robbery, prostitution). People observe and interpret the actions and reactions of others in relation to objects, conditions, and acts such as these. In the process, they acquire and internalize, in their cultures and subcultures, much of the meaning attached to things, to circumstances, and to behaviours.

Finally, Blumer notes that people take an active part in creating meaning. Meanings, he claims, are handled and modified through an active interpretive process invoked by individuals as they deal with the things that they encounter. The person is not simply a receptor for meaning. Because people actively interpret symbols, they may see slightly or even radically different meanings than others would under the same circumstances. People are partly passive receivers of meaning and partly its active creators.

Out of the meanings arising from interaction, people construct three important definitions that greatly affect their current and future actions, both conforming and deviant. From past interaction and the interpretation of meanings in those past interactions, the person constructs definitions of self, society, and situation. Each of these definitions significantly influences subsequent behaviour. The following sections consider each definition in detail.

Defining Self

A person constructs a conception of **self** through interaction with others. The reactions of others provide the person with symbolic information that, once interpreted, provides the individual with crucial details about the nature of his or her personal identity. For example, our conceptions of ourselves as attractive, kind, cowardly, or worthless arise from our interpretations of the symbolic reactions directed to us by those in our social environment. Our positive and negative evaluations of ourselves originate in our interpretations of the ways in which others react to us. In the long term, the positive and negative meanings that we attach to our senses of self come to affect more and more how we act both toward ourselves and toward others. Mead called this process of identity formation "the self as a social construct" (Mead, 1943). Another pioneer in sociology, Charles Horton Cooley, spoke of identity formation in terms of "the **looking-glass self**" (Cooley, 1902).

According to Mead, people make objects out of the self. They do so, he contends, by taking on the attitudes toward themselves that are expressed by the people with whom they interact. One's self, in these terms, is created by stepping out of one's own shoes and into the shoes of an onlooker. In this way,

people make efforts to see themselves "objectively." The sociology professor who considers turning off the lights, leaping onto a desk with candle in hand, and reciting the Shakespearean soliloquy on the demise of Lady Macbeth to make a point about death in the family is a case in point.

The professor, before this dramatic performance, momentarily steps outside of himself and into the shoes of his youthful audience. If he were a student, he reflects, would he see himself as a brilliant lecturer or a raving idiot? This reflection suggests the former and it motivates him to undertake this flamboyant action. A class moved to tears allows the professor to see himself, on reflection, in positive terms, as a gifted pedagogue. Why? Because if someone had moved him to tears under the same circumstances, he would have been profoundly impressed by the eloquence and emotion of a fine though unconventional performance. A class rolling in the aisles in hysterical laughter, however, would force the instructor to reflect that his technique, if not he himself, was a failure. Why? Because if he as a student had laughed under similar circumstances, he would have done so because he had been appalled by the ridiculous, inept, and immature display.

Mead separates the self into three components: the **"I,"** the **"me,"** and the **"generalized other."** The *I* is the action-oriented behavioural part of the individual, while the *me* is the person's contemplative reflective component. As such, the me reflects the attitudes and beliefs that people have about their own social and physical characteristics. The *generalized other* represents what people imagine others will think about them and their actions. When people ask themselves "What would people think?", they are invoking in themselves the generalized other. The generalized other is a composite of all the "significant others" who have made up or continue to make up our social world. Those whom people love and cherish and whose respect they keenly desire represent their significant others. When the child contemplating lighting up a cigarette wonders "What would Mom and Dad think?" or when a spouse considering adultery reflects "What would my children think?", they are taking account of significant others.

The me part of the self is particularly important to symbolic interactionism, and it is to the me that symbolic interactionists have devoted most of their attention. Understanding the conceptualization of the me offers an explanation of how one develops self-concept and identity. Charles Horton Cooley explains the development of this part of one's self with a rather catchy metaphor, "the looking-glass self."

Just as people's perfections and imperfections are reflected in a mirror, or looking-glass, so are their finer points and deficiencies reflected symbolically in the faces, voices, and even movements of those who make up their social environment. Cooley conceives of the looking-glass process in three stages: the initial conception, the test, and the feeling of pride or mortification. Cooley contends that, at first, people have an initial idea of how they and their actions will appear to others. Consider the child who voluntarily confesses to stealing an apple from the teacher's desk. The child confesses because he or she believes that the teacher's and other students' reactions to the confession will confirm his or her identity as a basically honest but ever-so-human person.

Cooley suggests that people's initial conception of how they will appear to others is subjected to a test as soon as they act and as soon as the act is observed. If the admission of theft is made and the teacher commends the child for honesty and inflicts a minor punishment, this confirms the child's self-conception as honest but perhaps subject to temptation now and then. If, on the other hand, the teacher brings out the strap and the other students begin to chant "You're a thief," the culprit will conclude that his or her image has been "spoiled."

Cooley argues that people feel pride or mortification as a result of their interpretations of others' responses to them. If the teacher commends the student, the student's positive image of the self as honest takes precedence over the negative image of the self as disreputable. If the teacher goes for the strap, the negative reaction emphasizes the child's disreputable image over his or her image as the honest person who made a little mistake. Feelings about self created by spoiled identity are unlikely to be positive. The dark reflection from the looking-glass produces mortification. The audience, according to Cooley, is a social mirror. Positive cues from others make people feel good about themselves, while negative cues make them feel bad. Cooley maintains that what the audience reflects in the long run profoundly shapes a person's sense of self.

Defining Society

Communication through symbols in the process of interaction shapes not only one's definition of self but also one's definition of society in general and of a variety of social situations in particular. For example, the individual's perception of society as either full of opportunity or inhospitable develops in interaction with various agents of socialization, including family members, friends, co-workers, and the media. Once this perception is created, it subsequently affects the way in which people behave. Perceiving social and economic opportunities as plentiful, whether or not this is true, results in the person happily working hard to get ahead. Conversely, the perception of restricted opportunities may produce unhappiness, disenchantment, and withdrawal despite the reality of economic well-being.

Defining Situations

People also **define situations** according to how the interaction process unfolds. Once the situation is defined in a certain way, its meaning influences people's actions. Consider, for example, how differences in the definition of the same situation can produce law-abiding behaviour in some and law-breaking behaviour in others. A motorist stops for a red light in the centre lane of a three-lane street. The driver repeatedly revs the car's engine. The car's windows are heavily shaded, hiding the person behind the wheel. Two other cars pull up on either side and also stop for the light. The driver of the centre vehicle continues to rev the engine. The light turns green. The car in the right lane pulls away slowly, while the car in the left lane crosses the intersection sideways, blue smoke rising from its squealing tires. The car in the centre lane stalls.

Each driver defined the situation differently and acted accordingly. The driver of the car on the right was a middle-aged executive on her way home from the office. Behind the wheel of the car on the left was a young male construction worker. For the businesswoman, the centre car and the sound of its engine are irrelevant. Her socialization left her ears untuned to the subtle variations in the tones emanating from idling engines. The construction worker, alternatively, interpreted the revving engine as a challenge to see who could cross the intersection first. For the driver of the centre car, the constantly revving engine was simply evidence of an annoyingly bad tune-up. How might the definitions of this situation and the drivers' subsequent actions have been affected by different times of day, different makes of cars, and, of course, different driver characteristics?

Symbolic interactionism makes several distinct points worth reviewing. Definitions of self, of society, and of situation are the product of symbolic exchanges that occur in one's interaction with oneself, when one thinks and reflects, with others when one communicates with them, and with external inanimate sources like books and newspapers when one absorbs information from them. Once created, the way in which people conceive of themselves, of society, and of specific situations affects their behaviour. Since individuals vary in the way in which they interpret things and since people actively engage their social world by thinking and responding, symbolic interactionism views behavioural outcomes as less deterministic in terms of cause and effect than do the causal theories presented in previous chapters.

THE SYMBOLIC INTERACTIONIST LABELLING PERSPECTIVE ON DEVIANCE

Symbolic interactionist theory as it is applied to the study of deviance is commonly referred to as the labelling perspective (Schur, 1971) and is outlined in Figure 6.1. Labelling theory does not define deviance as a straightforward violation of social norms in the way that human ecology, functional, differential association, and social control theories do. Rather, labelling theorists stress that it is not the act itself but the contextual meaning attached to it that defines whether or not it is deviant. According to interactionists, deviance, like beauty, is in the eye of the beholder. In developing an understanding of deviance, interactionists focus on three basic questions. Who gets defined or labelled deviant? How does this process occur? Finally, what are the consequences of being designated deviant?

The defined tend to differ from their definers on one significant dimension. Those who are either informally or formally labelled as deviant tend to occupy lower social statuses and to wield less social power than do those who successfully apply the labels. Possessing power means that dominant groups can force the less powerful to do their bidding. Power, however, is a matter of degree. The difference in power between those who define and those who are defined affects the ease with which deviant designations can be applied.

The degree of power wielded by individuals and groups frequently depends upon their statuses. Differences in income, occupation, property ownership, age, sex, ethnicity, and regional and national affiliation define social position and hence, to a large extent, determine social power. For example, all other things being equal, earners of high incomes, workers

FIGURE 6.1

GENERAL TENETS OF THE LABELLING PERSPECTIVE

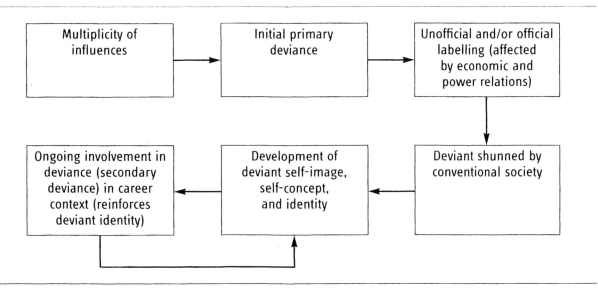

in "professional" occupations, owners of property, the middle-aged, men, whites, Ontarians, and Canadians are likely to be more powerful than the poor, blue-collar workers, renters, the very old and the very young, women, nonwhites, Newfoundlanders, and Ethiopians.

Furthermore, some in Canadian society are given special status with regard to power. The state invests those in officially mandated positions of legitimate authority with special legal power to assign deviant and criminal labels. Agents of the criminal justice system (e.g., police, Crown prosecutors, judges, and correctional workers), psychiatrists and psychologists, and workers in alcohol and drug rehabilitation centres are among those whose formal statuses and roles have attached to them this kind of special power.

FRANK TANNENBAUM AND THE DRAMATIZATION OF EVIL

The process by which the more powerful attach labels to the less powerful was initially outlined during the 1930s by a historian, Frank Tannenbaum. In his discussion of crime in the community, Tannenbaum (1938) developed an account of the way in which adolescents become delinquents. According to Tannenbaum, children participate in a wide range of activities every day. Many of these activities comprise behaviours that adults frequently find objectionable. Smoking cigarettes, flooding school washrooms, cutting classes, and throwing stones at passing trains are some of the joys of adolescent life. Not only do adults informally disapprove of such behaviours, regulations and laws prohibit and specify sanctions for each of these acts. If apprehended by teachers, parents, or police officers, miscreants can be and often are punished. According to Tannenbaum, severe sanctions represent a "dramatization of evil" that can easily stimulate the young to engage in more of the same misconduct.

Over the years, symbolic interactionists interested in explaining deviance and crime have enlarged this basic framework considerably. Various approaches emphasize different aspects of labelling. Edwin Lemert conceptualizes the process of labelling as a transition from primary deviance to secondary deviance. Howard Becker follows suit with an explanation of the labelling process that focuses on the deviant career model.

EDWIN LEMERT — FROM PRIMARY TO SECONDARY DEVIANCE

According to Edwin Lemert (1967), society comprises a wide variety of social and cultural segments divided along such lines as age, ethnicity, and class. These societal segments can be differentiated from one another, at least to some extent, by their unique norms, values, beliefs, and behaviours. Given this social diversity and given that power also varies along these lines, it is inevitable that some social segments come into conflict with other social segments. When this happens, the rules of the more dominant segments, more broadly construed as society's norms, will be violated from time to time as a matter of course. Lemert (1967) calls these initial acts, wherein individuals violate social rules, *primary deviance.*

A multitude of factors, many of which are identified as causes in the theories discussed in previous chapters, act alone or together to promote specific individual acts of deviant and illegal conduct. Deviant acts produced by accident, by unusual situations, by a desire to experiment, or by pressure from deviant associates, Lemert maintains, are common occurrences in the lives of virtually everyone. Deviance remains primary so long as it is occasional or hidden and so long as it does not result in strong and continuous negative social reaction.

Lemert argues that without a strong and continuous punitive response, the norm violator's sense of self is unlikely to be affected. Primary deviance implies that rule breakers, for several reasons, have not closely identified themselves with their deviant actions. In some cases, deviance goes undetected by others and the violator has no mirror to reflect the dark image necessary to develop a deviant identity. In other cases, the deviant act is noticed and elicits a negative sanction. On such occasions, a mirror is provided to reflect negative self-image. Nonetheless, rule breakers still have at hand several possible techniques to neutralize a repugnant self-image.

Gresham Sykes and David Matza (1957) specify five **neutralization techniques,** shown in Table 6.1, whereby those confronted with a deviant self-image may maintain a nondeviant self-concept. They may deny responsibility for their act, deny that injury to others is real, or deny that a victim is really a victim. They may also condemn those who are condemning them, and they may appeal to higher loyalties to

TABLE 6.1

TECHNIQUES OF NEUTRALIZATION

Technique	Examples
Deny responsibility	I had to do it. I had no choice. It was me or him.
Deny injury	They have insurance. What's one CD to a store like Wal-Mart?
Deny victim	They had it coming. She shouldn't have talked back to me.
Condemn condemners	Everyone is on the take. If I don't do it to them, they'll do it to me.
Appeal to a higher loyalty	Only cowards back down. I have to feed my family. National security required this action.

Sykes, G., and D. Matza. (1957). "Techniques of Neutralization: A Theory of Delinquency." *American Sociological Review* 22:664–70.

justify their actions. The unemployed parent who peddles drugs, claiming to be forced to do so by poverty, denies personal responsibility for the illegal conduct. The poacher who bags a moose without a licence, maintaining that there are plenty of the creatures out there in the woods, denies that illegal hunting is injurious. Police officers who administer violent doses of curbside justice to "street scum" deny that there is a "victim" in this assault. The "woman of the night" condemns her condemners when she dismisses her more conventional female critics as hypocrites, charging that they too exchange sexual favours in return for material considerations. Finally, high-ranking RCMP officials appeal to higher loyalties when they claim that concerns for national security required them to approve barn burnings, illegal wiretapping, and unlawful mail openings. In each of these situations, the actors make considerable effort to avoid self-definition as a deviant or lawbreaker.

Primary deviance is incidental to the perpetrator's self-concept because labels have not been successfully attached through a process of negative reflection. In many cases, however, negative responses may be strong and enduring because people persist in their nonconforming acts, because they are relatively powerless, or both. As the intensity of negative responses increases, efforts to maintain a nondeviant self-concept through neutralization or some other means become sorely taxed. When stigma is successfully applied and becomes all-encompassing, it can have negative effects on a person's social relations and economic opportunities. As someone becomes more and more broadly labelled as deviant, family members may withdraw their support, former friends may avoid social contact, employers may deny or take away jobs, and strangers may react with hostility. Moreover, official agents of social control may increase surveillance and harassment. The application of derogatory labels and the severing of connections to conventional spheres intensify the construction of a deviant identity by forcing the devalued person to seek out others in similar situations who can provide more favourable reflections of the self.

To retain a reasonably positive identity, to accept oneself as a "normal" person of some value, and to recast one's self-image in a more favourable light, the stigmatized person reorganizes life around the deviant status and the deviant role. When people transform their psychological outlooks and role performances into a defence from, attack against, or deep adjustment to negative labelling, **secondary deviance** has occurred (Lemert, 1967). The secondary deviant is a person with a deviant self-concept who participates fully in and is heavily committed to the deviant role. Deviant behaviour, for such persons, comes to be generated to a large extent by their definitions of self. The prostitute, the con artist, and the assassin who speak of their work in terms of professionalism and pride are secondary deviants. Their concepts of self are inexorably entwined with their statuses and their roles. They "are," therefore they "do."

HOWARD BECKER, MORAL ENTREPRENEURSHIP, AND THE DEVIANT CAREER

Howard Becker develops two lines of reasoning to extend the labelling perspective — moral entrepreneurship and the deviant career (Becker, 1963). Moral entrepreneurs are people with the power to create or enforce moral norms that are often translated into legal statutes and prohibitions. Becker emphasizes that some individual or group must actively focus public attention on social wrongdoing.

He sees deviance as the outcome of an enterprise in which those with vested moral or economic interests act accordingly to create and apply rules against those with less social and economic power. From this perspective, offenders are, in essence, created by rules that result in their being identified, apprehended, convicted, and, in the process, labelled.

Moral entrepreneurs are often successful at mobilizing support for social and legal sanctions developed and implemented in defence of what they view as core moral values. When they are successful, moral entrepreneurs can create full-blown moral panics out of incidents and events that represent relatively minor acts of nonconformity. Moral panics involve overreactions on the part of media, police, courts, the legislature, and the public. Far from eliminating deviant behaviour, such reactions tend to amplify it. Examples of moral entrepreneurship and the creation of moral panics include various forms of vice and morality violations, such as smoking marijuana, drinking alcohol, gambling, accessing pornography, and visiting prostitutes.

Becker also examines the process of becoming deviant by using the sociological concept of the career (Becker, 1963). While normally thought of in terms of occupations, people can have legitimate careers as students, parents, religious devotees, and golfers or illegitimate careers as drug users, gamblers, prostitutes, and shoplifters.

Sociologists define a career as a sequence of social statuses through which people pass in some sphere of their lives. In the most general of terms, the stages are novice, new recruit, veteran, and retiree. Using an occupation as an example, the typical career of an upwardly mobile police officer might involve working up through the ranks from patrol officer to sergeant, lieutenant, captain, inspector, superintendent, and perhaps even chief. Each career stage represents a social status in which the occupant is reacted to differently both by proximate and distant audiences. Reactions of others to one's status, Becker points out, affect, to varying degrees, one's self-esteem, self-concept, and identity.

Becker suggests that many forms of deviance can be seen as careers through which people pass on their way to becoming full-fledged "outsiders." Prostitutes, alcoholics, and the mentally ill, as well as the majority of professional criminals, pass through a recognizable pattern of stages beginning with the initiate, progressing with the confirmed, and ending with retirement or death. Becker suggests that at each stage

in a **deviant career,** some observers subject potential deviants to a variety of stigmatizing processes, while others, already committed to the devalued activity themselves, promote the redefinition of the deviant role in a more positive light. As a result of widespread homophobic attitudes, people wrestling with the thought that they might be gay often begin the homosexual career with feelings of anxiety, guilt, and shame. These repugnant feelings, in turn, promote a negative self-concept. In later stages of the career, some gays come into contact and interact with homosexuals in the context of a cohesive and supportive subculture. The gay subculture promotes homosexual identity, thereby encouraging gays to accept their sexuality, to "come out," and to declare their sexual orientation publicly and with pride (Troiden, 1979).

Another aspect of the career concept with which Becker deals is the notion of **"master status."** Essentially, a master status overrides other statuses regardless of the context in which the person is located when he or she is the subject of reaction. Someone at a party may occupy a number of different statuses, each of which might affect how other guests respond. For example, a party-goer might simultaneously occupy the statuses of wife, mother, president of a charitable organization, squash player, and physician. Occupying some statuses (e.g., being a doctor) can affect the reactions of others, regardless of the setting. Whether or not the context involves the delivery of health care, people tend to defer to doctors. If one status that a person occupies overrides all others, it is a master status.

Many deviants, when their devalued status becomes public knowledge, accordingly receive a negative response regardless of the context. Being homosexual and being mentally ill are often master statuses. Perhaps the best example is the "ex-con." People routinely treat with suspicion and distrust those who have served time in prison, regardless of their other status characteristics. Continuous negative reactions experienced by people with some form of deviant master status include gossip, ridicule, avoidance, and discrimination in housing and employment.

JOHN BRAITHWAITE AND REINTEGRATIVE SHAMING

The theory of **reintegrative shaming** is, as its creator points out, not highly original (Makkai and Braithwaite, 1994). The theory attempts to revitalize and provide context for the explanatory power of several existing frameworks that have enjoyed at least modest empirical support over the years. These theoretical traditions include strain, subcultural, differential association, social learning, control, and labelling theories. The reintegrative shaming framework poses two related questions. First, what are the conditions under which a criminal label is likely to produce a criminal self-concept and future criminal behaviour? Second, what are the conditions under which such a label is likely to have the opposite effect; that is, to prevent crime?

John Braithwaite (1989) begins by defining shaming as social disapproval that has the intention or the effect of producing remorse in the person being shamed. Shaming may also involve condemnation by others who become aware of the initial shaming. The central idea of the theory is what Braithwaite refers to as the "partitioning" of shaming into two principal components, each of which forms the opposite pole of a continuum. At one end of the scale is reintegrative shaming, while at the other end is shaming that stigmatizes. When shaming is reintegrative, the explanatory perspective inherent in control theory is mobilized. Shaming operates to reduce crime through informal and formal mechanisms of control. Alternatively, when shaming stigmatizes, the explanatory ideas of labelling and subcultural theory are operative. The stigma associated with shaming provokes and amplifies criminal behaviour.

Reintegrative shaming involves the following components. First, disapproval takes place in a context in which those who disapprove sustain a relationship of respect with those whose acts are rebuked. Second, ceremonies to certify deviance are followed and superceded by ceremonies to decertify it. Third, disapproval of the evil deed occurs without labelling people themselves as evil. Finally, disapprovers make efforts to avoid having deviance become a master status. Shaming through stigmatization, on the other hand, comprises disrespectful disapproval and humiliation. Ceremonies to certify deviance do not culminate in ceremonies designed to decertify it. Not only the act but also the person is designated as evil. Finally, deviance is allowed to become a master status.

According to the theory, shaming is likely to be reintegrative and anti-criminogenic under conditions where there is a high level of interdependency between the disapprovers and the disapproved. The theory posits that both individual and structural vari-

ables such as sex, age, employment, marital status, and mobility produce varying degrees of interdependence. Characteristics such as being male, young, unemployed, single, and transient combine to reduce the degree of interdependence between the disapprovers and the disapproved. Under such circumstances, shaming is likely to amplify rather than reduce crime, because stigmatization produces reactions comprising anger and vindictive escalation rather than remorse and conciliation (Makkai and Braithwaite, 1994).

INTERACTIONIST THEORY, LABELLING THEORY, AND SOCIAL POLICY

Interactionist approaches cite labelling and stigmatization, particularly by official agents of social control, as key precipitators in the development of an identity that promotes further deviance. The policy initiatives stemming from the labelling perspective call for a reduction in the degree to which official agents of social control negatively label and stigmatize the people whom they process. Strategies include a variety of undertakings aimed at limiting or eliminating the institutionalization of deviants. Diversion programs try to redirect accused persons out of the criminal justice system before official processing begins. Community-service orders seek to minimize official labelling by channelling those convicted of minor offences out of prisons and into court-mandated work in the community. Similarly, probation and parole programs aim to reduce stigma by minimizing periods of incarceration (Ekstadt and Griffiths, 1988).

The criminal justice system is not the only organization that has sought to incorporate the tenets of the labelling perspective. Many institutions for the mentally ill routinely release into the community people who are considered capable of functioning at an acceptable level on their own. Psychiatric centres have also moved toward reducing their admissions of persons with less serious mental problems (Marshall, 1982). Both these policy initiatives reflect efforts to reduce stigmatization.

Some labelling theorists have advocated more radical steps. Radical noninterventionists would limit official intervention to only the most serious forms of deviance (Schur, 1973). Decriminalization advocates would eliminate many forms of nonserious violation from the *Criminal Code* (Solomon, 1983); widespread illegalities such as the use of soft drugs, prostitution, and gambling would simply be dropped from the statutes. Reducing the numbers of minor but frequent offences would reduce the likelihood of someone becoming the object of official processing.

Table 6.2 summarizes the labelling perspective.

THE EVALUATION OF INTERACTIONIST AND LABELLING THEORIES

Micro theories in general and symbolic interactionism in particular have been criticized for paying little if any attention to history. Interactionists ignore the links between who or what is labelled deviant in the present and events that have occurred in the past. Moreover, interactionism downplays the importance, in the labelling process, of the social impacts of political and economic forces.

Another criticism levelled at labelling theorists is that they tend to ignore the causes of primary deviance (Gibbs, 1966). Consequently, they fail to offer adequate explanations for many forms of misconduct. Furthermore, types of deviance that do not lend themselves to incorporation in the career model cannot, in most cases, be adequately understood from the vantage point of labelling. Nevertheless, such acts (the majority of murders, assaults, and suicides) are significant problems in Canadian society.

Some people demonstrate real personality and behavioural differences long before deviant labels are applied to them. Not only do people become deviant without ever having been labelled as such, the application of stigma in itself often does not produce deviant behaviour. For some, the application of a negative label deters further nonconformity (West, 1980). While punishment may provoke the powerless to further acts of deviance, executives and professionals may be discouraged by punitive responses, especially when they receive public attention.

Labelling theory focuses on the powerful only as labellers; it pays little attention to the deviant behaviour of the socially privileged and economically advantaged (Thio, 1973). This emphasis, critics charge, is misplaced and perpetuates the conventional but mistaken belief that the disadvantaged in society are more deviant than the privileged. Ignoring the misconduct of the segments of society whose resources allow them to resist being labelled is a serious shortcoming.

The labelling perspective tends to treat the deviant as a passive receptor of the stigma that it holds ultimately produces secondary deviance (Piven, 1981). Some people, however, vigorously reject the imposition of these labels (Rogers and Buffalo, 1974). At least some prostitutes, mental patients, and homosexuals, for example, remain primary deviants in the sense that the stigma attached to their behaviours is not incorporated into their self-concepts and personal identities. As Nettler (1984) points out, the perspective is imprecise. It does not, for example, specify what behaviours and what kinds of personality are most susceptible to the application of labels. Nor does it indicate the stage in a person's life at which he or she is most easily labelled. Furthermore, labelling theory does not spell out how the kind of response, the type of actor responding, or the nature of the situation affects the likelihood that a label will stick.

The interactionist theory of deviance has strongly emphasized the importance of official labelling by the criminal justice system but has largely ignored the reactions of those within a person's own reference group (Vold and Bernard, 1986). Significant others play powerful roles in the development of deviant identity, in two ways. For those designated deviant by official agents, significant others may attach the official label even more securely. Alternatively, where deviants fall into the company of similarly predisposed comrades, these significant others may help recast stigma into a more positive mould.

The labelling perspective depicts the stigmatized as resistant to the application of derogatory labels. There are, however, occasions where this is not the case. Rather than struggle to avoid a label, some deviants seek out and embrace stigma (Vold and Bernard, 1986). Juvenile gang members, for example, frequently view their newly acquired disrepute as a badge of honour and a sign of group acceptance.

Attempts to empirically test labelling theory show mixed results (Gove, 1980). Some studies suggest that labelling does promote career deviance, while others fail to demonstrate the link.

From a policy perspective, labelling theory advocates that lawmakers reduce the number of offences and that the police, the courts, and the corrections

TABLE 6.2

LABELLING PERSPECTIVES ON DEVIANCE

Theory	Theorist	Central Premise	Key Concepts	Principal Contributions
Dramatization of evil	Frank Tannenbaum	Children participate in a variety of acts to which adults object. Severe sanctions dramatize evil and stimulate youth to do more of the same.	Dramatization of evil	Sensitization to the possibility that sanctions meant to deter may actually encourage deviant conduct.
Primary and secondary deviance	Edwin Lemert	A variety of factors produce initial or primary deviance. Strong persistent negative sanctions isolate deviants and produce deviant identities. Those who are stigmatized recast their identities in more favourable ways and organize their lives around deviant statuses and roles and continue deviant conduct as a process of secondary deviance.	Primary deviance; secondary deviance; neutralization; stigma	Emphasizes role of negative sanction in amplification as opposed to deterrence of nonconformity; stresses role of identity and self-concept as facilitators of deviance.
Deviant careers	Howard Becker	Moral entrepreneurs create or enforce moral norms that are translated into legal statutes and prohibitions that label as deviant those with less social and economic power. Deviance persists over time and may result in development of deviant self-concept; this process can be analyzed using the career model (novice, new recruit, veteran, retiree).	Moral entrepreneur, moral panic, career; master status	Provides a coherent analysis of criminal occupations; emphasizes the role of social-control agents in the creation of devalued master statuses.
Reintegrative shaming	John Braithwaite	Reintegrative shaming specifies conditions under which labelling constitutes a mitigating or aggravating circumstance influencing future criminal behaviour. Shaming that is reintegrative reduces crime, while shaming that is stigmatizing increases crime. Reintegration is likely where disapprovers and the disapproved are interdependent, and stigmatization is likely where they are not.	Partitioning of shaming; reintegrative shaming; stigmatization; certification and decertification of deviance	Blends insights from a variety of earlier theories, especially labelling, to explain criminal involvement and desistance.

system avoid officially processing accused persons wherever possible. It recommends that official intervention be initiated only for serious offences. However, decriminalization and nonintervention strategies are problematic in several ways. They may not work, and even if they do, they are too radical for a "law and order"–oriented public to accept (West, 1984). Moreover, even when strategies such as diversion programs, community-service orders, and other efforts aimed at de-institutionalization are undertaken, some labelling is inevitable. The application of at least some stigma by officials or by the deviant's acquaintances, friends, and family members is difficult to avoid.

Despite some of the difficulties associated with the interactionist or labelling approach, this orientation has dramatically influenced recent thinking in the areas of deviance, crime, and social control. Labelling theory has focused badly needed attention both on the social reaction to deviance and on the problems faced by those to whom stigma is attached. It has also highlighted the difficulties of reintegrating ex-offenders into the community. Finally, it has encouraged the criminal justice community to apply tough sanctions only as a last resort and only in cases involving serious crime (Stebbins, 1987).

While the theory is new and awaits thorough empirical testing (Akers, 1997), there is some evidence to suggest its usefulness in explaining crime. Braithwaite outlines several instances in which crime facts fit the theory. Moreover, a recent study of changes in nursing-home operators' compliance with regulations supports the reintegrative shaming perspective. Makkai and Braithwaite (1994) found, for example, that the interaction between inspectors' reintegrative ideology and their disapproval of violations produced the desired impact on the operators' subsequent degree of compliance.

SUMMARY

Symbolic interactionists stress the importance of communicating meaning through verbal and non-verbal symbols in a process of interaction. To the extent that the meanings attached to and conveyed by symbols are shared, interactionists maintain that culture exists. A person's interpretation of symbolic messages in cultural contexts positively or negatively affects the development of identity and self-concept.

The symbolic interpretations of the reactions of others act as a social mirror that reflects the actor's self.

Herbert Blumer, a sociologist, articulated the framework of symbolic interaction first set out by its founder, philosopher George Herbert Mead. Meaning is not inherent in things, but arises as people develop interpretations during their interaction with one another. Once developed, meanings affect people's actions and their definitions of self, of society, and of situation. The sense of self arises from how people interpret the reactions that others have to them. Mead termed the process "the self as a social construction," and Charles Horton Cooley called it "the looking-glass self." Mead partitioned the self into three components: the I, the me, and the generalized other. The me, the reflective part of the self, is central to an understanding of interactionism. In this vein, Cooley argued that through the looking-glass, the reflective social mirror represented by the audience, people test their initial conceptions of their selves. The results of these tests are either positive or negative, pride or mortification.

The generalized other has its origins in significant others, those whose opinions are of critical importance. Over time, the opinions of significant others like parents and immediate friends become internalized and transformed into the generalized other. The generalized other represents the ideas people have about what others would think of their actions. The generalized other represents a kind of conscience.

Definitions of society represent views of the social world as either hospitable and full of opportunity, or as hostile and unjust. Definitions of the situation refer to views of contexts. The way in which people define the same circumstances varies according to culture and background.

Out of this general framework of symbolic interaction, sociologists interested in deviance and crime developed the labelling perspective. The cornerstone of labelling is the notion that deviance, like beauty, rests in the eye of the beholder. Labelling proponents concern themselves with finding the answers to three fundamental questions: Who gets defined as deviant? How does this happen? What are the consequences for people who are designated as deviants? Labelling theorists point out that the designators can usually be differentiated from the designated on the basis of their more elevated status. In comparison with the labelled, labellers wield more social power.

The policy implications of labelling rest on the argument that labelling and stigmatization by official agents of social control promote deviant and criminal behaviour. Labelling theorists direct their policy initiatives at reducing or eliminating stigma by limiting or abolishing the formal processing and incarceration of offenders. The labelling perspective supports decriminalization, de-institutionalization, diversion, probation, parole, and community service orders.

Some critics point out that labelling is ahistorical and pays insufficient attention to the role of social and economic structures in generating deviance and crime. Others argue that labelling trivializes the causes of primary deviance and fails to provide an explanation of deviant acts, like murder, that do not fit the career model. In many cases, deviance precedes labelling and labelling discourages rather than encourages deviant and illegal conduct. Furthermore, empirical tests of the labelling process have produced mixed results.

Critics have also attacked labelling theory for its inability to explain the deviance of elites, for treating people as passive receptors, and for not paying sufficient attention to specifying the conditions under which labels are more or less likely to be successfully applied. Labelling has largely ignored the impacts of informal social groups on the development of negative self-concepts and deviant careers. Policy directives based on the labelling approach have fallen out of fashion of late because they tend to support non-interventionist, nonpunitive, and rehabilitative stances at a time when the corrections system is moving increasingly toward an exclusively punitive orientation.

Reintegrative shaming specifies conditions under which labelling constitutes a mitigating or aggravating circumstance influencing future criminal behaviour. Shaming that is reintegrative reduces crime while shaming that is stigmatizing increases crime. Reintegration is likely where disapprovers and disapproved are interdependent, and stigmatization is likely where they are not.

Labelling approaches have made important contributions to the understanding of social deviance and crime. They focus attention on the negative impacts of formal processing by criminal justice agencies. In particular, labelling theory has highlighted the problems of reintegrating into society those bearing the stigma of institutionalization. Labelling theory has added additional credence to the idea that severe negative sanctions like imprisonment should be used sparingly and as a last resort.

QUESTIONS FOR CRITICAL THINKING

1. Can there be objective standards of morality? Does the Canadian *Criminal Code* reflect contemporary moral standards that are agreed-upon coast to coast? Conversely, do laws banning sexual behaviours and substance abuse reflect the efforts of a handful of "moral entrepreneurs" who seek to control other people's behaviour in the name of what they consider to be proper and right?

2. Among other things, replacing the *Juvenile Delinquency Act* with the *Young Offenders Act* was intended to reduce the impact of the official labelling process. Questions were then raised about the deterrent effects, or lack thereof, of the *Young Offenders Act*. This legislation has been reformed into the *Youth Criminal Justice Act* and in part represents an effort to get tougher, particularly with more serious offending. Do you think that legal punishment of young offenders has more of a labelling effect or a deterrent effect? Can these competing outcomes be effectively balanced to reflect both the social and individual good?

3. Have you or someone you knew well ever been tagged with a negative label? Did the label result in social harm or was the behaviour in question simply deterred? Was the label escaped or did it endure? If negative labels are injurious, do positive labels serve to insulate people from criminogenic forces in their surroundings?

4. How would a labelling theorist explain the fact that many children begin offending at an early age and then desist as they mature?

5. Why is the Canadian government moving to legalize or decriminalize marijuana use? What are some of the social and cultural forces that have contributed to this change in policy?

CHAPTER 7

Conflict Theories I — Contemporary Marxism, Left Realism, Peacemaking, and Postmodernism

The aims of this chapter are to familiarize the reader with:

- the general fundamentals of Marxist conflict theory
- Marxist theories presenting deviance and crime as products of conditions: Bonger's foundation, Greenberg's age structure, and Friedrich's crisis of legitimacy
- Marxist perspectives emphasizing the role of the law in creating crime: instrumental Marxism and structural Marxism
- the left realist critique of left idealism
- the aims and objectives of the left realist approach
- the central ideas of peacemaking criminology
- the emergence of postmodernism as a criminological critique
- policy implications
- deficiencies
- the contributions of these conflict approaches to an understanding of deviance and crime

INTRODUCTION

There are two traditional types of conflict theories of crime: contemporary **Marxism** and liberal conflict. Both highlight the roles of social conflict and power in producing deviance and crime. Marxist perspectives see society as comprising two competing groups, one of which owns or controls the economy while the other does not. **Liberal conflict perspectives,** discussed in the next chapter, view society as composed of a variety of competing groups with different

and fluctuating sources of power. In Chapter 7, we investigate Marxist approaches, beginning with an examination of Marxist theory generally and then narrowing our focus to contemporary Marxist analyses of deviant behaviour and criminality. Also examined are more recent applications of conflict models in the form of left realism, peacemaking, and postmodernism. Chapter 8 considers several forms of liberal conflict theory as they have been applied to the understanding of deviance and crime: **culture conflict,** group conflict, authority–subject conflict, and the social construction of crime. It also examines an important development in the conflict tradition — feminism.

CONTEMPORARY MARXIAN CONFLICT PERSPECTIVES ON SOCIAL CONTROL, DEVIANCE, AND CRIME

Karl Marx did not have a great deal to say about crime (Bottomore, Keirnan, Milliband, and Harris, 1992; Taylor, Walton, and Young, 1973). However, criminologists working within the Marxist paradigm have tried to explain criminality by using as a foundation Marx's ideas about the exploitative nature of capitalist economy and about the way in which capitalist society is organized.

The Marxian Perspective in General

To make sense of European society during the latter part of the nineteenth century, Marx adopted a

94

historical perspective (Lefebvre, 1968). First, he argues that conflict has always been the basic element of social process. Second, he maintains that, for all eras in human history, **class** struggle is the critical factor in understanding both social structure and social process. Marx conceptualizes the principal historical social conflict as occurring between "the material forces of production" — the means by which the manufacture of goods is accomplished — and "the social relations of production" — the human contribution to this economic and material process; that is, the social organization of work.

In elaborating his vision of social conflict, Marx explains how the **material forces of production** (the mechanics of manufacturing goods) profoundly affect the **social relations of production** (the social organization of work). According to Marx, the social relations of production initially facilitate the material production of goods. When changes in the material forces of production (technology) occur so rapidly that changes in the social relations of production (work) cannot keep pace, the way in which work is socially organized impedes the efficient manufacture of goods. Such conditions result, Marx maintains, in abrupt and dramatic changes through which new social relations of production (new ways of organizing work) are established to better achieve efficient economic productivity. In his analysis of the events of the early industrial era, Marx argues that the social relations of production (organization of work), which functioned well during **feudalism,** came to impede the material forces of production during the process of **industrialization** in the nineteenth century. The result was the Industrial Revolution and the rapid restructuring of the social relations of production under capitalism.

The new social relations of production that emerged during and after the Industrial Revolution revolved around the development of private property under **capitalism.** For Marx, "private property" refers to resources used to generate wealth — land, machinery, and factories. Around the idea of private productive property, Marx develops his conception of a two-class system: the **bourgeoisie** (the haves) and the proletariat (the have-nots). The bourgeoisie are capitalists who own the land, the machinery, and the manufacturing plants. The proletariat are workers who must sell their labour to the capitalists and work in the mines, mills, and factories of the newly industrializing world.

Marx points out that the vested interests of the bourgeoisie and the proletariat are diametrically opposed. Capitalists strive to increase profits so that they can then reinvest this surplus wealth in additional capital-generating enterprises. Reinvestment of profits increases one capitalist's advantage over other capitalists. To build greater and greater surpluses of wealth, capitalists must maximize productivity while minimizing operating expenses. Since workers' salaries represent significant overhead costs, the bourgeoisie must keep wages as low as possible. Improvements to the workers' quality of life, on the other hand, depend largely on their ability to extract higher salaries from their capitalist employers. For either group to maximize its own economic interests, it must operate to the detriment of the other.

Capitalists, in addition to being in conflict with workers, must also compete with each other for increasingly larger shares of economic markets. As such, stronger capitalists put weaker capitalists out of business, in effect relegating them to the proletariat. As more and more unfit capitalists fail to survive the competition, the proletariat continues to increase in number and the private property of production becomes ever more concentrated in fewer hands. With increasing mechanization, capitalists need fewer workers to produce the same or greater amounts of goods. As the numbers of available workers grow while the demand for their labour tapers off, the bourgeoisie forces the proletariat to compete for fewer jobs at lower wages. This competition among labourers combines with rising rates of unemployment to make it possible for capitalists to easily replace one worker with another. All of these factors converge to erode the bargaining position of workers, thereby allowing capitalists to keep wages low.

Marx claimed that, in time, the number of capitalists would shrink. With smaller numbers, the wealth of individual capitalists would grow markedly. On the other hand, Marx predicted that the numbers of workers would expand dramatically while their incomes and standards of living would decline. He believed that members of the proletariat would become ever more concentrated in cities and that, as a result, their mutual awareness of a common plight would emerge. He predicted that periods of economic crisis would exacerbate the predicament of workers as capitalists cut costs by laying them off. Layoffs would increase poverty among the workers and accordingly result in a **polarization of classes** as the bourgeoisie's and proletariat's positions grew increasingly divergent. Marx argued that such a severe rift between the haves and have-nots would ignite a revolutionary restructuring wherein socialism would eventually replace capitalism. Under socialism, a **classless society** would emerge.

In elaborating his notion of dominance and self-interest, Marx discusses the importance of society's **"superstructure"** and **"infrastructure."** He defines the superstructure of society as its ideology and institutional structure. **Ideology** is the set of ideas that effectively govern people's lives — law, science and knowledge, popular beliefs, and religion. The institutional structure comprises the social organizations that promulgate these ideas — state, school, mass media, and church. Marx argues that society's superstructure (ideology and institutional structure) would impede the revolutionary transition from capitalism to socialism. The foundation or infrastructure of a society is its economy. While Marx views the relationship between a society's superstructure (ideas and institutions) and infrastructure (economy) as reciprocal, he makes it clear that both serve the interests of the capitalist class and enable capitalists to maintain their dominance over the proletariat.

The central ideas of any society, Marx points out, are the ideas of that society's ruling class. Under capitalism, the central ideas assert that freedom, opportunity, individualism, and equality are the cornerstones of modern society. All segments of the superstructure (political, legal, religious, educational, and mass communication) disseminate these precepts. Marx observes that the bourgeoisie and proletariat both believe in these precepts, but that such beliefs favour the capitalists.

Marx makes the point that, should the internalization of the dominant ideology falter or fail, certain branches of the state — the police and the army — are ready to force compliance. In *The Communist Manifesto* (written by Marx and Friedrich Engels), Marx states that the central justification of the political system under capitalism is to develop and administer a society's laws, using force if necessary. To the extent that the proletariat embrace society's ideological underpinnings, however, the creation and enforcement of law appear to reflect the common good of the entire society. Nonetheless, according to Marx, the enactment and the enforcement of statutes support the vested interests of those who own and control the economy.

Marx deals directly with deviance and crime only in passing (Bottomore et al., 1992; Taylor, Walton, and Young, 1973). He suggests that a productive and satisfying work life is essential both to human nature and to the realization of the human self. He presents underemployment and unemployment as unproductive and dissatisfying to the individual. According to Marx, marginalization and the demoralization associated with powerlessness, alienation, and low self-esteem produce strains. These pressures in turn result in the venting of frustration among the lowest class, the **"lumpenproletariat,"** in the form of crime and other vices.

Despite this rendition of the cause of crime, Marx shows little sympathy for the criminal class. He sees members of the lumpenproletariat as social parasites who make little contribution to society, who undermine labour as a potentially potent force, and who impede social change. Moreover, he argues that the deviance and crime of the lumpenproletariat simply expand and strengthen the power of the state's police forces, which may then be used to control legitimate labour unrest and insurrection.

Another theme emerging from Marx's discussion of crime and criminalization is the unequal distribution of wealth in capitalist society and, with it, the unequal distribution of power. Wealth provides power, and the wielding of power allows the wealthy to preserve their own interests. Marx hints that deviance and crime may be thought of as isolated expressions of rebellion against the deprivations inherent in oppressive circumstances.

To summarize, capitalism and private property give rise to a social system comprising two antagonistic classes. The bourgeoisie own productive property, while the proletariat who work for them do not. Marx predicted that the ever-worsening plight of the workers would eventually draw them together in a revolution that would replace capitalism with socialism. According to Marx, in situations where the ideology and the institutions promoting capitalist values and interests break down, society's wealthy and powerful elites use law and agents of social control to force the proletariat to comply. It is upon the themes of deprived circumstances and of the inequitable creation and application of law that Marx's followers have concentrated.

Contemporary Marxist Theories of Deviance and Crime

Modern Marxist theorists have not concentrated upon expanding the little that Marx had to say about deviance and crime. Rather, they have attempted to construct their explanations around central Marxian tenets about the nature of social conflict. Theories building upon Marx's ideas seek to provide insights into why some social norms are translated into law, why some laws are enforced while others are not, and why laws that are enforced are not applied equally to all social segments. Answering these questions, Marxists maintain, depends on a fundamental understanding of the way in which elites employ power both to create law and to criminalize people.

Willem Bonger's Marxist Criminology

Willem Bonger, whose work dates from the early part of this century, was the first criminologist to employ the Marxian approach. His argument is that while capitalism produces greed and selfishness in all members of society, only the avarice of the poor is criminalized. The acquisitiveness of the affluent, conversely, receives legitimate support. Bonger claims that a move to socialism would eliminate a great deal of criminal activity because legal biases favouring the wealthy would be removed (Bonger, 1916). After Bonger's early foray into the use of Marxist thought to explain crime, Marxist approaches did not resurface until the early 1970s.

Contemporary Marxist Approaches

Contemporary Marxist scholars attempt to account for deviance and crime in two principal ways. Some concern themselves with the ways in which certain conditions inherent in capitalism generate nonconforming behaviour, while others direct their attention toward the social origins of law and the criminalization process. The first approach, the "reaction to deprivation" thesis, views deviance and crime as calculated responses on the parts of rational individuals who must confront daily the miserable conditions endemic in the social relations of capitalism. People generally and in the long term think and behave in their own economic interests. Acquisitive property crime becomes a means of earning or supplementing income for those who are unemployed or who toil in low-paying, demeaning jobs. Violent crime, on the other hand, is either an unsophisticated means of

stealing (e.g., robbery) or a venting of the frustrations (e.g., wife battering) produced by occupying an economically marginal position. In a similar vein, this brand of Marxist thought views more-organized criminal endeavours as larger-scale rational responses of the poor to black markets and to their exclusion from legitimate money-making opportunities.

Against this ubiquitous backdrop of deprivation, marginalization, and strain, several contemporary Marxist criminologists, including David Greenberg and David Friedrichs, have developed more specialized theoretical frameworks. Greenberg (1980) offers an analysis of juvenile delinquency that begins by noting that today's youth are systematically excluded from the paid labour market. This exclusion, he suggests, results in severe strain for adolescents who find themselves unable to finance the leisure activities that have become such an integral part of teenage subcultures. The acute experience of strain induces adolescents to steal, while the daily negative experiences and degrading atmosphere that they confront in school encourage hostile responses to authority.

In another application of the Marxian model, Friedrichs (1980) views crime as a product of what he calls a **"crisis of legitimacy."** Social order, he maintains, is based on the perceived legitimacy of authority relations in society. According to Friedrichs, an erosion of faith in political leaders and governmental institutions has created a crisis of legitimacy, which itself has produced a breakdown in social control. Increasingly disillusioned with basic values, citizens come to perceive social institutions as ineffective. Loss of faith and disillusionment have spurred increases in crime, social protest, and rebellion. Under such circumstances, the government has little choice but to be ever more coercive to reinforce social order. This continued coercion has, according to Friedrichs, merely worsened the existing crisis of legitimacy, which continues to spiral out of control.

Some contemporary Marxist frameworks focus on the origin and application of law. There are two principal variants of this approach. The **instrumental theory of Marxism,** developed in the late 1960s and the 1970s, was replaced by the structural perspective in the 1980s. **Structural Marxism** was a response to criticisms levelled at the earlier instrumental approach. Instrumental and structural Marxist criminological theories present different views both of the law and of the ruling class (Chambliss and Seidman, 1982).

Instrumental Marxist Theories of Social Control

For instrumentalists, the ruling class is a unified and monolithic social group. The law, for this powerful elite, is designed to preserve and expand the group's economic and social interests (Smandych, 1985). The image of the ruling elite is one of a conspiratorial group plotting its own advantage at the expense of other social classes.

Quinney's theorizing in the early 1970s is an example of the instrumental position. Quinney claims that the fundamental conflict in society is between those who own the means of economic production and those who do not. The owners comprise a ruling elite that also controls relations in other spheres of social life, including politics, education, and religion. The state, in its authority to enact and enforce criminal law, is an important instrument used by the ruling class to perpetuate an economic and social order that reflects its own best interests. The economic elite influences the actions of the state either directly by affecting the legislative process or indirectly by bringing to bear various forms of economic pressure. On behalf of the ruling class, the state creates and selectively enforces the law when elite interests are threatened. Quinney argues that in those rare instances when statutes contravene ruling-class interests and the ruling class itself violates the law, the state seldom undertakes active enforcement. Instances of nonenforcement commonly arise where laws protect consumers and employees or where they preserve the environment at the expense of economic elites.

Quinney explains lower-class **overrepresentation** and upper-class underrepresentation in crime statistics by pointing to differences both in their economic roles and in their relative power to resist the encroachment of the state. He suggests that certain societal groups are susceptible to special strains that drive them toward higher rates of criminal activity. Street crime occurs because those breaking the law in this fashion are brutalizing their victims as they themselves have been brutalized under capitalism. To ensure its continued contribution to the capitalistic enterprise, the lower class becomes the target of law enforcement. By comparison, because the privileged have the capacity to resist enforcers, the upper classes tend not to become objects of legal control.

Quinney maintains that institutional structures buttress crime control in capitalist society. The ruling class establishes and maintains institutional structures specifically to provide definitions of morality that reinforce the existing domestic order. Schools teach people to obey statutes, claiming that they represent the common good. News and entertainment media present an image of harmful wrongdoing that situates the crime problem squarely in the laps both of the lower classes and of certain ethnic minorities. Religious teachings preach the sanctity of hard work and personal sacrifice, both of which will be rewarded, if not in this life, in the next. Religion, as a famous statement from Marx points out, is the "opium of the people." It dulls their senses to their predicament and, by putting a damper on the sparks of rebellion, supports the status quo.

Quinney argues that contradictions inherent in advanced capitalism fuel the oppression of subordinate classes. Competition among the bourgeoisie and the failure of many capitalists expand the ranks of the proletariat. Along with this expansion, the introduction of technology and the cyclical nature of the economy swell the ranks of the unemployed. The resultant growth in the numbers of the dispossessed in itself contains a potential threat to the established order that must be dealt with. Quinney points out that one strategy of mollifying the masses is to expand programs of social welfare. Another tactic is to escalate the coerciveness of society's main mechanism of formal social control, the criminal justice system (Quinney, 1970, 1973).

Structural Marxist Theories of Social Control

Like the instrumental approach, the structural perspective views the bourgeoisie and the proletariat as social segments occupying different positions in the social structure and, as a consequence, as having different values, beliefs, and behaviours. Structuralists differ from instrumentalists in that they do not view the ruling class as a cohesive group organized in conspiratorial fashion to defend its own economic and social interests. Moreover, they do not view governments simply as instruments in the hands of conspiratorial elites. While structuralists see the state as relatively more autonomous than do instrumentalists, they point out that the material well-being of a society and ultimately of the state itself depends upon the economic vitality of the industrial enterprises owned and controlled by the ruling class. If it is to survive, the state has little choice, in the long term, but to protect and enhance the overall interests of economic elites regardless of the consequences for other societal groups.

Structural Marxism takes account of different and competing factions or **"class fractions"** among the ruling class. Because some capitalist interests compete and interfere with other capitalist interests, structuralists portray the ruling class as highly fractionalized, even though all capitalists occupy a similar structural position in relation to the means of production and, as a result, possess similar values and beliefs. The role of the state when fractionalism occurs is to mediate among the competitive groups in the ruling class to protect the long-term interests of the entire capitalist class. From the state's perspective, the promotion of capital accumulation and social harmony is more important than the unbridled pursuit of self-interests by capitalist class fractions.

The structural position is an advance over instrumentalism because it explains how certain laws appear to contravene the best interests of the capitalist class (Smandych, 1985). Occasionally the state must serve the best interests of the proletariat, but only in the short term. It does this in order that the long-term interests of capitalists will not be undermined. By occasionally protecting proletariat interests in the short run, the state prevents the development of conditions that might eventually fuel the disruption or eventual disintegration of the capitalist economy. Governments pass laws designed to ensure consumer protection, worker health and safety, and environmental preservation. The existence and occasional enforcement of these laws lull citizens into believing that they are adequately protected. While the laws are without any real teeth, their existence quells protest and rebellion by consumers, employees, and the public. Thus, from the structuralist perspective, some laws may serve interests other than those of the capitalist elite, but only on occasion and in the short run (see Table 7.1).

LEFT REALISM

Left realism is a recent reaction to "traditional" radical theory, which itself was a response to the conservatism of the traditional positivist theories set forth by the Chicago school, the functionalists, and advocates of social control theory. One of the principal contributions of the radical approach was to highlight the roles played in the social construction of crime by economic and political elites. During the 1970s, radical conflict theories focused the attention of the criminological community on a number of inequities associated with deviance, crime, and social control. The creation and application of criminal law, police misconduct and abuse of power, biases inherent in the court's processing of accused persons, high rates of incarceration, and the deplorable living conditions in contemporary prisons came under intense scrutiny. While these contributions were important, radical theorists, particularly instrumentalists, tended to portray the street criminal as a person "more sinned against than sinning." Those accused and convicted of *Criminal Code* offences were romanticized as Robin Hood–like victims of oppression, fighting back however crudely against the authors of their subordination. In the process, it was implied that these socially and economically deprived bandits were merely "redistributing" wealth and exacting a measure of revenge.

During the 1980s, some who identified themselves as radicals became more critical of their own position. This spirit of reflection was spurred largely by feminist work undertaken during the 1970s. Much feminist writing on crime and legal issues during that period focused first on rape and then on violence against women and children generally. Feminist portrayals of male violence, its harm, and its propensity for demoralization shattered the romantic portrait of the aggressive predatory offender and, in so doing, fuelled a rethinking of the "criminal as victim" position (Matthews and Young, 1986).

Adherents of this emerging school of radical thought identify the existing radical approach as **"left idealism"** and define their new, more refined perspective as "left realism." Left realists argue that their approach is a response to a crisis now occurring in both the conservative mainstream and the radical camps of criminology (Young, 1986). The crisis among conservatives, according to left realists, is that positivism's scientific search for the causes of crime and for the sources of its control has been an abject failure. Having largely abandoned this mission, conservatives have replaced the search for causality with another form of criminological endeavour altogether. The new conservative regimen is an "administrative criminology" based on neoclassical thinking. According to left realists, administrative criminology emphasizes more punitive correctional measures

TABLE 7.1

TWO VERSIONS OF CONTEMPORARY MARXIST CONFLICT THEORIES

Theory	Theorist(s)	Central Premise	Key Concepts	Principal Contributions
Instrumental Marxism	Richard Quinney	A unified ruling class effects the creation and application of law to pursue its own interests and to preserve an economic and social order that reflects those vested interests. The state serves as an instrument of the ruling class. People in the lower classes commit crime as a consequence of deprivation and criminalization at the hands of powerful economic interest groups. The status quo is reinforced by social institutions (education, religion, media). The lower classes are controlled through social programs (welfare) and coercion (police, courts, corrections).	Instrumental Marxism	Represents the initial articulation of Marxist theory as an explanation of crime, class relations, and the operation of criminal justice systems.
Structural Marxism		The structural approach differs from the instrumental in two ways: the ruling class is not cohesive and conspiratorial, and the state is more autonomous. The ruling class is split into competing class fractions but shares similar values and beliefs. The state mediates among competitive elite groups to promote overall capital accumulation and social harmony in the face of the potential for unbridled pursuit of self-interest by elite groups, but only in the short term.	Bourgeoisie; proletariat; class fractions	Explains the origin and application of laws that do not serve directly the best interests of the entire capitalist class.

supported by recent innovations in coercive technologies.

The crisis in left idealism is equally severe; left idealism has overlooked the fact that street crime is a serious social problem, especially for victims, most of whom are from the lower class. The left realist critique of idealism begins by summarizing the radical position that has prevailed to date. First, left idealists view crime among the working class as a function of their poverty. They see the common criminal as possessing the ability to "see through" the inequities in society. The illegal conduct of these insightful rebels is an unsophisticated attempt to balance the ledger. According to the idealist position, to blame the offender who is both poor and oppressed is tantamount to blaming the victim.

Second, left idealists argue that the "real crime" in society stems from the actions of the political and economic ruling classes and from their power over lawmaking, policing, and the dispensation of justice. Idealists compare the high impact of corporate and state wrongdoing with the comparatively low impact of most street crime, which tends to be petty theft and minor violence. The causes of elite deviance, idealists maintain, rest in the single-minded pursuit of profit and power.

Third, left idealists portray criminal law as an expression of ruling-class efforts to protect private and productive property. The police role is essentially political, with constabularies acting more to maintain order in the capitalist interest than to control crime. The media create false impressions of crime by portraying threat and harm as products of lower-class inclinations and behaviours; the role of elites in creating social problems is ignored. These media myths deaden the masses' sense of their plight and inhibit popular support for radical reform (Young, 1986).

Having outlined what they see as the idealist position, left realists criticize it on several grounds. First, left idealism is simplistic; there is more to crime than moral panics and social reaction (DeKeseredy and Schwartz, 1991). Second, idealist portrayals of deviants and criminals as "seeing through" the inequities that surround them are misguided; the image of the actor is overly rational and that of the offender is unduly romantic. Also, the idealist perspective ignores the fact that many deviant groups are highly disorganized. Third, left idealism overlooks the fact that working-class offenders victimize working-class people more than they victimize capitalists and state officials.

Fourth, idealism ignores the question of why people become criminals and focuses exclusively on the ways in which the powerful criminalize the powerless. Structural determinants of crime are ignored or treated as self-evident.

The final criticism levelled at left idealism is that it closely resembles functionalism in its approach. Idealist formulations maintain that the actions of corporate enterprises and state agencies must be linked to the needs of the ruling capitalist class. The function of criminalization is to deflect society's attention from the social problems generated by capitalist enterprise, such as unemployment, inadequate social services, and corporate wrongdoing. The function of social welfare is to placate the masses and to defuse serious social unrest and open revolt. From the idealist perspective, rising crime rates do not reflect changes in the behaviour of criminals but result from police efforts to maintain order in the capitalist crisis that regularly manifests itself in economic depression and unemployment (Young, 1986).

Left realists argue that their radical position on the crime problem is more realistic than the one put forth by the left idealists. Left realism takes account of data from victimization studies conducted over the past 25 years. This body of research demonstrates that street crime is a serious problem and that it affects society's disadvantaged more so than its privileged. In charting the reality of crime, left realists advocate steering a middle course. Criminals are neither romantic nor pathological. Moreover, left realists would neither minimize nor exaggerate the volume of crime.

PEACEMAKING CRIMINOLOGY

Peacemaking criminology emerges from the concern among various critical criminologists that crime engenders real suffering. The theory's authors see the peacemaking tradition as emerging out of religious, humanist, feminist, and conflict approaches to understanding crime and justice (Pepinsky, 1991). Its chief proponents, Harold Pepinsky and Richard Quinney, portray crime and its control as a war, the solution to which involves the negotiation of peace between offenders and victims, police, and the public. Peacemaking criminology involves mediation, conflict resolution, reconciliation, and reintegration of the offender into the community in a dual effort to alleviate suffering and reduce crime. The peace-making perspective sees the criminal justice system itself as organized around a principle of violence that must be replaced with love and nonviolence if the crime problem is to be effectively resolved (Pepinsky and Quinney, 1991).

POSTMODERNISM

Postmodern criminological thought arose in the late 1980s as the principal successor to more radical forms of critical criminology and from perspectives such as feminism (see Chapter 8), left realism, and peace-making. In league with its predecessors, it argues that it is impossible to separate values from the research agenda and that there is a need to advance a progressive agenda favouring disprivileged peoples. Of the various perspectives that make up critical criminology, however, postmodern thought is perhaps the least developed and least understood (Schwartz and Friedrichs, 1994).

Schwartz and Friedrichs (1994) argue that **postmodernism** offers three possibilities for criminology. First, it is a method that can reveal how knowledge is constituted while at the same time uncovering pretensions and contradictions in traditional criminological scholarship. In so doing, postmodernists claim that the theory can provide an alternative to the "linear analysis" of traditional social science. Second, postmodernist theory highlights the significance of language and signs in the domain of crime and criminal justice. Finally, the theory provides a source of metaphors and concepts (e.g., "hyperreality") that capture elements of an emerging reality and the new context and set of conditions in which crime occurs.

Postmodernists emphasize that modernism embraces a naturalistic view of the social world in which science is seen as an objective process aimed at the prediction and control of action and behaviour. They reject the modernist scientific approach by asserting that all thought and knowledge are shaped by language, which itself lacks neutrality. Language, postmodernists claim, always advantages some points of view while disadvantaging others. They argue that modernism particularly privileges "scientific" thinking, according it, in comparison to other modes of thinking, special objectivity and validity. For their part, postmodernists do not grant scientific thinking privileged status, but rather describe it as neither

more nor less valid than competing forms of thought. Postmodernism maintains that linear thought processes, statements about cause and effect, syllogistic reasoning, objective analyses, and other standards of scientific thinking are no more valid than other forms of thinking. Postmodernists attempt to "deconstruct" language to identify implicit and unsupported assumptions that buttress the ways in which advantaged points of view are legitimized, while at the same time undermining the validity of alternative perspectives. They also identify disparaged points of view and seek to make them more explicit and rightful in order that different discourses can be simultaneously seen as legitimate and in order that diverse points of view are appreciated without assuming that one perspective is superior to others.

Postmodernism argues that modernism and its emphasis on science has increased oppression rather than bringing about liberation. Modernity has become a force for subjugation, oppression, and repression, extending and intensifying the scope of violence in the world. Even more critical is the fact that the major form of response to this rising violence involves rational organizations, such as those embodied in the criminal justice system, which themselves rely heavily on professional and scientific expertise. Such a response to violence merely reproduces domination in new but no less harmful forms.

Postmodernism seeks to uncover structures of domination in society as a strategy to enable the achievement of greater liberation. Domination occurs, according to postmodernists, through control of language systems because language structures thought. Whether people using those languages know it or not, the languages used to convey meaning are not neutral but rather support dominant world views.

In the pursuit of increased liberation, postmodernists examine relationships between human agency and language in the creation of meaning, identity, truth, justice, power, and knowledge. Their main method of investigating how people construct sense and meaning is called "discourse analysis." Discourse analysis takes account of the social position of those who are speaking or writing in an effort to understand the meaning of what is verbalized or written down. Discourse analysts pay specific attention to the values and assumptions inherent in the language used by a speaker or author. To understand fully what people mean when they speak as actors in specific roles, it is necessary to comprehend much about the roles in question as historically situated and structured positions in society. Examples of such "discursive subject positions" that are interconnected with their own language systems are police, correctional officers, and court workers on the one hand, and drug dealers, armed robbers, and juvenile gang members on the other.

Once people take on "discursive subject positions," the words that they articulate fail to express fully their own realities. Rather, they express, at least partially, the realities of the larger institutions in which they are embedded. With their language at least somewhat removed or disconnected from their own reality, people become "decentred." They are never precisely what their words describe and are continually pressed in the direction of being what their language systems expect or demand (Schwartz and Friedrichs, 1994; Vold, Bernard, and Snipes, 1998).

Vold, Bernard, and Snipes (1998) provide an example to illustrate these points. Victims and defendants must tell their stories to prosecutors and defence attorneys, who subsequently reconstruct and reformulate their narratives into the language of the courts. The testimony of victims and defendants cannot deviate from the accepted language system without jeopardizing either the prosecutor's conviction or the defence attorney's acquittal. Even if defendants are convicted, victims may feel that their stories were never fully told, and even if the accused are acquitted, they may believe that their stories, laid out before the court, bore so little resemblance to what actually happened that they too are dissatisfied. Regardless of who prevails, the process has comprised a ritualistic ceremony in which the reality of the courts has dominated the reality of both the victim and the accused. The legalistic language of the court expresses and institutionalizes the domination of the individual by social institutions.

According to postmodernists, the current situation is one in which discourse is either dominant (e.g., legalistic, professional, scientific language) or oppositional (e.g., the language of prison inmates). Their goal is to transform the situation to one in which many different discourses are recognized as legitimate by establishing "replacement discourses." A replacement discourse is a language that helps people to speak with a more authentic voice while remaining continuously aware of the authentic voices of others. The objective is to establish greater inclusivity, more diverse communication, and a pluralistic culture. To

do so, postmodernists advocate listening carefully to otherwise excluded perspectives while constituting the meaning of criminal acts. Creating a society in which alternative discourses liberate people from the domination of prevailing speech patterns will also legitimate the role of all citizens in the project of reducing crime and bringing about greater respect for social diversity. Postmodernists believe that the achievement of this objective ultimately will result in less victimization of other people by criminals and less official punishment of criminals by agents of the state (Vold, Bernard, and Snipes, 1998).

CONFLICT THEORIES AND SOCIAL POLICY

Conflict theorists advocate responding to crime either by changing the way in which governments create and enforce criminal laws or by altering the economic and political structure of capitalist society. Marxist theories of deviance and crime assume that meaningful social change is impossible without a massive restructuring of society from capitalism to socialism. Marxists advocate dismantling the capitalist economy and restructuring society on a socialist model wherein there is meaningful equality in economic and political decision making. When the pro-capitalist state is dismantled and the power to criminalize is eliminated, crime will disappear or at least be substantially reduced.

Marxists believe that the disintegration of capitalism and the emergence of socialism is inevitable. First, they predict that a massive proletariat will develop in the cities of the capitalist world. Members of this dispossessed class will communicate with one another and see their common plight. In the face of growing crises of unemployment, poverty, and crime — and with their consciousness raised — the lower classes will become ever more troublesome for the capitalist class and the state's law-enforcement agencies. To control the masses and keep the capitalist state operating, the government will implement more restrictive crime-control initiatives, which will be enormously costly and will bring about major violations of human justice. The situation will degenerate and increase in volatility until the masses eventually revolt and replace a capitalist economy and government with socialist institutions. The equality of human relations under socialism, according to

Marxists, will eliminate the need to criminalize and in so doing will substantially reduce if not eradicate crime.

Left realists outline several policy fronts upon which they wish to proceed. First, they would explode the myths about crime and its control that have been created and reinforced by the media. The inaccurate perception of crime risk and victimization as products of exchanges with strangers must also be corrected. Data from victimization studies and from other sources demonstrate that the perpetration and experience of crime are intra-class, intra-race, and intra-familial affairs. Similarly, police work is wrongly presented as glamorous, scientific, and successful. Nothing could be further from the truth; it is routine, straightforward, and boring. When police solve crimes, they do so by accident or because the answers are obvious. Most important, the police are highly dependent on the public to report crime and to cooperate in apprehending and convicting offenders.

Second, left realists advocate the use of a blend of micro and macro thinking about crime and its impact. They desire a theory that elaborates the micro–macro connections among victims, offenders, communities, and the state. Left realists also advocate the combination of qualitative and quantitative research to develop theory and policy. Of special use, they argue, are "local crime surveys" that focus on the neighbourhood or community (DeKeseredy and Schwartz, 1991). Crime-control policies should also be realistic; thus, realist initiatives would not be long-term, revolutionary, and virtually impossible to implement, as were the measures of left idealists. Rather, they would be short-term, practical, and achievable (Young, 1986).

Among the strategies for crime control advocated by the left realists are demarginalization, pre-emptive deterrence, the minimization of imprisonment, the democratizing of policing, and the involvement of the community in crime prevention (DeKeseredy, 1988). Demarginalization tactics involve alternatives to incarceration that promote the integration of offenders into the community rather than their separation from it. Suggested courses of action include community service orders and restitution programs. Pre-emptive deterrence involves altering physical environments to make them less crime-prone. This approach also encompasses changing people's day-to-day practices to reduce their vulnerability. Arguing that jails create as much or more criminality as they eradicate, left realists favour restricting imprisonment to serious offenders only. They also advocate making the prison experience more humane. Democratizing the police would transform the constabulary from a force apart from the community to a service within the community. It would also increase police accountability and promote the tolerance of disadvantaged groups (Lea and Young, 1985).

Third, the left realist approach emphasizes the importance first of assessing the risk of street crime and then of deciphering in precise terms its impact on people in certain areas and social groups. Finally, left realists stress the importance of identifying the relationships that connect victims to offenders. They observe that powerless working-class people are not only preyed on by offenders from the same backgrounds but also that these people are disproportionately victimized by the affluent and the powerful. Especially vulnerable are women, the lower classes, and visible ethnic minorities.

The peacekeeping perspective recommends restraining the purely punitive responses of the criminal justice system, which in themselves may cause crime. It advocates a humanist strategy in which mediation and conflict resolution facilitate reintegration and provide better means of alleviating the suffering caused by crime. Peacemakers prefer an alternative nonviolent model of criminal justice that responds to various forms of victimization with restorative justice approaches that involve communication and reconciliation among victims, perpetrators, and the community (Sullivan and Tifft, 2001).

Table 7.2 provides a summary of the conflict theories.

THE EVALUATION OF CONFLICT THEORIES

The early instrumental approaches drew much criticism from non-Marxists and Marxists alike. In response, Marxists developed the structural perspective, which continues to be refined. Several critiques of the more rudimentary instrumental position exist. First, instrumentalists' portrayal of the ruling class as a unified, monolithic elite is a gross oversimplification of reality: elites are divided and disagree about their economic and political interests. Moreover, instrumental Marxist claims of institutionalized elite conspiracies were both difficult to believe and

TABLE 7.2

RECENT CONFLICT-ORIENTED THEORIES OF DEVIANCE AND CRIME

Theory	Theorist(s)	Central Premise	Key Concepts	Principal Contributions
Left realism	Roger Matthews; Jock Young; Walter DeKeseredy; Martin Schwartz	Left realism examines street crime as a serious problem where left idealism offered only simplistic and romantic images of such offenders. Left realism explores the role of structural conditions in generating criminal activity. The theory seeks to destroy myths surrounding crime and control, integrate micro and macro theories, use qualitative and quantitative data, and generate practical and humane crime control strategies. It advocates demarginalization, pre-emptive deterrence, minimal imprisonment, the democratization of policing, and community involvement in crime prevention.	Left realism; left idealism; demarginalization; pre-emptive deterrence; minimal imprisonment; democratization of policing; crime prevention	A conflict theory that fully addresses issues concerning street crime perpetration and victimization
Peacekeeping	Harold Pepinsky; Richard Quinney	The criminal justice system is a violent response to crime. Peacekeeping advocates mediation and reintegration as better means of alleviating the suffering caused by crime.	Mediation; integration	Provides an alternative model of criminal justice de-emphasizing violence in favour of restorative justice
Postmodernism		Postmodernism reveals the hidden power of language to confer privilege and power on one explanatory perspective as opposed to another. Postmodernists are relativists who seek to avoid "privileging" any mode of thought or language. They challenge the validity and hegemony of modern science's search for testable explanations of crime.	Hyperreality; deconstruction; discourse analysis; discursive subject positions; decentring; replacement discourse; appreciative relativism	Points out contradictions in traditional scholarship. It emphasizes significance of language in spheres of crime and justice.

unsubstantiated by data (Klockars, 1979). Evidence suggests that the state is not a simple instrument of the economic elite (Denisoff and MacQuarie, 1975). For example, the state has often contravened the position of the dominant class by passing legislation that undermines its economic interests in favour of the lower classes' interests. Laws governing minimum wage, worker health and safety, restriction of trade, and pollution control are examples.

Critics dispute instrumentalist claims that laws always serve only the interests of ruling elites. They cite laws prohibiting murder, sexual assault, robbery, and theft, while emphasizing the consensus surrounding the legal definition of these acts as crimes (Rossi, Waite, Bose, and Berk, 1974). Not only do such statutes reflect the best interests of all, but those most frequently victimized by these crimes are the underprivileged.

Some instrumental Marxists have asserted that violent and predatory criminal activity is a political response to oppression, marginalization, and exploitation. Critics say these claims are overly romantic caricatures; killers, robbers, and thieves are not Robin Hoods and freedom fighters (Toby, 1980). Less extreme Marxist positions still present street crime as at least partly a response to deprivation, but they make no claims regarding the political nature of this sort of rebellion.

On the social policy dimension, both liberal conflict and Marxist theories have been criticized for their lack of realism (Wilson, 1975). Liberals require the privileged to forsake their advantage in the name of increased tolerance and equality. Critics, particularly of the liberal position, point out that efforts to transfer more power to the disadvantaged have been largely cosmetic and that the powerful have strongly resisted the erosion of their already advantaged position.

Instrumental Marxists' claims that crime will disappear under socialism have been assailed on two grounds. First, crime not only existed in pre-capitalist societies, but it was a major problem. Second, crime has thrived and has presented a serious dilemma for socialist republics such as China and, until it was dismantled, the USSR. Marxists retort that truly socialist states are nonexistent in the world today; they point out that the state bureaucracies of contemporary communist nations alienate and exploit their citizens. Other Marxists respond to the criticism of utopian expectations under socialism by suggesting that

crime, while not entirely eradicated, would be substantially reduced under a more egalitarian economic and political system. They admit that the claim that crime would disappear is extreme and suggest instead that the criminality of the poor would, under conditions approaching equality, more closely resemble the criminality of the more affluent in contemporary capitalist nations.

Structural Marxism explains how elites are neither unified nor necessarily conspiratorial, how the state is often autonomous and not a simple instrument of the ruling class, and how the law can and does undermine the vested interests of the powerful economic elite. It fails, however, to solve the classic criticism of Marxist social theory — that it is a vague and untestable *ex post facto* explanation.

Ex post facto means explanation after the fact. Instrumentalists first observe that a law exists and then set about showing how that legislation benefits the powerful. Their argument is that a law on the books must serve the interests of the powerful, or it would not have been passed in the first place. It is easy to make theories fit facts when the facts are already known. Such propositions are untestable, in the sense that they cannot be disproved scientifically (Jacobs, 1980).

Structuralists are as vague as their instrumental predecessors. After structuralists document the existence of a law, they show that the law either contravenes or supports the ruling elite. In the former case, structuralists argue that the law will undermine the position of the elite only in the short term. In the latter case, they contend that the law protects the powerful in the long term. *Ex post facto* explanations have no tests to establish whether they are right or wrong.

One of the difficulties of evaluating Marxist theories of deviance and crime is the different notion of theory in Marxist thought. Marxists emphasize that the purpose of theory is to raise consciousness. Consciousness-raising entails making the world aware of inequality, of its unfairness, and of the harm it engenders. Theory raises consciousness, and consciousness-raising in turn encourages action to remedy social inequality and the pains it produces. Marxist theory is less concerned with scientifically testing the adequacy of its propositions than with praxis — action to change the world. Critics from the more conventional perspectives, of course, maintain that theories that cannot be tested are more ideological than explanatory.

Unlike the theories discussed in previous chapters, conflict perspectives on deviance and crime are relatively new, dating mostly from the late 1960s. Since their rejuvenation, they have contributed substantially to sociological insights into inequality and the uses and misuses of legal power. Conflict frameworks focus attention on the origins of laws and the degree to which criminal statutes apply equally to all social segments. They have focused attention on the malfeasance of justice systems around the world and have fuelled initiatives to reform aspects of policing, the courts, and corrections. In a similar vein, the insufficiencies of law governing certain socially and economically harmful activities have also been seriously questioned. Moreover, conflict criminology has generated intense interest in research on the illegal conduct of business and political elites (Akers, 1985).

The conflict tradition has focused attention on ideology's previously ignored role in shaping both societal consensus and the social reality of crime. Conflict-oriented theorists have admonished positivistic criminologists for seeking both the causes and remedies of crime in the wrong places. According to Marxists, criminologists who cite strain, differential associations, or broken social bonds as precipitators of deviance and crime support the status quo. By ignoring issues of power and oppression, their analyses deflect attention from the wrongdoing of elites and thus reinforce their positions of advantage.

Although a relatively new approach, left realism is not without its critics. Left realists attack the most extreme position of the left idealists. Much of their criticism appears directed at the early instrumental rather than more recent structural perspectives. In this regard, the realist critique of the radical position closely resembles the barrage fired at instrumental Marxism by traditional positivists in the late 1970s and early 1980s. Some argue that the realist fusillade is directed at an idealist target that has moved on and taken new shape.

The realist criticism of traditional criminology is also somewhat directed at a "straw person." Realists note the rise of administrative criminology out of neoclassical ashes and decry its emphasis on deterrence and its draconian policy suggestions. However, they ignore the fact that other "traditional" criminologies are searching for a better understanding of the causes of deviance and crime. A good deal of causation research continues to be guided by human ecology, strain theory, differential association, and

informal social control perspectives as well as by relatively new approaches such as routine activities analysis and power–control theory.

Left realists argue that their perspective provides new focuses. Among other things, they call for the debunking of myths about crime and policing, the integration of theory and method across the macro–micro spectrum, the use of both qualitative and quantitative data, and the choice of pragmatic but humane control initiatives. But many of those who are labelled traditional criminologists by the realists claim that they have been pursuing these objectives for years and making significant strides.

Left realism advocates concentration on the importance of street crime as a social problem. One of the major contributions of radical criminology, however, has been to focus attention on elite deviance.

Finally, critics question whether left realism is as yet actually a theory of crime. Rather than an explanation of illegal conduct, left realism is more a set of philosophical and political statements concerning how society and the criminal justice system ought to function (Akers, 1997).

Left realism is in its formative stages. It is not without promise; if it is able to trace strands of macro-level theories of the state through meso-level community crime and control issues to the micro-level of individuals, left realism will make a significant mark on criminological theory.

Commentators point out that the peacemaking perspective is not a true theory of crime that can be empirically assessed. Rather, it is a philosophy that has at its core a utopian vision of an almost crime-free society with a justice system characterized by nonviolence, the peaceful resolution of conflict, and the restoration of offenders to the community. It does not, however, offer an explanation of why offenders commit crime or why the criminal justice system operates the way it does. Critics also maintain that the policy directives inherent in the peacemaking approach are not new. Both religious and lay organizations working in prisons have for years advocated love and peace in the reformation of offenders and have tried to persuade them of the value of a religious commitment and a lifestyle incompatible with committing crime and causing pain to others.

Some assessments of peacemaking emphasize the internal contradictions that arise from identifying conflict theory and feminist theory as foundations for the perspective. Neither of these origin theories advocates peacemaking. The major recommendation of Marxist theories is to combat power with power, ultimately to overthrow capitalist society. Peacemaking's observation that women support nurturing and caring values seems misplaced, in that feminism tends to portray the caring, loving, and peaceful orientation of women as part of the traditional feminine role. Feminists have rejected such roles as products of patriarchy and its inherent oppression of women. (For more on feminism, see Chapter 8.)

Finally, peacemakers assert that mainstream criminology has ignored the possibility of achieving peaceful and nonviolent means of addressing the real suffering caused by crime. In response, critics point to the existence of long-standing policies involving nonpunitive treatment, mediation, restitution, reintegration, and rehabilitation (Akers, 1997).

While some criminologists have embraced postmodernism with enthusiasm, many have not. The position of "appreciative relativism" that presents all points of view as equal and treats scientific discourse as having no more validity than any other language exceeds the tolerance of most criminologists who believe in the validity of the scientific process despite some very real, practical limitations.

Critics point out, as well, that postmodernists are infamous for their own use of highly specialized jargon, for inventing and discarding terms, and for "playing" with words. As Schwartz and Friedrichs (1994) observe, this occurrence raises a paradox. While postmodernists insist on not "privileging" the language of the powerful over the language of the powerless, they speak and write in a form and style that is highly inaccessible, not only to the powerless but also to most of those in a position to act on their behalf.

Postmodernism provides little practical guidance on policy. Some critics argue that postmodernism is idealistic and completely insensitive to the direct, concrete experiences and needs of victims and survivors of crime. Furthermore, some forms of postmodernist theory echo the romantic early days of radical criminology by regarding violence and insurrection as praiseworthy efforts to deny legitimacy to the state.

While not offering concrete policy suggestions, however, postmodernism does offer a basis for exposing pretences and illusions in the pursuit of a just policy. Postmodernism can be defended as intensely political in that it seeks to obliterate hegemonic discourses, thereby creating opportunities to construct alternative political structures. Postmodernism also promotes empowerment of victims, enabling them to engage more fully in a process of reconstituting the meaning of violence.

Postmodernism may be very useful in the future in developing insights into newly emerging forms of crime. These "information age" illegalities or "technocrimes" involve computers, telecommunications, the Internet, and other aspects of advanced technology. Postmodern analyses of crimes that take place in a symbolic universe or in the sphere of the "hyperreal" have the potential of enhancing criminological theory in the twenty-first century (Schwartz and Friedrichs, 1994).

SUMMARY

While Marx had little to say about crime, contemporary conflict criminologists have adapted many of his themes. Marx notes the development of private productive property, or what he calls the material means of production, following the Industrial Revolution. Around the development of productive property there arose a two-class system. One small class, the bourgeoisie, owns or controls the means of producing material goods, while another much larger class of workers, the proletariat, sells its labour for wages. Marx points out that these groups' vested self-interests — profits and earning a decent living — conflict. As conditions worsened for the less-powerful proletariat, Marx foresaw revolution and the replacement of capitalism with socialism and a classless society.

For Marx, the driving force of society was its infrastructure — the economy. Society's superstructure comprised the political, legal, religious, educational, and media systems controlled by capitalists. The superstructure's purpose is to promote pro-capitalist ideology. Marx suggested that when the institutions promoting ideology failed to communicate the pro-capitalist message effectively, capitalists would use coercion to preserve their dominance. In such cases, the law and agents of social control such as the police and the military would maintain order. Contemporary Marxist criminologists have echoed the Marxian themes of deprived social and economic conditions and the exercise of coercion.

Greenberg's theory shows how the conditions experienced by youth in modern capitalist societies produce strain and cause acquisitive crime. Friedrichs argues that social and economic conditions have undermined people's faith in social institutions and have stimulated deviance and crime. The nonconformity and violation of the law produced by this crisis of legitimacy are answered by the state's coercive responses. But coercion only escalates over time, as the need to maintain order and control becomes more critical.

Other Marxist approaches directly address the creation and application of laws. Primary among these perspectives are instrumental and structural Marxism. Instrumentalists present the ruling class as a unified and monolithic social group. The law and the state are instruments designed to preserve or expand its economic and social interests. The ruling elite is a conspiratorial group actively plotting its own advantage at the expense of other social classes. Structural Marxism builds upon its predecessor to take account of evidence indicating that the elite class is fractionalized, that the state enjoys a significant degree of autonomy from the economic elite, and that laws do not always directly serve elite interests.

Marxist theorists see the dismantling of capitalism as an essential step in eliminating social and economic inequality and the crime and criminalization stemming from that inequity.

Conflict theory, particularly the instrumental version of Marxism, has received a barrage of criticism. Among the more important critiques are those concerning the degree of unity among powerful elites, the degree of conspiratorial action, and the extent to which the law always and only serves the interests of the privileged. Other criticisms include the romanticization of crime and criminals, the lack of realism in social policy, and the dubiousness of the claim that socialism would eliminate crime. While the structural perspective has remedied some of these concerns, it continues the Marxist failing of *ex post facto* theorizing, or explanation after the fact. Part of this deficiency, however, stems from the different purposes of theory envisaged by Marxists on the one hand and by their more positivistic critics on the other. For Marxists, the goals of theory are consciousness-raising and praxis. Unlike positivists, they are less concerned with explaining and predicting events on the basis of theories emphasizing cause and effect.

Marxist conflict theorists have since the 1960s contributed immensely to the understanding of deviance and crime. Their work has greatly sharpened the social scientific and criminological community's focus on such important areas as social and economic inequality, the use and abuse of power, the workings and shortcomings of the criminal justice system, and elite deviance.

Radical theory emerged as a response to positivism, while left realism emerged as a response to radical theory and more positivist approaches. Stimulated by feminist insights in the 1970s, left realists criticize their idealist opponents for their "criminal as victim" perspective. Their attack on positivism centres on the rise of administrative criminology, which abandons the search for causality to pursue more coercive formal controls. Realists reject idealism for several reasons. Left idealism overlooks street crime as a serious social problem and focuses on elite deviance. Idealism, according to left realists, is simplistic and romanticizes offenders. It ignores the role of structural conditions in generating criminal activity and borders on functionalism when it suggests that actions of the state exist only to serve the vested interests of capitalists.

Left realism's goals include destroying myths surrounding crime and control, integrating micro and macro theories, using qualitative and quantitative data, and generating practical and humane control strategies. Among its recommended tactics are demarginalization, pre-emptive deterrence, minimal imprisonment, the democratization of policing, and community involvement in crime prevention. Critics of the left realist position point out that it sets up for attack the most extreme versions of radical and conservative approaches, that its insights closely resemble those of existing perspectives that operate outside of the conflict tradition, and that it underemphasizes elite deviance. Left realism, however, is in its formative stages and may well offer valuable insights in the future.

The peacekeeping perspective views the criminal justice system as a violent response to crime. Peacekeeping advocates mediation and reintegration as better means of alleviating the suffering caused by crime and in so doing provides an alternative model of criminal justice de-emphasizing violence in favour of restorative justice.

The postmodernist perspective exposes the hidden power of language to confer privilege and power on one theoretical perspective while undercutting the validity of others. Postmodernists are relativists who seek to avoid "privileging" any mode of thought or language. A central part of their mission is to challenge the validity and hegemony of modern science's search for testable explanations of crime.

QUESTIONS FOR CRITICAL THINKING

1. What would Marx, were he alive today, think about the economic prosperity enjoyed by much of the working class in industrial societies? Where do you think he would see an error in the prediction of change by revolutionary means? How might he alter his vision of the capitalist system and its deleterious impacts? Do you think he might become a proponent of capitalism under these conditions? Why or why not?

2. As a citizen of a modern capitalist industrial nation, you have experienced Marx's superstructure first hand. To what degree are Canada's political, legal, religious, educational, and media systems controlled by capitalists? In your experience, how well does our society's superstructure promote a pro-capitalist ideology?

3. Marxist criminologists see the dismantling of capitalism as an essential step in eliminating social and economic inequality and the resultant crime and criminalization. Considering recent developments in the former Soviet Union and in contemporary China, is there a future for socialism? And if there is, would socialism necessarily reduce crime?

4. Arguing that more traditional Marxist approaches (left idealism) have offered simplistic and romantic images of criminal acts and offenders, left realism examines street crime as a serious problem. The theory seeks to put an end to myths surrounding crime and control, integrate micro and macro theories, use qualitative and quantitative data, and generate practical and humane crime control strategies. Discuss the degree to which the theory has accomplished each of these aims (or has the potential to do so).

5. Does postmodernism represent a coherent theory of crime? Are you swayed by its arguments? Why or why not? Is there anything in the theory that points to a practical solution to problems posed by crime?

RECOMMENDED READINGS

Hinch, R. (1994). *Readings in Critical Criminology.* Scarborough: Prentice-Hall.
Canadian criminologist Ron Hinch's collection of readings in the field of critical criminology provides an excellent introduction to critical perspectives and their application to an increased understanding of the crime problem in contemporary societies such as Canada and the United States.

McMullin, J. (1992). *Beyond the Law: Corporate Crime and Law and Order.* Halifax: Fernwood.
Assesses the current state of corporate crime research and provides suggestions as to how this form of illegality might be more effectively addressed in a liberal democracy.

Okihiro, N. R. (1999). *Mounties, Moose, and Moonshine: Patterns and Context of Outport Crime.* Toronto: University of Toronto Press.
Examines the social implications of the manner in which an increasingly bureaucratized state uses police to wage war on a rural population by criminalizing behaviour that local custom does not regard as crime.

O'Reilly-Fleming, T. (1996). *Post-Critical Criminology.* Toronto: Prentice Hall.
Collection of largely Canadian readings focusing on the social construction of delinquency and street crime from the vantage points of rights, gender, race, and new critical theories.

Pepinsky, H. E., and R. Quinney. (1991). *Criminology as Peacemaking.* Bloomington, IN: Indiana University Press.
Sets out the foundations of a peacemaking approach to understanding and coping with crime.

Taylor, I., P. Walton, and J. Young. (1973). *The New Criminology: For a Social Theory of Deviance.* London: Routledge and Kegan Paul.
Presents the classic formulation of the critical criminological perspective in its modern form.

CHAPTER 8

Conflict Theories II — Liberal Conflict and Feminism

The aims of this chapter are to familiarize the reader with:

- liberal conflict perspectives: Sellin's culture conflict, Vold's group conflict, Turk's authority–subject conflict, and Quinney's social reality of crime
- the fundamentals of feminist theory, especially its analysis of patriarchy
- the similarities and differences among three types of feminist theory: liberal feminism, Marxist feminism, radical feminism
- policy implications
- deficiencies
- the contributions of these conflict approaches to an understanding of deviance and crime

INTRODUCTION

Liberal conflict perspectives view society as composed of a variety of competing groups with different and fluctuating sources of power (see Figure 8.1). Feminism offers a more recent and highly influential application of both Marxist and liberal conflict models. This chapter considers several forms of liberal conflict theory as they have been applied to the understanding of deviance and crime: **culture conflict,** group conflict, authority–subject conflict, and the social construction of crime. Subsequent sections examine feminist perspectives on deviant and criminal behaviour.

LIBERAL CONFLICT PERSPECTIVES ON DEVIANCE AND CRIME
Thorsten Sellin and Culture Conflict

In 1938, Thorsten Sellin proposed a theory of crime based on the notion of culture conflict (Sellin, 1938). Sellin noted that in societies where culture is homogeneous, the values to which people adhere and the norms to which they accede are essentially the same for all people. Cultures in which this sort of consensus reigns are governed by a single set of rules, which he termed "conduct norms." When different cultures come into contact with one another or when a variety of subcultures exists within a single society, the different groups will inevitably subscribe to different conduct norms. Where this is the case, the disparate groups are likely to come into conflict with one another.

Conflict increases in complex societies in which group norms overlap in some instances but are contradictory in others. Where the conduct norms of one group clash with those of another group, conflict ensues as each segment vies with the other for the right to have its norms recognized by competitors as legitimate. Most likely to be successful in this competition are the groups with access to the largest share of resources. Usually, Sellin points out, the dominant group in society translates its conduct norms into law. A society's laws, then, represent the conduct norms of the dominant cultural group or groups.

FIGURE 8.1

GENERAL MODEL OF CONFLICT THEORY

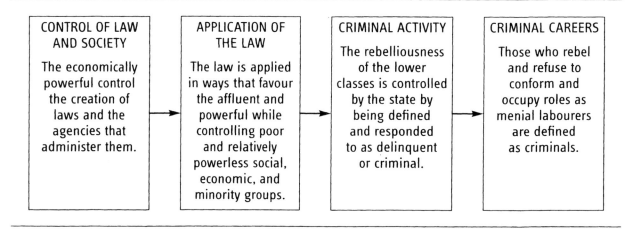

CONTROL OF LAW AND SOCIETY	APPLICATION OF THE LAW	CRIMINAL ACTIVITY	CRIMINAL CAREERS
The economically powerful control the creation of laws and the agencies that administer them.	The law is applied in ways that favour the affluent and powerful while controlling poor and relatively powerless social, economic, and minority groups.	The rebelliousness of the lower classes is controlled by the state by being defined and responded to as delinquent or criminal.	Those who rebel and refuse to conform and occupy roles as menial labourers are defined as criminals.

George Vold and Group Conflict

On the basis of some of Georg Simmel's ideas, George Vold in 1958 outlined another form of group conflict theory. Vold (1958) envisaged humans as compelled by necessity to become involved with one another in group contexts. Through working as individuals, people come to see that they can most effectively achieve their own best interests through collective action, so they form groups. When a number of different groups form and several of them pursue similar collective goals, it is common for one group to encroach upon the others' domains. When such encroachments occur, competition for scarce resources produces conflict.

Vold's view of society is one of competing groups locked in a continuing struggle to maintain or to improve their positions in relation to those of their competitors. Consequently, from Vold's perspective, conflict is an essential and endemic part of a functioning society. Social order emerges and continues at times when it is possible for groups to adjust to one another's demands. Vold argues that such adjustments are tenuous, however, and that social stability is fragile and quite often transitory.

According to Vold, when groups compete for scarce resources, they often seek the assistance of the state in achieving their goals. To protect or enhance its own interest, an ascendant group lobbies the state to create laws that will operate to its advantage and undermine the best interests of its competitors. This is a legislative political process. If some groups favour a law and other groups do not, the group with the greatest political support carries the day. If a group in favour of enacting a particular law can command more votes than an opposing group, it wins. If not, the law will die and the sponsoring group loses. When legislators enact a law, its promoters are in a position both to obey the new law and, in defence of their interests, to insist that the state enforce it. Opposition groups, or to use Vold's term, "minority power groups," can either obey the new law or break it. If they violate it, they become subject to the punitive machinery of the state.

Vold limits his group conflict theory to the explanation of a narrow range of conflicts that can result in criminalization. The theory is not, as he points out, applicable to crimes that are unplanned, irrational, or occur in the heat of passion. Rather, Vold focuses on explaining criminalization that results from a relatively powerful group invoking the law against a less powerful group to maintain or further improve its social and economic position. Examples of such conflicts include those arising between management and labour, among various ethnic groups, and between the state and civil rights advocates.

Austin Turk and Conflict between Authorities and Subjects

Austin Turk's conflict theory of crime (Turk, 1969) builds on the more general theory of conflict developed earlier by Ralf Dahrendorf (1959). Dahrendorf's theory of conflict emphasizes differences in power among various factions in society. Unlike Marxist theory, which cites ownership of the means of economic production as the sole source of power in modern society, Dahrendorf's theory views "institutional authority" as the primary basis of power. The foundation of social division is whether or not a group possesses the legitimate authority to control, through the institutional structure, the actions of other groups. While Dahrendorf sees the economy as an important factor in the distribution of power in society, he considers it neither central nor as critical as Marxists claim. According to Dahrendorf, control of the economy is only one source of power and may or may not overlap with the control of other institutional spheres including the church, the school, and the government.

Building upon the work of Dahrendorf, Turk divides society into two groups: those with power, "the authorities," and those without power, "the subjects." For Turk, social order emerges from the long-term institutionalized coordination of these two groups. To ensure coordination, authorities must maintain a delicate balance of consensus-building and coercion. There must be neither a preponderance of consensus-building nor a preponderance of coercion; balance is essential. According to Turk, the enduring maintenance of this balance psychologically conditions subjects to the social roles inherent in the authority–subject relationship. With successful conditioning, subjects do not question the legitimacy of their relationship to "super-ordinates." Like Dahrendorf, Turk believes power is invested in groups through their institutional authority rather than solely through their ownership of the means of economic productivity. Turk's focus also falls squarely on legal conflict and, in that context, upon criminalization.

When a balance exists between consensus-building and coercion and when social conditioning is successful, conflict in a society is minimal. Under certain conditions, however, group differences are likely to lead to social conflict and subjects are likely to be criminalized by active law enforcement. Turk specifies these conditions first by defining "cultural norms" and "social norms" and then by identifying the situations in which cultural and normative differences between authorities and subjects are most likely to result in conflict and criminalization. He defines cultural norms as verbal formulations of value, and social norms as actual behaviours. The former can be understood as laws on the books while the latter can be understood as laws as they are actually enforced.

Turk specifies three conditions under which cultural and normative differences between authorities and subjects lead to social conflict. The first condition begins with the requirement that the cultural and social norms of both authorities and subjects agree with one another; that is, each group actually translates its values into behaviour. When the values and the behaviours of authorities fall into line with one another but differ from the equally congruent values and behaviours of subjects, a contest of some sort is likely. In cases where one or the other group subscribes to values but does not translate them into behaviour, a struggle is unlikely. In such circumstances, groups will probably not deem significant the issues raised by differences in values alone.

Consider a hypothetical case in which the criminalization of subjects by authorities involves the use of soft drugs. Assume that authorities value industry, sobriety, and deferred gratification. Assume that they translate these cultural norms into behaviour by toiling in the mines, mills, and factories from dawn to dusk and by saving their hard-earned wages for the future. The cultural norms or values of the subject group, on the other hand, extol self-exploration, pleasure, and living for the moment. When subjects translate their cultural norms into social norms by actively dropping out, tuning in, and turning on with mind-altering drugs, the chances of conflict between the two groups and the criminalization of the latter escalate. Compare this situation with a circumstance in which either authorities or subjects, or both authorities and subjects, fail to translate their beliefs into action. Without both authorities and subjects translating cultural norms (values) into social norms (behaviour), the potential for conflict and criminalization is greatly reduced.

The second condition affecting the probability of conflict is the subject group's degree of social organization. Tightly organized subjects are in a better position to resist the subjugation efforts of authorities. Unorganized subject groups, by comparison, are much less capable of meaningful resistance.

The final condition contributing to the likelihood of conflict between authorities and subjects is the degree of sophistication demonstrated by the subjects in their attempts at resistance. The greater their sophistication, the less likely is overt conflict. Highly sophisticated subjects will be more likely to assess accurately the position taken by the authorities and, on the basis of that knowledge, will be able to manipulate them. Sophisticated subjects can frequently violate the norms of the authorities without engaging them in open conflict.

Having discussed the conditions precipitating conflict between authorities and subjects, Turk proceeds to outline three circumstances under which the authorities are most likely to enforce their legal norms, thereby criminalizing members of subject groups. First, when the authorities' cultural and social norms are not only congruent but also salient, authorities are likely to enforce legal norms. Within this context, Turk also points out that the meaning of a prohibited act for the first line of enforcement (the police) and for higher-level enforcers (the courts) is vital. If all levels of enforcement agree that a behaviour is offensive, a violation is likely to result both in high rates of arrest and conviction and in the imposition of severe penalties. In cases where the first line of enforcement finds a behaviour offensive but higher levels of enforcement do not, arrest rates will be high but convictions will be few and sentences lenient. Conversely, if the first line of enforcement views a violation as trivial while higher-level enforcers do not, arrest rates will be low but for those few arrested conviction rates will be high and punishment severe.

Second, the relative power of authorities and subjects plays a role in determining whether subjects can successfully resist authorities' efforts to criminalize them. The criminalization of subjects is highest when they are powerless to resist the authorities. In such cases, authorities expend few resources because subjects muster little opposition. Where the distribution of power between authorities and subjects is more equal, authorities must expend more of their own resources to bring about criminalization. In such cases, the social and economic costs of criminalization temper their initiatives. Enforcers under these circumstances become more cautious in their efforts. In those rare instances in which subjects manage to acquire a great deal of power, they may change the laws that criminalize them.

Third, the degree of realism with which either authorities or subjects undertake action one against the other influences the extent to which the powerful will criminalize the powerless. Unrealistic moves by either party increase the likelihood that subjects will become criminals. Subjects, for example, rather than adopt the realistic stance of maintaining a low profile, sometimes flagrantly violate existing laws. In these instances, authorities who might otherwise ignore such violations have no recourse but to invoke and to enforce the law. For their part, authorities generally demonstrate realism by opting for restrained coercion rather than unrealistic measures that might later be construed as brutal.

Richard Quinney and the Social Reality of Crime

Criminologists divide the theoretical contributions of Richard Quinney into two segments, depending upon whether the work dates from the period before 1970 or after 1970. Quinney (1970) outlines his initial conflict theory of criminality in his book *The Social Reality of Crime,* in which he elaborates the theory, in proposition form, as follows.

1. *Crime is a definition of human conduct that is created by authorized agents in a politically organized society.* With this statement, Quinney asserts that crime is a product of the way in which those in positions of authority choose to define it. Crime is not a product of some sort of individual pathology.

2. *Criminal definitions describe behaviours that conflict with the interests of the segments of society that have the power to shape public policy.* Quinney substitutes Vold's concept of "interest group" with his notion of "social segment." A social segment, according to Quinney, differs from a group in that it need not be comparatively small, organized, communicative, and in pursuit of a common goal through concerted action. He defines a segment as a broad statistical aggregate containing persons similarly disposed on certain characteristics such as age, sex, class, status, occupation, ethnicity, and religion.

3. *Criminal definitions are applied by the segments of society that have the power to shape the enforcement and administration of criminal law.* Some activities of relatively powerless segments become crimes because they aggravate or threaten those in possession of power. The powerful then mobilize to protect their vested interests. The preservation of privilege on the part of those with power produces intersegment conflict, the ultimate result of which is the criminalization of less powerful social segments. When Quinney links his third proposition to the one preceding it, he expands the range of criminal activity beyond that first outlined by Vold. For example, Quinney includes irrational and impulsive crimes in his framework. He sees these types of illegalities as individual acts of

rebellion that members of disorganized segments direct against their more privileged oppressors.

4. *Behaviour patterns are structured in segmentally organized society in relation to criminal definitions, and within this context persons engage in actions that have relative probabilities of being defined as criminal.* This proposition asserts that deciding what acts become violations of law depends on the power and influence of the segment engaging in them. If a social segment has little or no power, more of the behaviours of its members are likely to be legislated as crime. Alternatively, the more powerful a segment is, the smaller is the number of its behaviours that will be criminalized.

The final two propositions present a different conception of **criminogenesis.**

5. *Conceptions of crime are constructed and diffused in the segments of society by various means of communication.*

6. *The social reality of crime is constructed by the formulation and application of criminal definitions, the development of behaviour patterns related to criminal definitions, and the construction of criminal conceptions.* According to Quinney, crime is created and its essence is communicated so as to promote a set of values and interests that benefit the powerful. The media inculcate a social reality of crime as consisting of interpersonal violence and common property offences. Their message also conveys the image of rapidly increasing crime rates. By promoting these images of crime and by cultivating the widespread acceptance of their authority as legitimate, the powerful can implement, in the name of the common good, policies of social control that they themselves have created. The good, in Quinney's view, is far from truly "common," because these particularistic policies preserve the advantages of the privileged. In these last two propositions, Quinney explains why all segments of society, powerful and powerless alike, are inclined to view street crime as the real problem while ignoring the socially harmful acts of economic and political elites.

Table 8.1 summarizes liberal conflict theories.

FEMINIST THEORY

Noting that women and girls form more than half the population, feminists argue that *all* social experiences are transformed into women's concerns and poten-

tially into women's issues. Moreover, they point out that almost without exception, the social experiences of males dominate in explanations of gender differences. Male perspectives are used to explain gender differences in attitudes, beliefs, and behaviours. Feminists rebuke both sociology and criminology for their blindness to gender concerns, observing that women and their experiences of the world have been almost entirely ignored in the theoretical formulations of social science. In the relatively rare instances where attention has been paid to women in society, females have been superficially "plugged in" to masculine-oriented explanatory frameworks (Chesney-Lind, 1986).

Sociological theories of deviance and crime are **androcentric** — they are heavily governed by male experiences and understandings. Androcentric social theory treats women, where they are included at all, as being the same as men. Feminists maintain that the picture of deviant and criminal women as perpetrators, as victims, as persons accused before the law, and as individuals convicted by the criminal justice system is much more complex than mainstream, or "male-stream," social science suggests. With respect to theories of deviance and crime, feminist criminologists note that while the relationships between deviance and crime on the one hand and class, race, and age on the other have received considerable theoretical attention, gender has not. In addition, feminism strongly questions whether general social theory can explain nonconformity and wrongdoing equally well for both males and females (Daly and Chesney-Lind, 1988).

At the foundation of feminist thinking is the notion that gender inequality is the defining feature of society. Women suffer discrimination because of their sex, and as a result, their needs in comparison with those of men are negated and left unsatisfied. The remedy for this inequity involves radical change. In elaborating these basic premises, Daly and Chesney-Lind (1988) summarize five elements of feminist thinking that distinguish it from other forms of social and political thought.

1. Gender is not a natural fact but a complex social, historical, and cultural product; it is related to, but not simply derived from, biological sex difference and reproductive capacities.
2. Gender and gender relations order social life and social institutions in fundamental ways.
3. Gender relations and constructs of masculinity and femininity are not symmetrical but are based

TABLE 8.1

LIBERAL CONFLICT THEORIES

Theory	Theorist(s)	Central Premise	Key Concepts	Principal Contributions
Cultural conflict	Thorsten Sellin	Different cultures subscribe to different conduct norms. Conflict arises over whose conduct norms will be accepted as legitimate. Those with access to resources become dominant and translate their conduct norms into law.	Conduct norms	An early (1938) formulation of liberal conflict theory that influenced more contemporary versions.
Group conflict theory	George Vold	Of necessity, groups come into contact with one another in competition for scarce resources. Social order involves groups adjusting to one another's demands. Groups seek to use their power and other resources to influence the creation of laws that favour them and disadvantage competitors who are relegated to the status of "minority power groups."	Group conflict; minority power group	Provides a good explanation of certain types of legal conflict and criminalization that arise from problems involving labour relations, ethnic strife, and civil rights disputes.
Authority-subject conflict	Austin Turk	Social order emerges from long-term institutionalized coordination between authority and subject groups through a balance of consensus building and/or coercion. Conflict arises where cultural norms (values) and social norms (behaviours) differ, where subject groups are organized, and where subject resistance is unsophisticated. Authorities are likely to criminalize subjects where cultural and social norms are salient, where subjects are powerless, and where either group responds to the other unrealistically.	Institutional authority; authorities and subjects; cultural norms; social norms	Offers a parsimonious articulation of the sociological thinking of Weber and Dahrendorf as it applies to law, power, and processes of criminalization.
Social reality of crime	Richard Quinney	Authorized agents in a politically organized society use power to create a definition of human conduct called crime. By virtue of differing behaviour patterns in a segmented society, some are more likely to be defined as criminal than others. The social reality of crime is a product of the construction of criminal conceptions through various means of communication.	Social segmentation; social reality of crime	Stresses the importance of communication through the media of a social reality of crime that benefits powerful social and economic interests.

on an organizing principle of men's superiority and social and political–economic dominance over women.

4. Systems of knowledge reflect men's views of the natural and social world; the production of knowledge is gendered.

5. Women should be at the centre of intellectual inquiry, not peripheral, invisible, or appendages to men. (504)

Feminist social theory originated as a response to explanations of sex differences that originated in biology, psychobiology, and conservative sociology. Biological and psychobiological traditions combining anatomy, genetics, and hormonal make-up have presented differences in skill, aptitude, attitude, and temperament between males and females as having "natural" bases. Feminist and nonfeminist scholars alike have widely criticized physiological approaches, pointing out that they do not take account of heavily documented cross-cultural variations in sex differences. More importantly, as feminist theorists emphasize, biological and psychobiological theories cannot explain the unequal social and economic values attached to the traits and roles of men and women in contemporary society (Saunders, 1988).

In the realm of sociology, feminism is a distinct reaction to the conservatism of structural functionalism. Functionalists explain the origins and persistence of sex differences in terms of their contributions to social order and stability. Functional theorists begin their analysis by observing that the division of labour within the modern nuclear family occurs along the lines of sex. This gender-based division ensures role complementarity and interdependence and, in the larger picture, social solidarity. Functionalists argue that men perform instrumental functions outside the family in the workplace, a competitive and public sphere. Husbands work for wages that are then used to support their wives and children. Wives perform domestic chores and orchestrate family activities within the home, a cooperative and private sphere. The family roles performed by women are more expressive than instrumental; they provide emotional, moral, and domestic support to their husbands and children. From the functional perspective, much of women's effort defuses the tensions experienced by their children and by their husbands in the public spheres of school and work. According to the functionalist perspective, the family can hold together as an integrative social institution only if the roles performed by men and women do not conflict. Functionalists make no overt claims about the primacy of men's or women's roles; by remaining silent, they portray sex-role differentiation in egalitarian terms (Saunders, 1988).

Feminists disagree with functionalists on many points. They begin by pointing out that the roles of women and men in the private and public spheres are by no means equal. Women suffer discrimination and are systematically excluded from social statuses that are accorded the lion's share of income, prestige, and power in contemporary society. Feminists point out that discrimination against women, like other forms of discrimination, is enveloped in an ideology that justifies unequal treatment. In this case, the ideology suggests that women are incapable of performing certain types of tasks, making decisions and accepting responsibility in the public sphere, and exercising political and economic power (Saunders, 1988).

The key concept in various feminist analyses of gender inequality and gender stratification is **patriarchy** — a hierarchical system in which men in society enjoy more social and economic privilege and more autonomy than do women. The basic premise of this system is male superiority. Various agents of socialization, including the family, the school, organized religion, and the media, transmit and reinforce images that promote different temperaments, aspirations, self-images, and behaviours in males and in females. The ideology of male competence and superiority is a rationale through which men exercise institutional control and exclude women from competing for money, privilege, and power.

Feminism is not a unitary framework; rather, it is a set of perspectives that provides various explanations both for the oppression of women and for its amelioration. The three basic **feminist theories** are **liberal feminism,** socialist or **Marxist feminism,** and **radical feminism.**

Liberal feminism conceives of society as filled with barriers that block women's full participation in public spheres such as education, employment, and politics. Liberal feminists favour changing the system from within by redistributing opportunities as a means of restructuring gender power. They argue that society ought to be transformed into a real meritocracy, in which women's abilities receive full recognition. Merit should form the basis of reward, and women should be given the opportunity to compete on an equal footing with men. Liberal feminists call for initiatives that would change the prevailing sexist ideology by altering the process and content of socialization in the family, in the education system, and in the media. They also advocate legislative changes that would expand opportunities for women and outlaw gender discrimination.

Marxist feminists elevate social class over gender in their understanding of social and economic domination. For them, the control and exploitation of women reflects the larger issue of class oppression and represents the synthesis of class structure and patriarchy. Prominent in this formulation is the argument that women are exploited in two fundamental but related ways. First, husbands who are themselves exploited by capitalists dominate their wives and exploit both their domestic labour and their sexuality. Second, capitalists exploit women directly by using them as a reserve labour army. Women's work power can be used when necessary, often at wages lower than those paid to men, and easily dispensed with during economic contractions.

Marxist feminists draw upon the work of Friedrich Engels, a colleague and collaborator of Marx, to explain the subordination of women in capitalist society. Engels locates the origin of patriarchy in the privatization of property, noting that the development of private property required men to identify their heirs with certainty. This necessity required monogamous sexual relationships. With monogamy, women became increasingly encapsulated in the private sphere of the family. In time, husbands controlled all family property. Not having access to the productive income-generating public sphere of work or any control over property, women became increasingly subordinated to men. In time, subjugated women and children became the property of men. Through this process, the relations of production (work) and of reproduction (childbearing) were profoundly structured by capitalist patriarchy.

Marxist feminist strategies for social change are revolutionary. Only through revolt can capitalism be transformed into a truly democratic socialism free of class and gender stratification. Only through revolutionary means can women be full partners in economic production. Similarly, only through dramatic restructuring can marriage and sexual relations based on notions of private property be abolished and working-class economic subordination eradicated.

Radical feminism differs fundamentally from Marxist feminism in two ways. First, radical feminism sees the basis of gender inequality in the inherent aggression of men toward women and in the inherent needs and desires of men to control women's sexuality and reproductive potential. Women's smaller size and their dependency during childbearing years make them vulnerable to domination and control. Second, radicals maintain that patriarchy predates the rise of private property within capitalism.

According to the radical feminist framework, hierarchical power relations produce a "power psychology" that underlies female subordination. Society socializes both males and females to consider boys and men as superior to girls and women and teaches that males have the right to control females. The power differentials inherent in gender relations are accentuated by male-defined notions of heterosexual sexuality.

Strategies for eliminating the oppression of women hinge on dramatically increasing female autonomy. Modest initiatives for overthrowing patriarchy involve the creation of "women-only" organizations and institutions, while radical measures call for lesbian separatism and for reproductive technologies that would promote women's sexual autonomy (Saunders, 1988; Simpson, 1989).

While feminist scholarship has become firmly established in sociological theory over the past two decades, the same cannot be said for feminist work in the sociology of deviance and in criminology. While feminists have made gains in critiquing existing theories for their inattention to women, feminist explanations of deviance and crime are in the formative stage. The role of female subordination in both creating and responding to female crime has not been developed. Similarly, sociologists are only beginning to examine the impact of existing gender relations on the nonconformity and illegal behaviour of males.

Feminists take several approaches to the study of deviance and crime. They begin by demarcating the central issues and questions that require examination and explanation. Two of the most important theoretical issues about female offending concern generalizability and gender ratio (Daly and Chesney-Lind, 1988). With respect to generalizability, sociologists continue to explore the degree to which existing nonfeminist approaches such as strain, social control, differential association, and symbolic interactionism explain deviance and crime equally well for both sexes. The results of these efforts are mixed; some findings indicate similarity in the causal structure of male and female offending, while others explain deviant and illegal conduct much better for males than for females (Harris, 1977; Gomme, 1985a).

In critiquing the "add women" approach to resolving the generalizability issue, feminists make two arguments. First, they point out that using the same old theories "with women added" does not really represent a gender-neutral perspective. After all, the architects of these theories constructed them from "male-stream" conceptualizations of the social world. Second, many of these time-worn theoretical frameworks also fail to provide convincing explanations of male deviance and crime. If they cannot provide good explanations of male offending, their applicability to female offending is questionable (Daly and Chesney-Lind, 1988).

The gender-ratio issue concerns the dramatic gap that separates the frequency and type of male and female offending. In comparison with males, females are infrequent rule violators and rare participants in personal and violent crimes. Feminists question whether male and female offending can have the same causes in light of dramatic gender differences in the incidence and form of male and female deviance. Not surprisingly, they advocate the creation of innovative explanations that take as their starting points three important factors: the power differentials inherent in male–female relationships, the nature and extent of informal and official responses, and the control and commodification of female sexuality (Daly and Chesney-Lind, 1988).

Another issue, and one that has received considerable attention, is the sexism and misogyny that prevailed in social science theory and criminal justice practice before the 1970s. Until then, social scientists either ignored women or explained women's deviance, crime, and criminal justice experiences in stereotypical terms. Feminists have oriented their examination of both individualistic and institutional sexism around three concerns: females as victims, females as offenders, and females caught up in criminal justice processing as defendants, witnesses, victims, or prisoners (Simpson, 1989).

It is in the area of victimization that feminist scholarship has made the greatest contribution. For example, feminists have argued that violence, especially violence directed at women and children, cannot be adequately characterized as the random emotional outbursts of a relatively small number of men. Rather, violence is a form of social domination through which men control "their" women and "their" offspring. This insight has radically transformed the sociology of deviance and crime. Rape is now viewed not as an act of sex but as an act of power and violence. Considerable attention is now being directed toward understanding and controlling pornography, battering, incest, and sexual harassment. Not only are these activities widely considered harmful, but they almost exclusively involve the victimization of females.

As a consequence of feminist scholarship, what were formerly "hidden" crimes and "family secrets" are now in the public domain. Three reasons account for the success of feminism in making victims the top priority. First, these forms of victimization are serious and widespread. Second, the violent victimization of girls and women at the hands of men is an experience cogently accounted for by patriarchal theories. Third, the campaign for remedial action was enthusiastically embraced not only by feminists but also by nonfeminists. It was clear to all that something had to be done quickly to improve the protection of women and children.

Although they do so much less frequently than males, females do engage in deviance and crime. Not only were biology and psychology predominant in early explanations, but much female nonconformity and illegality was interpreted in sexual terms. Depictions of women in conflict with the rules of society portrayed them as morally corrupt, hysterical, manipulative, and devious (Simpson, 1989). Expressing the view that many of these supposedly feminine qualities were manifestations of the female nature, criminological accounts ignored the contributions to female deviance and crime of social and economic factors such as poverty, marginalization, and restricted opportunity (Klein, 1973; Smart, 1976).

During the 1970s, Freda Adler (1975) and Rita Simon (1975) developed explanations of female offending that shunned biological and psychological factors in favour of social circumstances and conditions. Both writers argued that low levels of female crime were linked to women's limited aspirations and restricted opportunities. They claimed that increases were taking place in rates of female crime and that these increases were occurring as a result of women's involvement in the liberation movement. As a result of women's liberation, women's roles changed and became more masculine. Adler and Simon maintained that this role convergence encouraged greater female participation in crime, thereby producing a "new female criminal."

The new female criminal argument was soon criticized on several grounds (Steffensmeier, 1978). First, sociologists pointed out that there had been little real change in the occupational structure. The argument that more women were entering the labour force at higher ranks and taking on the characteristics of similarly positioned men simply was not true. Second, researchers observed that arrested and imprisoned females embrace traditional sexist values. Finally, feminists strongly took issue with the works of Adler and Simon because the writers completely ignored the role of patriarchy in crime and justice. Their formulations paid little attention to the power that males wield over females in the realms of labour and sexuality. Finally, both Adler and Simon ignored women's economic marginality as a major factor in their illegal conduct (Simpson, 1989).

Feminists also argue that sexism manifests itself in the treatment of women by the criminal justice system. Justice is gendered in that an offender's sex affects decision making in the system. The chivalry hypothesis, for example, holds that women, in accordance with their image as powerless and in need of protection, are treated more leniently than men by male-dominated police organizations. It also suggests that the courts may be more lenient to women for offences considered "normal" for females. Where the offences contradict the court's sex-role expectations, the response to females may be harsher than to males committing the same offence under the same circumstances (Simpson, 1989). However, evidence suggests that when all other factors such as offence seriousness and the number of prior convictions are taken into account, women are not penalized more leniently than men (Chesney-Lind, 1986; Johnson, 1986).

Sexism has also been apparent in other criminal justice practices. Female deviance is often subject to "sexualization"; while men are thought to steal because they need money, women — even poor ones — steal because they are sexually frustrated. Also, women who violate rules and break laws are more likely than men to be considered mentally ill. For males who fight, the old adage "boys will be boys" applies, but females who engage in similar forms of violence are thought to need psychiatric treatment.

Table 8.2 summarizes feminist theories.

LIBERAL CONFLICT THEORIES, FEMINISM, AND SOCIAL POLICY

Theories in the liberal conflict tradition advocate a greater balance of power among factions with competing interests. Advocates of liberal conflict theory champion greater participation in political decision making for all social segments and greater equality in treatment under the law. One policy initiative is the decriminalization of many nonviolent street crimes that have no direct victims and that are disproportionately enforced against the underprivileged. In addition to calling for the legalization of some offences, liberal conflict theorists advocate the criminalization of certain harmful actions that are the exclusive domain of the rich and the powerful. They also promote more vigorous enforcement of existing laws prohibiting white-collar and corporate offences.

Liberal conflict theorists emphasize the importance of increasing access to lawmakers for the poor and the underprivileged while reducing the advantage of the affluent in this regard. Suggestions include creating and enforcing laws directed at controlling the lobbying of politicians and the making of political campaign donations. Other strategies aim at strengthening the capabilities of disadvantaged groups to resist the incursion into their lives of criminal justice agencies. Such undertakings include bolstering legal-aid programs, fostering inner-city community organizations, and strengthening the powers of independent boards that investigate and discipline police misconduct.

The cornerstone of feminist policy is, at best, the ending of patriarchy and the elimination of the disparity and inequality it produces. If that aim cannot be fully accomplished, feminists advocate at the very least changing gendered institutional and social relations in contemporary society in general and in the law and criminal justice in particular. Specifically, they advocate prevention and treatment options instead of the current emphasis on punitive measures. In so doing, they note that girls and women are much less violent and much more amenable to prevention and treatment in both residential and non-residential community-based correctional programs. Feminists bolster this argument for enhanced prevention and treatment programs by noting that females at various stages of their development experience comparatively special and unique life circumstances including sexual

TABLE 8.2

FEMINIST THEORIES OF DEVIANCE AND CRIME

Theory	Theorist(s)	Central Premise	Key Concepts	Principal Contributions
Feminism	Freda Adler; Carol Smart; Meda Chesney-Lind	Gender inequality is the defining feature of society and is explained in terms of patriarchy, a hierarchical system of power in which males are dominant and females and children are subordinate. Liberal feminism stresses restricted opportunities for women in a public sphere that should be made more meritocratic and less discriminatory. Marxist feminism emphasizes class and gender exploitation at home and work by the capitalist class that can be overcome only through revolutionary means. Radical feminism stresses a patriarchal power psychology in which male dominance is widely accepted as legitimate. It advocates women-only organizations, lesbian separatism, and women's control of reproductive technologies.	Gender inequality; patriarchy; liberal feminism; Marxist feminism; radical feminism; power psychology; generalizability; gender ratio	Focuses attention on gender inequality, sexism, the victimization of women and children, and gender discrimination in the criminal justice system

harassment and assault, violence at the hands of intimates, unplanned pregnancies, and adolescent motherhood.

THE EVALUATION OF LIBERAL CONFLICT THEORIES AND FEMINISM

Liberal conflict and Marxist theories of deviance and crime and their critics' responses have enlivened sociological debates linking power, law, and social control. These approaches have given birth to new forms of critical thinking and have encouraged sociologists and criminologists to reflect on their role vis-à-vis the criminal justice industry.

The experiences of women as perpetrators, victims, and agents of control were ignored until the late twentieth century. Theories about the causes and consequences of gender differences in offending and victimization are in their infancy. However, although feminist theorizing about deviance and crime is fairly recent, some noteworthy contributions exist. First, feminist scholars have focused attention on the inadequacies of existing social theories in explaining the deviance, crime, and victimization of both females and males. Second, feminist inquiry has brought to light the extensive, very serious but hitherto hidden victimization of two particularly vulnerable social segments, women and children. It has also focused attention on a particularly dangerous environment, the home. Third, feminism has provided, through the patriarchy construct, a coherent theoretical account of female victimization. Fourth, feminist approaches have emphasized economic necessity over female nature in the production of offences such as shoplifting, cheque forging, and prostitution. Other avenues of thought and other research questions are being explored. The most promising lines of inquiry involve determining the ways in which female deviance and crime are shaped by challenges to patriarchy, discovering the effect on female criminality of the sexism inherent in the social organization of criminal opportunity, and uncovering the ways in which gender relations affect the deviant and illegal conduct of females and males.

SUMMARY

Liberal conflict theorists view society as being composed of a variety of groups vying to maximize their own interests. Moreover, they see power bases as potentially involving more than economic advantage. Sellin emphasizes conflict among groups having different cultures. Vold focuses on the role of the state and the political enactment of law in power disputes involving labour, ethnic, and civil rights groups. Turk builds upon Dahrendorf's "institutional authority" as the basis of power. Turk sees society as comprising two competing groups: authorities and subjects. According to Turk, their coming into conflict depends on the congruence of their values and behaviours, the degree to which subjects are socially organized, and the subjects' level of sophistication in responding to authorities. Turk further specifies three circumstances wherein authorities are likely to actively enforce legal norms. Enforcement is most likely where norms are salient, where the discrepancy in power between authorities and subjects is large, and where the degree of realism demonstrated in the potential conflict is low.

Quinney's initial conflict theory of crime can be placed in the liberal conflict tradition. He understands crime as a definition of human behaviour that authorities create in a political framework. Crime is socially constructed to benefit the powerful. Quinney observes that public images of crime are created through interpersonal and media communications that direct attention toward street crime. The socially and economically harmful activities orchestrated in the executive suites of the powerful are ignored.

Policy recommendations springing out of liberal conflict perspectives call for balancing the power between the privileged and the underprivileged by providing the latter groups with better political and economic access to the mechanisms of creation and administration of the law. Liberal theorists advocate change from within the existing system. Conversely, Marxist theorists see the dismantling of capitalism as an essential step in eliminating social and economic inequality and the crime and criminalization stemming from that inequity.

Liberal conflict theorists, along with their Marxist counterparts, have since the 1960s contributed immensely to the understanding of illegal conduct and social control. Their efforts have greatly clarified the social scientific and criminological community's focus on such important areas as social and economic inequality, the use and abuse of power, and the functioning of the criminal justice system.

Feminist theorizing begins with the fundamental observation that while women make up at least half of society, their experience of the social world is ignored in social theory. Male experience dominates explanations of social structure and social process. Social science, in short, is "male-stream."

In reacting to biological, psychological, and conservative sociological approaches, feminists maintain that gender inequality is the defining feature of society. They reject the functionalist notion that male and female role complementarity facilitates harmony in the family and promotes social integration in the community. They consider the suggestion that male and female roles are separate but equal to be nonsense.

Feminists document the unequal rewards attached to male and female roles. They explain this inequality in terms of patriarchy, a hierarchical system of power in which males are dominant and females and children are subordinate.

Liberal feminism stresses the gender inequality inherent in a system that restricts opportunities for women in the public sphere. Liberal feminism favours change from within the system to make it more meritocratic. Other recommended changes involve socialization practices and legislation aimed at prohibiting discrimination against women. Marxist feminists emphasize links between class and gender dominance, pointing out how women are exploited by the capitalist class both in the home and in the workplace. The elimination of gender inequality depends on the elimination of class through revolutionary means. Radical feminists argue that society is governed by a patriarchal power psychology in which men's dominance is widely accepted as legitimate. Radicals advocate changes ranging from the creation of women-only organizations and institutions to lesbian separatism and the control of reproductive technologies.

Feminist theorizing about deviance and crime is in its infancy. Several questions are being debated. First, can "male-stream" theory be generalized to explain female deviance? Second, how can the gender ratio, the gap separating male from female deviance and crime, be accounted for? Third, given the extent of this gap, does it make sense to suggest a general theory of deviance?

QUESTIONS FOR CRITICAL THINKING

1. Is conflict inevitable in all cultures? To what extent and on what dimensions is Canadian society characterized by discord? Does criminal law figure prominently in cultural skirmishes? What can be done to reduce conflict in Canadian society?

2. Can you identify Canadian laws that protect mostly the rich or special interest groups? What kinds of activities are criminalized by such laws? Give a few examples. What are the origins of these statutes? Identify groups and their positions in favour of or against the legislation.

3. To what extent can the conflict perspective be applied to the study of recent incidents of terrorism and conflict involving rogue states?

4. Marxist and liberal feminism differ in their proffered solutions to the criminal victimization of women and children in Canadian society. In policy terms, which approach holds the most promise, and why?

5. How would making gender a central focus of criminological inquiry affect the ways in which criminologists study male criminality? What direction might feminism take in this regard and how useful might the theory be?

RECOMMENDED READINGS

Boritch, H. (1997). *Fallen Women: Female Crime and Justice in Canada.* Toronto: Nelson.
    Provides a comprehensive overview of women as crime perpetrators, suspects, accused, and convicted in Canadian context.

LeBlanc, L. (1999). *Pretty in Punk: Girls' Resistance in a Boy's Subculture.* New Brunswick, NJ: Rutgers University Press.
    Examines the origins and development of punk subculture and investigates the changing roles of women and girls in oppositional subcultures. Analysis is based on field research and interviews with self-identified punk girls in several North American cities including Montreal.

Quinney, R. (1970). *The Social Reality of Crime.* Boston: Little, Brown, and Company.
    Sets out Quinney's original formulation of crime in relation to the distribution of power across social segments.

Sommers, E. K. (1995). *Voices from Within: Women Who Have Broken the Law.* Toronto: University of Toronto Press.
    Through intensive interviews with fourteen Canadian women in prison, examines why and how women become involved in crime. Criticizes feminist criminology for overemphasizing and oversimplifying the links between crime and poverty.

Turk, A. (1969). *Criminality and the Legal Order.* Chicago: Rand McNally.
    Presents Turk's articulation of crime in the context of authority–subject relations.

Adler and Adler - Constructions
of Deviance

11

The Constructionist Stance

JOEL BEST

Best, one of the leading practitioners of the social constructionist approach, offers a historical analysis of the way theories of deviance have evolved. He notes the rise and decline in significance of several approaches to deviance theory, showing how social constructionism arose from its early roots in the sociology of deviance and moved into explaining social problems. The constructionist perspective represents a wedding of the views of labeling and conflict theories, as we noted in the General Introduction. It joins the microanalysis of the former by looking at how individuals encounter societal reactions and become labeled as deviants with the broader, more structural, social power contribution of the latter, isolating certain groups as more likely to have social reactions and definitions formed and applied by and against them. It is this social constructionist stance that will frame the organization and selections comprising the remainder of this book, as we examine the process by which groups vie for power in society and try to legislate their views into morality and then focus on how people develop deviant identities and manage their stigma as a result of those definitions and enforcements.

What does it mean to say that deviance is "socially constructed?" Some people assume that social construction is the opposite of real, but this is a mistake. Reality, that is everything we understand about the world, is socially constructed. The term calls attention to the processes by which people make sense of the world: we create—or construct—meaning. When we define some behavior as deviant, we are socially constructing deviance. The constructionist approach recognizes that people can only understand the world in terms of words and categories that they create and share with one another.

THE EMERGENCE OF CONSTRUCTIONISM

The constructionist stance had its roots in two developments. The first was the publication of Peter L. Berge and Thomas Luckmann's (1966) *The Social Construction of Reality*. Berger and Luckmann were writing about the sociology of knowledge—how social life shapes everything that people know. Their book introduced the term "social construction" to a wide sociological audience, and soon other sociologists were writing about the construction of science, news, and other sorts of knowledge, including what we think about deviance.

Second, labeling theory, which had become the leading approach to studying deviance during the 1960s, came under attack from several different directions by the mid-1970s. Conflict theorists charged that labeling theory ignored how elites shaped definitions of deviance and social control policies. Feminists complained that labeling ignored the victimization of women at the hands of both male offenders and male-dominated social control agencies. Activists for gay rights and disability rights insisted that homosexuals and the disabled should be viewed as political minorities, rather than deviants. At the same time, mainstream sociologists began challenging labeling's claims about the ways social control operated and affected deviants' identities.

THE CONSTRUCTIONIST RESPONSE

In response to these attacks, some sociologists sympathetic to the labeling approach moved away from studying deviance. Led by John I. Kitsuse, a sociologist whose work had helped shape labeling theory, these sociologists of deviance turned to studying the sociology of social problems. With Malcolm Spector, Kitsuse published *Constructing Social Problems* (1977)—a book that would inspire many sociologists to begin studying how and why particular social problems emerged as topics of public concern. They argued that sociologists ought to redefine social problems as claims that various conditions constituted social problems; therefore, the constructionist approach involved studying claims and those who made them—the claimsmakers. In this view, sociologists ought to study how and why particular issues such as date rape or binge drinking on college campuses suddenly became the focus of attention and concern. How were these problems constructed?

There were several advantages to studying social problems. First, constructionists had the field virtually to themselves. Although many sociology departments taught social problems courses, there were no rival well-established, coherent theories of social problems. In contrast, labeling had to struggle against functionalism, conflict theory, and other influential approaches to studying deviance.

The constructionist approach was also flexible. Analysts of social problems construction might concentrate on various actors: some examined the power of political and economic elites in shaping definitions of social problems; others focused on the role of activists in bringing attention to problems; and still others concentrated on how media coverage shaped the public's and policymakers' understandings of problems. This flexibility meant that constructionists might criticize some claims as exaggerated, distorted, or unfounded (the sort of critique found in several studies of claims about the menace of Satanism), but they might also celebrate the efforts of claimsmakers to draw attention to neglected problems

(for example, researchers tended to treat claims about domestic violence sympathetically).

Again, it is important to appreciate that "socially constructed" is not a synonym for erroneous or mistaken. All knowledge is socially constructed; to say that a social problem is socially constructed is not to imply that it does not exist, but rather that it is through social interaction that the problem is assigned particular meanings.

THE RETURN TO DEVIANCE

Although constructionists studied the emergence and evolution of many different social problems, ranging from global warming to homelessness, much of their work remained focused on deviance. They studied the construction of rape, child abduction, illicit drugs, family violence, and other forms of deviance.

Closely related to the rise of constructionism were studies of medicalization (Conrad and Schneider 1980). Medicalization—defining deviance as a form of illness requiring medical treatment—was one popular, contemporary way of constructing deviance. By the end of the twentieth century, medical language—"disease," "symptom," "therapy," and so on—was used, not only by medical authorities, but even by amateurs (for example, in the many Twelve-Step programs of the recovery movement).

A large share of constructionist studies traced the rise of social problems to national attention; for example, the construction of the federal War on Drugs was studied by several constructionist researchers. However, other sociologists began studying how deviance was constructed in smaller settings, through interpersonal interaction. In particular, they examined social problems work (Holstein and Miller 1993). Even after claimsmakers have managed to draw attention to some social problem and shape the creation of social policies to deal with it, those claims must be translated into action. Police officers, social workers, and other social problems workers must apply broad constructions to particular cases. Thus, after wife abuse is defined as a social problem, it is still necessary for the police officer investigating a domestic disturbance call to define—or construct—these particular events as an instance of wife abuse (Loseke 1992). Studies of this sort of social problems work are a continuation of earlier research on the labeling process.

CONSTRUCTIONISM'S DOMAIN

Social constructionism, then, has become an influential stance for thinking about deviance, particularly for understanding how concerns about particular forms of deviance emerge and evolve, and for studying how social control agents construct particular acts as deviance and individuals as deviants. Constructionism emphasizes the role of interpretation, of people assigning meaning, or making sense of the behaviors they classify as deviant. This can occur at a societal level, as when the mass media draw attention to a new form of deviance and legislators pass laws against it, but it can also occur in face-to-face interaction, when one individual expresses disapproval of anther's rule breaking. Deviance, like all reality, is constantly being constructed.

REFERENCES

Berger, Peter L., and Thomas Luckmann. 1966. *The Social Construction of Reality.* New York: Doubleday.

Conrad, Peter, and Joseph W. Schneider. 1980. *Deviance and Medicalization.* St. Louis: Mosby.

Holstein, James A., and Gale Miller. 1993. "Social Constructionist and Social Problems Work." Pp.151–72 in *Reconsidering Social Constructionism,* edited by James Holstein and Gale Miller. Hawthorne, NY: Aldine de Gruyter.

Loseke, Donileen R. 1992. *The Battered Woman and Shelters.* Albany: State University of New York Press.

Spector, Malcolm, and John I. Kitsuse. 1977. *Constructing Social Problems.* Menlo Park, CA: Cummings.

Loscke and Best –
Social Problems:
Constructionist Readings

1

The Changing Meanings of Spanking

PHILLIP W. DAVIS

Spanking is more than mild physical punishment to make children behave. It is also the focus of competing ideas, beliefs, and vocabularies put forth by critics and advocates in a debate over spanking's definition, appropriateness, and implications. There is a long history of religious and secular justifications for spanking. Beliefs that spanking is natural, normal, and necessary form a "spare the rod ideology" that may perpetuate the practice. Trivializing terms such as "smack," "spank," and "whack" are at the heart of a rhetoric of punishment that presupposes the legitimacy of parental authority and makes assumptions about the impersonality of adult motivation. Spanking is a socially constructed reality; it means what people say it means.

Controversial topics such as spanking cause people to trade competing images and moral vocabularies. They look selectively at certain parts of the "problem" and not at others. My purpose is to compare the traditional defense of spanking with the emergent criticism of spanking, identifying the claims and counterclaims spanking's advocates and critics have made in the popular press since mid-century. I will limit my focus to the debate over spanking by parents, recognizing that there is a parallel debate about spanking in schools. In general I argue that the debate over spanking has become more complex in its themes and vocabularies. New definitions of spanking supplement older ones, and what was once primarily a child-rearing issue has become a child-protection issue as well.

This chapter is excerpted from Davis, Phillip W. (1994). "The Changing Meanings of Spanking." Pp. 133–54 in *Troubling Children: Studies of Children and Social Problems*, edited by Joel Best. Hawthorne, NY: Aldine de Gruyter.

Spanking's advocates traditionally use a rhetoric and vocabulary that paint spanking as the reasonable reaction of responsible parents to their wayward children. They claim that spanking is (1) the sign of nonpermissiveness, (2) anticipatory socialization, (3) God's will, (4) a morally neutral childrearing tool, and (5) a psychic release.

The Sign of Nonpermissiveness

Advocates often present spanking as an answer to the problem of permissive parents who are responsible for much of the "youth problem." The argument is that parents' lax attitudes result in the "undercontrol" of their children who go on to become delinquents, hippies, political activists, liars, cheaters, and thieves who lack respect for authority. In this view, failure to spank becomes the benchmark of permissiveness. Advocates also argue that character flaws lie behind the permissiveness of parents who do not spank; they lack the courage and responsibility that spanking is said to require. According to these advocates, parents who don't spank have neglected their responsibilities, taken the easy way out, or let themselves be duped by experts into taking a scientifically progressive but unwittingly troubled path.

Anticipatory Socialization

A second claim is that spanking effectively prepares children for the tribulations of life and the vagaries of adulthood. Some advocates argue that children will profit from spankings once they enter the real world, a world that is characteristically more difficult and demanding than family life. One advocate wrote that going "back to the hairbrush" prepares children for life's "booby-traps": "…the poor kids, when they eventually break out of the cocoon of an undisciplined childhood, are completely unprepared for the fenced-in and booby-trapped pattern of conventional adult life." This statement appeals to the idea that modernity and nonspanking are an unfortunate combination and that old-fashioned approaches better prepare children for the confinements of adult life.

God's Will

Religious themes appear when authors mention "biblical sanctions" as a traditional argument for spanking. James Dobson, author of *Dare to*

Discipline, writes from the standpoint of Christian fundamentalism and is notorious among critics for his advocacy of spanking and switching: "I think we should not eliminate a biblically sanctioned approach to raising children because it is abused in some cases" (quoted in Neff 1993).

A Morally Neutral Childrearing Tool

Advocates often refer to spanking as a tool, technique, or method, writing about it as if its use were but the impersonal and mechanical application of a morally neutral procedure. The virtues of this technique are said to include speed, efficiency, and efficacy. Spanking creates obedience and respect with minimum effort and without long, "dragged-out" discussions. These claims contend that the good child is an obedient child and that faster techniques are superior to slower ones. Defining spanking as a tool or method suggests that spankers are purposive rather than aimless, and depicts spanking as a logical activity rather than an emotional outburst. The overall image of parents who spank is that their "applications" are part of a method that is reasonable, systematic, and even merciful. The definition of spanking as a childrearing tool or technique is especially clear in the widespread claim that spanking should be used as a last resort, only after other, presumably less harsh, efforts have failed. The rhetoric of "last resorts" implies that spankers possess the knowledge and ability to mete out penalties of varying severity in the proper sequence.

A Psychic Release

Another common contention is that spanking resolves particular conflicts by somehow allowing parents and their children to start over, because it "clears the air." Some authors claim that spanking frees children from guilt by providing them with an opportunity for repentance or offers a cathartic release of the parent's tension and anger. Advocates also contend that parents who don't spank will find other, less healthy, ways of expressing their anger. If they don't become neurotically guilty, insecure, or repressed, parents may erupt later and do greater harm to the child, for all their progressive efforts to conform to the new psychology.

THE CRITICS RESPOND

Critics of spanking claim that these traditional defenses are flawed for a variety of reasons. They argue that, rather than preventing youth problems, spanking creates them. For one thing, spanking makes children

untrustworthy because children might cheat or lie in order to avoid spankings. Critics also claim that, although spanking may "work" in the immediate situation, its effects are highly limited because it can cause children's rebellion and resentment. They also argue that, while it may be effective, it is effective for the wrong reason. Instead of complying voluntarily out of respect based on reason, children who are spanked comply out of fear. Critics claim that spankers are irresponsible, because they are avoiding the harder but superior alternatives. Spankers worry too much about teaching the values of respect and authority, oblivious to the fact that spanking really teaches the legitimacy of aggression, brute strength, and revenge. Critics also contend that spanking can easily escalate. Critics argue that the true meaning of discipline involves teaching children the lesson of self-control, whereas "physical discipline" only teaches them "might makes right."

In sum, since mid-century advocates and critics in the popular press have been invoking several different meanings of spanking. Advocates for spanking claim that children are "underdisciplined," that they need to be spanked, that parents who do not spank are mollycoddling their children, that being spanked doesn't harm children, and that nonspanking parents are irresponsible. Critics respond that spanking is futile at best and counterproductive at worst. In this traditional debate, advocates emphasize the drawbacks of permissiveness as a cause of delinquency and rebellion, and critics argue that discipline should involve teaching and self-control.

EMERGENT MEANINGS

The traditional claims about spanking persist. But spanking's critics bring newer, supplementary meanings to the debate, meanings that coincide with changing concerns and arguments borrowed from debates over other issues.

Spanking Is Compulsive

The critics' first new claim is that spanking is compulsive, habit-forming, or addictive. This claim depicts parents as people who have lost their autonomy by becoming dependent on a highly satisfying behavior that they can abandon only with considerable difficulty. Critics compare spanking to smoking, because both practices are legal, harmful, and habitual, and given the widespread criticisms of each, they are increasingly secretive practices. Responding to a report that time out is more popular with parents than spanking, for example, one pediatrician was skeptical, saying that "spankers today are like closet smokers."

Spanking Is a Demeaning, Violent Act

Critics routinely echo the view of most family violence researchers that spanking is a form of violence. They describe spanking as an act of violence that models violent behavior for the child and teaches children that violence is socially acceptable. Critics argue that spanking humiliates and devalues the child and demonstrates that physical violence is a good way to solve problems. For critics, spanking is a prime example of minor violence that later causes adult violence, especially by those who experience frequent, severe spankings as children. With increasing frequency, newspaper and magazine articles interweave references to spanking and abuse, and some emphasize that a "fine line" separates spanking and abuse, a line that is too easily crossed.

The Advocates Respond

Advocates have had little say about the idea that spanking is a compulsion, but they take issue with critics who claim it is violent or abusive. Some claim that critics are less concerned about raising children than they are about social appearances. Some writers make increasingly sharp distinctions between spanking and abuse, between "an occasional swat" and spankings, or between rare swats and corporal punishment. Some advocates tell parents just what to do so that they will not be considered abusive:

Spank only for a few specific offenses, such as blatant disrespect and defiance.... John Rosemond, in his Knight News Service newspaper column "Parent and Child," gives these guidelines: "With no threats or warnings, spank with your hand, not a wooden spoon, paddle, belt or switch. A spanking is not more than three swats to the child's rear end. A swat to any other part of the child's body is abuse. (Oliver 1987)

DISCUSSION

"Spanking" remains a fighting word, and what people are fighting about is both complex and changing. Over time, a topic traditionally approached as a childrearing issue in a debate over "what works" has also become a child-protection issue in a debate over whether spanking is violent and abusive.

Advocates of spanking extol its virtues in the name of tradition, effectiveness, efficiency, and responsibility, defining it essentially as a tool, technique, or method for making children behave. Spanking is said to offer an

antidote to the youth problem, release tension for both parent and child, and prepare children for life's hardships. Advocates generally ignore or trivialize children's suffering, portray nonspankers as irresponsible, and cite their own positive personal histories as spanked children. Critics counter that spanking promotes, rather than deters, misbehavior. They contend that it is usually an expression of the parent's anger and frustration and teaches children that violence and aggression are acceptable. More recent critics also define spanking as a bad habit, an act of violence, and a form of abuse. All too often, they argue, spanking leads to abuse later in life or is closely linked to the abuse of the spanked child.

In the context of increasingly broad definitions of child abuse, some advocates argue for narrow definitions of spanking (spank only on the bottom). Narrow definitions, as well as distinctions between planned spankings and the occasional smack, are ways of maintaining a "place" for spanking on the list of what parents can rightfully do to their children without lapsing into a category of "child abuser."

Activities in wider professional, scientific, religious, and political contexts have no doubt prompted and shaped these changing meanings for spanking. Psychological research and popular writings on aggression in the 1950s and 1960s challenged behaviorist assumptions about the role of punishment. Some well-publicized studies provided dramatic ironies such as physical punishment for aggressive behavior is associated with more, not less, aggression by children. Many of these scholarly ideas and facts made their way into articles and stories in the popular press.

Moreover, in the 1960s and early 1970s, the development of a modern child-protection movement, the discovery of child abuse, and the continuing emergence of violence as a major policy issue led to a series of controversies associated with the idea that children are increasingly "at risk." As these issues developed, spanking was mentioned, and sometimes its importance was highlighted.

There has also been a convergence of interests and activities among anticorporal punishment and antiabuse organizations. Organizations such as the National Coalition to Abolish Corporal Punishment in Schools, the National Center for the Study of Corporal Punishment and Alternatives, and End Violence against the Next Generation, although they focus on educational settings, regularly point to spanking and physical punishment by parents as an analogous issue. The National Committee for the Prevention of Child Abuse (NCPCA) has been actively seeking the primary prevention of child abuse through pamphlets, surveys, and press releases about physical punishment and spanking since the mid-1980s.

We cannot make a flat statement that the newer meanings of "spanking" are now dominant. The themes in the newer debate suggest only a partial transformation of the traditional childrearing issue into a contemporary child-protection controversy. There is certainly the potential for definitions related to abuse to become dominant. Whether the transformation proceeds further depends in part on the discourse, resources, and activities of advocates and critics in organizational, political, media, and movement contexts.

Activities in medical settings will have an impact. The Centers for the Study of Disease Control instituted a division for the study of domestic violence in 1992. The June 1992 issue of the *Journal of the American Medical Association* was devoted to family violence and included an article on spanking as a form of corporal punishment. Some physicians now claim that corporal punishment is child abuse. These medical developments, if they are recognized by the press, policymakers, and agency officials, should encourage spanking's association with child abuse.

Other activities, however, are likely to inhibit the ascendance of abuse meanings. Religious action groups are sensitive and alert to any move to broaden definitions of abuse to include spanking or to remove existing legal protections of parents who use reasonable physical discipline. We may see other spanking-related controversies develop as groups organize to resist further involvement by the state in family matters. In addition, some critics promote the idea that spanking is really a civil rights issue, and civil rights organizations may make spanking part of their agenda. Their constructions of the problem might easily bypass the issue of abuse or make it secondary to the issue of discrimination on the basis of age. Similarly, critics campaigning for state and national legislation may successfully promote the association of spanking with the violation of human or children's rights rather than child abuse. Whether spanking ever fully becomes a child-protection issue, these emergent meanings challenge the assumptions that spanking is natural, normal, and necessary on a fundamental level.

REFERENCES

Neff, D. 1993. "Dobson's New Dare" [interview with J. Dobson]. *Christianity Today* 37 (February 8):69–70.

Oliver, S. 1987. "How to Stop Spanking." *Essence* 18 (April):98.

8

Television Talk Shows Construct Morality

KATHLEEN S. LOWNEY

Lots of people seem to be uneasy with talk shows. A wide variety of people seem to think that talk shows have gone "too far," although not everyone agrees about what "too far" means. Some critics feel that the shows reflect a growing national moral decline. They assume that there is no moral code operating on these shows; they feel the shows simply celebrate the worst in sexual perversions, interpersonal violence, and family misfortunes. I disagree. There *is* a moral code on talk shows, and we need to explore it, asking: What is the code? And just whose morality is being espoused? These questions are critical for understanding the role of talk shows in American popular culture.

I want to explore the normative order on talk shows by examining the shows themselves. Having just written this sentence, I took a bit of a break and watched *The Jerry Springer Show*. The show focused on just one family. Amber was introduced first; she was 12 years old and had been dating, with her parents' approval, a 24-year-old guy named Glenn, who was another one of the guests. Her parents knew that she and Glenn were sexually involved. Amber's mother (Pam, the third guest) also was dating Glenn and wanted to marry him. About 20 minutes into the show, Amber's father, Frank, came out on the stage, promptly threatened Glenn with bodily harm, and had to be restrained by well-muscled guards. As the show progressed, emotions became extremely intense. Pam told her daughter that it was time that her own needs came first and her daughter would have to cope with Glenn as her new stepfather or else Amber would

This chapter is excerpted from Lowney, Kathleen S. (1999). *Baring Our Souls: TV Talk Shows and the Religion of Recovery* (Chapter 1). New York: Aldine de Gruyter.

just have to get lost. The mother went on to say more hurtful and embarrassing things about her daughter, such as the fact that she smelled due to poor hygiene.

On the surface, this show could be an excellent typifying example of what critics mean when they say that talk shows are destroying America's moral fabric. One whole television hour was devoted to discussing the sexual appetites of a 12-year-old girl and her mother. Viewers learn that Pam thought that Glenn was "stupid and slow"; Pam admitted to prostitution, a drug habit, and serving time in prison; Frank sort of admitted to having a violent relationship with Pam; Pam called Amber lots of names (many were bleeped out).

But there was more to the show. The host, Jerry Springer, played a significant role. He was constantly interrupting the guests, especially Pam, and most interruptions communicated one of two emotions. The first was incredulity—that a mother would say such hurtful, selfish things to her daughter. The second emotion was sarcasm. Jerry made pointed comments about Pam and Frank's parenting skills, Glenn's decision-making capabilities, and even Amber's choices (though he was careful to say repeatedly that she was a child and children make mistakes and that she shouldn't be judged too harshly). Jerry definitely was grounding his remarks in a moral code: children should not be having sex and parents should protect their children, even if it means putting the needs of the children above those of the parents. Near the end of the show, a psychologist joined the family on stage. He promptly added his critical voice by telling Glenn to leave this family alone. He told Pam to start acting like a mother to her daughter, and told both parents to start loving their daughter more if they wanted her to have any self-esteem.

Clearly there was a quite strong moral message to this show. It didn't come only at the end of the show; Springer wove it throughout the program. The morality was hard to ignore. In addition to Jerry's sarcasm and his outrage, the audience was there, booing and hissing Pam, Glenn, and Frank. They clapped wildly when Springer moralized; when he finished a three-minute harangue against Pam, the audience gave him a standing ovation. Jerry Springer, the audience, and the psychologist reiterated time and again a moral code that valued sexual restraint and honoring commitments to others (such as mother to daughter). Still, television talk show critics probably would say that this moral message should not be couched in the public humiliation of a 12-year-old girl. The viewing public now knows about her promiscuity and her troubled family life, and for what? What did that show cost Amber, her family, and perhaps our nation's very soul?

Such questions about the presence (or absence) of and the kinds of moral discourse on talk shows often occur in an intellectual vacuum. We think of television, and especially talk shows, as a relatively new, yet powerful medium of entertainment that can lead children and adults down the path to depravity. But there always has been some type of entertainment that has bothered a portion of the population. There are historical parallels to talk shows that bear investigating. I remember my parents hating some of the music that I liked; there was a national debate over Elvis' swinging hips and how much—or even if—they should have been shown on *The Ed Sullivan Show*. Both critics and apologists of talk shows need to understand the historical roots of talk shows in order to comprehend their role in American society today. Journey back in time with me for a moment.

SECULAR FUN: THE CIRCUS AS ENTERTAINMENT

It's the middle of the nineteenth century. For now, let's shun the big cities and instead go traveling in rural America. Most adult males worked on the land or were involved in a few central industries. The women were involved in agriculture as well as taking care of the home. Children worked hard to help the family economically. Book learning would be squeezed in around the patterns of planting, tending, and harvesting the crops. It's easy to think of this as a hard life by our twentieth-century standards. Appliances were rare, food took much longer to prepare, walking a few miles to a neighbor's home or into town was not seen as extraordinary.

What would these people do after a long day of working in the fields? Save for relaxing with other family members, most of their leisure time would be spent in two activities: church and secular entertainment. Carnivals and circuses provided much of the secular entertainment, in town for a few days and then gone for another year; religious revivals likewise were an important activity. These nineteenth-century carnivals and revivals are two roots—perhaps the most important roots—of modern talk shows. Each has left an important legacy that has shaped the moral discourse on talk shows.

Carnivals were significant national diversions by the 1830s. But although enjoyable, they were not without their critics. Many people felt that circuses and carnivals were morally ambiguous; people worried about their effects on impressionable children. But just what was so immoral about circuses? The laughter and the bawdiness of the activity under the big top fractured the routines of production and home life. There was a fascination with the giant, the bearded woman, the dwarf, and the daredevil humans with their animal acts. These were people quite different from one's neighbors. Townspeople joined in the revelry, not paying much attention to social status. The normative order was suspended during the performance; for example, many female circus performers wore

provocative clothing (for that time period, mind you) while they entertained the crowds, and fortune-tellers and seers transgressed religious admonitions. Ministers felt the dangers of disrupting the moral order, even if it was for momentary amusement. The thought of parishioners wasting time—and hard-earned money—in such frivolous pursuits flew in the face of the work ethic preached from pulpits every Sunday.

But despite warnings from the pulpit, people flocked to this form of amusement. And the most entertaining part of carnivals were the "freaks." Some had genetic abnormalities; others simply had physical characteristics they accentuated for monetary gain. They were displayed in ways emphasizing their distinctiveness from the "good citizens" who had paid to watch them. There was little public outrage over the exploitation of such performers (especially those who we would now call mentally handicapped) until early in the twentieth century.

Circuses not only brought new people into the town, they also brought an ambiance. The scurrying to put up the huge tent, the sights and smells of exotic animals, the strangely dressed entertainers—all these were part of the circus environment. An assemblage of strangers had invaded town; their behavior was not the same as the community's. Whether deserved or not, there was a veneer of fraud that permeated the circus company. Circus performers played with moral boundaries, in reality or through illusion. Thus the unique circus moral code, vehemently condemned by ministers, only highlighted to members of the audience that there were other ways of living, other ways of being human. The circus performers allowed spectators to imagine that their own lives could be different, but without much risk to the community's moral standards. The carnivals and circuses of that century provided entertainment, but it was all in fun. The next morning another day would dawn and the community would settle back into its routines, which focused on the institutions of work and family, with their sex/gender, racial, and socioeconomic systems of stratification. The circus would leave after a few days and, fostered by the community's religious institutions, life would go back to normal.

TURNING AWAY FROM SIN: RELIGIOUS REVIVALS AS OPPORTUNITIES FOR CONVERSION

America in the early 1800s was changing; it was growing territorially and with that growth came new people who somehow were to fit into the social contract. Technology began to transform how our ancestors lived, where they worked, and for whom they toiled. With such rapid change came anxiety, even fear of the future. People began to question the moral order—would it still work in these new times? How should one live in this

TELEVISION TALK SHOWS AS CIRCUS AND REVIVAL

We are not like our ancestors in these rural communities. Not as many of us identify ourselves as religious, we often have less familial interaction and support. We feel that our society is more violent, more out of control than ever before. We seek protection from each other by attending self-defense classes, by making our homes armed and secure fortresses, or by choosing to carry weapons. Poverty and drugs seem rampant and they worry us, even if we are not directly affected by either. We especially worry about our children: what they are downloading off the Internet, what they are or aren't learning in school. We are scared about the kind of future our children will inherit from us. As a nation we seem more interested in being assertive than compassionate, self-indulgent than self-sacrificing. We appear to be fascinated by those who break social norms rather than by those quiet, unassuming citizens who embody them.

We, of course, watch television whereas our ancestors could not. Perhaps the "lowest" form of entertainment we could publicly admit to watching is the talk show. But as a culture, watch them we do. We watch them just as we flocked to carnivals and revivals a century ago. Our reasons have changed little; talk shows serve useful social functions, just as carnivals and revivals did in the 1800s. Talk shows provide us with public entertainment, a time to play with and then ultimately affirm moral boundaries, and the opportunity to listen to people tell their stories of despair and then redemption.

The roots of the modern-day talk shows lie in the nineteenth century's carnivals and revivals. The parallels are striking. The talk show and the carnival both tempt us to watch portrayals of otherness. We see behaviors that are neither common nor publicly discussed exhibited for all to see. Just as the circus performers were displayed one dimensionally, so are talk show guests. Indeed, this atypical or deviant position is what earns them an invitation to appear on the show. And it is the talk show host, like the circus ringmaster of old, who identifies the guests' particular deviance for us from the outset, just in case those in the audience missed it. A person's complex life becomes summarized in a simplistic, made-for-TV label just as freaks were publicized for their unique characteristics on circus handbills. These labels are reinforced throughout the program by subtitles shown just under guests' faces. Just this one aspect of the guests' lives is lifted up for moral judgment.

Carnivals, circuses, and talk shows highlight behavior that falls outside the realm of normality for mainstream society. Most of us do not traipse on high wires, work with animal acts, or read the future; neither are most of us "mothers who covered up their daughters' pregnancies," "high-powered women derailed by menopause," or a "father who abused all four of his sisters." It seems unlikely that any one of us can personally relate to more

new time? What norms would be there to guide people's interactions with each other? For many, a turn, or return, to religion answered these questions. Religion became a comfort, a guidepost in unsettling times. No matter what faith people chose, most believers took their faiths very seriously. They examined their consciences and tried to reign in, if not extinguish, immoral behaviors. This period of religious fervor is usually referred to as the Second Great Awakening (1800–30).

A key feature of this Awakening was the religious revival. Preachers would come into a town for a few days and preach salvation to all who attended. These services were often held under a tent, perhaps on the very site occupied a few days earlier by a circus. The revivals were most often held at night during the workweek, so that all could attend and hear God's word. Frequently a large crowd would gather. The services were full of emotionality and drama. The key to a successful revival was excitement.

The revivalist's responsibility was to create this emotion-filled experience so that conversions would occur. The main way to accomplish this was preaching. Sermons had to deliver word pictures that gave graphic images of the damned eternally suffering in Hell, for then large numbers would convert or rededicate their lives to God. If it was necessary to make someone uncomfortable in the pit of the stomach, or in the depths of the soul, then these ministers were ready to make their audience very, very uncomfortable.

After the sermon, the testimonial was the most effective conversion technique in the revivalist's arsenal. Attendees would share stories of a life full of sinfulness now redeemed by a right relationship with God. The testimony about life before conversion needed to be truly horrific for others to want to convert. These revival meetings were full of sinners openly confessing to all sorts of sins—of failing to resist the temptations of alcohol, gambling, "the flesh," violence, theft, pride, self-indulgence, and so forth. The successful revivalist knew just what to do with these stories of sin. He used them to fill the mourner's bench, seeker's bench, or anxious seat, which was near the front of the tent, sometimes even on the stage. Sitting there was a public symbol that the person was undergoing an internal battle. Such visibility of self-identified deviants served a profound social function. Once a person had taken, voluntarily, a seat on the anxious bench, it was difficult not to complete the process with a confession and a promise to change one's life. Forgiveness and acceptance by one's neighbors flowed from giving testimony and from public conversion. This not only helped the individual find peace, but fostered solidarity in the community.

So it was that the carnival/circus and the revival were almost perfect opposites. The former were times when frivolity, deviance, and eternal damnation lurked under the big tent awaiting the sinner, whereas the latter beckoned the sinner to undergo public humiliation, in return for ultimate redemption.

than a small percentage of show topics. So why then do we watch? In the circus act, the performance was fraught with risk; we knew that no matter how practiced a performer might be, he or she was always flirting with injury, possibly even death. Likewise, guests on talk shows take risks. They expose their lives in ways that some of us might fantasize about and others might find repellent. We know that secrets are a moment away from being spilled. Anxiously we watch both the carnival and the talk show "acts," always aware of the precariousness of the situation. Talk shows become glimpses into the pain (much less often the joy) that is life. Watching deviant people suffer can make us rejoice at the life that we have while at the same time they can remind us of the need for a morality that binds people together. These shows do, then, feature a moral discourse.

Talk shows do not just entertain us—they are also a site for American revivalism, of a novel sort. They provide an "electronic tent" under which we can gather together and watch sinners confess, sometimes receiving absolution from the people whom they have hurt, and be reinstated into the moral community. The hosts are contemporary preachers, cajoling guests, studio audiences, and those of us at home to obey the normative order. And any good preacher knows that an excellent technique to facilitate conversion is to offer oneself as an exemplar of a sinner now redeemed. Talk show hosts make good use of this rhetorical strategy; thus audiences know about Oprah Winfrey and Ricki Lake's weight loss, Sally Jessy Raphael's drug use and subsequent death, and Geraldo Rivera's numerous sexual escapades. These admissions of failing are used to establish a parasocial sense of solidarity among host, guest, and audience members. This parasocial connection is exhibited when the public thinks that we "know" all about celebrities even though we haven't met them—and probably never will. And hosts manipulate this parasocial relationship.

The hosts' life stories, so well known to viewers due in part to repeated disclosures on the shows, invite others to share their pain. And how the guests talk and talk and talk some more about their troubles! We see them shamed by the host, audience, and other guests, and we are reminded of what is considered right and wrong. The hosts are pop cultural moralists and the audience accepts them in that role.

Therefore, talk shows parallel nineteenth-century Protestant revivals. The host is the visiting preacher bent on offering salvation to all those who seek it. The guests are primarily sinners, and the audience is the ardent congregation goading, chastising, and cajoling the sinners and celebrating repentance. Guests not in need of conversion are the aggrieved victims, demanding change in the sinner-guest's behavior. All the televisual attention is directed toward creating a conversion experience. The music, the

staging techniques, and the pace of the show all parallel the structure of revivals.

What mattered under the revivalist's tent is also what matters under the electronic tent of the talk shows—that people convert to a moral lifestyle. Turning away from sin is not a one-time event but something that has to happen every minute of every day. In the nineteenth century, the moral community of the local church was there for the former sinner. On talk shows, the host and the psychological expert, who appears at the end of many shows, share the conversion duties. The host and audience members diagnose and emotional experts certify the moral failings of the sinner-guests. Sinner-guests must earn our sympathy by admitting to sin and guilt *and* by agreeing to a process that will solidify their new status of convert. The experts show the way: therapy. Guests are chided until they agree to enter therapy or go to a 12-step program or some other support group. Like the sinners on the anxious bench, conversion on talk shows is understood as tenuous; backsliding is always a possibility. This is the *religion of recovery*.

We have come full circle: it is inaccurate to claim that there isn't morality on talk shows. Hosts, audiences, and experts all have a moral perspective that shapes their performance. Conservative critics have missed this point. The question is not whether there ought to be a moral code on talk shows, but *whose* morality it should be. Talk shows are frequent visitors in American homes. We can be enveloped in their "electronic tents" 24 hours a day if we want to, for just about any time of the day some channel is carrying one. But when we watch, to what altar, to use revivalists' language, are the guests—and viewers—being called? I think it is important that we understand this newest form of American civil religion. What kind of moral code is being offered to viewers?

14

Prostitutes Respond to AIDS

VALERIE JENNESS

The AIDS epidemic represents the most recent and the most dramatic change in the political environment of prostitutes' rights organizations. By the mid-1980s, the AIDS epidemic posed a recognizable health, social, and legal threat to prostitutes. As such, it represented a significant environmental constraint to the prostitutes' rights movement. As a result, COYOTE (Call Off Your Old Tired Ethics) and other sex workers' organizations have responded to the AIDS epidemic with considerable organizational activity. My focus is on the prostitutes' rights movement's efforts to respond to the many environmental constraints posed by the AIDS epidemic.

AIDS AS A SOCIAL PROBLEM

Although the media were slow to cover AIDS, once the issue finally became a story, the mysterious killer was constructed as a disease of *deviant sexuality*. As a way of accounting for the disease and the epidemic, the press focused not so much on the disease itself, as on groups whose life-style made them susceptible to AIDS. By focusing on the sociocultural characteristics of homosexual men, the largest group affected by AIDS, the press concentrated on the details of their life-style, claiming that it caused the spread of AIDS. By adopting a dual focus on deviant life-styles and the medical problem of AIDS, press coverage of AIDS tied the medical problem to a moral issue.

By 1985, however, AIDS was beginning to be understood as an explicit

threat to the heterosexual population. As the "gay plague" entered the general population, the AIDS epidemic was constructed as a fundamentally different type of social problem. Portrayed as a threat to the population at large, AIDS became a disease of the "normal" as well as a disease of the "deviant." As media attention turned to the emergent heterosexual threat, it began to focus on the issue of contagion with the same fervor it had previously focused on the lifestyles of those infected. As the danger of AIDS to heterosexuals attracted more media attention, the AIDS epidemic was redefined as a problem facing school children, married women, and college students. At the same time, concerns about halting the disease were heightened. Nonetheless, AIDS has not lost its original connection with deviants, deviant lifestyles, and promiscuous sex. The disease has been continually constructed as one implicating deviants in general and sexual deviants in particular.

The biological characteristics of AIDS, combined with the way in which the disease has been socially constructed, almost ensured that prostitutes would be implicated in the social problem of AIDS. This is not particularly surprising given that AIDS has been primarily conceived as a sexually transmitted disease, and that the historical association of prostitution with venereal disease, promiscuous sex, and moral unworthiness remains fixed in the minds of the public.

Prostitutes have been implicated in the AIDS epidemic as a primary bridge through which AIDS has been transmitted into the heterosexual population. The media contributed to making prostitution suspect as an avenue of transmission for the disease. For example, on a 1989 episode of the nationally televised *The Geraldo Show* entitled "Have Prostitutes Become the New Typhoid Marys?" the host offered the following introduction to millions of viewers:

> The world's oldest profession may very well have become among its deadliest. A recent study backed by the federal Centers for Disease Control found that one third of New York's prostitutes now carry the AIDS virus. If this study mirrors the national trend, then the implications are as grim as they are clear. Sleeping with a prostitute may have become a fatal attraction.

Supporting Rivera's introduction, a New York-based AIDS counselor appearing on the show argued:

> A high percentage of prostitutes infected with HIV pass it on to their sexual partners who are johns or the tricks, a lot of whom are married or have sex with a straight woman. I think this is how the AIDS epidemic is passed into the heterosexual population.

Throughout history, prostitution has been portrayed as a health threat as well as a moral threat. Many social historians have documented that,

---

This chapter is excerpted from Jenness, Valerie (1993). *Making it Work: The Prostitutes' Rights Movement in Perspective* (Chapter 5). Hawthorne, NY: Aldine de Gruyter especially during the nineteenth century, female sexual organs—particularly those of prostitutes—were associated with disease and decay. Thus, it is not particularly surprising that legislators have once again turned their attention to prostitution as an avenue of transmission for an epidemic. In the name of preventing the transmission of the HIV infection, legislation that intrudes into private, consensual sexual relations has sprung up around the country. A number of proposals have been introduced that would, in one way or another, make it a crime for someone who is HIV-positive to engage in sex with anyone else, regardless of the degree to which the behavior is mutually voluntary and whether or not condoms are used. At the same time, jurisdictions that have no AIDS-specific criminal law have begun to rely on traditional criminal laws (such as attempted murder and aggravated assault) to prosecute HIV-positive individuals who engage in behaviors that put seronegative individuals at risk.

THE SCAPEGOATING OF PROSTITUTES FOR AIDS

Not surprisingly, prostitutes' rights organizations and their representatives were quick to respond to the multitude of threats posed by AIDS, as well as public officials' response to the epidemic. As early as 1984, when prostitutes met at the second Annual International Hookers' Convention, prostitutes wanted to talk about how to avoid AIDS. In addition to sharing information on how to prevent the contraction and transmission of AIDS, in the mid-1980s prostitutes and their advocates focused on the threat of being implicated in the transmission of AIDS into the general population. Many of COYOTE's more recent claims-making activities are in direct response to the popular notion that prostitutes represent a social problem because they constitute a threatening avenue for the transmission of AIDS into the general population. In a press release entitled "Women and AIDS/Prostitutes and AIDS," COYOTE made explicit the popular conceptualization of prostitution as a health problem connected to AIDS:

Women who are infected with HIV or who have been diagnosed with AIDS are viewed its "vectors" for the transmission of AIDS to men or to children, not as people who get the disease and need services. Symbolic of this view is the frequent categorization of female prostitutes—in Africa, in Asia, in the United States—as "pools of contagion" or "reservoirs of infection." (COYOTE Howls 1988:1).

Similarly, Carol Leigh, an outspoken COYOTE member, argued in a 1987 Oakland Tribune editorial that "prostitutes become like other vulnerable victims of society, scapegoats and targets of backlash against this disease and the people who have it. Misfortune always hits hardest at those

on the bottom." In response to prostitutes being viewed as "deadly pools of contagion," COYOTE has undertaken numerous campaigns to dismantle the conceptualization of prostitutes as contractors, carriers, and transmitters of the virus.

COYOTE counters conceptualizations of prostitutes as pools of contagion by constructing such assertions as the political scapegoating of stigmatized, thus vulnerable, populations. For example, as part of the Sex Workers'/Outlaws in Civil Disobedience contingent of the National March on Washington for Lesbian and Gay Rights in 1987, COYOTE and its supporters pressed the following analysis:

During the AIDS crisis, populations with little power, societal acceptance or political representation are extremely vulnerable to social and legislative scapegoating. Prostitutes are the most obvious targets of those who wish to control the sexual behavior of the general population, often serving as symbols of promiscuity and illicit sex and disease.

Consistent with the politics of other minority groups, COYOTE construes the AIDS crisis as one that has led to the political scapegoating of prostitutes. As Gail Pheterson, the co-director of the International Committee on Prostitutes' Rights (ICPR) explained in the introduction to her 1989 book, The Vindication of the Rights of Whores:

The AIDS epidemic has reached alarming proportions and prostitutes are being scapegoated for spreading the disease. Like a hundred years ago during the syphilis epidemic, many governmental and medical establishments reacted to AIDS with increased regulation of prostitution.

COYOTE substantiates its assertions about prostitutes being scapegoated for the spreading of AIDS by pressing claims about prostitutes' HIV infection rates and by underscoring the civil rights violations involved in the forced testing of prostitutes.

RECONSTRUCTING CLAIMS ABOUT HIV INFECTION RATES

COYOTE has countered assertions that prostitutes represent a "pool of contagion" by claiming that prostitutes' rates of HIV infection are *lower* than other demographic groups. In the process, spokespeople for the prostitutes' rights movement invoke the use of many scientific studies and researchers to lend legitimacy to their claims. For example, at a press conference in 1988 ex-prostitute and COYOTE co-director Gloria Lockett claimed "Prostitutes test no higher for exposure to HIV than other women—when studies take into consideration IV drug use—since prostitutes use condoms."

In addition to asserting prostitutes' comparatively low infection rates, COYOTE has publicly explained that sex workers are not at risk for AIDS because of prostitution per se; viruses do not discriminate between those who exchange money for sex and those who do not. As Gail Pheterson claimed in her book, *A Vindication of the Rights of Whores*: "Prostitutes are demanding the same medical confidentiality and choice as other citizens. . . . They are contesting policies which separate them from other sexually active people, emphasizing that charging money for sex does not transmit disease."

Claims similar to these culminate in suggestions that prostitutes practice safe sex, get regular health checks, and insist that clients wear condoms. From COYOTE's perspective, prostitutes do not constitute an "at risk" group because, at least in part, they *always* have been cautious about sexually transmitted diseases out of concern for their own health and their ability to work. By extension, what separates prostitutes from "women in general" is prostitutes' higher rates of condom use.

Related to this, COYOTE accounts for prostitutes who have tested positive for the HIV infection by pointing to intravenous drug use among some prostitutes. COYOTE concedes that to the extent that prostitutes have become infected, their rate of infection has paralleled the rate among intravenous drug users in their communities. As Gloria Lockett argued on *The Geraldo Show* in 1989: "You're focusing mostly on prostitutes when you should be focusing on drug use. *That* is the problem."

Through claims such as these, the focus on prostitutes and prostitution as vectors of disease is purported to be misguided, while a distinction between drug-using and non-drug-using prostitutes is enforced.

OPPOSING MANDATORY TESTING

In addition to promoting the notion that prostitutes do not represent a "pool of contagion," COYOTE has distributed public announcements, attended conferences, issued press releases, and staged protests to oppose legislation requiring the mandatory testing of prostitutes for the AIDS virus. COYOTE has protested on the grounds that selective forced testing is discriminatory and thus a violation of individuals'—in this case prostitutes'—civil rights. As the codirector of COYOTE argued in 1988: "prostitutes should not be targeted for measures which so patently violate our civil rights." Many of COYOTE's recent protests are in direct response to the threat of mandatory testing. Newspaper editorials and press reports reiterate the theme that mandatory testing is a violation of individuals' civil rights, including those of prostitutes. For example, in response to the introduction of a series of state bills targeting mental patients, prisoners,

and prostitutes for mandatory AIDS testing, including one to repeal the guarantee of confidentiality of AIDS tests, a COYOTE spokeswoman offered the following plea in a 1987 guest editorial in the *Oakland Tribune*:

Mandatory testing for the AIDS virus has been discredited by almost the entire medical establishment as counterproductive in the battle against the disease. . . . However, these plans are promoted by our president and legislators who say they want to reduce the public's fear of contamination by the undesirables of our society. On the surface, mandatory testing of prostitutes and prisoners sounds like it makes sense, representing an effort to control "lawbreakers." But, if we look below the surface, we see people who are already victimized by unfair laws and the discriminatory enforcement of them: gays, prostitutes, and people of color.

Remarks such as these remain fairly consistent with the advocacy work of other minority groups protesting on their own behalf in light of the AIDS epidemic. Like these other groups, COYOTE protests the implementation of mandatory AIDS testing on the grounds that it is a violation of individuals' rights, especially the right to privacy.

The prostitutes' rights movement's AIDS-related claims also point to the selective nature of mandatory testing as further evidence of civil rights violations. At a press conference held to discuss a mandatory testing bill that passed both houses of the California legislature, Gloria Lockett stated: "If, in the name public health, there is to be a law against people who are HIV positive having sex, let it apply to everyone, not just the most politically vulnerable groups." COYOTE's AIDS-related claims contain themes of their earlier claims about the law and its selective enforcement as the source of prostitutes' victimization and prostitution as a civil rights issue. However, the urgency of pressing AIDS-related claims required a circumvention of the movement's original primary goals.

ORGANIZATIONAL GOAL DISPLACEMENT

It is not uncommon for social movement organizations to modify, transform, and occasionally even to subvert the objectives for which they were originally established. Occasionally, they abandon the goals for which they were originally created, and adopt goals that facilitate the immediate and/or long-range survival of the organizations. In the latter part of the 1980s, COYOTE constituted an instance of this sort of organizational goal displacement. Namely, there was a demonstrable shift away from COYOTE's original primary goal of decriminalizing prostitution to a focus on responding to the scapegoating of prostitutes for AIDS, and by extension, on combating the increased social control of prostitution. This made sense.

According to one COYOTE leader: "We [COYOTE] don't have time for focusing on a concerted effort on decriminalization—we're worried about quarantining [of prostitutes]."

AIDS education efforts have taken primacy as the substantive organizational goal of COYOTE, even as it still advocates the decriminalization of prostitution. No later than the summer of 1985, COYOTE began focusing on the social problem of AIDS full force, often almost exclusively. At the Second National Hookers' Convention, for example, participants spent the majority of their time discussing AIDS at great length and developing statements and policies on mandatory testing, quarantining, risk reduction measures, and the need for public education.

CONCLUSION

Clearly, the AIDS crisis significantly reshaped the course of COYOTE's crusade. It has resulted in moving the prostitutes' rights movement away from feminist discourse and into public health discourse. The substance of its claims increasingly has been attentive to the way in which the AIDS epidemic has implicated prostitutes by constructing them as diseased women who are a danger.

COYOTE has been quick to respond to the emergent view of prostitutes as "deadly pools of contagion" and the policy proposals deriving from such a view. From the mid-1980s on, the prostitutes' rights movement has been preoccupied with dismantling the image of prostitutes as contractors, carriers, and transmitters of the HIV virus. In an effort to do so, COYOTE has undertaken numerous campaigns that target public health officials, as well as local and state legislators. These campaigns have challenged responses to AIDS by pressing claims about prostitutes' lower HIV infection rates, as well as prostitutes' historic attentiveness to monitoring their health and the health of their clients. Combined, these claims support the larger effort to construe public officials' response to AIDS as one of political scapegoating; in this case, it is the scapegoating of prostitutes and other marginalized populations. With this view of the problem in hand, COYOTE has become recognizable as a watchdog organization engaging in a defensive crusade to defend prostitutes against frequently proposed and increasingly adopted legislation.

Conrad and Schneider - Deviance and Medicalization: From Badness to Sickness

1 DEVIANCE, DEFINITIONS, and the MEDICAL PROFESSION

A slow but steady transformation of deviance has taken place in American society. It has not been a change in behavior as such, but in how behavior is defined. Deviant behaviors that were once defined as immoral, sinful, or criminal have been given medical meanings. Some say that rehabilitation has replaced punishment, but in many cases medical treatments have become a new form of punishment and social control. This transformation is certainly not complete and has not been entirely unidirectional. These changes have not occurred by themselves nor have they been the result of a "natural" evolution of society or the inevitable progress of medicine. The roots of these changes lie deep in our social and cultural heritage, and the process itself can be traced through the workings of specific people, events, ideas, and techniques. We believe that, aside from its technical and intellectual aspects, this change is surely profoundly political in nature with real political consequences. This book presents an analysis of the historical transformation of definitions of deviance from "badness"* to "sickness" and discusses the consequences of these changes. It focuses on the medicalization of deviance in American society.

In this first chapter we introduce our study of deviance. We delineate the two major orienta-

tions to deviance and illustrate the interactionist view of deviance with the example of the infamous episode of deviance in 17th-century Salem Village. We discuss the universality and relativity of deviance and define the concept of social control. Because this book focuses on the importance of medicine in the changing definitions of deviance, we offer a capsule analysis of the development and structure of medicine in American society. The criminalization of abortion serves as an example of medical involvement in deviance definitions. Finally, at the end of the chapter we present an overview of the rest of the book.

SOCIOLOGICAL ORIENTATIONS TO DEVIANCE

There are many ways to study what sociologists call deviance. Even if we limit ourselves to sociological perspectives, there is a great variety of assumptions, definitions, and research methods from which to choose. We believe, however, that there are two general orientations to deviance in sociology that lead in distinct directions and produce different and sometimes conflicting conclusions about what deviance is and how sociologists and others should address it. We call these two orientations the positivist and the interactionist approaches. Others have made similar distinctions using different labels: correctional and appreciative (Matza, 1969), absolutist and relativist (Hills, 1977), scientific and humanistic (Thio, 1978), and objectivist and subjectivist (Goode, 1978). Such labels are merely signposts that summarize content. It is to the substance of these two orientations that we now turn.

The *positivist* approach assumes that deviance is real, that it exists in the objective experi-

---

*Although perhaps a bastardized term, we believe "badness" expresses best the *general* unequivocal morality typical of virtually all traditional major deviance designations, for example, "sin," "crime." Our subtitle, *From Badness to Sickness,* allows us to emphasize precisely the kinds of changes we believe inherent in the medicalization of deviance, that is, a shift from explicit moral judgments of deviants to the implicit and subtle morality of "sickness."

ence of the people who commit deviant acts and those who respond to them. This view of deviance rests on a second important assumption—that deviance is definable in a straightforward manner as behavior not within permissible conformity to social norms. These norms are believed part of a moral or value consensus in society that is both widely known and shared. Positivists devote much of their study of deviance to a search for causes of deviant behavior. In sociology such causes are usually described in terms of some aspect of social and/or cultural environment and one's socialization. Positivists outside sociology typically search for causes in physiology and/or psyche. In medicine, for example, this search is called etiology.* The major questions about deviants the positivist might ask are, Why do they do it? and How can we make them stop?

The *interactionist* orientation to deviance views the morality of society as socially constructed and relative to actors, context, and historical time. Fundamental to this view is the proposition that morality does not just happen; since it is socially constructed, there must be constructors. Morality becomes the product of certain people making claims based on their own particular interests, values, and views of the world. Those who have comparatively more power in a society are typically more able to create and impose their rules and sanctions on the less powerful. In consequence, deviance becomes actions or conditions that are defined as inappropriate to or in violation of certain powerful groups' conventions. Such deviance is believed to be caused not by mysterious forces beyond the individual's control but rather the consequence of particular definitions and rules being applied by members of certain groups to other people and/or situations. The interactionist view assumes that the behaviors called deviant are by and large voluntary and that people exercise some degree of "free will" in their lives. Deviance is then a social definition, and research focuses on how such definitions are constructed, how deviant labels are attached to particular people, and what the consequences

are both for those labeled and the authors of such attributions. The major questions about deviants an interactionist might ask are, Who made these deviants? How did they do it? and With what consequences?

This classification, of course, simplifies some complex and contentious theoretical issues. Some of these will be evident in later discussions. General categories such as these necessarily do a certain degree of violence to reality, but we believe this distinction is essentially faithful to broad patterns of sociological theory and research. Finally, we do not mean to suggest that these two orientations are never combined in research on deviance; in fact, some of the best studies have adopted elements of both.

The approach taken in this book is decidedly interactionist. Our main concern is with changing definitions of deviance and the consequences of these changes. The interactionist study of deviance usually focuses on the social processes of defining and labeling deviants in contemporary society. Only rarely have interactionists ventured into history and attempted to use similar assumptions to understand the development of historical definitions of deviance. What makes this book different from most interactionist studies is that we focus explicitly on the sociohistorical development of the definitions of deviance. To the extent we succeed in adding this *historical dimension* to the interactionist study of deviance, we have made a contribution to the development and clarification of the interactionist approach.

This book is a study of deviance, but it is also a study of morality. In the interactionist view the morality of a society—the application of notions of "right" and "wrong"—are relative and socially constructed. There is no absolute morality, although in a world of competing moralities we may prefer some over others because they seem to us more human and life-supporting. Morality and deviance are both products of complex social interaction. In our study of changing definitions of deviance we are also studying changing morality. The individuals and collectivities engaged in defining deviance are at the same time defining morality. Although we mention this several times throughout this text, it might be useful to keep in mind

---

*It may be helpful to remember throughout this book that the medical model of deviance is essentially a positivist or correctional one.

that this is as much a study of morality as it is a study of deviance.

A word should be said about the term "deviance." We use it in its technical, sociological sense to refer to behavior that is negatively defined or condemned in our society. When we use the term, we do not imply any specific judgment or that we think the behavior is bad or sick. On the contrary, in some cases a considerable disjunction exists between our views and the dominant societal view. We use the term "deviance" to depict how the behavior or activity is generally defined in society.

To introduce our study of deviance and morality, we turn now to an event of 17th-century Massachusetts: the witchcraft phenomenon of Salem Village. Our intention is to illustrate what deviance is and how it is created in a particular social setting.

WITCHCRAFT IN SALEM VILLAGE

In 1692 in the New England community of Salem Village occurred one of the most remarkable and notorious episodes of deviance production in American history.* In the cold January winter of that year a number of young girls were stricken with a strange malady and began to behave in alarming ways. The first two affected were Betty Parris (age 9) and Abigail Williams (age 11). Betty became forgetful, distracted, and preoccupied. She sometimes would sit staring fixedly at an invisible object and, if interrupted, would scream and begin an incomprehensible babble.

> [Abigail] too was absent-minded . . . and began to make babbling and rasping sounds. . . . She got down on all fours and ran about under the furniture, barking and braying, and sometimes fell into convulsions when she writhed and screamed as if suffering the torments of the damned. (Starkey, 1949, p. 40)†

In addition to the "fits," the victims frequently

---

*Our discussion provides only a brief summary of the events at Salem. For more detailed description and analysis, see Marion L. Starkey (1949), Kai T. Erikson (1966, pp. 137-59), Chadwick Hansen (1969), and Paul Boyer and Stephen Nissenbaum (1974).

†Reprinted by permission of Curtis Brown, Ltd. Copyright © 1949 by Marion Lena Starkey, renewed 1977.

suffered a temporary loss of hearing and loss of memory and often felt as if they were being choked and suffocated. Vivid and frightening hallucinations tormented and terrified them. Whatever this fearful malady was, it was also contagious. Other girls soon were stricken.

The girls were taken by their parents to physicians who examined them but found no medical problems and were puzzled by this strange behavior. A local physician, however, believed that he understood the problem but that it was out of his realm of expertise. "The evil hand is on them," he announced. The girls were victims of witchcraft.

The Devil was at work in Salem Village. Within a short time half a dozen young girls were stricken. Fears and suspicions mounted. Who, the community leaders asked, were the Devil's accomplices? Who had afflicted these poor children? Ministers from nearby communities were summoned to help Salem Village deal with its emergency. These observers confirmed the community's worst fears: the girls' maladies were real and resulted from supernatural forces.

> "The motions of their fits," wrote the Reverend Deodat Lawson, "are preternatural, both as to the manner, which is so strange as a well person could not screw their body into; and as to the violence also it is preternatural, being much beyond the ordinary force of the same person when they are in their right mind." The Reverend John Hale of Beverly confirmed Lawson's description. "Their arms, necks and backs," he wrote, "were turned this way and that way, and returned back again, so it was impossible for them to do of themselves, and beyond the power of any epileptic fits, or natural disease to effect." (Hansen, 1969, p. 11).

The community leaders and the ministers reached a decision. "The girls must be induced to name their tormenters; the witches must be ferreted out and brought to justice" (Starkey, 1949, p. 45).*

With little urging, the girls named the three witches who were terrorizing them: Tituba, a slave from the West Indies who was acquainted with voodoo and magic; Sarah Good, a pipe-

---

*Reprinted by permission of Curtis Brown, Ltd. Copyright © 1949 by Marion Lena Starkey, renewed 1977.

smoking woman known for her slovenliness and begging and considered neglectful of her children; and Sarah Osborne, a woman of higher standing, but who was negligent in her church attendance and had scandalized the community a year or so earlier by living with a man for a short time before he became her husband (Erikson, 1966). The accused women were all marginal members of the community; in effect, they were outsiders even before the accusations.

The preliminary hearings took place in the meeting house. They were presided over by colony magistrates, who were to ascertain whether enough evidence existed for an actual trial. This was serious business in Salem because the Puritans took literally the biblical injunction "Thou shalt not permit a witch to live." Conviction of witchcraft meant sure death. Certain rules of evidence were agreed on.

They would accept as proof of guilt the finding of any "teat" or "devil's mark," that is to say any unnatural excrescence on the bodies of the accused. They would accept as ground for suspicion of guilt any mischief following anger between neighbours. And most important of all, they would accept the doctrine that "the devil could not assume the shape of an innocent person in doing mischief to mankind." (Starkey, 1949, p. 53)*

It was this final criterion of evidence that was critical. It simply meant that the Devil could not appear in the form of anyone who was not guilty of witchcraft. This was called "spectral evidence." It enabled hallucinations, dreams, and visions to be accepted in court "as factual proof not of the psychological condition of the accuser but of the behavior of the accused" (Starkey, 1949, p. 54). It was evidence that was impossible to disprove, for if one of the girls accused a person's "specter" or "shade" of haunting them, the accused was left without a defense. It was prima facie evidence for association with the Devil and thus guilt of witchcraft.

The hearings must have been quite a scene. There was a somber excitement in town, and

many people packed the meeting house to see the alleged witches examined. The afflicted girls were given a place of honor in front of the hall. When the accused were brought in, the girls began to yell, writhe, and convulse in apparent agony. When questioned, the girls pointed to specters of the accused flying around the room, pinching and tormenting their victims. (Of course, none of the observers could see these specters.) Sarah Good and Sarah Osborne categorically denied their guilt. But when Tituba spoke, a hush settled over the meeting house, for Tituba was confessing to consorting with the Devil. For 3 days she told the astonished court about the "invisible world" of spirits and apparitions with which she had contact. She suggested there were still others in the community with whom she (and the Devil) had consorted. These three women were dispatched to jail to await trial, but the witch-hunt had only begun.

Salem Village was in crisis. Somber excitement was giving way to fearful panic. The Devil was out to take people's souls, and the good God-fearing people of Salem must fight him to the hilt. The afflicted girls were the instruments through which the dastardly witches could be discovered. They performed their witch-finding chores with zeal and gusto. The girls seemed to relish all the attention they received and the power they were given. Within the next 6 months this troop of young girls accused nearly 200 people of consorting with the Devil. Some righteous and upstanding citizens were accused, as well as individuals from distant communities. Farmers, grandmothers, children, even a reverend; if the girls claimed the individual's specter was haunting them, the accused was taken to prison to await a hearing. The community was stunned, but the fear of witchcraft prevailed.

Dozens of the accused were brought to trial, and before the year was out, 19 witches had been executed by hanging, two had died in jail, and one was crushed to death during an interrogation. When the girls began to accuse some of the town's most respected individuals, however, doubts about their infallible judgment began to grow. Toward the year's end people were openly expressing concern about the trials

---

*Reprinted by permission of Curtis Brown, Ltd. Copyright © 1949 by Marion Lena Starkey, renewed 1977.

and executions and especially about the validity of "spectral evidence." After the magistrates reversed their earlier decision and decided to disallow spectral evidence, there remained no way other than confession to ascertain guilt in witchcraft. Nearly all those still accused were acquitted. The hundred or so yet residing in jails were released, and the few who had confessed or had been found guilty were granted reprieves. The witchcraft hysteria of Salem Village was over.

Witchcraft as deviance is a fascinating subject to study. Numerous scholars have attempted to understand what happened in Salem Village in 1692. Most agree that the girls' behaviors today would be diagnosed as "hysteria," a psychological disorder rather than a result of witchcraft, and that nearly all the accused were innocent. Several theories have been postulated as to the causes of the witchcraft outbreak. Starkey (1949) suggests that it was a case of mass hysteria caused by Puritan repression and guilt. Erikson (1966) theorizes that the witch trials were an attempt to resolve a "crisis" over the social boundaries of the changing Puritan colony. Hansen (1969) asserts that there were undoubtedly a few practitioners of witchcraft in Salem, and the girls' fear of bewitchment made them hysterical. We need not choose between these theories here because we present the Salem witchcraft example only to illustrate the social construction of deviance rather than to explain the behaviors involved. The example will serve us through the next few pages as we begin to develop our study of deviance.

UNIVERSALITY AND RELATIVITY OF DEVIANCE

What is deviance? For the moment, let us say simply that deviance consists of those categories of condemnation and negative judgment which are constructed and applied successfully to some members of a social community by others. We intentionally avoid the notion that the essence of deviance is in actors' behaviors; rather, we argue that it is a quality attributed to such persons and behaviors by others. For example, "witchcraft" and all it entailed in 17th-century Salem Village was deviance. We

will develop this concept of deviance considerably as we proceed.

Deviance is a universal phenomenon. All societies have definitions of some behaviors or activities as deviant or morally reprehensible. The very notion that a society has social norms or rules ensures the existence of deviance. There can be no deviance without social rules (and, as far as we know, there can be no society without rules and norms, either). As Emile Durkheim (1895/1938) pointed out, deviance is "normal" to society. "Imagine.a society of saints," wrote Durkheim,

a perfect cloister of exemplary individuals. Crimes [or deviance], properly so called, will there be unknown; but faults which appear venial to the layman will create there the same scandal that the ordinary offense does in ordinary consciousnesses. If, then, this society has the power to judge and punish, it will define these acts as criminal [or deviant] and will treat them as such. (pp. 68-69)*

Durkheim touches on many important aspects of deviance in this short passage: deviance is universal, deviance is a social definition, social groups make rules and enforce their definitions on members through judgment and social sanction, deviance is contextual, and defining and sanctioning deviance involves power. Let us consider these one at a time.

1. Deviance is universal, but there are no universal forms of deviance. There are few acts, if any, that are defined as deviance in all societies under all conditions. Incest probably conforms most closely to a universal definition of deviance. Yet different societies consider different activities to be incest: some societies prohibit only brother-sister relations, whereas others consider relations between third cousins to be incestuous. A few societies encourage sexual relationships between parents and children, and in several, siblings may engage freely in all sexual activity until puberty. Premeditated murder is also considered deviant in most societies, but there are societies in which a man who kills an-

*From Durkheim, E. *Rules of the sociological method.* New York: The Free Press, 1938. Copyright 1938 by the University of Chicago. (Originally published, 1895.)

other man for committing adultery with his wife is deemed justified. Even incest and murder are not universally deviant.

Deviance is also relative. Different societies define different activities as deviant. In contemporary American society the young girls of Salem might find their behavior defined as deviant (i.e., hysterical) rather than the behaviors of those they accused of witchcraft. Certain forms of homosexuality were acceptable among the cultural elite in classical Greece, but in America such conduct is condemned and stigmatized. Suicide is considered deviant and ungodly in most of the Christian world, whereas in Imperial Japan it could be an honorable act. The extremely suspicious and treacherous behavior of the Dobu of Melanesia would be labeled "paranoid" by modern psychiatric standards, but it would be the accepting and unsuspicious individual who would be a deviant among the Dobu. Ruth Benedict's (1934) notion of "cultural relativity" is useful here: each society should be viewed by its own conceptions and standards. What is deviant for a society is relative to that society: witchcraft among the Puritans, hysteria and paranoia in American society.

2. Deviance is a social definition. That is, deviance is not "given" in any behavior, act, or status. It must be so defined intentionally by "significant" actors in the society or social group. In Erikson's (1966) words, "Deviance is not a property *inherent in* any particular kind of behavior; it is a property *conferred upon* that behavior by the people who come into direct or indirect contact with it" (p. 6). Deviance may be seen as a label attached to an act or behavior or as a category by which certain behaviors are defined. Thus deviance is a socially *attributed* condition, and "deviant" is an *ascribed* status. Deviance does not inhere in the individual or the behavior; it is a social judgment of that behavior. In short, it is not the act but the definition that makes something deviant.

This view of deviance allows us to separate the *definition* of the behavior and the *behavior* itself. Each may be studied separately. In this light we see deviance as a *system of social categories* constructed for classifying behavior, persons, situations, and things. Puritan society inherited a long tradition of defining certain behaviors as witchcraft (Currie, 1968). Witchcraft, regardless of whether we believe in it, was a generally accepted category for "deviant" behavior to the Puritans. In Puritan society there were certain more or less agreed-on criteria for assignment to this deviant category (p. 4, just as we have criteria for applying our contemporary definitions of deviance. As sociologists we may study the origins of witchcraft as a category of deviance, as well as study the "causes" of witchcraft behavior. In other words, we may examine the etiology of social definitions of deviance separately from the etiology of the behaviors labeled as deviant. We can ask, for example, how it was that abortion was defined as deviant until recently rather than ask what caused people to have or perform the abortions (we present this example later in this chapter). Again, the definition is separated from the behavior or act. Deviance definitions may change over time. Witchcraft is no longer a relevant type of deviance in American society, but juvenile delinquency, opiate addiction, and child abuse, unknown to the Puritans, are well-accepted contemporary categories of deviance. The approach we take in this book is to analyze the changing definitions of deviance, which may or may not be related to actual changes in "deviant" behavior. We develop this further in Chapter 2.

3. Social groups make rules and enforce their definitions on members through judgment and social sanction. Although we view deviance definitions as social categories, in reality they are not separate from their use and application. Definitions do not create themselves: "social groups create deviance by making the rules whose infraction constitutes deviance, and applying those rules to particular people and labeling them as [deviants]" (Becker, H. S., 1963, p. 9). The leaders of Salem Village "created" deviance by making and enforcing rules whose infraction constituted deviance. (Had they ignored the girls' behavior, the witch trials probably never would have occurred.) Admittedly, most instances of deviance are not nearly as clear examples of the creation and application of rules to produce deviance as the Salem episode, but collective rule making, social

judgment, and the application of sanctions (penalties) are central to all types of deviance. What is important to remember is that "societies" do not make rules and define deviance; people acting collectively do.

4. Deviance is contextual. By this we mean that what is labeled as deviant varies by social context—especially according to such conditions as society, subculture, time, place, who is involved, and who is offended. Willfully taking another's life usually is considered deviant, but not on a battlefield when the victim is defined as the enemy. Marijuana smoking is by law deviant in most states, but in many youth subcultures it would be the nonsmoker who would be defined deviant. Masturbation was defined as a sin and disease in Victorian times but today is considered healthy. Suicide by an 80-year-old man with terminal cancer may be considered by many as justifiable, whereas a suicide attempt by a college student ordinarily is seen as deviant and usually leads to psychiatric treatment. Thus "what" and "who" are "deviant" depends significantly on social context.

5. Defining and sanctioning deviance involves power. In general, powerful people and groups are able to establish and legitimate their morality and definitions of deviance. Those belonging to the more powerful groups in society, in terms of social class, age, race, ethnicity, profession, sex, etc., can enforce their categories of deviance on less powerful groups. It is seldom vice versa. In the witchcraft example the community and religious leaders of Salem Village (all men) were able to implement their categories of deviance on the accused witches (mostly women). Similarly adults make rules children must live by, the middle and upper classes define deviance in the lower classes (perhaps that is one reason why so much deviance is found among the lower classes), and a prestigious profession such as medicine makes rules whose violation is nearly universally termed sickness. We shall discuss the power dimension further in Chapter 2.

In summary, deviance is universal yet widely variable. It is in essence a social judgment and definition and therefore culturally relative. Deviance is socially created by rule making and

enforcement, usually by powerful groups over people in less powerful positions.

SOCIAL CONTROL

Social control is a central and important concept in sociology. Developed by Edward A. Ross (1901) around the turn of the century, the term was used to describe the processes societies developed for regulating themselves. Social control meant social regulation. In the past two decades, however, its common sociological usage has changed. Perhaps dating from the work of Talcott Parsons (1951), social control began to be used in a narrower sense to mean the control of deviance and the promotion of conformity. This is the common usage today, although there are some who call for a return to its original meaning as societal regulation (Janowitz, 1975).

Social control is usually conceptualized as the means by which society secures adherence to social norms; specifically, how it minimizes, eliminates, or normalizes deviant behavior. Even when we limit our discussion of social control to the control of deviance, it is still a broad and complex topic. We introduce here a few dimensions of social control most directly relevant to our argument in this book (for more complete discussions see Pitts, 1968, and Roucek, 1978). Social control operates on both informal and formal levels and through "positive" and "negative" forms. Informal controls include self-controls and relational controls. Self-controls reside within individuals (although their source is external and therefore social) and include internalized norms, beliefs, morals, self-concept, and what is commonly called "conscience." Relational controls are a regular feature of the face-to-face interactions of everyday life. They include such common interactions as ridicule, praise, gossip, smiles, disapproving glances and "dirty looks," mythmaking, group ostracism and support, and essentially any negative or positive sanction for behavior. Informal controls both inhibit individuals from behavior that might be considered deviant and encourage conformity by positive sanction. In most cases these informal controls do not lead to an individual being defined and labeled as deviant, for we are all subject to these controls daily. Formal social control is less ubiquitous in everyday life, but its consequences are usually much more profound and enduring to the individual and society. (Sociologists have studied negative and formal social control far more thoroughly than informal and positive social control, perhaps because the latter are much more difficult to study.) Formal social controls are institutionalized forms of social control. Although they include "the 'official' laws, regulations, and understandings that are supposed to encompass all the members of a group or society" (Buckner, 1971, p. 14), sociologists usually think of formal social control in terms of *institutions* and *agents* of social control. They may be depicted as social control apparatuses that operate, explicitly and implicitly, to secure adherence to a particular set of values and norms, and in this work, to sanction deviance. In our society we usually think of the criminal justice system, with the police, courts, correctional facilities, and auxiliary personnel, as the major institution of social control. Other institutions such as education, welfare, the mass media, and medicine are also frequently depicted as having social control functions.

The greatest social control power comes from having the authority to define certain behaviors, persons, and things. This right to define may reside in an abstract authority such as "the law" or God but is implemented commonly through some institutional force such as the state or church. Such institutions, then (or, perhaps better, the people who represent them), have the mandate to define the problem (e.g., as deviance), designate what type of problem it is, and indicate what should be done about it. In our witchcraft example, representatives of the church (ministers) and the state (magistrates) agreed on the definition of the problem, witchcraft (so, incidentally, did the physician), but it was essentially a theological definition that prevailed (i.e., it was a question of witchcraft, or consorting with the Devil). As we mentioned earlier, a modern psychiatrist might have defined the problem as the young girls' being "hysterical," but there were no psychiatrists with any authority in Salem to challenge the witchcraft definition.

Social control, then, can be seen as the power

to have a particular set of definitions of the world realized in both spirit and practice. To the extent that such definitions receive widespread and/or "significant" social support, this power becomes authority and thereby considerably more secure from attack and challenge. This authority, not uncommonly, may become vested in a dominant institution. For example, during the Middle Ages and through the Inquisition the Church had the authority and power to define activities as deviant. With the decline of the Church and the subsequent secularization, the state increasingly gained authority to define deviance. When an institution (e.g., the church, state, medical profession) gains the power and authority to define deviance, that is, to say what kind of a problem something is, the responsibility for dealing with the problem often comes to that institution. In this sense we can say institutions can define their own social control "turf." Representatives of an institution may linguistically stake claims to deviance territory and thus attempt to justify their authority and legitimacy. In areas where an institution's definitions become dominant and accepted, it is capable of defining the territory of its work. The institution and the practitioners within it become designated "experts" in dealing with the problem, or at least stewards of its social control.

It is important to remember that any given "problem" can be viewed by different eyes and thus may be defined and analyzed in different ways. For example, the problems of deviant drinking can be seen as "caused" by sinfulness, moral weakness, psychological disturbance, genetic predisposition, adaptation to stress, or other influences (the problem could also be defined as caused by the promotion and distribution of the liquor industry). What the problem "really" is may be debated and argued; deviant drinking is not obviously one certain type of problem. The right to define a "problem," and thereby locate it within a particular social control turf, is achieved typically through enterprise, strategy, and struggle. We will encounter numerous examples of this throughout the book.

This book examines how increasing forms of deviant behavior have been defined as medical problems and thereby properly under medical social control. We examine how medicine achieved the authority to define problems as "sickness" rather than "badness" and analyze the consequences of this transformation. We begin this discussion in the next chapter. Before we start this examination, however, it is important to review briefly medicine's rather recent rise to dominance in American society.

THE MEDICAL PROFESSION AND DEVIANCE IN AMERICA

Since the dominant theme of this book concerns the change in definitions of deviance from badness to sickness and the expansion of medicine as an agent of social control, it is important to have some understanding of the historical development of medical practice and the medical profession. Medicine has not always been the powerful, prestigious, successful, lucrative, and dominant profession we know today. The status of the medical profession is a product of medical politicking as well as therapeutic expertise. This discussion presents a brief overview of the development of the medical profession and its rise to dominance.

Emergence of the medical profession: up to 1850

In ancient societies, disease was given supernatural explanations, and "medicine" was the province of priests or shamans. It was in classical Greece that medicine began to emerge as a separate occupation and develop its own theories, distinct from philosophy or theology. Hippocrates, the great Greek physician who refused to accept supernatural explanations or treatments for disease, developed a theory of the "natural" causes of disease and systematized all available medical knowledge. He laid a basis for the development of medicine as a separate body of knowledge. Early Christianity depicted sickness as punishment for sin, engendering new theological explanations and treatments. Christ and his disciples believed in the supernatural causes and cures of disease. This view became institutionalized in the Middle Ages, when the Church dogma dominated theories and practice of medicine and priests were physicians. The Renaissance in Europe brought a renewed interest in ancient Greek medical knowledge. This marked the beginning of a

drift toward natural explanations of disease and the emergence of medicine as an occupation separate from the Church (Cartwright, F. F., 1977).

But European medicine developed slowly. The "humoral theory" of disease developed by Hippocrates dominated medical theory and practice until well into the 19th century. Medical diagnosis was impressionistic and often inaccurate, depicting conditions in such general terms as "fevers" and "fluxes." In the 17th century, physicians relied mainly on three techniques to determine the nature of illness: what the patient said about symptoms; the physician's own observations of signs of illness and the patient's appearance and behavior; and, more rarely, a manual examination of the body (Reiser, 1978, p. 1). Medicine was by no means scientific, and "medical thought involved unverified doctrines and resulting controversies" (Shryock, 1960, p. 52). Medical practice was a "bedside medicine" that was patient oriented and did not distinguish the illness from the "sick man" (Jewson, 1976). It was not until Thomas Sydenham's astute observations in the late 17th century that physicians could begin to distinguish between the patient and the disease. Physicians possessed few treatments that worked regularly, and many of their treatments actually worsened the sufferer's condition. Medicine in colonial America inherited this European stock of medical knowledge.

Colonial American medicine was less developed than its European counterpart. There were no medical schools and few physicians, and because of the vast frontier and sparse population, much medical care was in effect self-help. Most American physicians were educated and trained by apprenticeship; few were university trained. With the exception of surgeons, most were undifferentiated practitioners. Medical practices were limited. Prior to the revolution, physicians did not commonly attend births; midwives, who were not seen as part of the medical establishment, routinely attended birthings (Wertz and Wertz, 1977). William Rothstein (1972) notes that "American colonial medical practice, like European practice of the period, was characterized by the lack of any substantial body of usable scientific knowledge" (p. 27). Physicians, both educated and otherwise, tended to treat their patients pragmatically, for medical theory had little to offer. Most colonial physicians practiced medicine only part-time, earning their livelihoods as clergymen, teachers, farmers, or in other occupations. Only in the early 19th century did medicine become a full-time vocation (Rothstein, 1972).

The first half of the 19th century saw important changes in the organization of the medical profession. About 1800, "regular," or educated, physicians convinced state legislatures to pass laws limiting the practice of medicine to practitioners of a certain training and class (prior to this nearly anyone could claim the title "doctor" and practice medicine). These state licensing laws were not particularly effective, largely because of the colonial tradition of medical self-help. They were repealed in most states during the Jacksonian period (1828-1836) because they were thought to be elitist, and the temper of the times called for a more "democratic" medicine.

The repeal of the licensing laws and the fact that most "regular" (i.e., regularly educated) physicians shared and used "a distinctive set of medically invalid therapies, known as 'heroic' therapy," created fertile conditions for the emergence of *medical sects* in the first half of the 19th century (Rothstein, 1972, p. 21). Physicians of the time practiced a "heroic" and invasive form of medicine consisting primarily of such treatments as bloodletting, vomiting, blistering, and purging. This highly interventionist, and sometimes dangerous, form of medicine engendered considerable public opposition and resistance. In this context a number of medical sects emerged, the most important of which were the homeopathic and botanical physicians. These "irregular" medical practitioners practiced less invasive, less dangerous forms of medicine. They each developed a considerable following, since their therapies were probably no less effective than those of regulars practicing heroic medicine. The regulars attempted to exclude them from practice; so the various sects set up their own medical schools and professional societies. This sectarian medicine created a highly *competitive* situation for the regulars (Rothstein, 1972). Medical sectarianism, heroic therapies, and ineffective treatment con-

tributed to the low status and lack of prestige of early 19th-century medicine. At this time, medicine was neither a prestigious occupation nor an important economic activity in American society (Starr, 1977).

The regular physicians were concerned about this situation. Large numbers of regularly trained physicians sought to earn a livelihood by practicing medicine (Rothstein, 1972, p. 3). They were troubled by the poor image of medicine and lack of standards in medical training and practice. No doubt they were also concerned about the competition of the irregular sectarian physicians. A group of regular physicians founded the American Medical Association (AMA) in 1847 "to promote the science and art of medicine and the betterment of public health" (quoted in Coe, 1978, p. 204). The AMA also was to set and enforce standards and ethics of "regular" medical practice and strive for exclusive professional and economic rights to the medical turf.

The AMA was the crux of the regulars' attempt to "professionalize" medicine. As Magali Sarfatti Larson (1977) points out, professions organize to create and control *markets*. Organized professions attempt to regulate and limit the competition, usually by controlling professional education and by limiting licensing. Professionalization is, in this view, "the process by which producers of special services sought to constitute *and control* the market for their expertise" (Larson, 1977, p. xvi). The regular physicians and the AMA set out to consolidate and control the market for medical services. As we shall see in the next two sections, the regulars were successful in professionalization, eliminating competition and creating a medical monopoly.

Crusading, deviance, and medical monopoly: the case of abortion

The medical profession after the middle of the 19th century was frequently involved in various activities that could be termed social reform. Some of these reforms were directly related to health and illness and medical work; others were peripheral to the manifest medical calling of preventing illness and healing the sick. In these reform movements, physicians became medical crusaders, attempting to influence public morality and behavior. This medical crusading often led physicians squarely into the moral sphere, making them advocates for moral positions that had only peripheral relations to medical practice. Not infrequently these reformers sought to change people's values or to impose a set of particular values on others or, as we shall soon see, to create new categories of social deviance. Throughout this book we will often encounter medical crusaders. We now examine one of the more revealing examples of medical crusading: the criminalization of abortion in American society.*

Most people are under the impression that abortion was always defined as deviant and illegal in America prior to the Supreme Court's landmark decision in 1973. This, however, is not the case. American abortion policy, and the attendant defining of abortion as deviant, were specific products of medical crusading. Prior to the Civil War, abortion was a common and largely legal medical procedure performed by various types of physicians and midwives. A pregnancy was not considered confirmed until the occurrence of a phenomenon called "quickening," the first perception of fetal movement. Common law did not recognize the fetus before quickening in criminal cases, and an unquickened fetus was deemed to have no living soul. Thus most people did not consider termination of pregnancy before quickening to be an especially serious matter, much less murder. Abortion before quickening created no moral or medical problems. Public opinion was indifferent, and for the time it was probably a relatively safe medical procedure. Thus, for all intents and purposes, American women were free to terminate their pregnancies before quickening in the early 19th century. Moreover, it was a procedure relatively free of the moral stigma that was attached to abortion in this century.

After 1840 abortion came increasingly into public view. Abortion clinics were vigorously and openly advertised in newspapers and mag-

azines. The advertisements offered euphemistically couched services for "women's complaints," "menstrual blockage," and "obstructed menses." Most contemporary observers suggested that more and more women were using these services. Prior to 1840 most abortions were performed on the ummarried and desperate of the "poor and unfortunate classes." However, beginning about this time, significantly increasing numbers of middle- and upper-class white, Protestant, native-born women began to use these services. It is likely they either wished to delay childbearing or thought they already had all the children they wanted (Mohr, 1978, pp. 46-47). By 1870 approximately one abortion was performed for every five live births (Mohr, 1978, pp. 79-80).

Beginning in the 1850s, a number of physicians, especially moral crusader Dr. Horatio Robinson Storer, began writing in medical and popular journals and lobbying in state legislatures about the danger and immorality of abortion. They opposed abortion before and after quickening and under Dr. Storer's leadership organized an aggressive national campaign. In 1859 these crusaders convinced the AMA to pass a resolution condemning abortion. Some newspapers, particularly the *New York Times,* joined the antiabortion crusade. Feminists supported the crusade, since they saw abortion as a threat to women's health and part of the oppression of women. Religious leaders, however, by and large avoided the issue of abortion; either they didn't consider it in their province or found it too sticky an issue to discuss. It was the physicians who were the guiding force in the antiabortion crusade. They were instrumental in convincing legislatures to pass state laws, especially between 1866 and 1877, that made abortion a criminal offense.

Why did physicians take the lead in the antiabortion crusade and work so directly to have abortion defined as deviant and illegal? Undoubtedly they believed in the moral "rightness" of their cause. But social historian James Mohr (1978) presents two more subtle and important reasons for the physicians' antiabortion crusading. First, concern was growing among medical people and even among some legislators about the significant drop in birth-

---

* We rely on James C. Mohr's (1978) fine historical account of the origins and evolution of American abortion policy for data and much of the interpretation in this section.

rates. Many claimed that abortion among married women of the "better classes" was a major contributor to the declining birthrate. These middle- and upper-class men (the physicians and legislators) were aware of the waves of immigrants arriving with large families and were anxious about the decline in production of native American babies. They were deeply afraid they were being betrayed by their own women (Mohr, 1978, p. 169). Implicitly the antiabortion stance was classist and racist; the anxiety was simply that there would not be enough strong, native-born, Protestant stock to save America. This was a persuasive argument in convincing legislators of the need of antiabortion laws.

The second and more direct reason spurring the physicians in the antiabortion crusade was to aid their own nascent professionalization and create a monopoly for regular physicians. As mentioned earlier, the regulars had formed the AMA in 1847 to promote scientific and ethical medicine and combat what they saw as medical quackery. There were, however, no licensing laws to speak of, and many claimed the title "doctor" (e.g., homeopaths, botanical doctors, eclectic physicians). The regular physicians adopted the Hippocratic oath and code of ethics as their standard. Among other things, this oath forbids abortion. Regulars usually did not perform abortions; however, many practitioners of medical sects performed abortions regularly, and some had lucrative practices. Thus for the regular AMA physicians the limitation of abortion became one way of asserting their own professional domination over other medical practitioners. In their crusading these physicians had translated the social goals of cultural and professional dominance into moral and medical language. They lobbied long and hard to convince legislators of the danger and immorality of abortion. By passage of laws making abortion criminal any time during gestation, regular physicians were able to legislate their code of ethics and get the state to employ sanctions against their competitors. This limited these competitors' markets and was a major step toward the regulars' achieving a monopolization of medical practice.

In a relatively short period the antiabortion crusade succeeded in passing legislation that made abortion criminal in every state. A by-product of this was a shift in American public opinion from an indifference to and tolerance of abortion to a hardening of attitudes against what had until then been a fairly common practice. The irony was that abortion as a medical procedure probably was safer at the turn of the 20th century than a century before, but it was defined and seen as more dangerous. By 1900 abortion was not only illegal but deviant and immoral. The physicians' moral crusade had successfully defined abortion as a deviant activity. This definition remained largely unchanged until the 1973 Supreme Court decision, which essentially returned the abortion situation to its pre-1850 condition.

This was not the first nor the last medical venture into the moral world of norm creation and deviance. German physicians in the 18th century proposed development of a "medical police" who would supervise the health and hygiene of the population as well as control activities such as prostitution (Rosen, 1974). Physicians were actively involved in the Temperance and "eugenics" movements of the 19th century. The first legal and involuntary medical sterilizations performed in the United States were on "criminals" by crusading physicians seeking both to curb crime and protect the racial stock (Fink, 1938). The following impassioned defense of such selective and "reformist" sterilization appeared in the *New York Medical Journal* in 1902, written by a surgeon at the Indiana Reformatory:

It is my judgment, founded on research and observation, that this is the rational means of eradicating from our midst a most dangerous and hurtful class. Too much stress cannot be placed upon the present danger to the race. The public must be made to see that radical methods are necessary. Even radical methods may be made to seem just if they are shown to be rational. In this we have a means which is both rational and sufficient. It remains with you—men of science and skill—to perpetuate a known relief to a weakening race by prevailing upon your legislatures to enact such laws as will restrict marriage and give those in charge of State institutions the authority to render every male sterile who passes its portals, whether it be almshouse, insane asylum, institute for the feebleminded, reformatory, or prison. The medical profession has never failed in an attempt, and it will not fail in this. (Sharp, 1902, pp. 413-414).

In the 20th century, physicians were central figures in crusades for social hygiene (Burnham, 1972) and birth control (Gordon, 1975). Physicians often saw their scientific and professional values as the values that ought to guide the behavior of others. Frequently they argued for certain positions in the name of science when the issues were actually moral. As John C. Burnham (1972) observes, "Repeatedly the leaders of American medicine sought to impose such values upon others, that is, to exercise social control" (p. 19).

American medicine and physicians have had a long-lived, historic involvement with deviance and social control. Some diseases were considered indistinguishable from deviant behavior; sufferers were treated as both deviant and sick. Physicians perhaps always have had a significant role in the control and treatment of conditions such as leprosy and epilepsy. Leprosy, a long-term degenerative disease that severely and horribly mutilates its victims, was widespread in the 12th and 13th centuries. It was a highly feared disease (although it is *not* very contagious), and its sufferers were stigmatized and treated as deviants because of their frightful appearance. Since no physical cure was known, the only means of dealing with the disease was social. Physicians were the diagnosticians. If the diagnosis was firmly established, the leper was segregated for life.

He was expelled from human society and deprived of his civil rights; in some places a Requiem was held for him, and thus he was declared dead as far as society was concerned. He lived in a *leprosarium* outside the city walls in the company of other lepers, all of whom were dependent on charity for their sustenance. (Sigerist, 1943, p. 73)

Epilepsy was considered both a disease and a sign of supernatural demonic possession (i.e., deviance) until the 20th century. Surely uncontrolled seizures were a frightening form of deviant behavior, and epileptics were severely stigmatized and frequently segregated (Temkin, 1971). Thus the lines between sickness and deviance sometimes were not clearly drawn: some diseases were considered deviance, and, as we shall demonstrate in upcoming chapters, some deviance became defined as disease. The medical profession would have an increasing role in defining and controlling deviance. This "power" rested at least in part on the growth of medical expertise and professional dominance.

Growth of medical expertise and professional dominance

Although the general public's dissatisfaction with heroic medicine remained, the image of medicine and what it could accomplish was improving by the middle of the 19th century. There had been a considerable reduction in the incidence and mortality of certain dread diseases. The plague and leprosy had nearly disappeared. Smallpox, malaria, and cholera were less devastating than ever before. These improvements in health engendered optimism and increased people's faith in medical practice. Yet these dramatic "conquests of disease" were by and large *not* the result of new medical knowledge or improved clinical medical practice. Rather, they resulted from changes in social conditions: a rising standard of living, better nutrition and housing, and public health innovations like sanitation. With the lone exception of vaccination for smallpox, the decline of these diseases had nearly nothing to do with clinical medicine (Dubos, 1959; McKeown, 1971). But despite lack of effective treatments, medicine was the beneficiary of much popular credit for improved health.

The regular physicians' image was improved well before they demonstrated any unique effectiveness of practice. The AMA's attacks on irregular medical practice continued. In the 1870s the regulars convinced legislatures to outlaw abortion and in some states to restore licensing laws to restrict medical practice. The AMA was becoming an increasingly powerful and authoritative voice representing regular medical practice.

But the last three decades of the century saw significant "breakthroughs" in medical knowledge and treatment. The scientific medicine of the regular physicians was making new medical advances. Anesthesia and antisepsis made possible great strides in surgical medicine and improvements in hospital care. The bacteriological research of Koch and Pasteur developed the "germ theory of disease," which had important applications in medical practice. It was the accomplishments of surgery and bacteriology that put medicine on a scientific basis (Freidson, 1970a, p. 16). The rise of scientific medicine marked a death knell for medical sectarianism (e.g., the homeopathic physicians eventually joined the regulars). The new laboratory sciences provided a way of testing the theories and practices of various sects, which ultimately led to a single model of medical practice. The well-organized regulars were able to legitimate their form of medical practice and support it with "scientific" evidence.

With the emergence of scientific medicine, a unified paradigm, or model, of medical practice developed. It was based, most fundamentally, on viewing the body as a machine (e.g., organ malfunctioning) and on the germ theory of disease (Kelman, 1977). The "doctrine of specific etiology" became predominant: each disease was caused by a specific germ or agent. Medicine focused solely on the internal environment (the body), largely ignoring the external environment (society) (Dubos, 1959). This paradigm proved fruitful in ensuing years. It is the essence of the "medical model" we discuss in Chapter 2.

The development of scientific medicine accorded regular medicine a convincing advantage in medical practice. It set the stage for the achievement of a medical monopoly by the AMA regulars. As Larson (1977) notes, "Once scientific medicine offered sufficient guarantees of its superior effectiveness in dealing with disease, the state willingly contributed to the creation of a monopoly by means of registration and licensing" (p. 23). The new licensing laws created regular medicine as *a legally enforced monopoly of practice* (Freidson, 1970b, p. 83). They virtually eliminated medical competition.

The medical monopoly was enhanced further by the Flexner Report on medical education in 1910. Under the auspices of the Carnegie Foundation, medical educator Abraham Flexner visited nearly all 160 existing medical schools in the United States. He found the level of medical education poor and recommended the closing of most schools. Flexner urged stricter state laws, rigid standards for medical educa-

tion, and more rigorous examinations for certification to practice. The enactment of Flexner's recommendations effectively made all nonscientific types of medicine illegal. It created a near total AMA monopoly of medical education in America.

In securing a monopoly, the AMA regulars achieved a unique professional state. Medicine not only monopolized the market for medical services and the training of physicians, it developed an unparalleled "professional dominance." The medical profession was *functionally autonomous* (Freidson, 1970b). Physicians were insulated from external evaluation and were by and large free to regulate their own performance. Medicine could define its own territory and set its own standards. Thus, Eliot Freidson (1970b) notes, "while the profession may not everywhere be free to control the *terms* of its work, it is free to control the *content* of its work" (p. 84).

The domain of medicine has expanded in the past century. This is due partially to the prestige medicine has accrued and its place as the steward of the "sacred" value of life. Medicine has sometimes been called on to repeat its "miracles" and successful treatments on problems that are not biomedical in nature. Yet in other instances the expansion is due to explicit medical crusading or entrepreneurship. This expansion of medicine, especially into the realm of social problems and human behavior, frequently has taken medicine beyond its proven technical competence (Freidson, 1970b). In this book we examine a variety of cases in which personal problems or deviant behaviors become defined as illness and therefore within medical jurisdiction.

The organization of medicine has also expanded and become more complex in this century. In the next section we briefly describe the structure of medical practice in the United States.

Structure of medical practice

Before we leave our discussion of the medical profession, it is worthwhile to outline some general features of the structure of medical practice that have contributed to the expansion of medical jurisdiction.

The medical sector of society has grown

enormously in the 20th century. It has become the second largest industry in America. There are about 350,000 physicians and over 5 million people employed in the medical field. The "medical industries," including the pharmaceutical, medical technology, and health insurance industries, are among the most profitable in our economy. Yearly drug sales alone are over $4.5 billion. There are more than 7000 hospitals in the United States with 1.5 million beds and 33 million inpatient and 200 million outpatient visits a year (McKinlay, 1976).

The organization of medical practice has changed. Whereas the single physician in "solo practice" was typical in 1900, today physicians are engaged increasingly in large corporate practices or employed by hospitals or other bureaucratic organizations. Medicine in modern society is becoming bureaucratized (Mechanic, 1976). The power in medicine has become diffused, especially since World War II, from the AMA, which represented the individual physician, to include the organizations that represent bureaucratic medicine: the health insurance industry, the medical schools, and the American Hospital Association (Ehrenreich & Ehrenreich, 1970). Using Robert Alford's (1972) conceptualizations, corporate rationalizers have taken much of the power in medicine from the professional monopolists.

Medicine has become both more specialized and more dependent on technology. In 1929 only 25% of American physicians were full-time specialists; by 1969 the proportion had grown to 75% (Reiser, 1978). Great advances were made in medicine, and many were directly related to technology: miracle medicines like penicillin, a myriad of psychoactive drugs, heart and brain surgery, the electrocardiograph, CAT scanners, fetal monitors, kidney dialysis machines, artificial organs, and transplant surgery, to name but a few. The hospital has become the primary medical workshop, a center for technological medicine.

Medicine has made a significant economic expansion. In 1940, medicine claimed about 4% of the American gross national product (GNP); today it claims about 9%, which amounts to more than $150 billion. The causes for this growth are too complex to describe here, but a few factors should be noted. American medicine has always operated on a "fee-for-service" basis, that is, each service rendered is charged and paid for separately. Simply put, in a capitalist medical system, the more services provided, the more fees collected. This not only creates an incentive to provide more services but also to expand these medical services to new markets. The fee-for-service system may encourage unnecessary medical care. There is some evidence, for example, that American medicine performs a considerable amount of "excess" surgery (McCleery et al., 1971); this may also be true for other services. Medicine is one of the few occupations that can create its own demand. Patients may come to physicians, but physicians tell them what procedures they need. The availability of medical technique may also create a demand for itself.

The method by which medical care is paid for has changed greatly in the past half-century. In 1920 nearly all health care was paid for directly by the patient-consumer. Since the 1930s an increasing amount of medical care has been paid for through "third-party" payments, mainly through health insurance and the government. About 75% of the American population is covered by some form of medical insurance (often only for hospital care). Since 1966 the government has been involved directly in financing medical care through Medicare and Medicaid. The availability of a large amount of federal money, with nearly no cost controls or regulation of medical practice, has been a major factor fueling our current medical "cost crisis." But the ascendancy of third-party payments has effected the expansion of medicine in another way: more and more human problems become defined as "medical problems" (sickness) because that is the only way insurance programs will "cover" the costs of services. We will say more about this in Chapter 9.

In sum, the regular physicians developed control of medical practice and a professional dominance with nearly total functional autonomy. Through professionalization and persuasion concerning the superiority of their form of medicine, the medical profession (represented by the AMA) achieved a legally supported monopoly of practice. In short, it cornered the medical market. The medical profession has succeeded in both therapeutic and economic expansion. It has won the almost exclusive right to reign over the kingdom of health and sickness, no matter where it may extend.

OVERVIEW OF THE BOOK

In this chapter we introduced the sociological study of deviance and social control and offered a brief analysis of the development of the medical profession and practice. We locate our study in the labeling-interactionist sociology of deviance that has emerged in the past two decades. Our emphasis differs from most interactionist work in that we focus on historical construction and change of deviance definitions.

Chapter 2 presents the analytic perspective used for the remainder of the book: the politics of deviance definitions and designations. We also present some introductory thoughts about the medicalization of deviance. Chapters 3 through 8 consist of substantive sociohistorical analyses of the changing definitions of various categories of deviance. Throughout we attempt to focus on people, groups, and organizations as they contend about particular definitions of deviance. Chapter 3 examines the oldest and most widely accepted example of medicalization, the medical model of madness. It traces the events, discoveries, and people involved with the promotion and diffusion of the concept of mental illness. Chapter 4 focuses on the development of the disease concept of alcoholism, highlighting how nonmedical groups can use medical means to their own ends. Chapter 5 examines the fall and rise of opiate addiction as a medical problem, illuminating with particular clarity the political struggles between supporters of criminal and medical definitions of addiction. Chapter 6 reviews the development and legitimation of the designations of juvenile delinquency, hyperkinesis, and child abuse and suggests that children, because of their position in society, are a population at risk for medicalization. Chapter 7 traces the definitions of homosexuality from sin to sickness to life-style, noting the profound moral continuity in definition and social response. The recent demedicalization by the American Psychiatric Association is examined and found more symbolic than real. Chapter 9 (written by Richard Moran) outlines the long search for the "born criminal" and the medical treatments used to "cure" and control criminals.

The final two chapters present a general analysis and conceptual understanding of the medicalization of deviance. Chapter 10 describes and analyzes three types of medical social control, elaborates on the important social consequences of medicalizing deviance, and examines implications of recent and future social policy on medicalization. Chapter 11 endeavors to present a theoretical statement on the medicalization of deviance, serving both as a summary of what we understand about the process of medicalizing deviance and suggestions about issues those who study the problem need to pursue.

SUGGESTED READINGS

Erikson, K. T. *Wayward puritans*. New York: John Wiley & Sons, Inc., 1966.
An excellent and highly readable account of deviance among the 17th-century Puritans. Erikson explores the Antinomian controversy, the Quaker invasion, and Salem witchcraft as "crime waves" and develops a theory of deviance as boundary marking.
Freidson, E. *Professional dominance*. Chicago: Atherton Press, 1970.
A critical analysis of the social structure of medical practice. Freidson outlines the perquisites and consequences of professional dominance from a sociology-of-work perspective.
Goode, E. *Deviant behavior: an interactionist approach*. Englewood Cliffs, N.J.: Prentice-Hall, Inc., 1978.
A thoughtful and intelligent introduction to the relativist-interactionist approach to the study of deviance. The first eight chapters are especially useful.
Rubington, E., & Weinberg, M. S. *Deviance: the interactionist perspective* (3rd ed.). New York: Macmillan Publishing Co., Inc., 1978.
A well-integrated collection of articles that includes some of the best examples of the interactionist approach to deviance. Either this book or Goode's could profitably be read as a companion to *Deviance and Medicalization*.
Wertz, R. W. & Wertz, D. C. *Lying in: a history of childbirth in America*. New York: The Free Press, 1977.
Traces the definition and treatment of childbirth from a family event to a medical event. This is a well-presented case of the medicalization of a nondeviant activity.

2 FROM BADNESS to SICKNESS

CHANGING DESIGNATIONS of DEVIANCE and SOCIAL CONTROL

This chapter departs from the historical frame that organizes most of this book to present the theoretical perspective we have used in our study of deviance. The perspective serves as a general conceptual framework for the ensuing substantive chapters. The first part of this chapter presents what we call a historical-social constructionist approach to deviance. Ours is a broadly conceived sociology-of-knowledge approach to the construction and change of deviance designations and is rooted in the labeling-interactionist tradition of deviance research. This allows us to focus on how certain activities or behaviors become defined as deviant and how they come to be designated as one particular form of deviance rather than another. We attempt to analyze the factors involved in the changes in dominant deviance designations from moral or legal categories to medical ones, or more simply, from "badness" to sickness. This requires a historical view of deviance definitions and designations. The second part of this chapter introduces the general discussion first, of the concepts illness and deviance, and then of the social construction of illness. The final section summarizes the theoretical approach developed in this chapter.

A HISTORICAL-SOCIAL CONSTRUCTIONIST APPROACH TO DEVIANCE

Since deviance is an attributed designation rather than something inherent in individuals, our approach focuses on the historical, social, and cultural processes whereby individuals, behavior, attitudes, and activities come to be

defined as deviant. The power to so define and construct reality is linked intimately to the structure of power in a society at a given historical period. This is another way of saying that historical constructions of deviance are linked closely to the dominant social control institutions in the society. Our perspective emphasizes a dual point of view: the attribution of deviance as a historical, social construction of reality and the activities involved in constructing new deviance definitions or designations for social control. We view religion and the state as social control agents that have lost, or in the case of the state, transferred, some of their control prerogatives in the development of modern societies. Medical science, in particular, typically buoyed by state legitimation, has grown to assume these age-old control functions.

In this section we outline our approach to the study of deviance. Our concern is not so much with deviants per se but with the social processes through which certain forms of behavior are defined collectively as one type of problem or another. In this sense, ours is a sociology of deviance designations or categories. These categories are socially constructed entities, "neither immutable nor 'given' by the character of external reality" (Gusfield, 1975; p. 286), that shift and change over time and place. More specifically, our approach focuses on how certain categories of deviant behavior become defined as medical rather than moral problems and how medicine, rather than, for example, the family, church, or state, has become the dominant agent of social control for those so identified. In short, our concern is with how certain forms of deviant behavior have become problems for medical jurisdiction and been designated as sickness rather than badness.

We present our analytical approach here somewhat inductively, tracing its roots from the labeling-interactionist tradition and the sociology of knowledge.

Deviance as collective action: the labeling-interactionist tradition

As noted in the previous chapter, the labeling-interactionist perspective views deviance as relative to time, place, and audience and as an attribute that is conferred on people by others. This perspective posits that the processes of identifying, defining, and labeling behavior as deviant should be central concerns of the sociology of deviance. The labeling-interactionist approach turns the analysis away from the individual and the "causes" of his or her behavior, which have so long preoccupied the sociologist, to the "societal reaction." Rather than being viewed as an objective condition, deviance is regarded as a social product, produced by the joint action of the "deviant" and various social audiences.

Although the labeling perspective emerged from a symbolic interactionist social psychology, the focus on social process allowed for analysis of a wide range of activities related to deviance production. As Howard Becker (1973) points out, a central tenet of such an interactionist view is that deviance is "collective action." "In its simplest form, the theory insists that we look at all people involved in any episodes of alleged deviance" (p. 183). Edwin Schur (1971) clarifies the essence of this approach:

Processes of social definition, or labeling, that contribute to deviance outcomes are actually found on at least three levels of social action, and all three require analysis. Such processes—as they occur on the levels of *collective rule-making, interpersonal reactions* and *organizational processing*—all constitute important concerns of the labeling school. (p. 11).*

Most studies of deviance from a labeling-interactionist perspective have focused on the social psychological and microsociological

aspects of deviance: especially the levels of interpersonal reactions (e.g., identification, definition, and contingencies of deviant labeling) and organizational process (e.g., official labeling and its attendant consequences). Thus we have developed considerable knowledge about contingencies in labeling, deviant careers, deviant subcultures, deviant identities, and the effects of stigma.

The "macrosociological" aspects of the labeling perspective have received less attention and consequently are not as developed in the sociological literature. Thus we know considerably less about the "collective definition of deviance" (Davis & Stivers, 1975) than we do about deviance-processing organizations, deviant careers, and stigmatized identities. Certainly this imbalance is not inherent in the labeling perspective itself. There have been a few studies that focus on this collective process of deviance definition and designation. Becker, in his seminal discussion of the Marijuana Tax Act of 1937, which rendered the sales and use of marijuana deviant, developed the concept of moral entrepreneurs to describe those who "lobby" for the creation of social rules. Such works as Kai Erikson's (1966) study of deviance in the Puritan colonies, Anthony Platt's (1969) study of the child-saving movement and the "invention of delinquency," Joseph Gusfield's (1963) analysis of the Women's Christian Temperance Union's crusade for prohibition, Elliot Currie's (1968) analysis of the control of witchcraft in Renaissance Europe, William Chambliss's (1964) study of the origin and change of vagrancy laws, and David Matza's (1966) essay on the disreputable poor are perhaps the classic labeling-interactionist studies that have examined the origin of deviant categories.* Although a few other studies

---

*Schur, E. *Labeling deviant behavior.* New York: Harper & Row, Publishers, Inc., 1971.

*A few studies that focused on the collective definition of deviance were done before the emergence of the labeling tradition, most significantly Sutherland's (1950) analysis of the diffusion of sexual psychopath laws and Kingsley Davis' (1938) paper on the ideology of the mental hygiene movement (see Chapter 3). Nonsociologists have also explored the collective definition of deviance, such as Thomas Szasz's (1970) essays on mental illness and David Musto's (1973) analysis of the history of opiate addiction in America.

have appeared recently, relatively less attention is still given to how "society" defines an act as deviant.

Sociologists whose work falls within the labeling-interactionist tradition have themselves pointed to this underdeveloped aspect of the perspective. Howard Becker (1973), in his discussion of deviance as collective action, notes that all parties involved in deviance production are fit objects for study.

At a second level, the interactionist approach shows sociologists that a major element in every aspect of the drama of deviance is the imposition of definitions —of situations, acts, and people—by those powerful enough or sufficiently legitimated to be able to do so. A full understanding requires the thorough study of those definitions and the processes by which they develop and attain legitimacy and taken-for-grantedness. (p. 207)*

Eliot Freidson suggests that sociologists of deviance have recognized only one of the two major sociological tasks in the study of deviance. He points out, as do we, that sociologists have investigated rather thoroughly the etiology of various forms of deviant behavior but largely have "failed to recognize the other task" of studying the etiology of deviance designations. Freidson's (1970a) notions are similar to the perspective we develop here:

[Sociological researchers] have followed the model of medicine in setting as their task the determination of some stable, objective quality or state of deviance (e.g., criminal behavior) and have sought to determine its etiology. They have failed to recognize the other task of studying the way conceptions of deviance are developed and the consequences of the application of such conceptions to human affairs. . . . *This task does not require explanation of the cause of behavior so much as it requires the explanation of the cause of the meaning attached to the behavior.* (pp. 213, 216, emphasis added)

Since the labeling-interactionist approach argues that deviance is an imputed or attributed condition, a social construction, it makes the study of the imputer or definer as important as

the study of those defined as deviant. A fully developed labeling-interactionist perspective must also account for the development and change of deviance designations.

Malcolm Spector and John Kitsuse (1977) recently have taken a similar approach to the study of social problems. In contrast to traditional functionalist and normative approaches to social problems, Spector and Kitsuse suggest that sociologists study the collective activities involved in how certain conditions come to be defined as social problems. They are not concerned with how such social conditions developed but rather with how these alleged conditions came to be seen as social problems. Social problems emerge and are legitimated through the action of various "claims-making" groups in society. Spector and Kitsuse suggest that sociologists need to study the interaction between these claims-makers and responders concerning the definition of social conditions and what ought to be done about them. They see a parallel situation in the study of deviance:

Central to the subject matter of the sociology of deviance is the processing of the definitions of deviance which may result in the development of informally recognized and enforced categories, as well as the establishment of official categories and populations of deviants. The theoretical problem is to account for how categories of social problems and deviance are produced, and how methods of social control and treatment are institutionally established. (Spector & Kitsuse, 1977, p. 72).*

One final point concerning the labeling-interactionist perspective of deviance is important. Labeling studies have been criticized for being "apolitical" and for avoiding structural considerations in their analysis (e.g., Taylor, I., et al., 1973). By investigating the collective and historical dimensions of the development of deviance categories in a given society, we can begin to examine these structural and political elements involved in defining this or that behavior as deviant: Who defines what as deviant? How does one group manage to have their definition of deviance legitimated? How do deviance designations change as political and economic conditions change? Whose interests do deviance designations serve? The definition of any behavior or action as deviant is essentially a political matter, as Becker (1963, p. 7) has noted. In large part the success of such definitional process is decided by who has the power to legitimate their definitions. Such a perspective must eventually lead to the study of the distribution of power in a society, how those with power are able to effect the production of deviance designations, and whose interests these designations support.*

The labeling-interactionist sociologists, although actually producing few studies on the process of the collective definition of deviance, have developed a framework that allows for study of the macrosociological process of deviance definition. In that this perspective views deviance as an attribution, it allows us to study the etiology of definitions separately from the etiology of behavior. Thus the investigation of the origin, development, and change of deviance designations becomes a central task for the sociology of deviance.

SOCIAL CONSTRUCTION OF REALITY: A SOCIOLOGY OF KNOWLEDGE

Although the labeling-interactionist perspective presents us with the questions to ask concerning the development of deviance designations, it is a sociology-of-knowledge approach that is necessary to answer them. The sociology of knowledge involves relating ''knowledge'' or cultural facts to specific social and structural forms in a given society. It sees knowledge as linked intimately to social organization or interaction that can be located in a historical frame. The basic assumption of a sociology-of-

knowledge approach is that ideas do not develop in a vacuum but rather are generated and elaborated in a specific social milieu. Using this approach, we view deviance designations as products of the society in which they exist. The task of such an analysis is to investigate, usually in a historical frame, the social sources of these ideas and to trace their development or demise.

A few labeling-interactionist sociologists have pointed clearly in the direction of the sociology of knowledge to aid in this ''other task'' of sociologists studying deviance, examining how conceptions of deviance are developed (e. g., Goode, 1969). As Freidson (1970a) states,

> The other task is one that is essentially defined by the sociology of knowledge. It is created by the recognition that deviance is not a state as such, so much as an evaluation of the meaning of a state. Its problem for analysis then becomes not the etiology of some state so much as the etiology of the *meaning* of a state. Thus, it asks questions like: How does a state come to be considered deviant? How does it come to be considered one kind of deviance rather than another? . . . What does the imputation of a particular kind of deviance do to the organization of the interaction between interested parties? (pp. 215-216)

The only way to answer such questions about the emergence of dominant deviance designations is to attempt to locate their origins in history and identify the social groups and activities that generate and support them. In this fashion we can begin to understand the meanings we attribute to certain forms of behavior.

There are several different paths we could take toward a sociology-of-knowledge analysis of deviance designations. We have chosen to follow the phenomenological and conflict perspectives. Both view ideas—and in our case, deviance designations—as products of historically locatable social interaction or social organization. But they vary as to where they would ultimately locate the source of the idea and what factors they would take into account in their analysis.

The *phenomenological* perspective views deviance designations as ''socially constructed realities,'' typifications (commonly understood categories or types) that are products of social

---

*Sociologists with perspectives other than labeling-interactionist may also see the collective definition of deviance as a central sociological concern. As Steven Spitzer (1975) points out in his theoretical discussion of a Marxian approach to the study of deviance, ''Most fundamentally, deviance production involves the development of and changes in deviant categories and images'' (p. 640). Although Spitzer would call for a class-based analysis of deviance designations, he agrees that such designations should be central in the study of deviance.

interaction and central in our interpreation of the world. "Reality" is defined not as something that exists "out there" for the scientist or anyone else to discover but as a social construction that emerges from and is sustained by social interaction. The social world is thus both interpreted and constructed through the medium of language. Language and language categories provide the ordered meanings by which we experience ourselves and our lives in society. They make the social world (objects, behavior, etc.) meaningful.

Peter Berger and Thomas Luckmann (1966) are perhaps the major proponents of this perspective. They view reality construction as a social process of three stages: externalization, objectivation, and internalization. Externalization is the process by which people construct a cultural product (e.g., the idea that strange behaviors can be caused by a mental illness). Objectivation occurs when cultural products take on an objective reality of their own, independent of the people who created them, and are viewed as part of objective reality (e.g., mental illness causes strange behaviors). Internalization is when people learn the "objective facts" of a culture through socialization and make them part of their own "internal" consciousness (e.g., taking for granted that strange behaviors are caused by mental illness). Objectivation is the institutionalization of the socially produced cultural product; it becomes, then, part of the available stock of knowledge of any society. Language becomes a depository of institutionalized collective "sedimentations" (e.g., mental illness), which we acquire "as cohesive wholes and without reconstructing the original process of formation" (Berger & Luckmann, 1966, p. 69). In a real sense they become part of the taken-for-granted everyday vocabulary of a society. It follows that if reality is socially constructed by human activity, it can be changed by human activity. Indeed, in Berger and Luckmann's view, realities are constantly being constructed and reconstructed in a dialectic process between interacting individuals and their social world qua society.

The *conflict* perspective views deviance designations as the products of social and political conflict, and it defines social control as a political mechanism by which certain groups can dominate others. There are two general schools of deviance conflict theorists, the pluralists and the Marxians. The pluralist conception sees society as made of a variety of competing interest groups in conflict for dominance, status, wealth, and power (e.g., Lofland, 1969; McCaghy, 1976). The Marxian perspective views conflict as a product of the class structure of society and the relation people have to the economic system (e.g., Quinney, 1974; Taylor, I. et al., 1973). For the pluralist, the conflict is most often played out in the conventional arena of institutionalized partisan politics, with different interest groups attempting to legislate their laws or laws that benefit them. The Marxian view sees law as much more a reflection of the interests of a ruling class. In this view, laws and deviance designations are part of the "superstructure," the culture and knowledge of a society, which is determined by the economic "substructure." Dominant or socially "popular" ideas bear the insignia of the ruling economic class and serve to reinforce its interests. A conflict approach sees "the subjective conceptions and definitions of deviance that exist to a given society as ideological products of interest group competition or class conflict" (Orcutt et al., 1977). Deviance designations are produced and influenced more by the powerful and applied more to the powerless.

These two sociologies of knowledge are not fully compatible (nor need they be). For example, Marxians would take issue with the phenomenologists' "social construction of reality" and argue that "reality" is based on the interests and visions of the ruling class rather than emerging out of social interaction. Phenomenologists, on the other hand, would have difficulty with the "hidden forces" (e.g., the economic system or means of production) that Marxians see as determining social life. Important as these differences may be, however, we need not concern ourselves here with such disputes. Although our approach is more phenomenological and pluralist than Marxian, both these approaches are insightful in studying the development and change of deviance designations. The phenomenological perspective sensitizes us to the socially constructed nature of deviance designations—that they emerge from social interaction and that they are humanly constructed and hence can be humanly changed. The conflict perspective sensitizes us to the fact that not all people are equal in their power to construct reality—that deviance designations may serve political interests and that they are created usually through some type of social conflict. We call this conflict the politics of definition.

Politics of definition

What is considered deviant in a society is a product of a political process of decision making. The behaviors or activities that are deviant in a given society are not self-evident; they are defined by groups with the ability to legitimate and enforce their definitions. As Becker (1963, p. 162) notes, deviance is always a product of enterprise. It is through some type of political process, using "political" in its broad meaning of conflict about power relations, that deviance designations emerge and are legitimated. There are several ways this can occur. An individual or group may champion a cause that this or that behavior should be considered deviant (Blumer, 1971; Mauss, 1975). The antebellum abolitionist movement, antipornography crusades in various communities (Zurcher et al., 1971), the Women's Christian Temperance Union's campaign for Prohibition (Gusfield, 1963), the present-day antiabortion ("right to life") groups, and Anita Bryant's recent crusade against gay rights legislation are examples of this. Such campaigns for deviance designations can be seen as the work of *moral entrepreneurs*, those who crusade for the creation of new rules.*

The prototype of the rule creator . . . is the crusading reformer. He is interested in the content of rules. The existing rules do not satisfy him because

---

*Becker discusses both rule creators and rule enforcers as moral entrepreneurs, but only the former concern us here. Becker, and some of the other authors of labeling studies we present in this section, did not conceptualize their work in terms of the sociology of knowledge. However, when sociology of knowledge is used as we present it here, these works are clearly within that perspective.

there is some evil which profoundly disturbs him. He feels that nothing can be right in the world until the rules are made to correct it. He operates with an absolute ethic; what he sees is truly and totally evil with no qualification. Any means is justified to do away with it. The crusader is fervent and righteous, often self-righteous. (Becker, 1963, pp. 147-148)*

Becker notes that the claims of most moral crusaders have humanitarian overtones; they truly think that they know what is good both for themselves *and* other people. But the crusader or crusading group is also often a self-interested participant in the deviance-defining process. The crusader (or the group) is not only crusading for a moral change in social rules, but there also may be a hidden agenda which is of equal or greater import and not immediately obvious.

Becker (1963, pp. 135-146) describes the passage of the Marijuana Tax Act of 1937 as an exemplar of moral entrepreneurship. He suggests that there was little public interest in marijuana before a publicity campaign by the Bureau of Narcotics. This campaign, led by Commissioner Henry J. Anslinger, aroused public interest and was followed by Congress passing a law that essentially made marijuana illegal. The marijuana smokers, whoever they were, were unorganized, powerless, and without publicly legitimate grounds for defense. They did not appear at the congressional hearings to oppose the law. The bureau had helped create a new category of deviants, marijuana sellers and users (Becker, 1963; p. 145). Another sociologist, Donald Dickson (1968), a few years later reanalyzed the origin of the Marijuana Tax Act and concluded that Anslinger and the bureau lobbied for its passage for organizational rather than moral reasons. He suggests that the bureau, faced with the threat of a steadily decreasing budget, tried to present itself as essential to the public welfare as a defender against the peril of marijuana.

---

*From Becker, H. S. *Outsiders; studies in the sociology of deviance*. New York: The Free Press of Glencoe, Inc., 1963. Copyright © 1963 by The Free Press of Glencoe.

It attempted to increase its powers and scope of operations by lobbying for the inclusion of marijuana in its jurisdiction. Dickson suggests it was bureaucratic survival and growth rather than moral righteousness that prompted the bureau's efforts in promoting the antimarijuana legislation (the fact that most states already had some type of antimarijuana laws supports his interpretation). In either case, however, it appears that the new deviance designation was a product of enterprise, moral or bureaucratic, and was legitimated through the political process.*

Although the legal process is the most formal and institutionally obvious political avenue by which individuals and groups can influence and promote their definitions of deviance, it is by no means the only one. Moral entrepreneurs and other champions of deviance definitions can operate in any social system that has power and authority to impose definitions of deviance on the behaviors and activities of its members. One could expect to find champions of deviance definitions in schools, factories, bureaucracies, and religious and medical organizations — virtually in any system that has rules and authority. However, in modern industrial society, only law and medicine have the legitimacy to construct and promote deviance categories with wide-ranging application. With medicine this application even transcends social and national boundaries. The labeling of a disease or illness, the medical designation for deviance, is usually considered to have universal application. As Freidson (1970a) points out, the medical profession takes an active role in influencing deviance definitions and designations, discovering new "illnesses," and intervening with "appropriate" medical treatment.

In these activities the physician can be seen as a moral entrepreneur:

[Medicine] is active in seeking out illness. The profession does treat the illnesses laymen take to it, but it also seeks to discover illness of which laymen may not even be aware. One of the greatest ambitions of the physician is to discover and describe a "new" disease or syndrome and to be immortalized by having his name used to identify the disease. Medicine, then, is oriented to seeking out and finding illness, which is to say that it seeks to create social meanings of illness where that meaning or interpretation was lacking before. And insofar as illness is defined as something bad — to be eradicated or contained — medicine plays the role of what Becker called the "moral entrepreneur." (Friedson, 1970a, p. 252)

Medical work can lead to the creation of new medical norms, whose violation is deviance, or, in the cases we present, new categories of illness. This increases the jurisdiction of medicine or some segment of it and legitimates the medical treatment of sick deviants. Sociological analysis of the 19th-century medical involvement in the definition of madness (Scull, 1975) and the more recent cases of the medical definition of hyperkinesis (Conrad, 1975) and child abuse (Pfohl, 1977) are prime examples of the medical profession's championing of certain definitions of deviance. These examples will be presented in detail in later chapters. Although the "politics of definition" may be more obscured in the construction of medical designations than in legal ones, the decision to define certain behaviors, activities, or conditions as deviant still emerges from a political process that produces and subsequently legitimates the imposition of the deviant categories. And, most often, the consequences of medical definitions, especially when they concern human behavior, are also political. The second section of this chapter, which discusses deviance, illness, and medicalization, as well as subsequent chapters, elaborates this point.

Interests, status, and class in the politics of definition. Moral entrepreneurship and other championing of deviance definitions are not the only types of politics of definition. Another powerful influence on creating deviance designations is what we call *interest politics:*

---

*A recent reappraisal of the passage of this legislation posits that since most states already had antimarijuana laws, the bureau's publicity campaign was actually rather limited, the public interest was minimal, there was virtually no opposition, and there was no budget increase for the bureau; the act was a symbolic piece of legislation, symbolically reassuring congresspeople and others in what they already commonsensically believed (Galliher & Walker, 1977).

the promotion, directly or indirectly, of definitions of deviance that specifically support and buttress certain class or status interests. This approach aligns neatly with the conflict approach to the sociology of knowledge. In these cases we usually find groups or ''power blocs'' rather than individual entrepreneurs attempting to create rules that uphold their needs and interests. The deviance designation may become an instrumental or symbolic way in which to achieve ends that are totally unrelated to the deviance or deviance designations themselves. Interest politics may focus on interest groups, status interests, or class interests. Each will be discussed briefly.

Richard Quinney is one of the major conflict sociologists writing on deviance today. His more recent work (Quinney, 1974) assumes a Marxian view, but his earlier work is more pluralistic. In one of these early works Quinney presented a sociological theory of criminal law, in which he outlined an interest group model for the origin and development of law and deviance designations. Building on the work of legal scholar Roscoe Pound, Quinney developed a theory strikingly similar to the early work of Edwin Sutherland. It is based on the pluralist assumptions that society is characterized by diversity, conflict, and change rather than consensus; that law, and therefore deviance definitions, are *created* by interest groups in conflict with one another; and that law usually represents these specific interests rather than all the members of society. Quinney departs from the standard pluralist conception, which sees law as a compromise of diverse societal interests; in his view, law ''supports some interests at the expense of others.'' He proposes four propositions to explain the origin of law through interest group conflict:

1. Law is the creation and interpretation of specialized rules in a politically organized society.
2. Politically organized society is based on an interest structure.
3. The interest structure of politically organized society is characterized by unequal distribution of power and conflict.
4. Law is formulated and administered within the interest structure of a politically organized society. (Quinney, 1969, pp. 20-30)

Quinney sees law as a political instrument used by specific groups to further their own interests; as a tool of those with power to shape the law at the expense of others. Definitions of deviance thus created and/or legitimated through law represent those interests.

But what the interests are, and even whose interests are involved, is not always obvious. Joseph Gusfield (1963) presents us with an interesting example in his analysis of the Women's Christian Temperance Union's crusade for Prohibition. Why would the members of the WCTU, a largely rural, Protestant, middle-class group of women, crusade so fervently for the prohibition of alcohol when problem drinking was not a major concern in their own rural communities? And why did they support only complete prohibition of alcohol use rather than restriction and control? They were moral crusaders for sure, but why engage in a moral crusade against a problem that appeared, at least on the surface, not to affect them?

Gusfield places the Temperance movement and especially the WCTU in a social-historical context to attempt to understand this crusade. The movement gained its strength in the late 19th and early 20th centuries. The United States was changing rapidly from a land dominated by native-born, rural, Protestant farmers and small-townspeople to one increasingly influenced by urban, immigrant, Catholic industrial workers and other urban folk. The drinking of alcohol was part of the everyday life of these urban workers. The rural Protestant culture was beginning to decline in influence; they saw their dominant status as endangered. Gusfield suggests that the Temperance movement for prohibition of alcohol was an instance of *status politics,* with the rural Protestant people trying to legislate their morality and norms. The conflict, according to Gusfield, was one of divergent styles of life, and the issue of alcohol was the symbol of this conflict. Thus he sees the Temperance movement as a ''symbolic crusade'' to try to maintain status in a changing society. The fact that Temperance advocates were much less concerned with the enforcement of Prohibition legislation than with its passage supports Gusfield's interpretation. The success of the Eighteenth Amendment outlawing alcohol was a public affirmation of their morals; it was clear to all concerned, regardless of enforcement, *whose* law it was (Gusfield, 1967). This analysis depicts how definitions of deviance (e.g., drinking alcohol) can be symbolic representations of one group's struggle against another about issues of morality and style of life.

Karl Marx argued law supports the dominant class's economic interests in society, which in industrial society is that of the bourgeoisie, or the owners of the means of production. It is nearly axiomatic among Marxian theorists that law reflects the interests of the *ruling class*. Sociologist William Chambliss (1964) presents an analysis of the origin and change in the deviance called "vagrancy" that points clearly to the effects of economic changes on law and deviance designations. The first vagrancy statutes emerged in England in the 14th century after the Black Death decimated the labor force. The lack of an adequate supply of labor forced the feudal landowners to pay higher wages for "free" labor and made it more difficult for them to keep serfs on the land. Opportunities for wages were available, and the landowners were hardpressed to keep them from fleeing. Chambliss (1964) concludes that the vagrancy law was to keep serfs from migrating: "There is little question but that these statutes were designed for one express purpose: to force laborers (whether personally free or unfree) to accept employment at a low wage in order to insure the landowner an adequate supply of labor at a price he could afford to pay" (p. 69). By the 16th century the focus of vagrancy laws shifted from a concern with the movement of laborers to a concern with criminal activities. A vagrant became defined in the law as one who "can give no reckoning how he lawfully makes his living." Punishment was severe: public whipping and, for repeated offenses, cutting off an ear. Chambliss points out that this change in vagrancy laws came about when feudalism was crumbling and there was increased emphasis on commerce and industry. This led to an increase in trade, on which English commerce was dependent. Transportation, however, was hazardous, and the traders were frequently attacked and robbed of their goods. The vagrancy law was revived with the changed focus to con-

trol persons suspected of being "highwaymen" who preyed on merchants transporting goods. Thus, as the economic structure changed, the law shifted and continued to support the dominant economic class in society—first the landowners, then the merchants.

In summary, the politics of definitions is a process whereby definitions of deviance are socially constructed. In a world where there are multiple "realities" and definitions of behavior, these definitions are constructed through a political process and legitimated in legal statutes, medical vocabulary, or religious doctrine. Although negotiations may occur, more powerful interests in society are better able to implement their version of reality by creating and legitimating deviance definitions that support their interests.

Politics of deviance designation

The definition of certain behaviors or activities does not necessarily tell us what particular *designation* of deviance will be applied. For example, is the offending conduct a sin, a moral problem, a crime, or a sickness? The particular deviance designation is often a matter of controversy: Is deviant drinking a moral weakness or a disease? Are criminals genetically defective, psychologically abnormal, morally vacuous, or unsocialized brutes?

The professional and popular literatures on deviance are replete with discussions on what constitutes the nature of nearly any form of deviant behavior. Such discussion usually takes the form of an analysis of the etiology and characteristics of the deviant behavior. It is assumed generally that if one could only know the cause and thus the "true" nature of the deviant behavior, one could prevent or, more likely, control it closer to its source. But there is an unacknowledged political dimension to these academic debates. That is the question of who is the appropriate official agent of social control for such deviance. Put another way, in whose turf does the deviance lie? It is when we view discussions of deviance from this angle that such debates descend from the language of intellectual and technical specialization to political battles over turf. If drug addiction and alcoholism are diseases, then the medical profession is the legitimate agent of social control; if they are crimes, then they are in the jurisdiction of the criminal justice system. Needless to say, in a society as complex as ours the jurisdictional lines are not mutually exclusive, and considerable overlap may exist. This, however, does not negate the fact that arguments of etiology may be in essence jurisdictional disputes (this is perhaps clearest in the case of opiate addiction, presented in Chapter 5). As Erich Goode (1969) points out, "naming" itself has important political implications: "By devising a linguistic category with specific connotations, one is designing the armaments for a battle; by having it accepted and used, one has scored a major victory" (p. 89). In our view, deviance designations are not ipso facto one type of problem or another, and it is similarly not evident which social control agency is most appropriate. Decisions concerning what is the proper deviance *designation* and who is the proper *agent of control* are political questions decided frequently through political contest.

Recent analyses of social problems present an analogous situation. We have already noted that Spector and Kitsuse (1977) suggest that the distinctive focus of the sociology of social problems and deviance should be the social processing of definitions. Sociologists need to focus on the "claims-making activities" of the various groups asserting their definitions of deviance and analyze "how categories of social problems and deviance are produced, and how methods of social control and treatment are institutionally established" (Spector & Kitsuse, 1977, p. 72). This latter task is analogous to the one we propose here: the examination of "claims-making" activities that lead to the establishment of a deviance designation and the appropriate agent of social control. Joseph Gusfield (1975), in his analysis of the appropriate designation and control agent for automobile accidents and deaths attributed to "drinking-driving," suggests we investigate how one agency attains "ownership" of a social problem and thus establishes its designation of deviance. For example, why are traffic fatalities and drinking-driving defined as an individual's alcohol problem rather than as a problem in transportation (i.e., getting safely from one place to another)? Although it is usually believed that decisions about proper designations of deviance (i.e., a crime versus a sickness) are made on a rational, even scientific, basis, as social scientists we cannot assume this. The public identity of the problem is not apparent; rather it is constructed through human interaction.

The "discovery" of public facts is a process of social organization. Someone must engage in monitoring, recording, aggregating, analyzing and transmitting the separate and individual events into the public reality of "auto accidents and deaths." At every stage in this process human choices of selection and interpretation operate. Events are given meaning and assumptions and values guide the selection. Public "facts" are not like pebbles on the beach, lying in the sun and waiting to be seen. They must instead be picked, polished, shaped and packaged. Finally ready for display they bear the marks of their shapers. (Gusfield, 1975, p. 291)

These facts may be part of claims-making activities of an agency or organization. Spector and Kitsuse (1977) note that their perspective leads them "to view scientific facts and knowledge about social conditions as products of that organization, not as reflections of the phenomena they purport to explain" (p. 67). In this view, public "facts" about social conditions that render deviance properly in one jurisdiction or another, even those claimed to be scientific ones, are viewed skeptically as "social constructions" that may support certain claims of legitimacy.* This perspective is particularly appropriate when "scientific evidence" is presented by an agency or organization in support of their deviance designation or to refute the claims of others. In short, such data may become vitally important ammunition in the battle among competing groups and control agencies.

---

*It is in this light that Goode (1969) notes that "empirical reality, being staggeringly complex, permits and even *demands* factual selection. We characteristically seek support for our view: contrary opinions and facts are generally avoided. This opens the way for the maintenance of points of view which are contradicted by empirical evidence. And there is invariably a variety of facts to choose from. It is a comparatively simple matter to find what one is looking for in any moderately complex issue" (p. 87).

Some prestigious claims-makers or organized collectivities have greater power than others to define what is true and false, respectable and disrespectable, normal and abnormal, etc. Howard Becker (1967) suggests there are "hierarchies of credibility" whereby prestigious organizations such as the American Medical Association, the American Bar Association, the Department of Health, Education and Welfare, the Justice Department, and representatives of these organizations have a greater power to define and legitimate reality (and deviance designations) than do other groups. They often use scientific findings selectively to support their particular policies (see, for example, Chapter 5).

Deviance designations and social change. Changes in deviance designations have consequences beyond justifying the suitable social control agent:

1. It may change the legitimate "authority" concerning a particular variety of deviant behavior. In the late 17th century, physicians rather than priests or magistrates became the experts on madness.

2. It may change the meaning of behavior. The behavior of restless, disruptive schoolchildren is no longer rebelliousness or willful opposition, but symptomatic of the illness hyperkinesis.

3. It may change the legal status of the deviance. The Harrison Act of 1914 created a new group of criminals—opium peddlers; the 1973 Supreme Court decision made abortion a conventional medical procedure.

4. It may change the contents of a deviance category or the norm itself. Prohibition, the Eighteenth Amendment, altered, at least symbolically, the norm of acceptable drinking behavior—there could be none. With repeal, only certain drinkers were defined as deviant—the underage and the chronic inebriate.

5. It may change the arena where identification and labeling of deviance takes place, as well as the vocabulary used. When homosexual conduct is viewed as a "crime against nature," labeling occurs in judicial processes; when it is defined as an illness, labeling takes place in the psychiatric arena through medical processes.

6. It may produce a change in the mode of intervention. When opiate addicts are defined as criminals, they are given legal punishments; when they are defined as sick, they are given methadone.

7. It may operate as a road sign as to what type of data to collect and on what to focus one's attention. By defining drinking-driving as the "cause" of auto fatalities, we focus on problem characteristics of the individual driver and collect data about him or her, rather than collecting data about the auto industry or analyzing the transportation system. By defining hyperactive children as sick, we turn our attention from the school and the child's situation and focus on the child's physiological characteristics.

8. It may shift the attribution of responsibility. Sinful and criminal deviants are responsible for their behavior; sick deviants are not.

All these changes and others should become apparent in various combinations throughout this book in our examination of changing deviance designations.

When certain types of deviance become accepted and taken for granted as reality, we have something analogous to Thomas Kuhn's concept of paradigm (i.e., a fundamental image of the subject matter). Paradigms structure the way the "faithful" construct and interpret the world. When paradigms change, after a crisis and the emergence of a new paradigm, views of reality change also. According to Kuhn (1970), "though the world does not change with a change in paradigm, the scientist afterwards works in a different world" (p. 121). Different data are collected, the world is seen and interpreted differently, and the new paradigm becomes the dominant manner by which to interpret experience.

We propose that three major paradigms may be identified that have held reign over deviance designations in various historical periods: deviance as sin; deviance as crime; and deviance as sickness. Overlap and competition among these "paradigms" are apparent over time, but they provide, nonetheless, distinct perspectives and images for constructing deviant reality. When a theological world view dominated, deviance was sin; when the nation-states emerged from the decay of feudalism, most deviance became designated as crime; and in our own scientifically oriented world, various forms of deviance are designated increasingly as medical problems. Thus we view the medical paradigm as the ascending paradigm for deviance designations in our postindustrial society.

In a given society a particular paradigm may be dominant. In contemporary American society a tension exists frequently between the legal-crime and medical-sickness paradigms, although opponents can develop comfortable accommodations. Each paradigm has institutional supporters of relatively high status (i.e., lawmakers and judges, medical researchers and physicians). In a world that views science as the ultimate arbiter of reality, deviance designations that can be supported by scientific research are more likely to gain credence. We say ''more likely,'' since the factors in the politics of deviance designation are complex. However, all other things being equal, medical conceptions of deviance are more likely to be proposed in the name of science. When medical designations of deviant reality are in competition with other designations, we may well witness a *hegemony* of medical definitions; that is, a preponderant influence or acceptance of medical authority as the ''final'' reality and a diminishing of other potential realities. Needless to say, there can be and are challenges to this hegemony, but some see a type of cultural and structural medical hegemony of deviance designations as increasingly apparent in American society (see Illich, 1976; Radelet, 1977a).

We use the approach just outlined in the remainder of this book to study the changing designations of deviance, especially as designations become medical and physicians are involved in treatment and social control. In the next section of this chapter we identify some of the more general issues in ''the medicalization of deviance.'' In all the following substantive chapters (3 to 8), we try to be true to the complexities of the changing definitions and designations of deviance for each particular case. This involves giving attention to such specifics as historical events, relevant settings of conflict and change, attributions of cause, political conflict, social control mechanisms, scientific

discoveries, claims-making activities, and negotiation of jurisdictional boundaries. It is important to remember that deviance designations do not change by themselves; social action engaged in by real people or collectivities is necessary to create definitional change. We aim at constructing a historical overview and staying close to the data in each case, rather than trying to fit all cases into a rigid model of medicalization. In a sense, we view each substantive chapter as revealing some aspect of the process of medicalization. In Chapter 10 we attempt to integrate these into a theoretical statement on the medicalization of deviance.

DEVIANCE, ILLNESS, AND MEDICALIZATION*

Consider the following situations. A woman rides a horse naked through the streets of Denver claiming to be Lady Godiva and after being apprehended by authorities, is taken to a psychiatric hospital and declared to be suffering from a mental illness. A well-known surgeon in a Southwestern city performs a psychosurgical operation on a young man who is prone to violent outbursts. An Atlanta attorney, inclined to drinking sprees, is treated at a hospital clinic for his disease, alcoholism. A child in California brought to a pediatric clinic because of his disruptive behavior in school is labeled hyperactive and is prescribed methylphenidate (Ritalin) for his disorder. A chronically overweight Chicago housewife receives a surgical intestinal bypass operation for her problem of obesity. Scientists at a New England medical center work on a million-dollar federal research grant to discover a heroin-blocking agent as a ''cure'' for heroin addiction. What do these situations have in common? In all instances medical solutions are being sought for a variety of deviant behaviors or conditions. We call this ''the medicalization of deviance'' and suggest that these examples illustrate how medical defi-

---

*The remainder of this chapter is an extended and amended version of ''On the Medicalization of Deviance and Social Control'' by Conrad, P. In D. Ingleby (Ed.), *Critical psychiatry*. Copyright © 1980 by Peter Conrad. Reprinted by permission of Penguin Books Ltd.

nitions of deviant behavior are becoming more prevalent in modern industrial societies like our own. The historical sources of this medicalization, and the development of medical conceptions and controls for deviant behavior, are the central concerns of our analysis.

Medical practitioners and medical treatment in our society are usually viewed as dedicated to healing the sick and giving comfort to the afflicted. No doubt these are important aspects of medicine. In recent years the jurisdiction of the medical profession has expanded and encompasses many problems that formerly were not defined as medical entities. Ivan Illich (1976) has called this "the medicalization of life." There is much evidence for this general viewpoint—for example, the medicalization of pregnancy and childbirth, contraception, diet, exercise, child development norms—but our concern here is more limited and specific. Our interests focus on the medicalization of deviant behavior: the defining and labeling of deviant behavior as a medical problem, usually an illness, and mandating the medical profession to provide some type of treatment for it. Concomitant with such medicalization is the growing use of medicine as an agent of social control, typically as medical intervention. Medical intervention as social control seeks to limit, modify, regulate, isolate, or eliminate deviant behavior with medical means and in the name of health (Zola, 1972). The remainder of this book examines sociologically the medicalization of deviance and the development of medical social control. It presents an analysis of the transformation of deviance from *badness* to *sickness* and the adoption of the medical model for a number of specific categories of deviant behavior.

Before beginning our introduction to the medicalization process, we discuss two general sociological notions that pertain to the perspective developed here. These are the social construction of illness and the relationship of illness and deviance.

The social construction of illness

What are disease and illness? On the face of it they seem rather straightforward concepts. A commonsense viewpoint might see disease as something that exists "out there," apart even from the human body, that may enter the body and do harm; ideas of avoiding viruses, germs, and other "diseases" follow from this view. A systematized variant of a commonsense view might be that disease is "a specific destructive process in an organism, with specific causes and specific symptoms" (Webster's New Ideal Dictionary). Sometimes disease is seen simply as a departure from health. Illness, if differentiated from disease, is taken as the condition of being diseased, or more commonly, the state of being sick. Yet, as we will point out, disease and illness are highly complex entities, far more problematic than these commonsense views indicate. It is not our goal here to settle a longstanding academic controversy on the nature of disease and illness, but rather to sensitize the reader to a number of approaches and to some characteristics of illness designations.

A positivist conception of illness is most similar to the commonsense view. Illness is the presence of disease in an organism that inhibits the functioning, or, in Leon Kass's (1975) terms, "well-working" of the physiological organs (in a most inclusive sense) of the organism. This strict and limiting definition includes only malfunctioning organs as diseases. It contains an implicit assumption that there is some norm of functioning or well-working that can be used as a standard and that this normal condition is recognizable by the medical observer. One need only think about the recent medical controversies surrounding tonsillectomies and what constitutes "healthy" or "unhealthy" tonsils to realize that the concept of "well-functioning organs" is itself problematic. Moreover, does such a notion limiting illness and disease to organ malfunctioning include undiscovered diseases or organ changes that may be adaptations to an environment (e.g., the sickle cell trait)? By focusing only on "objective" organ conditions, the medical positivists (at least in theory) limit their concept of disease. It is important to point out that most of the difficulties we call mental illness, especially the so-called functional disorders, do not match this definition at all.

Others have argued that disease and illness are separate entities and can be so analyzed. For example, Abram Feinstein has conceptualized disease

in purely morphologic, physiologic, and chemical terms. What the physician directly observes in his dialogue [examination] . . . that he terms the *illness* consists of subjective sensations (symptoms) and certain findings (signs). The illness is described as the result of the interaction of the disease with the host or person, emphasis being given to the mechanism by which the disease develops and "produces" or is associated with the illness. (Feinstein, 1967, as summarized and cited in Fabrega & Manning, 1972, p. 95)*

According to this view, disease is a physiological state, and illness is a social state presumably caused by the disease. Although the pathologist sees the disease, the physician sees only signs and symptoms of illness and infers disease. This allows, conceptually at least, for illness without diseases and diseases without illnesses. Such a body/social dichotomy has the advantage of permitting analysis on both the physiological and social levels.

In sharp contrast to the positivist viewpoint is the cultural relativist position: an entity or condition is a disease or illness only if it is recognized and defined as one by the culture. For example, in one South American Indian tribe, dyschromic spirochetosis, a disease characterized by colored spots appearing on the skin, was so common that those who did not have it were regarded as deviant and excluded from marriage (Mechanic, 1968, p. 16). Among the Papago Indians of the American Southwest, obesity has a prevalence of nearly 100%. The Papago do not regard this condition as abnormal; in fact, they often bring babies whose development is normal by Western standards to the medical clinic and ask the physician why their baby is so skinny and sickly. To the Papago, obesity is not an illness; by Western standards nearly all the Papago are ill. Which definition is more valid? René Dubos (1959), an esteemed microbiologist, has argued that the

notion that a universal condition exists that is "health" is a mirage and that health and illness are limited by cultural knowledge and adaptations to the environment. Certainly such a relativist stance allows important insight, perhaps especially with what we call mental illness, but it is criticized easily for minimizing the organic-physiological nature of illness and disease. Cultural relativists, however, do sensitize us to the variability in the interpretation and definition of physiological phenomena.

Although all these approaches have some utility and validity in the contexts in which they are used, from a sociological perspective they miss a crucial aspect of illness: they take for granted how something becomes *defined* as an illness in the first place. Illness and disease are human constructions; they do not exist without someone proposing, describing, and recognizing them. There are processes we commonsensically call "disease," but that does not make them a priori diseases. As Peter Sedgwick (1972) points out, "the blight that strikes at corn or potatoes is a *human invention*, for if man wished to cultivate parasites (rather than potatoes or corn) there would be no 'blight,' but simply the necessary foddering of the parasite-crop" (p. 211). An animal may be feebled, have parasites, or be in pain but that in no way means it is suffering from an "illness." As Sedgwick (1972) states,

Animals do not have diseases either, prior to the presence of man in a meaningful relation with them. A tiger may experience pain or feebleness from a variety of causes. . . . It may be infected by a germ, trodden by an elephant, scratched by another tiger, or subjected to the [aging] process of its own cells. It does not present itself as being *ill* (though it may present itself as being highly distressed or uncomfortable) except in the eyes of a human observer who can discriminate illness from other sources of pain or enfeeblement. Outside the significances that man voluntarily attaches to certain conditions, *there are no illnesses or diseases in nature.* (p. 211)

Another way of saying this is that there are no illnesses in nature, only relationships. There are, of course, naturally occurring events, including infectious viruses, malignant growths, ruptures of tissues, and unusual chromosome constellations, but these are not ipso facto ill-

---

*From "Disease, illness, and deviant careers," by Horatio Fabrega, Jr. and Peter K. Manning, in *Theoretical perspectives on deviance,* edited by Robert A. Scott and Jack D. Douglas, p. 95, © 1972 by Robert A. Scott and Jack D. Douglas, Basic Books, Inc., Publishers, New York.

nesses. Without the social meaning that humans attach to them they do not constitute illness or disease:

The fracture of a septuagenarian's femur has, within the world of nature, no more significance than the snapping of an autumn leaf from its twig; and the invasion of a human organism by cholera germs carries with it no more the stamp of "illness" than the souring of milk by other forms of bacteria. (Sedgwick, 1972, p. 211)

Thus one could argue that biophysiological phenomena are what we use as a basis to label one condition or another as an illness or disease; the biophysiological phenomena are not in themselves illness or disease. (As we shall see in later chapters, however, a suspicion or hypothesis of biophysiological phenomena may be sufficient to label something as illness.)

Illnesses represent human judgments of conditions that exist in the natural world. They are essentially *social constructions* —products of our own creation. "Illness," as Gusfield (1967) has written, "is a social designation, by no means given by the nature of medical fact" (p. 180). The fact that there is high agreement on what constitutes an illness does not change this. The high degree of consensus on what "objectively" is disease is not independent of the social consensus that constructs these "facts" and renders them "important." For physical illness, the consensus is so extensive and taken for granted that we are inclined to forget that it represents a reality wholly dependent on our collective agreement (Freidson, 1970a, pp. 214-215).

As illnesses are social judgments, they are negative judgments. Can we think of any illness designations that are positive judgments or any illness conditions that are viewed as desirable states? Common sense also tells us that an entity labeled an illness or disease is considered undesirable. In the human world this is as true for tuberculosis* and cancer as it is for mental

illness and alcoholism. Biological aberration is neither necessary nor sufficient for something to be labeled an illness: a 7-foot basketball player is outside the normal biological range but not considered ill. Early and late onset of puberty are both biologically deviant conditions, yet only late puberty is viewed as evidence for physiological abnormalities and disorders (Conrad, 1976, p. 69). Nearly all functional mental disorders have no or at best questionable physiological evidence, yet they are defined and treated as diseases. In Western societies most illnesses are assumed to have some biophysiological or organic basis (and most do), but this is not a necessary condition for something to be defined as an illness. Occasionally an undesirable physiological condition such as baldness is not considered an illness. Most physiological conditions found troublesome, however, are defined as illnesses or medical disorders.

As Eliot Freidson (1970a) observes, calling something an illness in human society has consequences *independent* of the effects on the biological condition of the organism:

When a veterinarian diagnoses a cow's condition as an illness, he does not merely by diagnosis change the cow's behavior: to the cow, illness remains an experienced biophysical state, no more. But when a physician diagnoses a human's condition as illness, he changes the man's behavior by diagnosis: a social state is added to a biophysical state by assigning the meaning of illness to disease. (p. 223)

Think for a moment of the difference in consequences if a person's inability to function is attributed to laziness or to mononucleosis, seizures to demon possession or epilepsy, or drinking habits to moral weakness or alcoholism. Medical diagnosis affects people's behavior, attitudes they take toward themselves, and attitudes others take toward them.

In summary, illness is a social construction based on human judgments of some condition in the world. In some fashion, illness, like beauty (and like deviance), is in the eye of the beholder. Although it is based partly on current cultural conceptions of what disease is, and more often than not in Western society grounded in biophysiological phenomena, this social evaluative process is central rather than peripheral to the concept of illness and disease.

---

*Susan Sontag's (1978) recent characterization of tuberculosis in the 19th century as having an appealing symbolic significance within a small circle of literary and artistic figures appears to be an exception that, when viewed from a more general social perspective, serves to support the rule.

It follows logically that both diagnoses (as systematized classifications) and treatments are founded on these social judgments; they cannot be separated. Just as profound consequences followed from the recognition of microorganisms as agents of "disease," so are there consequences from recognizing illnesses as social judgments. Needless to say, the social construction of illness designations for deviant behaviors is subject to more ambiguity and interpretation than manifestly biophysiological problems. In this light it is understandable that conditions defined as illness reflect the social values and general Weltanschauung of a society.

Illness and deviance

As Talcott Parsons pointed out in his classic writings on the "sick role," both crime and illness are designations for deviant behavior (Parsons, 1951, pp. 428-479). Parsons conceptualized illness as deviance primarily because of its threat to the stability of a social system through its impact on role performance. Although both crime and illness are violations of norms (social and medical) and can be disruptive to social life, the attributions of cause are different. Deviance considered *willful* tends to be defined as crime; when it is seen as *unwillful* it tends to be defined as illness (see Aubert & Messinger, 1958). Since crime and illness are both designations of deviance, it becomes necessary to distinguish between the two, especially with reference to appropriate mechanisms of social control. It is in this regard that Parsons developed his notion of the sick role.

The social responses to crime and illness are different. Criminals are punished with the goal of altering their behavior in the direction of conventionality; sick people are treated with the goal of altering the conditions that prevent their conventionality. Parsons further argues that there exists for the sick a culturally available "sick role" that serves to conditionally legitimate the deviance of illness and channel the sick into the reintegrating physician-patient relationship. It is this relationship that serves the key social control function of minimizing the disruptiveness of sickness to the group or soci-

ety. The sick role has four components, two exemptions from normal responsibilities and two new obligations. First, the sick person is exempted from normal responsibilities, at least to the extent necessary to "get well." Second, the individual is not held responsible for his or her condition and cannot be expected to recover by an act of will. Third, the person must recognize that being ill is an inherently undesirable state and must want to recover. Fourth, the sick person is obligated to seek and cooperate with a competent treatment agent (usually a physician).* For sickness, then, medicine is the "appropriate" institution of social control. Both as legitimizer of the sick role and as the expert who strives to return the sick to conventional social roles, the physician functions as a social control agent.

In light of the socially constructed nature of both crime and illness, it should not be surprising to find that there has been a fluidity or drift between designations of crime deviations and illness deviations. One of the major concerns of this book is to explore the factors contributing to the change from moral-criminal definitions of deviance to medical ones, what we call the medicalization of deviance.

MEDICALIZATION OF DEVIANCE

Conceptions of deviant behavior change, and agencies mandated to control deviance change also. Historically there have been great transformations in the definition of deviance—from religious to state-legal to medical-scientific. Emile Durkheim (1893/1933) noted in *The Division of Labor in Society* that as societies develop from simple to complex, sanctions for deviance change from repressive to restitutive or, put another way, from punishment to treatment or rehabilitation. Along with the change in sanctions and social control agent there is a corresponding change in definition or conceptualization of deviant behavior. For example, certain "extreme" forms of deviant drinking (what is now called alcoholism) have been

---

*There have been a number of critiques and modifications of the sick role. See, for example, Gordon (1966), Mechanic (1968), Sigler and Osmond (1974), and Parsons (1975).

defined as sin, moral weakness, crime, and most recently illness. Nicholas Kittrie (1971) has called this change the divestment of the criminal justice system and the coming of the therapeutic state. Philip Rieff (1966), in his sociological study of the impact of Freudian thought, terms it the "triumph of the therapeutic."

In modern industrial society there has been a substantial growth in the prestige, dominance, and jurisdiction of the medical profession (Freidson, 1970a). It is only within the last century that physicians have become highly organized, consistently trained, highly paid, and sophisticated in their therapeutic techniques and abilities. Eminent American social scientist Lawrence J. Henderson observed that "somewhere between 1910 and 1912 in this country, a random patient, with a random disease, consulting a doctor chosen at random, had, *for the first time* in the history of mankind, a better than fifty-fifty chance of profiting from the encounter" (quoted in Blumgart, 1964; emphasis added). This observation suggests the poor state of medicine prior to the 20th century. With the apparent success of medicine in controlling communicable diseases (Dubos, 1959), the growth of scientific biomedicine, the regulation of medical education and licensing, and the political organization and lobbying by the American Medical Association, the prestige of the medical profession has increased. The medical profession dominates the organization of health care and has a virtual monopoly on anything that is defined as medical treatment, especially in terms of what constitutes "illness" and what is appropriate medical intervention. As Freidson (1970a) has observed, "The medical profession has first claim to jurisdiction over the label illness and *anything* to which it may be attached, irrespective of its capacity to deal with it effectively" (p. 251). Rieff (1966) contends that the hospital has replaced the church and parliament as the symbolic center of Western society. Although Durkheim did not predict this medicalization, perhaps in part because medicine of his time was not the scientific, prestigious, and dominant profession of today, it is clear that medicine is the central restitutive agent in our society.

The effectiveness of physicians and modern medicine in treating many illnesses has certainly contributed to the authority they are given. This has been especially true in the case of infectious diseases. With the mid–19th-century discovery of the germ theory of disease, a "doctrine of specific etiology" developed (Dubos, 1959). This doctrine implied that each disease had a single, specific, external, and objectively identifiable cause that could be discovered and treated accordingly. The success of this doctrine enhanced the prestige and reputations of medical professionals. However, as Freidson (1970a, p. 83) cautions, the reputations of the medical profession should not be seen only as a result of actual achievement but also as the product of negotiation, persuasion, and impression management by powerful interests involved in health care (recall our discussion of the monopolization of medicine in Chapter 1). This distinction between the reputation and reality of modern medicine is a point we return to in the next chapter in our discussion of how madness became entrenched in medical jurisdiction.

Medical treatments for deviant behavior are heralded frequently as examples of the "progress" typical of modern society, believed to unfold in a linear fashion, leaving beneficial advances in its wake. Medical progress is particularly likely to be seen as holding promise for solutions to age-old human problems. What "progress" is, however, on inspection, is not as clear as it might initially appear. "Progress" is only meaningful in relation to some other point in time and to a specific audience. Progress is a positive evaluation of some change. But social change is not clearly linear and rarely totally beneficial or detrimental. Social change nearly always produces positive and negative effects that are distributed differentially in the affected population (Corzine, 1977). For plantation owners the development of slavery was progress, but for the slaves it was the beginning of oppressive bondage. Perhaps in some respects the medicalization of opiate addiction, deviant drinking, obesity, hyperactivity, madness, and the other behaviors discussed in this book was progress. But changes defined as progress must be viewed as progress for a specific audience; all do not necessarily benefit equally from these changes. And to have a more complete picture, it is important to point out the accompanying problems and consequences created by the alleged progress. When the picture is more complete, change may not appear as clearly to be progress.

Expansion of medical jurisdiction over deviance

When treatment rather than punishment becomes the preferred sanction for deviance, an increasing amount of behavior is conceptualized in a medical framework as illness. As noted earlier, this is not unexpected, since medicine has always functioned as an agent of social control, especially in attempting to "normalize" illness and return people to their functioning capacity in society. Public health and psychiatry have long been concerned with social behavior and have functioned traditionally as agents of social control (Foucault, 1965; Rosen, 1972). What is significant, however, is the expansion of this sphere where medicine functions in a social control capacity. In the wake of a general humanitarian trend, the success and prestige of modern biomedicine, the technological growth of the 20th century, and the diminution of religion as a viable agent of control, more and more deviant behavior has come into the province of medicine. In short, the particular, dominant designation of deviance has changed; much of what was badness (i.e., sinful or criminal) is now sickness. Although some forms of deviant behavior are more completely medicalized than others (e.g., mental illness), recent research has pointed to a considerable variety of deviance that has been treated within medical jurisdiction: alcoholism, drug addiction, hyperactive children, suicide, obesity, mental retardation, crime, violence, child abuse, and learning problems, as well as several other categories of social deviance. Concomitant with medicalization there has been a change in imputed responsibility for deviance: with badness the deviants were considered responsible for their behavior; with sickness they are not, or at least responsibility is diminished (see Stoll, 1968). The social response to deviance is "therapeutic" rather than punitive. Many have viewed this as "humanitarian and

scientific" progress; indeed, it often leads to "humanitarian and scientific" treatment rather than punishment as a response to deviant behavior. As Barbara Wootton (1959) notes:

Without question . . . in the contemporary attitude towards anti-social behavior, psychiatry [i.e., medicine] and humanitarianism have marched hand in hand. Just because it is so much in keeping with the mental atmosphere of a scientifically-minded age, the medical treatment of social deviants has been a powerful reinforcement of humanitarian impulses; for today the prestige of humane proposals is immensely enhanced if these are expressed in the idiom of medical science. (p. 206)

There are, however, other, more disturbing consequences of medicalizing deviance that will be discussed in later chapters.

A number of broad social factors underlie the medicalization of deviance. As psychiatric critic Thomas Szasz (1974) observes, there has been a major historical shift in the manner in which we view human conduct:

With the transformation of the religious perspective of man into the scientific, and in particular the psychiatric, which became fully articulated during the nineteenth century, there occurred a radical shift in emphasis away from viewing man as a *responsible agent acting in and on the world* and toward viewing him *as a responsive organism being acted upon* by biological and social "forces." (p. 149)*

This is exemplified by the diffusion of Freudian thought, which since the 1920s has had a significant impact on the treatment of deviance, the distribution of stigma, and the incidence of penal sanctions.

Nicholas Kittrie (1971), focusing on decriminalization, contends that the foundation of the therapeutic state can be found in determinist criminology, that it stems from the *parens patriae* power of the state (the state's right to help those who are unable to help themselves), and that it dates its origin with the development of juvenile justice at the turn of the century. He further suggests that criminal law has failed to deal effectively (e.g., in deterrence) with criminals and deviants, encouraging a use of alter-

---

*From Szasz, T. *Ceremonial chemistry*. New York: Doubleday & Co., Inc., 1974. Copyright © 1974 by Thomas Szasz.

native methods of control. Others have pointed out that the strength of formal sanctions is declining because of the increase in geographical mobility and the decrease in strength of traditional status groups (e.g., the family) and that medicalization offers a substitute method for controlling deviance (Pitts, 1968). The success of medicine in areas like infectious disease has led to rising expectations of what medicine can accomplish. In modern technological societies, medicine has followed a technological imperative — that the physician is responsible for doing everything possible for the patient — while neglecting such significant issues as the patient's rights and wishes and the impact of biomedical advances on society (Mechanic, 1973). Increasingly sophisticated medical technology has extended the potential of medicine as social control, especially in terms of psychotechnology (Chorover, 1973). Psychotechnology includes a variety of medical and quasimedical treatments or procedures: psychosurgery, psychoactive medications, genetic engineering, disulfiram (Antabuse), and methadone. Medicine is frequently a pragmatic way of dealing with a problem (Gusfield, 1975). Undoubtedly the increasing acceptance and dominance of a scientific world view and the increase in status and power of the medical profession have contributed significantly to the adoption and public acceptance of medical approaches to handling deviant behavior.

The medical model and "moral neutrality"

The first "victories" over disease by an emerging biomedicine were in the infectious diseases in which specific causal agents — germs — could be identified. An image was created of disease as caused by physiological difficulties located *within* the human body. This was the medical model. It emphasized the internal and biophysiological environment and deemphasized the external and social psychological environment.

There are numerous definitions of "the medical model." In this book we adopt a broad and pragmatic definition: the medical model of deviance locates the source of deviant behavior within the individual, postulating a physiological, constitutional, organic, or, occasionally,

psychogenic agent or condition that is assumed to cause the behavioral deviance. The medical model of deviance usually, although not always, mandates intervention by medical personnel with medical means as treatment for the "illness." Alcoholics Anonymous, for example, adopts a rather idiosyncratic version of the medical model — that alcoholism is a chronic disease caused by an "allergy" to alcohol — but actively discourages professional medical intervention. But by and large, adoption of the medical model legitimates and even mandates medical intervention.

The medical model and the associated medical designations are assumed to have a scientific basis and thus are treated as if they were morally neutral (Zola, 1975). They are not considered moral judgments but rational, scientifically verifiable conditions. As pointed out earlier, medical designations *are* social judgments, and the adoption of a medical model of behavior, a political decision. When such medical designations are applied to deviant behavior, they are related directly and intimately to the moral order of society. In 1851 Samuel Cartwright, a well-known Southern physician, published an article in a pretigious medical journal describing the disease "drapetomania," which only affected slaves and whose major symptom was running away from the plantations of their white masters (Cartwright, 1851). Medical texts during the Victorian era routinely described masturbation as a disease or addiction and prescribed mechanical and surgical treatments for its cure (Comfort, 1967; Englehardt, 1974). Recently many political dissidents in the Soviet Union have been designated mentally ill, with diagnoses such as "paranoia with counterrevolutionary delusions" and "manic reformism," and hospitalized for their opposition to the political order (Conrad, 1977). Although these illustrations may appear to be extreme examples, they highlight the fact that all medical designations of deviance are influenced significantly by the moral order of society and thus cannot be considered morally neutral.

SUMMARY

This chapter has outlined the conceptual framework that informs the remainder of this book. We call it a "historical-social constructionist" approach to deviance. Of the two orientations to deviance noted in Chapter 1, it is clearly interactionist and has its roots in the labeling-interactionist tradition. In addition, it employs a sociology-of-knowledge perspective to examine the emergence and change of definitions and designations of deviance. Rather than focusing on individual deviants and the causes of their behavior, the focus is on the *etiology of definitions* of deviance. In this sense it can be viewed as a sociology of deviance designations. Deviance definitions are treated as products of a political process, as social constructions usually implemented and legitimated by powerful and influential interests and applied to relatively powerless and subordinate groups.

Even after a social definition of deviance becomes accepted or legitimated, it is not evident what particular type of problem it is. Frequently there are intellectual disputes over the causes of the deviant behavior and the appropriate methods of control. These battles about deviance designation (is it sin, crime, or sickness?) and control are battles over turf: Who is the appropriate definer and treater of the deviance? Decisions concerning what is the proper deviance designation and hence the appropriate agent of social control are settled by some type of political conflict.

How one designation rather than another becomes dominant is a central sociological question. In answering this question, sociologists must focus on claims-making activities of the various interest groups involved and examine how one or another attains ownership of a given type of deviance or social problem and thus generates legitimacy for a deviance designation. Seen from this perspective, public facts, even those which wear a "scientific" mantle, are treated as products of the groups or organizations that produce or promote them rather than as accurate reflections of "reality." The adoption of one deviance designation or another has consequences beyond settling a dispute about social control turf; these will become more apparent and will be articulated in subsequent chapters.

When a particular type of deviance designation is accepted and taken for granted, some-

thing akin to a paradigm exists. There have been three major deviance paradigms: deviance as sin, deviance as crime, and deviance as sickness. When one paradigm and its adherents become the ultimate arbiter of "reality" in society, we say a hegemony of definitions exists. In Western societies, and American society in particular, anything proposed in the name of science gains great authority. In modern industrial societies, deviance designations have become increasingly medicalized. We call the change in designations from badness to sickness the medicalization of deviance.

Illness, like deviance, is a social construction based on social judgments of some condition in the world. Although based partly on current cultural conceptions of what constitutes disease, and (in Western societies) typically grounded in biophysiological phenomena, the social evaluative process of classifying some condition or event as a disease is central rather than peripheral to the concept of disease and illness. In this fundamental sense a disease designation is a moral judgment, for to define something as a disease or illness is to deem it undesirable.

Sociologists since Parsons have viewed illness and crime as alternate designations for deviance. Deviance that is considered willful is defined as crime; when it is considered unwillful, it tends to be defined as illness. Thus when illness is a designation for deviant behavior, medicine becomes the agent of social control.

Designations of deviance have increasingly shifted from the moral to the medical sphere. With the apparent success of medicine in controlling communicable diseases, the growth of scientific biomedicine, the political organization and lobbying of the American Medical Association, and the profession's control over medical education and licensing, medicine has become a prestigious profession in the 20th century. The medical profession dominates the organization of health care and has a virtual monopoly over anything that is defined as an illness or a "medical" treatment.

Although our portrayals of the social and historical sources of changing deviance designations are painted with a broad brush, and certainly cannot include all the contextual characteristics involved in such complex shifts, clear outlines of the change and development of each deviance designation are delineated. In depicting these individual cases we use a finer brush and give attention to specific detail. Thus we give consideration to historical events, relevant settings of conflict and change, attributions of cause, social control mechanisms, scientific discoveries, and claims-making activities for each case presented in the following six chapters.

SUGGESTED READINGS

Freidson, E. *Profession of medicine*. New York: Dodd, Mead & Co., 1970.
Considered a seminal and path-breaking sociological analysis of the profession of medicine. Of particular interest is the section on the social construction of illness (pp. 203-331).
Gusfield, J. R. Moral passage: the symbolic process in the public designations of deviance. *Soc. Prob.*, 1967, **15**, 175-188.
Builds on Gusfield's earlier (1963) work on the Temperance movement and analyzes changing public designations of deviant drinking. Although his emphasis is on the symbolic qualities of changing designations, this paper exemplifies the approach outlined in this chapter.
Illich, I. *Medical nemesis*. New York: Pantheon Books, Inc., 1976.
A readable and controversial analysis of the place of medicine in modern society. Illich argues that medicine has become more a threat to health than a healing agent and needs to be dismantled, decentralized, and replaced by various forms of self-help. The section on "social iatrogenesis" is most relevant to medicalization of deviance.
Kittrie, N. N. *The right to be different: deviance and enforced therapy*. Baltimore: Johns Hopkins University Press, 1971.
A superbly documented overview focusing on the legal aspects of medicalization. Kittrie documents the growth of the therapeutic state in relation to the growth of 19th-century deterministic theories, emphasizes lack of legal "safeguards" for deviants, and makes specific recommendations for action.
Parsons, T. *The social system*. New York: The Free Press, 1951.
Parsons' major theoretical treatise. His analysis of "the sick role" (pp. 428-479) is the classical sociological discussion of the relation of crime and illness as deviance designations and medicine as an agent of social control.

9 MEDICINE as an INSTITUTION of SOCIAL CONTROL

CONSEQUENCES for SOCIETY

In the final two chapters we leave behind the specific cases and focus on some general features of the medicalization of deviance.

These are important chapters, for together they outline the sources and consequences of medicalizing deviance in American society. Chapter 9 examines medicine as an institution of social control, and Chapter 10 offers a statement of what a theory of medicalization of deviance might look like, based on the cases presented in earlier chapters. We attempt, in essence, to provide a more succinct sociological analysis of the medicalization of deviance.

In our society we want to believe in medicine, as we want to believe in religion and our country; it wards off collective fears and reduces public anxieties (see Edelman, 1977). In significant ways medicine, especially psychiatry, has replaced religion as the most powerful extralegal institution of social control.

□ This chapter is an adapted, amended, and extended discussion from Conrad, P. Types of social control. *Soc. Health & Illness*, 1979, *1*, 1-12, by permission of Routledge & Kegan Paul Ltd.; and Conrad, P., The discovery of hyperkinesis. *Social Problems*, 1975, *23*, 12-21. Portions of this chapter also taken from "Medicine" by Conrad, P., and Schneider, J., in *Social control for the 1980s: a handbook for order in a democratic society* edited by Joseph S. Roucek, 1978, pp. 346-358, and used with the permission of the publisher, Greenwood Press, Inc., Westport, Conn., and our forthcoming article in *Contemporary Crises,* reprinted by permission of Elsevier Scientific Publishing Co., Amsterdam.

Physicians have been endowed with some of the charisma of shamans. In the 20th century the medical model of deviance has ascended with the glitter of a rising star, expanding medicine's social control functions. In earlier substantive chapters we focused on the changing definitions and designations of deviance, frequently alluding to medical social control. In this chapter we focus directly on medicine as an agent of social control. First, we illustrate the range and varieties of medical social control. Next, we analyze the consequences of the medicalization of deviance and social control. Finally, we examine some significant social policy questions pertaining to medicine and medicalization in American society.

TYPES OF MEDICAL SOCIAL CONTROL

Medicine was first conceptualized as an agent of social control by Talcott Parsons (1951) in his seminal essay on the "sick role" (see Chapter 2). Eliot Freidson (1970a) and Irving Zola (1972) have elucidated the jurisdictional mandate the medical profession has over anything that can be labeled an illness, regardless of its ability to deal with it effectively. The boundaries of medicine are elastic and increasingly expansive (Ehrenreich & Ehrenreich, 1975), and some analysts have expressed concern at the increasing medicalization of life (Illich, 1976). Although medical social control has been conceptualized in several ways, including professional control of colleagues (Freidson, 1975) and control of the micropolitics of physician-patient interaction (Waitzkin & Stoeckle, 1976), the focus here is narrower. Our concern, as is evident throughout this book, is with the medical control of deviant behavior, an aspect of the medicalization of deviance (Conrad, 1975; Pitts, 1968). Thus by medical social control we mean the ways in which medicine functions (wittingly or unwittingly) to secure adherence to social norms—specifically, by using medical means to minimize, eliminate, or normalize deviant behavior. This section illustrates and catalogues the broad range of medical controls of deviance and in so doing conceptualizes three major "ideal types" of medical social control.

On the most abstract level medical social control is the acceptance of a medical perspective as the dominant definition of certain phenomena. When medical prespectives of problems and their solutions become dominant, they diminish competing definitions. This is particularly true of problems related to bodily functioning and in areas where medical technology can demonstrate effectiveness (e.g., immunization, contraception, antibacterial drugs) and is increasingly the case for behavioral and social problems (Mechanic, 1973). This underlies the construction of medical norms (e.g., the definition of what is healthy) and the "enforcement" of both medical and social norms. Medical social control also includes medical advice, counsel, and information that are part of the general stock of knowledge: for example, a well-balanced diet is important, cigarette smoking causes cancer, being overweight increases health risks, exercising regularly is healthy, teeth should be brushed regularly. Such directives, even when unheeded, serve as road signs for desirable behavior. At a more concrete level, medical social control is enacted through professional medical intervention, qua medical treatment (although it may include some types of self-treatment such as self-medication or medically oriented self-help groups). This intervention aims at returning sick individuals to compliance with health norms and to their conventional social roles, adjusting them to new (e.g., impaired) roles, or, short of these, making individuals more

comfortable with their condition (see Freidson, 1970a; Parsons, 1951). Medical social control of deviant behavior is usually a variant of medical intervention that seeks to eliminate, modify, isolate, or regulate behavior socially defined as deviant, with medical means and in the name of health.

Traditionally, psychiatry and public health have served as the clearest examples of medical control. Psychiatry's social control functions with mental illness, especially in terms of institutionalization, have been described clearly (e.g., Miller, K. S., 1976; Szasz, 1970). Recently it has been argued that psychotherapy, because it reinforces dominant values and adjusts people to their life situations, is an agent of social control and a supporter of the status quo (Halleck, 1971; Hurvitz, 1973). Public health's mandate, the control and elimination of conditions and diseases that are deemed a threat to the health of a community, is more diffuse. It operates as a control agent by setting and enforcing certain "health" standards in the home, workplace, and community (e.g., food, water, sanitation) and by identifying, preventing, treating, and, if necessary, isolating persons with communicable diseases (Rosen, 1972). A clear example of the latter is the detection of venereal disease. Indeed, public health has exerted considerable coercive power in attempting to prevent the spread of infectious disease.

There are a number of types of medical control of deviance. The most common forms of medical social control include medicalizing deviant behavior—that is, defining the behavior as an illness or a symptom of an illness or underlying disease—and subsequent direct medical intervention. This medical social control takes three general forms: medical technology, medical collaboration, and medical ideology.

Medical technology

The growth of specialized medicine and the concomitant development of medical technology has produced an armamentarium of medical controls. Psychotechnologies, which include various forms of medical and behavioral technologies (Chorover, 1973), are the most common means of medical control of deviance.

Since the emergence of phenothiazine medications in the early 1950s for the treatment and control of mental disorder, there has been a virtual explosion in the development and use of psychoactive medications to control behavioral deviance: tranquilizers such as chlordiazepoxide (Librium) and diazepam (Valium) for anxiety, nervousness, and general malaise; stimulant medications for hyperactive children; amphetamines for overeating and obesity; disulfiram (Antabuse) for alcoholism; methadone for heroin, and many others.* These pharmaceutical discoveries, aggressively promoted by a highly profitable and powerful drug industry (Goddard, 1973), often become the treatment of choice for deviant behavior. They are easily administered under professional medical control, quite potent in their effects (i.e., controlling, modifying, and even eliminating behavior), and are generally less expensive than other medical treatments and controls (e.g., hospitalization, altering environments, long-term psychotherapy).

Psychosurgery, surgical procedures meant to correct certain "brain dysfunctions" presumed to cause deviant behavior, was developed in the early 1930s as prefrontal lobotomy, and has been used as a treatment for mental illness. But psychosurgery fell into disrepute in the early 1950s because the "side effects" (general passivity, difficulty with abstract thinking) were deemed too undesirable, and many patients remained institutionalized in spite of such treatments. Furthermore, new psychoactive medications were becoming available to control the mentally ill. By the middle 1950s, however, approximately 40,000 to 50,000 such operations were performed in the United States (Freeman, 1959). In the late 1960s a new and technologically more sophisticated variant of psychosurgery (including laser technology and brain implants) emerged and was heralded by some as a treatment for uncontrollable violent outbursts (Delgado, 1969; Mark & Ervin, 1970). Although psychosurgery for violence has been criticized from both within as well as outside the medical profession (Chorover, 1974b), and relatively few such operations have been performed, in 1976 a blue-ribbon national commission reporting to the Department of Health, Education and Welfare endorsed the use of psychosurgery as having "potential merit" and judged its risks "not excessive." This may encourage an increased use of this form of medical control.*

Behavior modification, a psychotechnology based on B.F. Skinner's and other behaviorists' learning theories, has been adopted by some medical professionals as a treatment modality. A variety of types and variations of behavior modification exist (e.g., token economies, tier systems, positive reinforcement schedules, aversive conditioning). While they are not medical technologies per se, they have been used by physicians for the treatment of mental illness, mental retardation, homosexuality, violence, hyperactive children, autism, phobias, alcoholism, drug addiction, eating problems, and other disorders. An irony of the medical use of behavior modification is that behaviorism explicitly denies the medical model (that behavior is a symptom of illness) and adopts an environmental, albeit still individual, solution to the problem. This has not, however, hindered its adoption by medical professionals.

Human genetics is one of the most exciting and rapidly expanding areas of medical knowledge. Genetic screening and genetic counseling are becoming more commonplace. Genetic causes are proposed for such a variety of human problems as alcoholism, hyperactivity, learning disabilities, schizophrenia, manic-depressive psychosis, homosexuality, and mental retardation. At this time, apart from specific genetic disorders such as pheylketonuria (PKU) and certain forms of retardation,

---

*Another pharmaceutical innovation, birth control pills, also functions as a medical control; in this case, the control of reproduction. There is little doubt that "the pill" has played a significant part in the sexual revolution since the 1960s and the redefinition of what constitutes sexual deviance.

*A number of other surgical interventions for deviance have been developed in recent years. Surgery for "gender dysphoria" (transsexuality) and "intestinal by-pass" operations for obesity are both examples of surgical intervention for deviance. The legalization of abortions has also medicalized and legitimated an activity that was formerly deviant and brought it under medical-surgical control.

genetic explanations tend to be general theories (i.e., at best positing "predispositions"), with only minimal empirical support, and are not at the level at which medical intervention occurs. The most well-publicized genetic theory of deviant behavior is that an XYY chromosome arrangement is a determinant factor in "criminal tendencies." Although this XYY research has been criticized severely (e.g., Fox, 1971), the controversy surrounding it may be a harbinger of things to come. Genetic anomalies may be discovered to have a correlation with deviant behavior and may become a causal explanation for this behavior. Medical control, in the form of genetic counseling (Sorenson, 1974), may discourage parents from having offspring with a high risk (e.g., 25%) of genetic impairment. Clearly the potentials for medical control go far beyond present use; one could imagine the possibility of licensing selected parents (with proper genes) to have children, and further manipulating gene arrangements to produce or eliminate certain traits.

Medical collaboration

Medicine acts not only as an independent agent of social control (as above), but frequently medical collaboration with other authorities serves social control functions. Such collaboration includes roles as information provider, gatekeeper, institutional agent, and technician. These interdependent medical control functions highlight the extent to which medicine is interwoven in the fabric of society. Historically, medical personnel have reported information on gunshot wounds and venereal disease to state authorities. More recently this has included reporting "child abuse" to child welfare or law enforcement agencies (Pfohl, 1977).

The medical profession is the official designator of the "sick role." This imbues the physician with authority to define particular kinds of deviance as illness and exempt the patient from certain role obligations. These are general gatekeeping and social control tasks. In some instances the physician functions as a specific gatekeeper for special exemptions from conventional norms; here the exemptions are authorized because of illness, disease, or dis-

ability. A classic example is the so-called insanity defense in certain crime cases. Other more commonplace examples include competency to stand trial, medical deferment from the draft or a medical discharge from the military; requiring physicians' notes to legitimize missing an examination or excessive absences in school, and, before abortion was legalized, obtaining two psychiatrists' letters testifying to the therapeutic necessity of the abortion. Halleck (1971) has called this "the power of medical excuse." In a slightly different vein, but still forms of gatekeeping and medical excuse, are medical examinations for disability or workman's compensation benefits. Medical reports required for insurance coverage and employment or medical certification of an epileptic as seizure free to obtain a driver's license are also gatekeeping activities.

Physicians in total institutions have one of two roles. In some institutions, such as schools for the retarded or mental hospitals, they are usually the administrative authority; in others, such as in the military or prisons, they are employees of the administration. In total institutions, medicine's role as an agent of social control (for the institution) is more apparent. In both the military and prisons, physicians have the power to confer the sick role and to offer medical excuse for deviance (see Daniels, 1969; Waitzkin & Waterman, 1974). For example, discharges and sick call are available medical designations for deviant behavior. Since physicians are both hired and paid by the institution, it is difficult for them to be fully an agent of the patient, engendering built-in role strains. An extreme example is in wartime when the physician's mandate is to return the soldier to combat duty as soon as possible. Under some circumstances physicians act as direct agents of control by prescribing medications to control unruly or disorderly inmates or to help a "neurotic" adjust to the conditions of a total institution. In such cases "captive professionals" (Daniels, 1969) are more likely to become the agent of the institution than the agent of the individual patient (Szasz, 1965; see also Menninger, 1967).

Under rather rare circumstances physicians may become "mere technicians," applying the sanctions of another authority who purchases their medical skills. An extreme example would be the behavior of the experimental and death physicians in Nazi Germany. A less heinous but nevertheless ominous example is provided by physicians who perform court-ordered sterilizations (Kittrie, 1971). Perhaps one could imagine sometime in the future, if the death penalty becomes commonplace again, physicians administering drugs as the "humanitarian" and painless executioners.*

Medical ideology

Medical ideology is a type of social control that involves defining a behavior or condition as an illness primarily because of the social and ideological benefits accrued by conceptualizing it in medical terms. These effects of medical ideology may benefit the individual, the dominant interests in the society, or both. They exist independently of any organic basis for illness or any available treatment. Howard Waitzkin and Barbara Waterman (1974) call one latent function of medicalization "secondary gain," arguing that assumption of the sick role can fulfill personality and individual needs (e.g., gaining nurturance or attention) or legitimize personal failure (Shuval & Antonovsky, 1973).† One of the most important functions of the disease model of alcoholism and to a lesser extent drug addiction is the secondary gain of removing blame from, and constructing a shield against condemnation of, individuals for their deviant behavior. Alcoholics Anonymous, a nonmedical quasireligious self-help organization, adopted a variant of the medical model of alcoholism independent of the medical profession. One suspects the secondary gain serves their purposes well.

---

*It is worth noting that in the recent Gary Gilmore execution a physician was involved; he designated the spot where the heartbeat was loudest and measured vital signs during the execution ceremony. A few states have actually passed death penalty legislation specifying injection of a lethal drug as the means of execution.

†Although Waitzkin and Waterman suggest that such secondary gain functions are latent (i.e., unintended and unrecognized), the cases we have discussed here show that such "gains" are often intentionally pursued.

Disease designations can support dominant social interests and institutions. A poignant example is prominent 19th-century New Orleans physician S. W. Cartwright's antebellum conceptualization of the disease drapetomania, a condition that affected only slaves. Its major symptom was running away from their masters (Cartwright, S. W., 1851). Medical conceptions and controls often support dominant social values and morality: the 19th-century Victorian conceptualization of the illness of and addiction to masturbation and the medical treatments developed to control this disease make chilling reading in the 1970s (Comfort, 1967; Englehardt, 1974). The recent Soviet labeling of political dissidents as mentally ill is another example of the manipulation of illness designations to support dominant political and social institutions (Conrad, 1977). These examples highlight the sociopolitical nature of illness designations in general (Zola, 1975).

In sum, medicine as an institution of social control has a number of faces. The three types of medical social control discussed here do not necessarily exist as discrete entities but are found in combination with one another. For example, court-ordered sterilizations or medical prescribing of drugs to unruly nursing home patients combines both technological and collaborative aspects of medical control; legitimating disability status includes both ideological and collaborative aspects of medical control; and treating Soviet dissidents with drugs for their mental illness combines all three aspects of medical social control. It is clear that the enormous expansion of medicine in the past 50 years has increased the number of possible ways in which problems could be medicalized beyond those discussed in earlier chapters. In the next section we point out some of the consequences of this medicalization.

SOCIAL CONSEQUENCES OF MEDICALIZING DEVIANCE

Jesse Pitts (1968), one of the first sociologists to give attention to the medicalization of deviance, suggests that "medicalization is one of the most effective means of social control and that it is destined to become the main mode of *formal* social control'' (p. 391, emphasis in original).* Although his bold prediction is far-reaching (and, in light of recent developments, perhaps a bit premature), his analysis of a decade ago was curiously optimistic and uncritical of the effects and consequences of medicalization. Nonsociologists, especially psychiatric critic Thomas Szasz (1961, 1963, 1970, 1974) and legal scholar Nicholas Kittrie (1971), are much more critical in their evaluations of the ramifications of medicalization. Szasz's critiques are polemical and attack the medical, especially psychiatric, definitions and treatments for deviant behavior. Szasz's analyses, although path breaking, insightful, and suggestive, have not been presented in a particularly systematic form. Both he and Kittire tend to focus on the effects of medicalization on individual civil liberties and judicial processes rather than on social consequences. Their writings, however, reveal that both are aware of sociological consequences.

In this section we discuss some of the more significant consequences and ramifications of defining deviant behavior as a medical problem. We must remind the reader that we are examining the *social* consequences of medicalizing deviance, which can be analyzed separately from the validity of medical definitions or diagnoses, the effectiveness of medical regimens, or their individual consequences. These variously ''latent'' consequences inhere in medicalization itself and occur *regardless* of how efficacious the particular medical treatment or social control mechanism. As will be apparent, our sociological analysis has left us skeptical of the social benefits of medical social control. We separate the consequences into the ''brighter'' and ''darker'' sides of medicalization. The ''brighter'' side will be presented first.

Brighter side

The brighter side of medicalization includes the positive or beneficial qualities that are at-

*From Pitts, J. Social control: the concept. In D. Sills (Ed.), *International encyclopedia of social sciences* (Vol. 14). New York: Macmillan Publishing Co., Inc., 1968. Copyright 1968 by Crowell Collier and Macmillan, Inc.

tributed to medicalization. We review briefly the accepted socially progressive aspects of medicalizing deviance. They are separated more for clarity of presentation than for any intrinsic separation in consequence.

First, medicalization is related to a longtime *humanitarian* trend in the conception and control of deviance. For example, alcoholism is no longer considered a sin or even a moral weakness; it is now a disease. Alcoholics are no longer arrested in many places for ''public drunkenness''; they are now somehow ''treated,'' if only to be dried out for a time. Medical treatment for the alcoholic can be seen as a more humanitarian means of social control. It is not retributive or punitive, but at least ideally, therapeutic. Troy Duster (1970, p. 10) suggests that medical definitions increase tolerance and compassion for human problems and they ''have now been reinterpreted in an almost nonmoral fashion.'' (We doubt this, but leave the morality issue for a later discussion.) Medicine and humanitarianism historically developed concurrently and, as some have observed, the use of medical language and evidence increases the prestige of human proposals and enhances their acceptance (Wootton, 1959; Zola, 1975). Medical definitions are imbued with the prestige of the medical profession and are considered the ''scientific'' and humane way of viewing a problem. (Concerning the actual scientific basis for medical definitions, recall our discussion of the disease concept of alcoholism in Chapter 4.) This is especially true if an apparently ''successful'' treatment for controlling the behavior is available, as with hyperkinesis.

Second, medicalization allows for the extension of the *sick role* to those labeled as deviants (see Chapter 2 for our discussion of the sick role). Many of the perceived benefits of the medicalization of deviance stem from the assignment of the sick role. Some have suggested that this is the most significant element of adopting the medical model of deviant behavior (Sigler & Osmond, 1974). By defining deviant behavior as an illness or a result of illness, one is absolved of responsibility for one's behavior. It diminishes or *removes blame* from the individual for deviant actions. Alcoholics are no longer held responsible for their uncontrolled drinking, and perhaps hyperactive children are no longer the classroom's "bad boys" but children with a medical disorder. There is some clear secondary gain here for the individual. The label "sick" is free of the moral opprobrium and implied culpability of "criminal" or "sinner." The designation of sickness also may reduce guilt for drinkers and their families and for hyperactive children and their parents. Similarly, it may result in reduced stigma for the deviant. It allows for the development of more acceptable accounts of deviance: a recent film depicted a child witnessing her father's helpless drunken stupor; her mother remarked, "It's okay. Daddy's just sick."*

The sick role allows for the "conditional legitimation" of a certain amount of deviance, so long as the individual fulfills the obligations of the sick role.† As Renée Fox (1977) notes:

The fact that the exemptions of sickness have been extended to people with a widening arc of attitudes, experiences and behaviors in American society means primarily that what is regarded as "conditionally legitimated deviance" has increased. . . . So long as [the deviant] does not abandon himself to illness or eagerly embrace it, but works actively on his own or with medical professionals to improve his condition, he is considered to be responding appropriately, even admirably, to an unfortunate occurrence. Under these conditions, illness is accepted as legitimate deviance. (p. 15)‡

---

*It should be noted, however, that little empirical evidence exists for reduced stigmatization. Derek Phillips' (1963) research suggests that people seeking medical help for their personal problems are highly at risk for rejection and stigmatization. Certain illnesses carry their own stigma. Leprosy, epilepsy, and mental illness are all stigmatized illnesses (Gussow & Tracy, 1968); Susan Sontag (1978) proposes that cancer is highly stigmatized in American society. We need further research on the stigma-reducing properties of medical designations of deviance; it is by no means an automatic result of medicalization.

†On the other hand, Paul Roman and Harrison Trice (1968, p. 248) contend that the sick role of alcoholic may actually reinforce deviant behavior by removing responsibility for deviant drinking behavior.

‡Reprinted by permission of *Daedalus,* Journal of the American Academy of Arts and Sciences, Boston, Mass. Spring 1977, *Doing better and feeling worse: health in the United States.*

The deviant, in essence, is medically excused for the deviation. But, as Talcott Parsons (1972) has pointed out, "the conditional legitimation is bought at a 'price,' namely, the recognition that illness itself is an undesirable state, to be recovered from as expeditiously as possible" (p. 108). Thus the medical excuse for deviance is only valid when the patient-deviant accepts the medical perspective of the inherent undesirability of his or her sick behavior and submits to a subordinate relationship with an official agent of control (the physician) toward changing it. This, of course, negates any threat the deviant may pose to society's normative structure, for such deviants do not challenge the norm; by accepting deviance as sickness and social control as "treatment," the deviant underscores the validity of the violated norm.

Third, the medical model can be viewed as portraying an *optimistic* outcome for the deviant.* Pitts (1968) notes, "the possibility that a patient may be exploited is somewhat minimized by therapeutic ideology, which creates an optimistic bias concerning the patient's fate" (p. 391).† The therapeutic ideology, accepted in some form by all branches of medicine, suggests that a problem (e.g., deviant behavior) can be changed or alleviated if only the proper treatment is discovered and administered. Defining deviant behavior as an illness may also mobilize hope in the individual patient that with proper treatment a "cure" is possible (Frank, J., 1974). Clearly this could have beneficial results and even become a self-fulfilling prophecy. Although the medical model is interpreted frequently as optimistic about individual change, under some circumstances it may lend itself to pessimistic interpretations. The attribution of physiological cause coupled with the lack of effective treatment engendered a somatic pessimism in the

---

*For a contrasting viewpoint, see Rotenberg's (1978) work, discussed in the next chapter.

†From Pitts, J. Social control: the concept. In D. Sills (Ed.), *International encyclopedia of social sciences* (Vol. 14). New York: Macmillan Publishing Co., Inc., 1968. Copyright 1968 by Crowell Collier and Macmillan, Inc.

late 19th-century conception of madness (see Chapter 3).

Fourth, medicalization lends the *prestige of the medical profession* to deviance designations and treatments. The medical profession is the most prestigious and dominant profession in American society (Freidson, 1970a). As just noted, medical definitions of deviance become imbued with the prestige of the medical profession and are construed to be the "scientific" way of viewing a problem. The medical mantle of science may serve to deflect definitional challenges. This is especially true if an apparently "successful" treatment for controlling the behavior is available. Medicalization places the problem in the hands of healing physicians. "The therapeutic value of professional dominance, from the patient's point of view, is that it becomes the *doctor's* problem" (Ehrenreich & Ehrenreich, 1975, p. 156, emphasis in original). Physicians are assumed to be beneficent and honorable. "The medical and paramedical professions," Pitts (1968) contends, "especially in the United States, are probably more immune to corruption than are the judicial and parajudicial professions and relatively immune to political pressure" (p. 391).*

Fifth, medical social control is more *flexible* and often more *efficient* than judicial and legal controls. The impact of the flexibility of medicine is most profound on the "deviance of everyday life," since it allows "social pressures on deviance [to] increase without boxing the deviant into as rigid a category as 'criminal'" (Pitts, 1968, p. 391).* Medical controls are adjustable to fit the needs of the individual patient, rather than being a response to the deviant act itself. It may be more efficient (and less expensive) to control opiate addiction with methadone maintenance than with long prison terms or mental hospitalization. The behavior of disruptive hyperactive children, who have been immune to all parental and teacher sanc-

*From Pitts, J. Social control: the concept. In D. Sills (Ed.), *International encyclopedia of social sciences* (Vol. 14). New York: Macmillan Publishing Co., Inc., 1968. Copyright 1968 by Crowell Collier and Macmillan, Inc.

tions, may dramatically improve after treatment with medications. Medical controls circumvent complicated legal and judicial procedures and may be applied more informally. This can have a considerable effect on social control structures. For example, it has been noted that defining alcoholism as a disease would reduce arrest rates in some areas up to 50%.

In sum, the social benefits of medicalization include the creation of humanitarian and nonpunitive sanctions; the extension of the sick role to some deviants; a reduction of individual responsibility, blame, and possibly stigma for deviance; an optimistic therapeutic ideology; care and treatment rendered by a prestigious medical profession; and the availability of a more flexible and often more efficient means of social control.

Darker side

There is, however, another side to the medicalization of deviant behavior. Although it may often seem entirely humanitarian to conceptualize deviance as sickness as opposed to badness, it is not that simple. There is a "darker" side to the medicalization of deviance. In some senses these might be considered as the more clearly latent aspects of medicalization. In an earlier work Conrad (1975) elucidated four consequences of medicalizing deviance; building on that work, we expand our analysis to seven. Six are discussed here; the seventh is described separately in the next section.

Dislocation of responsibility. As we have seen, defining behavior as a medical problem removes or profoundly diminishes responsibility from the individual. Although affixing responsibility is always complex, medicalization produces confusion and ambiguity about who is responsible. Responsibility is separated from social action; it is located in the nether world of biophysiology or psyche. Although this takes the individual officially "off the hook," its excuse is only a partial one. The individual, the putative deviant, and the undesirable conduct are still associated. Aside from where such conduct is "seated," the sick deviant is the medium of its expression.

With the removal of responsibility also comes the lowering of status. A dual-class citizenship is created: those who are deemed responsible for their actions and those who are not. The not-completely-responsible sick are placed in a position of dependence on the fully responsible nonsick (Parsons, 1975, p. 108). Kittrie (1971, p. 347) notes in this regard that more than half the American population is no longer subject to the sanctions of criminal law. Such persons, among others, become true "second-class citizens."

Assumption of the moral neutrality of medicine. Cloaked in the mantle of science, medicine and medical practice are assumed to be objective and value free. But this profoundly misrepresents reality. The very nature of medical practice involves value judgment. To call something a disease is to deem it undesirable. Medicine is influenced by the moral order of society—witness the diagnosis and treatment of masturbation as a disease in Victorian times—yet medical language of disease and treatment is assumed to be morally neutral. It is not, and the very technological-scientific vocabulary of medicine that defines disease obfuscates this fact.

Defining deviance as disease allows behavior to keep its negative judgment, but medical language veils the political and moral nature of this decision in the guise of scientific fact. There was little public clamor for moral definitions of homosexuality as long as it remained defined an illness, but soon after the disease designation was removed, moral crusaders (e.g., Anita Bryant) launched public campaigns condemning the immorality of homosexuality. One only needs to scratch the surface of medical designations for deviant behavior to find overtly moral judgments.

Thus, as Zola (1975) points out, defining a problem as within medical jurisdiction

is not morally neutral precisely because in establishing its relevance as a key dimension for action, the moral issue is prevented from being squarely faced and occasionally from even being raised. By the acceptance of a specific behavior as an undesirable state the issue becomes not whether to treat an individual problem but how and when. (p. 86)*

Defining deviance as a medical phenomenon involves moral enterprise.

Domination of expert control. The medical profession is made up of experts; it has a monopoly on anything that can be conceptualized as an illness. Because of the way the medical profession is organized and the mandate it has from society, decisions related to medical diagnoses and treatment are controlled almost completely by medical professionals.

Conditions that enter the medical domain are not ipso facto medical problems, whether we speak of alcoholism, hyperactivity, or drug addiction. When a problem is defined as medical, it is removed from the public realm, where there can be discussion by ordinary people, and put on a plane where only medical people can discuss it. As Janice Reynolds (1973) succinctly states,

The increasing acceptance, especially among the more educated segments of our populace, of technical solutions—solutions administered by disinterested and morally neutral experts—results in the withdrawal of more and more areas of human experience from the realm of public discussion. For when drunkenness, juvenile delinquency, sub par performance and extreme political beliefs are seen as symptoms of an underlying illness or biological defect the merits and drawbacks of such behavior or beliefs need not be evaluated. (pp. 220-221)†

The public may have their own conceptions of deviant behavior, but those of the experts are usually dominant. Medical definitions have a high likelihood for dominance and hegemony: they are often taken as the last scientific word. The language of medical experts increases mystification and decreases the accessibility of public debate.

Medical social control. Defining deviant

---

*Reprinted with permission from Pergamon Press, Ltd.

†From "The medical institution: the death and disease-producing appendage" by Janice M. Reynolds, first published in *American society: a critical analysis* edited by Larry T. Reynolds and James M. Henslin. Copyright © 1973 by Longman Inc. Reprinted by permission of Longman.

behavior as a medical problem allows certain things to be done that could not otherwise be considered; for example, the body may be cut open or psychoactive medications given. As we elaborated above, this treatment can be a form of social control.

In regard to drug treatment, Henry Lennard (1971) observes: "Psychoactive drugs, especially those legally prescribed, tend to restrain individuals from behavior and experience that are not complementary with the requirements of the dominant value system" (p. 57). These forms of medical social control presume a prior definition of deviance as a medical problem. Psychosurgery on an individual prone to violent outbursts requires a diagnosis that something is wrong with his brain or nervous system.Similarly, prescribing drugs to restless, overactive, and disruptive schoolchildren requires a diagnosis of hyperkinesis. These forms of social control, what Stephan Chorover (1973) has called "psychotechnology," are powerful and often efficient means of controlling deviance. These relatively new and increasingly popular forms of medical control could not be used without the prior medicalization of deviant behavior. As is suggested from the discovery of hyperkinesis and to a lesser extent the development of methadone treatment of opiate addiction, if a mechanism of medical social control seems useful, then the deviant behavior it modifies will be given a medical label or diagnosis. We imply no overt malevolence on the part of the medical profession; rather, it is part of a larger process, of which the medical profession is only a part. The larger process might be called the individualization of social problems.

Individualization of social problems. The medicalization of deviance is part of a larger phenomenon that is prevalent in our society: the individualization of social problems. We tend to look for causes and solutions to complex social problems in the individual rather than in the social system. William Ryan (1971a) has identified this process as "blaming the victim": seeing the causes of the problem in individuals (who are usually of low status) rather than as endemic to the society. We seek to change the "victim" rather than the society. The medical practice of diagnosing an illness

in an individual lends itself to the individualization of social problems. Rather than seeing certain deviant behaviors as symptomatic of social conditions, the medical perspective focuses on the individual, diagnosing and treating the illness itself and generally ignoring the social situation.

Hyperkinesis serves as a good example of this. Both the school and parents are concerned with the child's behavior; the child is difficult at home and disruptive in school. No punishments or rewards seem consistently effective in modifying the behavior, and both parents and school are at their wits' end. A medical evaluation is suggested. The diagnosis of hyperkinetic behavior leads to prescribing stimulant medications. The child's behavior seems to become more socially acceptable, reducing problems in school and home. Treatment is considered a medical success.

But there is an alternative perspective. By focusing on the symptoms and defining them as hyperkinesis, we ignore the possibility that the behavior is not an illness but an adaptation to a social situation. It diverts our attention from the family or school and from seriously entertaining the idea that the "problem" could be in the structure of the social system. By giving medications, we are essentially supporting the existing social and political arrangements in that it becomes a "symptom" of an individual disease rather than a possible "comment" on the nature of the present situation. Although the individualization of social problems aligns well with the individualistic ethic of American culture, medical intervention against deviance makes medicine a de facto agent of dominant social and political interests.

Depoliticization of deviant behavior. Depoliticization of deviant behavior is a result of both the process of medicalization and the individualization of social problems. Probably one of the clearest recent examples of such depoliticization occurred when political dissidents in the Soviet Union were decared mentally ill and confined to mental hospitals (Conrad, 1977). This strategy served to neutralize the meaning of political protest and dissent, rendering it (officially, at least) symptomatic of mental illness.

The medicalization of deviant behavior depoliticizes deviance in the same manner. By defining the overactive, restless, and disruptive child as hyperkinetic, we ignore the meaning of the behavior in the context of the social system. If we focused our analysis on the school system, we might see the child's behavior as a protest against some aspect of the school or classroom situation, rather than symptomatic of an individual neurological disorder. Similar examples could be drawn of the opiate addict in the ghetto, the alcoholic in the workplace, and others. Medicalizing deviant behavior precludes us from recognizing it as a possible intentional repudiation of existing political arrangements.

There are other related consequences of the medicalization of deviance beyond the six discussed. The medical ideal of early intervention may lead to early labeling and secondary deviance (see Lemert, 1972). The "medical decision rule," which approximates "when in doubt, treat," is nearly the converse of the legal dictum "innocent until proven guilty" and may unnecessarily enlarge the population of deviants (Scheff, 1963). Certain constitutional safeguards of the judicial system that protect individuals' rights are neutralized or by-passed by medicalization (Kittrie, 1971). Social control in the name of benevolence is at once insidious and difficult to confront. Although these are all significant, we wish to expand on still another consequence of considerable social importance, the exclusion of evil.

Exclusion of evil

Evil has been excluded from the imagery of modern human problems. We are uncomfortable with notions of evil; we regard them as primitive and nonhumanitarian, as residues from a theological era.* Medicalization contributes to the exclusion of concepts of evil in our society. Clearly medicalization is not the sole

cause of the exclusion of evil, but it shrouds conditions, events, and people and prevents them from being confronted as evil. The roots of the exclusion of evil are in the Enlightenment, the diminution of religious imagery of sin, the rise of determinist theories of human behavior, and the doctrine of cultural relativity. Social scientists as well have excluded the concept of evil from their analytic discourses (Wolff, 1969; for exceptions, see Becker, E., 1975, and Lyman, 1978).

Although we cannot here presume to identify the forms of evil in modern times, we would like to sensitize the reader to how medical definitions of deviance serve to further exclude evil from our view. It can be argued that regardless of what we construe as evil (e.g., destruction, pain, alienation, exploitation, oppression), there are at least two general types of evil: evil intent and evil consequence. Evil intent is similar to the legal concept mens rea, literally, "evil mind." Some evil is intended by a specific line of action. Evil consequence is, on the other hand, the result of action. No intent or motive to do evil is necessary for evil consequence to prevail; on the contrary, it often resembles the platitude "the road to hell is paved with good intentions." In either case medicalization dilutes or obstructs us from seeing evil. Sickness gives us a vocabulary of motive (Mills, 1940) that obliterates evil intent. And although it does not automatically render evil consequences good, the allegation that they were products of a "sick" mind or body relegates them to a status similar to that of "accidents."

For example, Hitler orchestrated the greatest mass genocide in modern history, yet some have reduced his motivation for the destruction of the Jews (and others) to a personal pathological condition. To them and to many of us, Hitler was sick. But this portrays the horror of the Holocaust as a product of individual pathology; as Thomas Szasz frequently points out, it prevents us from seeing and confronting man's inhumanity to man. Are Son of Sam, Charles Manson, the assassins of King and the Kennedys, the Richard Nixon of Watergate, Libya's Muammar Kaddafi, or the all-to-common child beater sick? Although many may

---

*Writing in the early 1970s, Kittrie (1971) noted, "Ours is increasingly becoming a society that views punishment as a primitive and vindictive tool and is therefore loath to punish" (p. 347). Some recent scholarship in penology and the controversy about the death penalty has slightly modified this trend.

well be troubled, we argue that there is little to be gained by deploying such a medical vocabulary of motives.* It only hinders us from comprehending the human element in the decisions we make, the social structures we create, and the actions we take. Hannah Arendt (1963), in her exemplary study of the banality of evil, contends that Nazi war criminal Adolph Eichmann, rather than being sick, was "terribly, terrifyingly normal."

Susan Sontag (1978) has suggested that on a cultural level, we use the metaphor of illness to speak of various kinds of evil. Cancer, in particular, provides such a metaphor: we depict slums and pornography shops as "cancers" in our cities; J. Edgar Hoover's favorite metaphor for communism was "a cancer in our midst"; and Nixon's administration was deemed "cancerous," rotting from within. In our secular culture, where powerful religious connotations of sin and evil have been obscured, cancer (and for that matter, illness in general) is one of the few available images of unmitigated evil and wickedness. As Sontag (1978) observes:

But how to be . . . [moral] in the late twentieth century? How, when . . . we have a sense of evil but no longer the religious or philosophical language to talk intelligently about evil. Trying to comprehend "radical" or "absolute" evil, we search for adequate metaphors. But the modern disease metaphors are all cheap shots . . . Only in the most limited sense is any historical event or problem like an illness. It is invariably an encouragement to simplify what is complex. . . . (p. 85)

Thus we suggest that the medicalization of social problems detracts from our capability to see and confront the evils that face our world.

In sum, the "darker" side of the medicalization of deviance has profound consequences for the putative or alleged deviant and society. We now turn to some policy implications of medicalization.

---

* We *do not* suggest that these individuals or any other deviants discussed in this book are or should be considered evil. We only wish to point out that medicalization on a societal level contributes to the exclusion of evil. To the extent that evil exists, we would argue that social structures and specific social conditions are the most significant cause of evil.

MEDICALIZATION OF DEVIANCE AND SOCIAL POLICY

"Social policy" may be characterized as an institutionalized definition of a problem and its solutions. There are many routes for developing social policy in a complex society, but, as John McKnight (1977) contends, "There is no greater power than the right to define the question" (p. 85). The definition and designation of the problem itself may be the key to the development of social policy. Problem definitions often take on a life of their own; they tend to resist change and become the accepted manner of defining reality (see Caplan, N., & Nelson, 1973). In a complex society, social policy is only rarely implemented as a direct and self-conscious master plan, as, for example, occurred with the development of community mental health centers (see Chapter 3). It is far more common for social policies to evolve from the particular definitions and solutions that emerge from various political processes. Individual policies in diverse parts of society may conflict, impinge on, and modify one another. The overall social policy even may be residual to the political process. The medicalization of deviance never has been a formalized social policy; as we have demonstrated throughout this book, it has emerged from various combinations of turf battles, court decisions, scientific innovations, political expediences, medical entrepreneurship, and other influences. The medicalization of deviance has become in effect a de facto social policy.

In this discussion we explore briefly how some changes and trends in medicine and criminal justice as well as the recent "punitive backlash" may affect the future course of the medicalization of deviance.

Criminal justice: decriminalization, decarceration, and the therapeutic state

Over the past two decades the percent of officially defined deviants institutionalized in prisons or mental hospitals has decreased. There has been a parallel growth in "community-based" programs for social control. Although this "decarceration" has been most dramatic with the mentally ill, substantial deinstitutionalization has occurred in prison populations and with juvenile delinquents and opiate addicts as well (see Scull, 1977a). Many deviants who until recently would have been institutionalized are being "treated" or maintained in community programs—for example, probation, work release, and community correctional programs for criminal offenders; counseling, vocational, or residential programs as diversion from juvenile court for delinquents; and methadone maintenance or therapeutic community programs in lieu of prison for opiate addicts.

This emerging social policy of decarceration has already affected medicalization. Assuming that the amount of deviance and number of deviants a society recognizes remains generally constant (see Erikson, 1966), a change in policy in one social control agency affects other social control agents. Thus decarceration of institutionalized deviants will lead to the deployment of other forms of social control. Because medical social control is one of the main types of social control deployed in the community, decarceration increases medicalization. Since the *Robinson* Supreme Court decision and the discovery of methadone maintenance the control of opiate addicts has shifted dramatically from the criminal justice system to the medical system. Control of some criminal offenders may be subtly transferred from the correctional system to the mental health system; one recent study found an increase in the number of males with prior police records admitted to psychiatric facilities and suggested this may be an indication of a medicalization of criminal behavior (Melick, Steadman, & Cocozza, 1979). There is also some evidence that probation officers, in their quest for professional status, adopt a medical model in their treatment of offenders (Chalfant, 1977). Although some observers have suggested that the apparent decarceration of mental patients from mental hospitals and the rise of community mental health facilities has at least partially demedicalized madness (see Chapter 3), this is an inaccurate interpretation. Moreover, the extent of decarceration has been exaggerated; many of the former or would-be

mental patients are located in other institutions, especially nursing homes (Redlich & Kellert, 1978). Here they remain under medical or quasimedical control. In short, decarceration appears to increase the medicalization of deviance.

Decriminalization also affects medicalization. Decriminalization means that a certain activity is no longer considered to be a criminal offense. But even when criminal sanctions are removed, the act may still maintain its definition as deviance. In this case, other noncriminal sanctions may emerge. Alcohol use and deviant drinking provide a useful example. We noted in our discussion of the definition of deviant drinking (Chapter 4) that the disease model of alcoholism did not begin its rise to prominence until after the repeal of Prohibition, that is, after alcohol use in general was decriminalized. More specifically, we can examine the response to the decriminalization of "public drunkenness" in the 1960s. A recent study has shown that although alcohol and drug psychoses comprised only 4.7% of the mental health population (inpatient and outpatient) in 1950, in 1975 "alcoholism accounted for 46 percent of state hospital patients" and became the largest diagnostic category in mental hospitals (Redlich & Kellert, 1978, p. 26). It is likely that the combination of the declining populations in state mental hospitals and the decriminalization of "public drunkenness" (e.g., police now bring drunks to the mental hospital instead of the drunk tank) is in part reflected in this enormous increase of alcoholics in the mental health system.

Medicalization allows for the decriminalization of certain activities (e.g., public drunkenness, some types of drug use) because (1) they remain defined as deviant (sick) and are not vindicated and (2) an alternative form of social control is available (medicine). If an act is decriminalized and also demedicalized (e.g., homosexuality), there may well be a backlash and a call for recriminalization or at least reaffirmation of its deviant status rather than a vindication. We postulate that if an act is decriminalized and yet not vindicated (i.e., still remains defined as deviant), its control may be transferred from the criminal justice to the medical system.*

In the 1960s and early 1970s considerable concern was voiced in some quarters concerning the "social policy" that was leading to the divestment of criminal justice and the rise of the therapeutic state (Kittrie, 1971; Leifer, 1969; Szasz, 1963). As pointed out in Chapter 8, there has been some retreat from the "rehabilitative ideal" in criminal justice. On the other hand, both decarceration and decriminalization have increased medicalization. Thus we would conclude that although the "therapeutic state" is not becoming the dominant social policy as its earlier critics feared, neither is it showing signs of abating. We would suggest that to the extent that decarceration and decriminalization remain social policies, medicalization of deviance can be expected to increase.

Trends in medicine and medicalization

The medicalization of deviance has been influenced by changes in the medical profession and in social policy regarding medical care. The prestige of medicine has been growing since the turn of the century. Medical practice has become increasingly specialized; whereas only 20% of physicians were specialists in 1940, by the early 1970s nearly 80% considered themselves specialists (Twaddle & Hessler, 1977, p. 175). This is in part the result of the increasingly technological nature of medicine. The number of personnel employed in the medical sector has increased considerably since the Second World War. But the most spectacular growth has been in the cost and investment in medical care in the past three decades.

In 1950 the expenditures for medical care comprised 4.6% of the Gross National Product (GNP); by 1976 they accounted for 8.3%, for

---

*The decriminalization of abortion has led to its complete medicalization. It is interesting to speculate whether the decriminalization of marijuana, gambling, and prostitution would lead to medicalization. It is likely that with marijuana and gambling, "compulsive" and excessive indulgence would be defined as "sick"; with prostitution, medical certification might be required, as is presently the case in several European countries.

a total of over $130 billion spent on medical care. Since 1963 health expenditures have risen more than 10% yearly, while the rest of the economy has grown by 6% to 7%. In other words, medicine is the fastest expanding part of the service sector and one of the most expansive segments of our economy. In one sense we might see these increasing expenditures themselves as an index of increasing medicalization. But more likely, the increasing economic resources allocated to medical care create a substantial pool of money to draw from, thereby increasing the resources available for medical solutions to human problems. It should be noted, however, that the inflation of medical costs could ultimately become a factor in decreasing the medicalization of deviance, simply because medical solutions have become too costly.

Much of the rising cost of medical care has been attributed to the growth in third-party payments (i.e., when medical care is paid not by the patient or the provider of the care but by a third party). The major source of third-party payments has been Blue Cross and Blue Shield and the health insurance industry, and, since the enactment of Medicare and Medicaid in 1965, also the federal government. More than 51% of medical costs was paid directly by the patient in 1966; by 1975 this figure had dipped to less than 33% (Coe, 1978, p. 387). The largest increase in third-party payments has been the amount paid by the federal government; in 1975, 27.7% of medical costs was borne by the federal government, and this is expected to continue to increase. What this all means for the medicalization of deviance is that "third parties" are increasingly deciding what is appropriate medical care and what is not. For example, if medical insurance or Medicaid will pay for certain types of treatment, then the problem is more likely to be medicalized. Although the medical profession certainly has influence in this area, this removes the control of medicalization from medical hands and places it into the hands of the third-party payers. Although 90% of America's Blue Cross plans provide some hospital coverage for alcoholism, less than 10% of the cost of treatment is currently covered by private insurance and health-care protection programs (*Behavior Today*, June 21, 1976). Although many physicians consider obesity to be a bona fide medical condition, virtually no health insurers will pay for intestinal by-pass operations as a treatment for obesity. Clearly, changes in policies by third-party payers can drastically affect the types or amount of deviance medicalized.

Until about the past two decades, the dominant organization of medical practice was private, solo practice. There has been a growing bureaucratization of medical practice. The hospital rather than the private office is becoming the center for health care delivery. These large modern hospitals are both a result of, and an inducement for, the practice of highly specialized and technological medicine. Hospitals have their own organizational priorities of sustaining a smoothly running bureaucracy, maximizing profitable services, justifying technological equipment, and maintaining the patient-bed load at near full capacity. Although bureaucratic organizations reduce medical professional power, the institutional structure of the hospital is better suited to function as an agent of social control than the singular office practice. Hospital medicine can be practiced at a high biotechnological level, is less client dependent (because of third-party payments), has less personal involvement, and is more responsive to demands of other institutions, especially the state, on whom it is increasingly dependent for financial support.

For many years American medicine was considered to be suffering from a shortage of physicians. In the 1960s federal programs to expand medical schools increased greatly the number of physicians being trained. We have just begun to experience the effects of the rising number of physicians. Between 1970 and 1990 we can expect an 80% increase in the number of physicians—from about 325,000 to almost 600,000. And if present population and medical trends continue, as we expect they will, by 1990 there will be one physician for every 420 people in the United States and an even greater enlargement in the number of nurses and allied health workers (U.S. Department of Health, Education and Welfare, 1974).

One result of the growing number of medi-

cal personnel could be an increase in the number of problems that become defined as medical problems (after all, we have all these highly trained professionals to treat them). Although the greater number of physicians could result in better delivery of medical services, it could also increase medicalization as new physicians attempt to develop new areas of medical turf as old ones become saturated. David Mechanic (1974, p. 50) suggests, for instance, that for "family practice" to become a viable discipline in medicine, family practitioners would have to develop a "scientific and investigatory stance" toward common family practice problems such as "alcoholism, drug abuse, difficulties in sexual development, failure to conform to medical regimen and the like." The potential for the expansion of the medical domain here is great.

But there are also some countertrends in medicine. There is an emphasis on both self-care and individual responsibility for health (see Knowles, 1977). Health is becoming defined as more of a personal responsibility. As Zola (1972) observes, "At the same time the label 'illness' is being used to attribute 'diminished responsibility' to a whole host of phenomena, the issue of 'personal responsibility' seems to be re-emerging in medicine itself" (p. 491). Increased personal responsibility for sickness could cause the responsibility for the behavior to return to the individual. For instance, alcoholics would be deemed responsible for deviant drinking, obese people for their deviant bodies, and opiate addicts for their habits. This could ultimately spur some demedicalization.*

But the most important social policy affecting the future of medicalization hinges on the notion of a "right to adequate health care" and

---

*Reneé Fox (1977, pp. 19-21) contends that the recent trends of viewing patients as consumers, the emergence of physician extenders such as nurse practitioners and physicians' assistants, and "the increased insistence on patients' rights, self-therapy, mutual aid, community medical services and care by non-physician health professionals" constitute evidence for demedicalization. We think Fox is mistaken. *Demedicalization does not occur until a problem is no longer defined in medical terms and medical treatments are no longer seen as directly relevant to its solution.* Fox confuses deprofessionalization with demedicalization.

the development of a National Health Insurance (NHI) program. The proposal of an NHI program has become a significant political issue. In the past decade dozens of bills advocating different NHI plans have been submitted to various congressional committees. No specific NHI plan as yet has emerged as the most probable candidate for passage, but there is a high likelihood that some type of NHI plan will be enacted within the next decade. Because of the recent fiscal crunch and the strong lobbying of powerful vested interests (e.g., the health insurance industry, the medical profession, the hospital associations), it is unlikely that it will be an NHI program providing comprehensive coverage. More likely, NHI will not alter the present structure of the medical system and will resemble present insurance programs (although with increased public accountability); it will be at least partly federally financed and extend insurance coverage to all Americans. Regardless of which NHI bill is enacted, it will have an effect on medicalization. What the effect will be, however, is uncertain. There are at least three possible scenarios.

SCENARIO ONE: Because the cost of paying for treatment is high and deemed prohibitive, fewer deviant behaviors are defined as medical problems. Perhaps alcoholism, marital problems, drug addiction, psychosurgery, and treatment for obesity will be excluded from NHI coverage.

SCENARIO TWO: Because NHI will pay for the treatment of anything defined as a medical problem, more deviance becomes medicalized. Gambling, divorce, boredom, narcissism, and lethargy will be defined as illnesses and treated medically.

SCENARIO THREE: Individuals are not considered responsible for their illnesses; so activities that are seen as leading to medical problems become defined as deviant. Smoking, eating poorly, getting insufficient exercise, or eschewing seat belts all will be defined as deviant. Certain medical problems could be excluded from NHI coverage because they are deemed to be willfully caused (i.e., "badness").

This final scenario takes us full circle, as we would develop the notion of "sickness as sin."* Scenarios two and three would further

---

*Paradoxically this could also encourage demedicalization, for the medical model then becomes less functional in removing the culpability for deviance.

the convergence of illness and deviance. At this point, it is difficult to predict which, if any, of these scenarios might result from the enactment of NHI.

Punitive backlash

Since about 1970 there has been a "backlash" against the increasing "liberalization" of the treatment of deviance and the Supreme Court decisions that have granted criminal suspects and offenders greater "rights." This public reaction, coming mostly from the more conservative sectors of society, generally calls for more strict treatment of deviants and a return to more punitive sanctions.

This "punitive backlash" takes many forms. In 1973 New York passed a "get tough" law with mandatory prison sentences for drug dealers. Other legislative attempts have been made to impose mandatory minimum sentences on offenders. There is considerable public clamor for the return of the death penalty. A current New York state law has allowed juveniles between ages 13 and 15 to be tried as adults for some offenses. The antiabortion crusade has made inroads into the availability of abortions and is aiming for the recriminalization of abortion. Recently antihomosexuality crusades have appeared from Florida to Oregon, defeating antidiscrimination referenda and limiting the rights of homosexuals.

This swell of public reaction may be in part a response to the therapeutic ideology and the perceived "coddling" of deviants. Should this backlash and other recent public reactions such as California's Proposition 13 taxpayer revolt continue to gather strength and grow in popularity, they well may force a retreat from the medicalization of deviance.

Some social policy recommendations

Our examination of the medicalization of deviance in American society has led us to some conclusions related to social policy. In this discussion we briefly outline some social policy recommendations.

1. The medicalization of deviance needs to be recognized as a de facto social policy. Recognized as such, issues like those pointed to in this chapter could be raised and debated. It is

important that public discussion by physicians, politicians, and lay persons alike be encouraged and facilitated. In recognition of the salience of medicalization and its consequences, perhaps ''medicalization impact statements'' should be required of social policy proposals affecting medicalization. For example, it is important to weigh the impact of NHI on medicalization.

2. Research is needed on the extent of medicalization, its benefits, and its costs. This includes research into the efficacy, the financial and social costs, and the extent of actual medicalization. We need continued research into the politics of medicalization and further investigation into the areas of medicalized deviance covered in this book as well as those not covered, such as the medicalization of suicide, old age and senility, obesity, abortion, and mental retardation. We need to compare these with uncontested medical problems that were at one time defined as deviance, such as epilepsy and leprosy. Close attention needs to be given to the efficacy, costs, and benefits for each type of medicalization. Hopefully such knowledge and understanding will better guide social policy decisions concerning medicalization.

3. Medicalization removes the constitutional safeguards of the judicial process (see Kittrie, 1971). Because of this, it is important to create some type of medical due process or redress for putative deviants who are the objects of therapeutic interventions. Since this type of due process would probably be resisted by the medical profession and labeled antitherapeutic, we propose the development of some type of ''counterpower'' to medical social control. This could take the form of patient or deviant advocates, intervention review organizations, or even a Nader-type watchdog group. This would help ensure that individual rights were not circumvented in the name of health.

4. It is our belief that we need to develop social policies toward deviance that hold people *accountable* for their actions but do *not blame* them. This is a delicate but possible balance. One proposal is bypassing such slippery concepts as responsibility and guilt, substituting an assumption of human fallibility combined with accountability for human action. As Kittrie (1971) suggests,

Every person who lives in a society is accountable to it for his anti-social behavior. Society, in return, may seek to curb his future misdeeds, not as a punishment for the improper exercise of free will but as a remedy for his human failings.

Although the notions of guilt, moral responsibility, and accountability are profound philosophical (and political) questions that cannot begin to be addressed here, we believe they must be directly discussed and reevaluated, since many people's lives are profoundly affected by them.

Presently our society's only ''no blame'' model for deviant behavior is the medical model. We need to develop new models of deviance that do not assume ultimate individual moral responsibility and yet do not define those who are not considered responsible as ''sick.'' Presently the only alternative to the criminal-responsibility model is the medical-no-responsibility model. It is imperative that we free ourselves from the dichotomous crime or sickness models that create largely either-or situations, as well as from unworkable and contradictory crime-sickness hybrids, as with sex offenders.

New models of deviance need to be reconciled with social scientific knowledge about deviance. There is considerable evidence that economic, social, and family factors contribute to deviant behavior, and it is important to understand that the individual has only limited control over these factors. Yet it is also important, because of our understanding of human behavior, not to completely neglect its voluntary components. Thus we concur with Robert Veatch (1973) that rather than assuming that human behavior is caused by biophysiological elements (''sickness''), ''it is preferable to make clear the missing categories—namely nonculpable deviancy caused psychologically, socially and culturally, for example, by lack of various forms of psychological, social, and cultural welfare'' (p. 71). We need to create a ''no blame'' role for deviants that still holds the individual accountable for his or her action. We need to create a social role analogous to the sick role that does not assume sickness or remove responsibility and yet reconciles our understanding that there are ''forces'' beyond the scope of the individual that affect human behavior. For example, one can envision the conception of a "victim role"; the individual is viewed as a "victim" of life circumstances; these circumstances are known to increase the probability for certain types of "deviant" behavioral responses as well as attributions, yet because the behavior is not regarded as "determined" by the circumstances, the individual is accountable for deviant behavior. In other words, given the circumstances, the individual is accountable for the behavioral strategies chosen in a situation. Needless to say, this is a complex and sticky issue, replete with philosophical and pragmatic pitfalls. It provides an important challenge for social scientists and philosophers. We present this example only to suggest the possibility of alternatives to the medical-criminal model dichotomy. As Clarice Stoll (1968) observes, our "image of man" is central in determining our social response to deviance; we call for the development of an alternative image that reconciles societal response with the understandings of social and behavioral science.

Finally, because social control is necessary for the existence of society, we urge the development of alternative, noncriminal and nonmedical modes of social control appropriate to the new model of deviance.

MEDICALIZING DEVIANCE: A FINAL NOTE

The potential for medicalizing deviance has increased in the past few decades. The increasing dominance of the medical profession, the discovery of subtle physiological correlates of human behavior, and the creation of medical technologies (promoted by powerful pharmaceutical and medical technology industry interests) have advanced this trend. Although we remain skeptical of the overall social benefits of medicalization and are concerned about its "darker" side, it is much too simplistic to suggest a wholesale condemnation of medicalization. Offering alcoholics medical treatment in lieu of the drunk tank is undoubtedly a more humane response to deviance; methadone maintenance allows a select group of opiate addicts to make successful adaptations to society; some schoolchildren seem to benefit from stimulant

medications for hyperkinesis; and the medical discovery of child abuse may well increase therapeutic intervention. Medicalization in general has reduced societal condemnation of deviants. But these benefits do not mean these conditions are in fact diseases or that the same results could not be achieved in another manner. And even in those instances of medical "success," the social consequences indicated in this chapter are still evident.

The most difficult consequence of medicalization for us to discuss is the exclusion of evil. In part this is because we are members of a culture that has largely eliminated evil from intellectual and public discourse. But our discomfort also stems from our ambivalence about what can meaningfully be construed as evil in our society. If we are excluding evil, what exactly are we excluding? We have no difficulty depicting such conditions as pain, violence, oppression, exploitation, and abject cruelty as evil. Social scientists of various stripes have been pointing to these evils and their consequences since the dawn of social science. It is also possible for us to conceive of "organizational evils" such as corporate price fixing, false advertising (or even all advertising), promoting life-threatening automobiles, or the wholesale drugging of nursing home patients to facilitate institutional management. We also have little trouble in seeing ideologies such as imperialism, chauvinism, and racial supremacy as evils. Our difficulty comes with seeing individuals as evil. While we would not adopt a Father-Flanagan-of-Boys-Town attitude of "there's no such thing as a bad boy," our own socialization and "liberal" assumptions as well as sociological perspective make it difficult for us to conceive of any individual as "evil." As sociologists we are more likely to see people as products of their psychological and social circumstances: there may be evil social structures, ideologies, or deeds, but not evil people. Yet when we confront a Hitler, an Idi Amin, or a Stalin of the forced labor camps, it is sometimes difficult to reach any other conclusion. We note this dilemma more as clarification of our stance than as a solution. There are both evils in society and people who are "victims" to those evils. Worthwhile social scientific goals include uncovering the evils, understanding and aiding the victims, and ultimately contributing to a more humane existence for all.

SUMMARY

In the 20th century, medicine has expanded as an institution of social control. On the most abstract level medical social control is the acceptance of a medical perspective as the dominant definition of certain phenomena. Medical social control of deviant behavior usually takes the form of medical intervention, attempting to modify deviant behavior with medical means and in the name of health. We identify three general forms of the medical social control of deviance: medical technology, medical collaboration, and medical ideology. Medical technology involves the use of pharmaceutical or surgical technologies as controls for deviance. Medical collaboration emphasizes the interwoven position of medicine in society and occurs when physicians collaborate with other authorities as information providers, gatekeepers, institutional agents, and technicians. Medical ideology as social control involves defining a behavior or condition as an illness primarily for the social and ideological benefits accrued by conceptualizing it in medical terms. Although these three "ideal types" are likely to be found in combination, they highlight the varied faces of medical social control.

There are important social consequences of medicalizing deviance. The "brighter" side of medicalization includes (1) a more humanitarian conception of deviance; (2) the extension of the sick role to deviants, minimizing blame and allowing for the conditional legitimation of a certain amount of deviance; (3) the more optimistic view of change presented by the medical model; (4) lending the prestigious mantle of the medical profession to deviance designations and treatments; and (5) the fact that medical social control is more flexible and sometimes more efficient than other controls. However, there is a "darker" side of medicalization, which includes (1) the dislocation of responsibility from the individual; (2) the assumption of the moral neutrality of medicine; (3) the problems engendered by the domi-

nation of expert control; (4) powerful medical techniques used for social control; (5) the individualization of complex social problems; (6) the depoliticization of deviant behavior; and (7) the exclusion of evil. It is this darker side that leaves us skeptical of the social benefits of medicalizing deviance.

The medicalization of deviance has become a de facto social policy. Changes in other "social policies" affect medicalization. Decarceration leads to the increasing deployment of medical social control, since it is one of the most effective social controls "in the community." Decriminalization may also increase medicalization because medicine provides an alternative social control mechanism. We postulate that if an act is decriminalized and not vindicated, its control may be transferred from the criminal justice system to the medical system. Although the therapeutic state has not become the dominant social policy, neither does it show any signs of withering away. Medicalization is also influenced by changes and trends in medicine. Medical practice is becoming increasingly specialized, technological, and bureaucratic. Society's economic investment (in terms of percentage of GNP) in medical care has nearly doubled in the past three decades. This is both an index of and incentive for medicalization. Bureaucratic medical practice removes some definitional power from the medical profession and places it in the hands of third-party payers (including the state) and hospital administrators. The number of physicians and other medical personnel will double by 1990; this may well cause further medicalization. On the other hand, the increased emphasis on self-care and individual responsibility for health, as well as the "fiscal crisis" of rapidly rising medical costs, may limit medicalization and spur demedicalization. The passage of a National Health Insurance program may have a profound effect on medicalization, although it is difficult to predict precisely what it will be. If the "punitive backlash" to perceived liberalized treatment of deviants gains strength, it may force some retreat from the medicalization of deviance.

We conclude with some brief social policy recommendations:

1. The medicalization of deviance needs to be recognized as a de facto social policy.

2. More research is needed on the extent, politics, benefits, and costs of medicalizing deviance.

3. Some form of ''counterpower'' to medical social control needs to be created.

4. A new model of deviance that holds people accountable for their actions but does not blame them needs to be developed, perhaps as a ''victim'' model. We need to be freed from the dichotomous crime or sickness models that create limiting either-or situations.

Loscke and Best –
Social Problems:
Constructionist Readings

15

Science Constructs PMS

ANNE E. FIGERT

Is Premenstrual Syndrome a mental illness? On June 23, 1986, after a year of bitter dispute, the Board of Trustees of the American Psychiatric Association said yes and placed a premenstrually related diagnosis in an appendix of the soon to be published revised third edition of its *Diagnostic and Statistical Manual of Mental Disorders (DSM-III-R)*. The psychiatric manifestations of PMS became something called Late Luteal Phase Dysphoric Disorder (LLPDD). Since 1994, LLPDD has been known as Premenstrual Dysphoric Disorder (PMDD) and is listed in the main text of the *DSM*'s fourth edition. So, the short answer to the question is yes, a form of PMS is an official mental disorder. It is official because the *DSM* is seen as a basic reference book for all mental health professionals. It provides standardized diagnostic criteria used by most insurance carriers and is recognized by the federal government and the courts as the psychiatric profession's consensus over the diagnoses of mental disorders.

But deliberations to include this diagnosis in the *DSM III-R*—on their surface an obvious case of scientific consensus over a proposed diagnosis—quickly erupted into a major public problem. A campaign organized by women psychiatrists and mental health professionals to stop the inclusion was soon underway. The decision to include LLPDD in the *DSM-III-R* was so controversial and consequential because it concerned many people—not just women and psychiatrists—who were trying to define and claim ownership of PMS. This brief article will focus on the history of constructing PMS before it became reconstructed as LLPDD.

This chapter is excerpted from Figert, Anne E. (1996). *Women and the Ownership of PMS: The Structuring of a Psychiatric Disorder* (Chapter 1). Hawthorne, NY: Aldine de Gruyter.

127

IS PMS REAL?

The primary way in which new ideas or diseases achieve legitimacy or recognition in modern society is for scientists or physicians to call them "real." Scientists and physicians have the cultural authority in society to define realms of reality. When M.D.s or Ph.D.s in chemistry or biology believe something is real, the public in general usually goes along with them. This is what happened to PMS in its various forms and incarnations in the twentieth century: PMS became real as a medical diagnosis and condition.

An American gynecologist first published scientific studies about a condition he called "premenstrual tension" 1931. The list of patient complaints included "husband to be pitied," "psychoneurotic," "suicidal desire," and "sexual tension." Medical prescription for severe cases of premenstrual tension was either complete removal of or radiation therapy upon the ovaries to decrease estrogen production in the body and thus to restore order in both the home and the workplace.

Between 1931 and 1980 there were steady references to premenstrual issues in the medical literature. Authors generally constructed PMS as a medical condition requiring management and treatment by a physician or a psychiatrist/psychologist. However, PMS was *not* seen as a major problem for the majority of women at that time. Nor was PMS seen as a major research problem for most scientists.

PMS as a medical disorder received steady but relatively little attention until an English doctor, Katharina Dalton, began to investigate it. In 1953, Dalton coauthored an important article on PMS in the *British Medical Journal*. This article first introduced the term, "Premenstrual Syndrome," emphasizing that women need not accept the physical and emotional discomfort of PMS every month, and that modern medicine could help them. Dalton has conducted research and written articles and books on PMS for over 40 years. She defines PMS as "any symptoms or complaints which regularly come just before or during early menstruation but are absent at other times of the cycle. It is the absence of symptoms after menstruation which is so important in this definition" (Dalton 1983:12). According to Dalton's research, PMS is responsible for decreased worker productivity (in both the sufferer and "her husband"), increased divorce rates, and even murder.

Dalton's own popularity, notoriety, and authority as a PMS "expert" heightened when she served as the chief defense medical expert in a 1981 murder trial in London, in which she successfully argued that the defendant was not responsible for murdering her lover because she suffered from a severe form of PMS. The publicity generated from this trial and Dalton's claims of successful progesterone treatments found many different audiences in the United States and brought publicity to PMS.

Due in part to the publicity generated by these trials, PMS and related diagnoses have been called the "disease of the 1980s." A disease that thousands of women previously had been told did not exist suddenly become a media event. More importantly, PMS also acquired medical legitimacy. A specifically biomedical orientation to PMS defines it as a medical problem requiring a specific type of scientific research, diagnosis, and intervention. The result is that PMS is real in the scientific and medical sense.

PMS AS A FEMINIST SCIENTIFIC ARTIFACT

It was feminist researchers (especially in nursing and psychology) who were responsible for conducting a significant portion of the scientific research done on PMS during the 1970s and 1980s. Since the 1970s, feminist scientists have actively worked within the field of science to study PMS and to make sure that the research was conducted. Feminist critics of traditional menstrual and premenstrual studies have long argued for different and better scientific methodologies, more appropriate research designs, and nonstigmatizing labels and assumptions. So, feminist scientists took responsibility for the majority of scientific research on menstruation in the 1970s and 1980s because they believed otherwise it would not be conducted. Thus, these early feminist researchers sought to "demystify" the negative stereotypical images of women and PMS by conducting "good" and "sound" science. These writers are quick to assert that the very use of the term "premenstrual syndrome" is an attempt by scientists to make premenstrual "tension" a more scientific term, and takes the control of women's bodies out of their own hands. These writers point out that the use of the word "syndrome" instead of "symptoms" itself suggests that there is an underlying disease process in women's bodies.

So, what scientifically constitutes PMS, and how PMS research should be legitimately carried out, were questions raised by feminists within the scientific profession in the 1970s and 1980s. The aim (and possibly its result as well) of feminist scientific work on menstruation was to use the tools and rhetoric of "science" to refute negative images of PMS. These feminists believed that changes in public perception and attitudes about the previously understudied topic of menstruation and PMS were achievable from within science.

Scholarly and Social Science Explanations of PMS/Menstruation

While physicians and scientists studied and tried to define PMS and other menstrual disorders in terms of *biology*, mainly feminist anthropologists, sociologists, and other scholars tried to place and account for PMS in its *social* and *cultural* context. Studies of the history of menstruation in human society point out that menstrual related disorders are often associated with the practice of labeling women and their behaviors crazy (dating back to ancient Greek writings).

Scholars have linked PMS to ancient descriptions of hysteria and other modern characteristics (lethargy, moodiness, and depression) previously attached to menstruation itself.

For example, in some cultures, menstruation has been portrayed as an evil spirit that invades women of childbearing age once a month. Cultural taboos and negative stereotypes—such as not touching a menstruating woman and physically separating her—also have existed. The ancient Greeks believed that the uterus "wandered" in women's bodies and caused all sorts of unusual behaviors—behaviors that today are attributed to PMS.

Other authors have tried to combat negative stereotypes of madness and PMS by tracing the diagnosis (as a cultural and political artifact) to capitalist patriarchal society. Some authors argue that PMS is historically located within the stresses of modern capitalism in western culture. Such authors might ask, how is it that a majority of all women are afflicted with a physically abnormal hormonal cycle? Within this view, it is not surprising that original interest in PMS arose during the economic Depression in the 1930s. Although women had made gains in labor force participation during World War I, the Depression led to women being forced to give up wage work because jobs were needed by men.

Post–World War II studies that emerged in the 1950s appear to fit into this traditional pattern of using medical rhetoric to diagnose and treat social and cultural problems in the home and workplace. These traditional medical studies have a distinct focus on the effect of a woman's PMS on her social roles of wife, mother, and worker. This early scientific work on PMS stressed how disruptive it is in the home, factory, and social order. By focusing on this "disruption," the medical community attempted to claim ownership over PMS and to medicalize women's bodies. In this respect, medicine attributes problems in families (unhappiness, arguments, and violence) to women in general and PMS in particular, and claims that these problems can be solved medically. Of course, this medical reasoning discourages us from looking at the social sources of problems.

Another author identifies the specifically male composition of the medical profession as the source of control and power over women's bodies and PMS. Still other feminist writers and health care providers have tried to communicate the need for every woman to take control over her body and its byproducts, such as menstruation and PMS.

The social, scientific, and feminist analyses suggest that the diversity of meanings assigned to PMS in contemporary Western culture (bitchy, moody, not responsible for behavior, uncontrolled emotional states) is

related to the societies in which they are developed and is also indicative of the movement in modern society to assign a medical label or explanation for human behaviors. Within such constructions, PMS is a problem to be resolved socially and culturally, not medically).

In brief, what scientifically constitutes PMS, and how PMS research should be legitimately carried out were questions raised from within science itself as well as from political critics outside science.

The nature and content of pre-1980s PMS research is important. In 1983, one writer remarked that because PMS symptoms are behavioral, psychological, and physiological in nature, researchers have included biologists as well as social scientists. All types of scientific research (social science as well as biological science) were being conducted and funded by different types of researchers (biologists, gynecologists, psychologists, and psychiatrists). The major difference among PMS researchers was whether they held a purely biological/biomedical orientation or a feminist and thus more sociocultural orientation. A feminist or sociocultural perspective challenges traditional biomedical control of women's bodies and experiences, while a biomedical orientation to PMS considers it a medical problem requiring medical scientific research, diagnosis, and intervention.

THE 1983 CONFERENCE AND SCIENTIFICALLY DEFINING PMS

A marked shift in the PMS research community took place at a May 1983 conference sponsored by the National Institute of Mental Health (NIMH). This conference played a major role in bringing together a diverse group of research scientists, psychiatrists, and psychologists doing PMS-related research. The main product of this 1983 NIMH conference was a working scientific definition of Premenstrual Syndrome: "a diagnosis of premenstrual syndrome should be made when symptom intensity changes at least 30 percent in the premenstrual period (six days before menses) compared with the intermenstrual period (days 5–10 of the cycle) for two consecutive months."

The 1983 definition of PMS was seen as a scientific advance in a field in which no previous agreement or definition had been reached. A consistent definition could tighten research and clinical standards of evaluation. Yet the 1983 NIMH conference did not fully resolve all definitional and methodological issues of PMS research. Scientists still pointed to the lack of clarity and to the absence of solid scientific data to fully support it as a diagnosis. Given the increasing level of interest in PMS by the public and by other health and mental health professionals, more research was called for. For example, according to scientific and medical reports of the 1983 NIMH conference in the *Journal of the American Medical Association* (JAMA), panelists couldn't precisely define the disorder and they admitted that their research had many methodological problems. Even well-known and respected PMS researchers noted in the *American Journal of Psychiatry* that researchers did not agree on the definition of PMS, that they had not found specific biological correlates and that no one had demonstrated that any specific medical treatment worked better than no treatment at all. Another PMS researcher pointed out in an editorial in the *New England Journal of Medicine* in 1984 that there was much speculation but very little was actually understood about the pathophysiology of PMS.

Public interest in scientific research is generally perceived by researchers as vital. In fact, the impetus and pressure for PMS research came not from within the scientific community but from consumers or the public. A "proper" public image of PMS research was important for reasons both external and internal to the scientific community. If PMS research was seen as inconclusive and plagued by methodological or epistemological difficulties, it might not get funded by government agencies and other patrons, or published by scientific journals. If some scientists do not perceive PMS research as legitimate science, then the public might not believe PMS experts or seek out their advice and treatments.

Reports about methodological difficulties of scientific and medical research on PMS were indeed making their way into the popular press. *Ms.* magazine in 1983 and *Vogue* in 1984 informed their readers that there was little agreement on what causes PMS or how it should be treated. Yet this perception of scientific uncertainty conveyed by the public press was not necessarily a bad thing for scientists and PMS researchers. Because PMS was portrayed as the "new" disease of the 1980s, uncertainty meant that funding and more research were needed. Science and medicine had not yet come up with "answers" about PMS. But with proper support and attention from scientists and health professionals, science would eventually provide them.

Scientists' response to scientific and public accounts of PMS was important. Given the confused slate of symptoms and treatment possibilities, PMS attracted many "alternative" healers with "nonscientific" treatments and prescriptions. If PMS was indeed the "disease of the 1980s" then scientists needed to ensure that its study was "legitimate science," clearly demarcated from "quackery" or scientifically "unsound" treatments. One way to ensure scientists' control of PMS was to codify its definition and formally outline "legitimate" treatment protocols.

The 1983 NIMH conference and later interpretations of its guidelines played an important role in the controversy over LLPDD, a DSM category for the psychiatric manifestations of PMS. The apparent lack of scientific consensus about symptoms and treatments of PMS was played out by scientists in two different ways. First, beginning with the strategy supported by proinclusion researchers, efforts were made to push for a PMS-related psychiatric diagnosis in the revision of the DSM-III. Second, inclusion would ensure its scientific legitimation as a psychiatric disorder and was needed to secure funding for further scientific/medical research.

THE PMS INDUSTRY

While scientists continued to complain about the research underlying the "realness" of PMS, a PMS industry was being formed. One important aspect of this PMS industry involved the pharmaceutical industry, which began offering over-the-counter PMS drugs and more PMS-related products in the 1980s. At the time when scientists were arguing about whether or not to include PMS as a psychiatric diagnosis, total consumer spending in 1984 for menstrual pain relievers, including PMS products, was $111,132,000 a year.

What is the nature of the relationship of PMS-related products to PMS research in the scientific community? Simply stated, drug companies would not fund research unless PMS was accorded the status of a "real diagnosis" because they could not sell products to respond to a medical condition that didn't formally exist. But the relationship between the pharmaceutical companies and scientific researchers was more complex: There was much debate *within* the scientific community about whether to formally classify PMS as a *psychiatric* disorder. If PMS were classified only as a physical disorder then medical doctors would claim ownership; if LLPDD was included in the *DSM-III-R* then it would be a psychiatric disorder and psychologists/psychiatrists would claim ownership.

Chattem Pharmaceutical's advertisement in *People* magazine (June 30, 1986) represents a challenge to the scientific and medical expertise of psychiatrists over PMS. It portrays a psychiatrist's couch, with the words "Premenstrual Tension is not a psychological issue. It is a physical condition." The advertisement could be read as an effort to demarcate the boundary between physical treatment of PMS (which can be treated with products such as Premsyn PMS) and the "mental" treatment of PMS (which has no over-the-counter pharmaceutical products). It directly and not-so-subtly suggests to women that physical conditions such as headaches, bloating, and swelling can be taken care of with their products. Increased attention to the creation of PMS as a biomedical problem would appear to benefit drug sales. So, in the end, while the psychiatric manifestations of PMS were formally accorded a psychiatric diagnosis, the key for the pharmaceutical industry was defining PMS as something that can be helped with pills, diets, or other products offered in the PMS industry.

WHAT'S AT STAKE IN THE CONSTRUCTION OF PMS?

For some women, the publicity and legitimization of PMS and its symptoms as real, a natural part of their body and its processes, have led to a positive sense of control over this phenomenon. However, a more negative image of PMS as something that controls women once a month, that makes them "crazy" and subject to their hormones, is much more pervasive in our contemporary Western culture. This image has allowed women to use PMS as an excuse to express their emotions or to account for their otherwise "strange" behaviors. Other people (husbands, children, doctors, lawyers, judges, juries, coworkers) have also used PMS to explain women's behaviors.

How PMS is defined—and who controls or owns the diagnosis related to it—has been and continues to be a matter of social, political, and economic concern. The degree to which PMS has become a major issue is best understood in light of current estimates that anywhere between 20 and 90 percent of all women would qualify as having some of the more than 150 recognized symptoms of PMS.

PMS has been defined in a variety of ways (scientific, feminist, cultural, and economic) over the years, but there is no consistent or agreed upon definition. If the estimates given above are indeed true, and if almost all menstruating women do have at least some of these symptoms, then the "stability" of women's moods and behaviors can be called into question by scientists, doctors, politicians, bosses, and lawyers. What is considered "normal" for women itself is at the heart of the debate in the PMS controversy.

REFERENCE

Dalton, Katrina. 1983. *Once a Month*. Claremont, CA: Hunter House.

17

The "Homeless Mentally Ill" and Involuntary Hospitalization

DONILEEN R. LOSEKE

What should the public do about a person who wants to live on the streets? What is the public's responsibility for this type of person? What can the public demand from such a person? These practical questions became central to controversies surrounding a policy of removing the "homeless mentally ill" from New York City's streets in the 1980s. I want to explore the roots of these controversies and examine how the *New York Times (NYT)* constructed the morality of the public policy resolution to them.

Two general social constructionist understandings about *all* social policy inform my analysis. First, central to my argument is the belief that socially constructed images of *types* of conditions and *types* of people underlie social policies of all types and that these images are important. Second, because my interest is in a social policy that allowed people to be removed from the streets and placed into mental hospitals against their will, it is important to note that any level of government in the United States can intervene in private lives for only two reasons: intervention must be justified as either necessary to protect the public by controlling those who violate social rules, or as necessary to help people requiring assistance.

This chapter is excerpted from Loseke, Donileen R. (1995). "Writing Rights: The Homeless Mentally Ill and Involuntary Hospitalization." Pp. 261–86 in *Images of Issues, Typifying Contemporary Social Problems*, 2nd edition, edited by Joel Best. Hawthorne, NY: Aldine de Gruyter.

Using data from 132 articles in the *NYT* between 1981 and 1992, I turn now to a perplexing question facing people living in New York City during that time. What should the public do about people who live on the streets? This controversy occurred within a historical backdrop: The 1960s and 1970s in the United States were characterized as a time when "mental illness" increasingly was accepted as a normalized response to poor environments, an era when most mental hospitals were closed, when powers of police, psychiatrists and other institutional representatives had been greatly curtailed in favor of self-determination for many types of people, including the "mentally ill." Yet during the 1980s in New York City a question arose: Did the public have the right to involuntarily commit to mental facilities the people who lived on the streets of the city? My argument is that answers to this question depend on images of both the problem, "homelessness," and the people, "the homeless."

CLAIMS-MAKERS AND PUBLIC POLICY

The pages of the *NYT* contain the voices of many claims-makers debating what to do about people who wanted to live on the streets of New York City. In historical retrospect, the victors in these debates were those promoting the policy of involuntary hospitalization. One person, then-Mayor Edward Koch, was identified by the *NYT* as the primary person advocating this policy. Yet while the mayor was the original, and the most vocal, spokesperson for policies of involuntary hospitalization, the pages of the *NYT* also can be read as containing a choir of supporting voices. For example, policies of involuntarily hospitalization were supported by *NYT* editorials as early as 1982; on these pages the policy of involuntary hospitalization was supported by such powerful claims-makers as a state senator, the president of the American Psychological Association, and city and state health officials. There also were supportive opinion editorials, letters to the editor, and reports that the plan won praise in "man-on-the-street" polls.

The other side of this controversy, as constructed through the pages of the *NYT*, was twofold. First, many claims constructed practical, procedural, legal, or monetary problems associated with involuntary hospitalization policies. These were claims about practical problems of reversing changes in the 1960s and 1970s that made it very difficult to force hospitalization and which made hospital space itself very limited. My interest, though, is with claims constructing the morality of policy: *Should* policies promoting involuntary hospitalization be implemented? Although Mayor Koch often identified social workers, homeless advocates and civil liber-

---

tarians as his moral opposition, this construction is both too broad and too narrow. First, it is misleading to claim that some groups always opposed policies of involuntary confinement or that they opposed these policies on moral grounds. For example, Robert Hayes, representing the Coalition for the Homeless, said that his group had "absolutely no objection" to proposals advocating involuntarily confinement when the weather was very cold. In the same way, another advocacy group, Partnership for the Homeless, endorsed policies of involuntary hospitalization as long as they were "compassionately implemented." And, social workers could agree that involuntary commitment should be easier.

Clearly, such policies promoting hospitalization reversed those of "community treatment" that had been very much in vogue during the 1960s and 1970s; policies making involuntary commitment easier reversed the prior trend of making commitment increasingly more difficult. Such changes did not come quickly or easily: Mental hospitals needed to be reopened and laws needed to be changed. Yet practical changes could be made only if the morality of policy was successfully constructed.

CONSTRUCTING IMAGES OF SANITY AND INSANITY

New constructions of types of conditions and people must compete with others already present in the social order. For the case in point, people who opposed policies of involuntary hospitalization constructed the problem as first and foremost one of a lack of housing; they constructed "mental illness" as a normal condition; they constructed the "mentally ill" person as a rational actor capable of self-determination. In other words, the types of constructions that had been the positive support for community mental health policies became defensive claims criticizing proposed new policies of involuntary hospitalization.

Some of these claims criticized the social order and constructed environmental explanations for the condition of people living on the streets. Within this construction, the problem was the lack of low-income housing creating "homelessness" in the first place, or the lack of "safe and decent" places for people to sleep once they were without homes. Claims constructed the city's shelter system as "big, barracks like quarters," that were "depressing" and sometimes "dangerous." According to these claims, people on the street because they could not afford homes; they remained on the street because the city shelter system was despicable. Within this construction, people on the street would go to shelters willingly if shelters were better.

Constructing the social order as the problem yields an image of people on the street as rational actors no different from people who have homes.

After all, readers are reminded, the majority of Americans would not like the "long lines and regimentation" in shelters; most people might choose to live on the streets if their "only alternative was despicable, regimented, and downright dangerous shelters." Within this construction, the decision to remain on the streets rather than enter a city shelter becomes a "sign of" mental health rather than of mental illness."

In addition, claims could produce what might be classified as indications of "mental illness" to rather be normal reactions to oppressive environments. Such claims warned readers to not confuse behavior realistically resulting from the experience of street living with "actual" psychiatric disorder. Even seemingly bizarre behaviors could be normalized. For example, while commonsense reasoning might judge "burning money" as an indication of "mental illness," one story told of a woman who burned money only when it was rudely thrown at her. "Burning money" becomes constructed as an act of "self-respect." This woman also "burned money" only when she did not need it for that particular day. This, according to a claims-maker promoting her normality, indicated her rational understanding that it is dangerous to have money and live on the street. Likewise, while urinating or defecating on a public sidewalk might be judged a sign of "mental illness," some writers constructed these as merely unfortunate consequences of a lack of publicly available toilets.

Constructions promoting the normality of such behaviors simultaneously promote the right to self-determination. Indeed, people who live on the street could be constructed as exemplary Americans who have a "fiercely independent lifestyle." Hence, a woman living on the street argued "I like the streets, and I am entitled to live the way I want to live." Another woman turned down an offer for transportation to a shelter because "I want to be independent." These can be read as comments of rational actors exemplifying the highly valued American love of freedom.

In brief, constructions of "mental illness" that were popular in the 1960s and 1970s associated with the community mental health policy did not simply disappear. They remained a part of the social scene in the 1980s and promoted the normality—or at least the rationality—of people living on the streets.

Within commonsense reasoning, it *should* be very difficult to take away the right to self-determination for rational actors who are not harming others. Hence, the morality of laws making involuntary commitment very difficult is accomplished by constructing the rationality of people living on the streets.

Yet if people living on the streets are *not* rational, then laws making commitment easier are justified. I turn now to a second construction of people living on the streets that supports policies promoting the morality of suspending their individual rights to self-determination. Within this construction, people choosing to live on the streets are not rational, so laws making it difficult to hospitalize them are morally wrong. Or, in the often-quoted opinion of Mayor Koch, "the law is an ass," and needs to be changed.

Claims constructed the commonsense *content* of the problem. According to these claims, normalizing mental illness and promoting unlimited rights to self-determination might lead to "stimulating dinner party conversation and Philosophy I discussions," but commonsense dictated that people living on the streets were not "normal." Within this construction, the "homeless mentally ill" was a person whose decisions and behaviors could not be normalized by practical reasoning.

First, claims promoting the need for involuntary hospitalization formed the unacceptability of living on the street as one knowable from the *practical experience of NYT readers*. There were articles about the large number of people living on the streets, and editorials claimed the number of such people "has sharply increased." Readers were informed by editors that "four out of five city residents said they saw such people every day." Hence, this was "one of the city's most visible problems." Readers were instructed to "trust the reality of your senses"; if they simply looked, they would see "craziness."

While claims forming the rationality of people living on the streets constructed behaviors in terms of their *causes or meanings*, "craziness" was constructed by purely *behavioral* descriptions. For example, readers learned of Rebecca Smith, a woman who froze to death in a cardboard box rather than accept a ride to a shelter, and Judy, a woman who sat docile all day but arose each and every night at 11:00 p.m. and spent the next several hours "screaming obscenities and intimate details about her life into the night." The "homeless mentally ill" were constructed as people who "stumble about addressing strangers . . . or unseen deities . . ., sometimes shouting obscenities or urinating against buildings"; they were "dirty, disheveled, and malodorous"; and they committed "filthy nuisances on streets and gutters." Such descriptions of appearance and behavior cannot easily be read as forming a "normal" citizen. The type of person known as the "homeless mentally ill" was rather constructed as a "wild presence on the streets of New York City."

But how do we know that a person living on the street is "mentally ill"? We know because the person is on the street. Within middle-class folk reasoning, problems with the city shelter system might lead rational people to live on the streets during summer months. But a person who continues to live on the streets in subzero temperatures when *any* choices are available is, by definition, not rational. Therefore, in response to claims-makers who argued that people made rational choices to remain on the streets in the winter, Mayor Koch replied: "baloney, baloney." According to the mayor, people remained on the street because they were "deranged."

By commonsense logic, a deranged person is not normal. Readers are told such people "don't have their wits about them," suffer from "disorientation and impaired judgment," are "incapable of logical thinking," "incapable of taking care of themselves," and "incompetent." The act of being on the street is constructed as a sufficient sign of incompetence: "Anyone who chooses to be on the streets in the cold when we offer that person . . . a shelter, that person is not competent." "Incompetence" is doubly constructed. First, this type of person is not competent at *self-diagnosis*: They are "too sick to know they are sick," "so sick they imagine they need no help." It follows that such a person also is incapable of making *rational decisions*. "A person who is seriously mentally ill often doesn't realize that he's sick. He will deny that he is ill and refuse to be treated." Such a person "often resists treatment precisely because he [is] mentally ill." Therefore, it goes without saying that others must make decisions because such people "can not be held competent to choose beds of stone and to resist help."

The value of the right to self-determination, of course, is challenged by this construction of the "homeless mentally ill" as a mad person who is, by definition, incompetent. Within middle-class logic, "the freedom to sleep in doorways is no freedom at all." The right to self-determination for people living on the streets becomes constructed as the "freedom to die in the streets," the freedom to "remain wrapped in their agonies of illness of the mind," the "freedom to be left enslaved to madness." Freedom becomes constructed as slavery.

What, then, constitutes freedom for this type of person? According to claims-makers, this was the "freedom from the prison of mental illness." Involuntary commitment was a "rescue" allowing people to "regain rationality." Involuntary commitment could "save the homeless from themselves." So, although the U. S. Supreme Court ruled that involuntary incarceration in a mental institution was a "massive deprivation of liberty," for the "homeless mentally ill" such hospitalization was freedom.

These obviously are moral constructions; they justify hospitalization as the only conceivable policy toward a type of person who, if allowed self-determination, would die. Because policy was justified in terms of how it literally saved lives, it follows that failure to support this policy was constructed as *immoral*: As readers are reminded, "Government cannot be forgiven for letting them just lie there"; a "civilized society has an obligation to help those so deranged that they are likely to die if left alone on the streets." Failure to treat "mental illness" is constructed as "a cruel neglect on the part of society." This was not simply a civil obligation—it was a "*human* obligation to intervene" (emphasis added). Hence, the humanity of the policy of involuntary commitment was constructed as "beyond challenge."

As in earlier eras, claims-making justified practical changes in the social environment. As compared with the early 1980s, by the end of the decade it was procedurally easier to involuntarily commit people to mental hospitals, and there were now many more facilities. But claims-makers promoting more involuntary commitment constructed such change as insufficient. By the early 1990s, readers were told that people living on the streets had become an "unmanageable presence." When the public expressed sympathy for a man who had killed an aggressive homeless person, the *NYT* claimed such sympathy reflected the "community's disgust, and fear, about a continuing assault on public decency posed by people living on the streets." The "homeless mentally ill" now was constructed as a type of person who "befouled private and public property," a type of person whose "very presence devalued everything in the city." Citizens were described as "increasingly irritated," neighborhoods were constructed as "living in absolute terror." While claims in the early- and mid-1980s emphasized *helping* people living on the streets, by the late 1980s, the *NYT* claimed that the public mood had "soured," and that compassion from earlier years had been "replaced with a simple desire to get them out of here." The condition was constructed as "madness in the streets," and "madness is not an acceptable alternative lifestyle to sanity."

The scales of tolerance had tipped, and so, too, had the scales balancing the rights of a public with the rights of individuals. Stated bluntly by a radio talk show host: "What about the rights of people like me who walk past the people who urinate on the sidewalk? I'm a taxpayer. What about my rights?" An editorial bemoaned: "when and why did this country accept madness in the streets as a part of the city scenery?" Concern about the rights of the public—defined implicitly as people who have homes—now became central. Rhetoric shifted to justifying policy in terms of social control: Involuntary commitment was necessary to protect the public from the contagion of madness. But shifting from a rhetoric of help to one of social control did not pose a moral dilemma: By the late 1980s it was simply taken for granted that involuntary confinement was good for the "homeless mentally ill." If policies also were constructed as good for the public then all was as it should be—the policy was beneficial for all and detrimental to none.

SOCIAL CONSTRUCTION AND PUBLIC POLICIES

What should the public do about people who want to live on the streets? What is the public's responsibility for such a person? What can the public demand from such a person? While this examination certainly has not answered questions about what *should* be done, exploring how moral justifications are constructed has practical implications.

My major argument is that images of what the public *should* do depend on our images of types of people. So, for example, a policy of "community mental health" is sensible given an image of "mental illness" as a more-or-less "normal" condition, and the "mentally ill" person as a more-or-less rational actor. Policies of involuntary confinement in mental hospitals are justified by images of the "mentally ill" person as dangerous to self and/or others. Differing images justify different types of public responses toward types of people.

Changes in laws in New York City during the 1980s that made it far easier to involuntarily commit to mental hospitals people who lived on the street came after much public dialog about the characteristics of those people who lived on the street. What should be done about people who live on the streets? The answer to that question depends on constructed images of who these people are.

25

Medicalizing Childhood

DOROTHY PAWLUCH

Over the last several decades the practice of pediatrics has changed radically—so much so that pediatricians often describe their specialty today as the "new pediatrics," or refer to the problems they treat as the "new morbidity" in pediatrics. What makes these new pediatrics "new" is its shift away from the physical problems of children, which once dominated pediatrics, to problems of a nonphysical nature. While in the past pediatricians were primarily concerned with treating and preventing life-threatening infectious diseases, those practicing the specialty in most of North America today deal with problems such as temper tantrums, sibling rivalry, bedwetting, eating and sleeping disorders, fears and phobias, shyness, nightmares, thumb-sucking, nervous tics, nail-biting, glue-sniffing, stealing, fire-setting, running away, using obscene language, overdependent relationships with parents, school difficulties, reactions to chronic illness, adoption, and traumatic experiences such as child abuse.

This is only a partial list of the wide range of difficulties that now fall under the pediatric purview. The "new pediatrics" oversees not only children's physical growth and development, but their emotional, psychological, social, and even, as some pediatricians have interpreted it, their spiritual well-being.

Another feature of the new pediatrics is its concern with adolescents. Until the 1950s, pediatricians primarily treated children under the age of 12. Today, many pediatricians follow their patients through their teens, and, in some cases, into young adulthood. Adolescent health care has its

---

This chapter is excerpted from Pawluch, Dorothy (1996). *The New Pediatrics: A Profession in Transition* (Chapters 1, 7). Hawthorne, NY: Aldine de Gruyter.

own distinctive problems: acne, sports injuries, and the gynecological needs of young women.

But since adolescence is the healthiest stage in the life cycle in physical terms, providing health care for teenagers really means attending to behavioral and psychosocial concerns such as sexual activity and birth control, gender preference, peer relationships, relationships to authority figures, truancy and school dropouts, as well as drug abuse.

As dramatic as these changes have been for pediatricians, their impact has not been limited to the practitioners of the profession. The new pediatrics is linked to a shift in the way that we as a society think about children, teenagers, and their difficulties. In redefining pediatrics and extending the limits of their professional responsibilities, pediatricians have, in effect, redefined and medicalized many behaviors that they now treat. Behaviors that were once unnamed or unnoticed, those that we once thought we could do nothing about, or that we might have been prepared to overlook or to accept as a normal part of growing up, now evoke concern. Conditions that were once attributed to random variation in character, aptitude, appetite, and energy level, or to "normal" teenage rebelliousness, we now understand within a medical frame of reference as symptoms of an underlying condition. Behaviors that we once punished are now referred to pediatricians and other doctors or experts. Labels such as "hyperkinesis" or "hyperactivity," "minimal brain dysfunction," "attention deficit disorder," "learning disability," have replaced labels such as "naughty," "mischievous," "rambunctious," "lazy," "shy," "stupid," "wild," and "delinquent." Deviance has become a disease and medical treatment has replaced discipline as the appropriate way to deal with many troublesome behaviors.

Many people, especially parents, have welcomed and even pushed for greater involvement of pediatricians in children's lives, with its promise of more effective management, if not a total "cure," for their nonphysical difficulties and a less troubled, disrupted, and conflict-ridden passage for them into adulthood. But there have been critics as well, charging that the medicalization of childhood misbehaviors is no more than a massive and insidious program of child control and a justification for using medical techniques, including drug therapy, to bring into line those behaviors in children that adults find objectionable, annoying, or bothersome. Some observers have argued that medical labels and treatment for childhood deviance became popular with the advent of the children's rights movement of the 1960s and the general liberalization of attitudes that made overtly coercive means of maintaining order unpopular, if not illegal. Disease labels met the political and social necessities of an age searching for an explanation to the classic problems of deviance. These disease labels continue to be popular, especially among the middle class because they are

less stigmatizing than moral labels such as "delinquent," and they absolve parents of blame for their children's misbehaviors. Other critics describe Ritalin, an amphetamine prescribed for hyperkinesis, as a way of regimenting and restraining spirited kids. Others suggest that medical labels for childhood misbehaviors are often thin disguises for the difficulties that children experience in adjusting to specific social, family, or scholastic situations.

In practicing a medical specialty devoted to children, pediatricians have been in a position to arbitrate questions dealing with the health and illness of children. By incorporating problematic behaviors into the boundaries of proper pediatric care and providing services in these areas, pediatricians have implicitly legitimized and given official approval to the medical definitions of children's nonphysical problems. If we are now more likely to see children's behavior as a health care concern, it is largely because pediatricians have endorsed this view. Why have pediatricians been willing to assume responsibility for the problematic behaviors of children and teenagers, and to provide services that they never previously considered part of their specialty?

THE RISE OF THE NEW PEDIATRICS

The new pediatrics was an outcome of a series of crises that shook the specialty after 1950. Over the first half of the twentieth century, the infectious diseases of childhood came under control and the health of children improved. Pediatrics began to experience difficulties. The rates of infant and childhood death (mortality) and illness (morbidity) fell. This did not directly affect the university-based professors of pediatrics who continued to teach and do research on the physical problems of children. Nor did the change affect the small group of consulting pediatric subspecialists who concentrated on studying and treating the serious, though relatively rare, medical conditions that still struck children. The group hardest hit by the improvements in children's health were the thousands of general pediatricians in private, primary care practice.

The problem was not that these pediatricians had fewer patients to treat. On the contrary, the growing popularity of pediatricians as doctors of choice for children and the postwar baby boom combined to create an overwhelming demand for pediatric services. The problem for primary care pediatricians lay in the kind of medicine they found themselves practicing. Their practices increasingly consisted of preventive work—weighing and measuring babies and otherwise supervising the normal growth and development of their young patients—and the treatment of minor illnesses that were easily handled or disappeared on their own without any treatment at all. The growing frustration and boredom with such practice generated a crisis of purpose for the specialty. The crisis, which pediatricians themselves referred to as the "dissatisfied (or disgruntled) pediatrician syndrome" was a pervasive sense of malaise among primary care pediatricians who doubted whether their specialized, disease-oriented skills were serving any real purpose in child health care. It was in the context of the dissatisfied pediatrician syndrome that some within the specialty began to suggest that primary care pediatrics could be revitalized if pediatricians addressed themselves to children's unmet needs, particularly those that were not strictly medical. Pediatricians were encouraged to be creative in their exploration of new areas of care.

Key segments within the profession resisted the expansion of pediatrics into nonphysical areas. But the specialty's ambitions in these new areas were fortified during the 1970s when a new crisis hit—a supply crisis. Pediatricians found themselves competing for a dwindling child population with new groups of health care practitioners eager to provide their services to children, pediatric nurse practitioners, and the budding specialty of family practice. This supply crisis pushed the specialty further toward the new pediatrics. The new pediatrics became more than just a way to make the practice of primary care pediatrics rewarding and fulfilling. It was now the linchpin in pediatricians' assertions that they were the professional group best equipped to deal with children's total health care concerns.

Pediatricians, then, were not seeking to gain a greater measure of control over children's lives. What they were seeking to do was to preserve a place for themselves in primary child health care at a time when their role in the area was threatened. By redefining what proper pediatric care involves to include the new pediatrics, they hoped to secure a future for themselves as primary care practitioners. But in the process, they altered fundamentally our view of children, their problems, and their lives.

GOAL TRANSFORMATIONS AND SOCIAL PROBLEMS

There are parallels between pediatricians who transformed the mission of pediatrics and organizations and social movements that have transformed themselves. The Foundation for Infantile Paralysis (FIP), for example, was established to raise funds to support research into infantile paralysis (poliomyelitis) and to assist victims of the disease. Once Jonas Salk developed the vaccine for polio, the FIP became redundant. Rather than disappearing, however, it changed its name to the March of Dimes and found a

new objective in fighting arthritis and birth defects. Other examples of movement change include the Red Cross, whose initial concerns revolved around wars and other national emergencies, but after World War I it became involved in public health. Also, a movement to stem the dangerous and unethical marketing practices of companies supplying infant food formulas to third world countries—the Infant Formula Action Coalition (INFACT)—was formed in 1977 and initiated a national campaign aimed at changing the practices of American companies and the Swiss giant, Nestlé. INFACT led a seven-year boycott of Nestlé products and eventually forced the company to alter and restrict its marketing tactics. In the aftermath of its victory, INFACT broadened its objectives to include international campaigns to stop abuses of transnational corporations that endanger the health and survival of people all over the world.

These professions, organizations, and movements share with pediatricians the experience of having to reinvent themselves to survive. But in doing so, most promote new views of the behaviors and/or conditions they take on as goals. The March of Dimes, the Red Cross, and groups such as INFACT have drawn public attention to a broad range of previously unnoticed health issues. And pediatricians have fundamentally altered children's "misbehaviors" and adolescents' "growing pains."

CHILDREN, PEDIATRICIANS, AND MEDICALIZATION

Certain groups have been particularly vulnerable to the medical labeling of their behaviors and circumstances. Women are one such group; children are another. The relative powerlessness of women and children and their limited ability to resist medicalization have made them prime targets. Several studies examine claims-making efforts related specifically to children. While some of these focus on children's problematic behaviors—for example, studies on hyperactivity and learning disabilities and juvenile delinquency—others have examined issues that are, in other ways, child-related, including child abuse, missing children, sudden infant death syndrome, child custody and child support laws, and accidental poisoning.

Many of these studies touch on the role played by the medical profession and its tacit approval of, if not active involvement in, the campaigns that turned these issues into public concerns. Once certain forms of childhood deviance were labeled as "hyperkinesis" or "hyperactivity," the medical profession assumed the responsibility for managing and controlling them. Some studies single out pediatricians as key players. Pediatricians were the first to draw attention to poisoning as an alarming danger to children and were at the forefront of the poison control movement. In fact, the first poison control center, established in 1953, was organized in Chicago under the sponsorship of the Illinois chapter of the American Academy of Pediatrics. A paper in the *Journal of the American Medical Association*, reviewing the development of poison control over five years after the first center was established, noted: "Probably the most noteworthy of these developments is the realization by the medical profession, especially by pediatricians, that poison accidents constitute a major health problem."

But none of the studies examines the forces that propelled pediatricians to involve themselves in the medicalization of so many childhood issues. Pediatricians' involvement in the seemingly relentless medicalization of children's lives was linked to the crises that the specialty faced over the past half century and their efforts to adapt to the changing circumstances around them. The new pediatrics was rooted not in any naturally expansionary or imperialistic tendencies of the medical profession to extend its privileges and prerogatives—a conclusion that some analysts come to about medicalization—but in the concerns of a primary care specialty struggling to survive. An understanding of the dilemmas that pediatricians faced and the professional concerns that have preoccupied them since the 1950s is critical to understanding their involvement in the medicalization of children's deviant behaviors and other problems in their lives.

SOCIAL PROBLEMS AND PROFESSIONS

The new pediatrics raises questions about the forms that professional claims-making can take. If the discovery of new medical diseases and the creation of medical diagnoses is claims-making, another, more obvious, form that claims-making takes is social or political activism in relation to issues that a profession feels strongly about and that it often claims it is uniquely equipped to solve. Pediatricians, individually and collectively, have engaged in both types of claims-making. They have been among the "discoverers" of specific new behavioral conditions in children and have participated in the political campaigns that have brought such issues as child abuse, seatbelt use, and accidental poisoning to light as social problems.

But the incorporation of so many childhood and adolescent difficulties within a medical frame of reference was more subtly the consequence of a redrawing of the boundaries of pediatric practice. In changing and expanding their definition of their political task, pediatricians cleared the way for the production of specific disease labels and for political activism on the part of pediatricians as well as others. This suggests that forms that

professional claims-making can take, and how various forms relate to each other, need to be more clearly specified. We need a better understanding not only of why professions become involved in the social problems process, but also in what ways they do so.

20

The Size Acceptance Movement

Jeffery Sobal

Social problems are often tightly intertwined with organized social movements that work to define, draw attention to, and change the conditions associated with those particular problems. This chapter will examine how a social movement that opposes the stigmatization of obese individuals has played a role in the way body weight is constructed as a social problem in the United States and other postindustrial societies.

Over the course of the twentieth century an increasing emphasis on slimness has emerged and developed. The emphasis on thinness has broadened and intensified since the 1960s, with weight concerns salient and even obsessive among women. The rise in emphasis on thinness was accompanied by a parallel rejection of fatness. Obesity became a stigmatized condition, a discredited characteristic that was perceived as a moral failure of fat people. Prejudice against fatness led to labeling large people as deviant.

The cultural focus on slimness in recent decades led to the development of a system of weight industries that developed vested social, economic, and political interests in portraying high levels of body weight as a social problem. These included the weight loss, medical, pharmaceutical, fitness food, dieting, apparel, fashion and insurance industries, all of which operated in the role of moral entrepreneurs who have vested interests in promoting slimness and rejecting fatness.

This chapter is excerpted from Sobal, Jeffery (1999). "The Size Acceptance Movement and the Social Construction of Body Weight." Pp. 231–49 in *Weighty Issues: Fatness and Thinness as Social Problems*, edited by Jeffery Sobal and Donna Maurer. Hawthorne, NY: Aldine de Gruyter.

THE EMERGENCE OF THE SIZE ACCEPTANCE MOVEMENT

The size acceptance movement focuses on advocating for fat people who are stigmatized and discriminated against. Many movement participants use the term *fat* to describe themselves, and attempt to neutralize its connotations. Body size dimensions other than weight could be, but have not been, dealt with by a size acceptance movement. Thin people are typically admired and have not developed a social movement to advance their acceptance. Tall people are also socially valued, although short people are negatively evaluated, but they have not been part of the size acceptance movement.

Size acceptance did not begin to emerge as a social movement until the late 1960s and early 1970s. Before then, a few individual pioneers spoke out for size acceptance, but a broader consciousness about the problem and organization around the issue did not exist. Understanding the development and growth of the size acceptance movement requires consideration of its social location with respect to other precursor and parallel social movements and particular social conditions related to the movement.

Precursor Movements

Postwar society in the United States bred skepticism and opposition to many established social patterns and institutions. A variety of social movements developed, many challenging inequalities in the way particular segments of society were treated. Civil rights, women's rights, age rights, gay rights, and other movements emerged, mobilized resources, and changed social identities. Social movements of the 1960s and 1970s captured the attention and imagination of the public, and led to a climate of protest that generated a variety of oppositional movements that dealt with other causes, such as the antiwar, antinuclear, and antipollution movements.

The size acceptance movement was a product of race, gender, age, sexuality, and other precursor movements that blazed the trail, established methods for creating social change, and served as a training ground for some size activists. However, few fat feminists have come from or been tied to the mainstream women's movement and often feel alienated by the lack of recognition and attention to size acceptance issues.

Nondieting as an Allied Movement

In addition to larger precursor movements, an alliance with another movement catalyzed attention and resources for body weight. What was

widely called the nondiet movement became a close ally of size acceptance, even though the two movements draw from different populations of leaders and participants. The nondiet movement was a backlash against dieting and a reaction to public concerns about thinness and eating disorders, which fit well with size acceptance ideas, although people associated with nondieting may not actually endorse acceptance of very large people.

By the 1980s there were increasing attacks on the emphasis on thinness and dieting. The orientations of these challenges ranged from feminist to sociological. Dieting to lose weight had become almost obligatory among many women, but was plagued by a terrible lack of reported success in achieving and maintaining weight loss. Backlash against stringent thinness standards, compulsive aspects of dieting, low weight loss success rates, and fraudulent and even harmful side effects of some diets fueled the nondiet movement. The nondiet movement is partially a reaction to overmedicalization of eating and weight.

Social Conditions

Demographic changes that resulted from the aging of the baby boom cohort contributed to conditions that facilitated the earlier culture of thinness and later reactions of size acceptance. During the 1960s an accelerating emphasis on thinness was based in the growing focus on the youth culture of the baby boom, with thin adolescents adopted as ideals for body shape. Mass media and mass marketing in the fashion industry blossomed to emphasize thinness during this period. The general aging of the population grew as the baby boom matured and the rise in fatness in the United States in the 1980s moved many away from the earlier youth culture and its focus on appearance.

THE STRUCTURE AND PROCESSES OF THE SIZE ACCEPTANCE MOVEMENT

Size acceptance ideas developed in the United States in the late 1960s as reactions to pervasive stigmatization and discrimination against fat people. The movement grew and developed a structure that included a loose collective of organizations, groups, and individuals connected through interpersonal relationships and more formal communications channels such as publications, and, more recently, the Internet. The underlying ideology of the size acceptance movement focused on exposing, combating, and preventing fatism, weightism, and sizism; promoting size diversity and tolerance; and developing a size-accepting, size-neutral, and size-friendly society. Size acceptance became a new conceptual model that was used in the broader construction of body weight, opposing the moral and medical models that dominated discourse about fatness and thinness. The major strategies of the size acceptance movement were to use political changes to collectively challenge mainstream beliefs and practices and, at the same time, create cultural change in ideas about weight in their emphasis on fat pride, fat liberation, and fat power.

Like most social movements, several organizations have played a crucial role in advancing the size acceptance movement. The National Association to Advance Fat Acceptance (NAAFA) was founded in 1969. The Association for the Health Enrichment of Large Persons (AHELP) held its first conference in 1991 as an organization for health professionals, including psychologists, dieticians/nutritionists, nurses, exercise professionals, social workers, educators and researchers tied more to the nondieting movement than the size acceptance movement. Many other allied groups have existed in the size acceptance network, including diverse small activist groups (Fat Underground, Fat Liberation Front, Council on Size and Weight Discrimination) and other types of groups (Abundia, Ample Opportunity, Body Image Task Force, Largesse). The structure of the size acceptance movement has been and continues to be highly diffuse. NAAFA, the largest organization, has forty local chapters, which all have considerable autonomy.

The number of people involved in the size acceptance movement is relatively small. NAAFA is the largest and only national organization, claiming approximately five thousand members. This is only a tiny fraction of the estimated third of the U.S. adult population defined by health researchers as overweight. Size activists who form the size acceptance movement's leadership, act as crusaders, and serve as experts probably number only in the hundreds.

The size acceptance movement includes two major components: (1) political activism that attempts to reform the values and practices of society about body weight, and (2) social support that provides a refuge for large people from the intolerance of a thin society through assistance and companionship.

Political Activism

The size acceptance movement organizes and engages in a variety of political activities to promote its causes. Several types of protest events are employed, including rallies (the Million Pound March was held in 1998), boycotts (of Coca-Cola, Southwest Airlines, and other companies), and other forms of civil disobedience like protests and picketing. Other strate-

gic tactics include activism to gain attention to size issues by designating events (International No-Diet Day, Size Acceptance Month), support groups, letter writing, educational services, and programs.

An important component of the size acceptance movement is producing materials to communicate its concerns and ideas. These include popular books describing the problems of being large and promoting size acceptance, self-help books offering practical and instrumental support for large people, and glossy magazines for large people. Formal size acceptance organizations and informal groups also distribute newsletters. Numerous computerized Web sites, listservers, and other electronic services function to promote the movement and facilitate communication among those who are involved but scattered across various locations.

Social Support

As an organized social movement, size acceptance offers several forms of social support to its participants. Emotional social support is an important resource. In the broader society thinness is the reigning value, but the size acceptance movement offers its large-sized participants who may weigh 300, 400, 500 or more pounds a refuge from a world organized for thinner people. By offering large people acceptance and positive evaluation, the movement can become a functional "family" for individuals oppressed because of their size.

Another function of the size acceptance movement is to provide instrumental social support for its members. The women's fashion industry has largely emphasized extreme slimness and is seen by many in the movement as a barrier or even an opponent to size acceptance. Obtaining clothing is a problematic experience for large people, particularly for women. However, a segment of the fashion world is recently beginning to cater to larger women, and members of the size acceptance movement offer important marketing opportunities.

SIZE ACCEPTANCE AND THE SOCIAL CONSTRUCTION OF BODY WEIGHT

The size acceptance movement has struggled to gain acknowledgment in the body weight arena, and appears to have gained a place on the agenda. In the weight arena, size activists and size acceptance organizations have broken into the circle of sources that the news media seek out. This may not have led to large changes in the way most of the general population deals with weight, but has influenced some individuals and groups. Most significantly, size acceptance has gained sufficient attention to offer a political counterpoint to the largely medical and moral discussion of body weight.

The impacts of size acceptance on the public construction of body weight reflect the size and structure of the movement, with the relatively small and diffuse organizations, groups, and individuals influencing a variety of specific and local decisions, but not leading to sweeping social changes. The power of the movement tends to be cultural, rather than economic and political, with few financial or governmental resources to draw upon. While there are powerful moral entrepreneurs that profit from encouraging thinness, such as pharmaceutical companies, there is less overt profit to be made in promoting size acceptance. That has led to difficulty in producing allies with financial and political power.